RECKNOCKSHIRE

MONMOUTHSHIRE

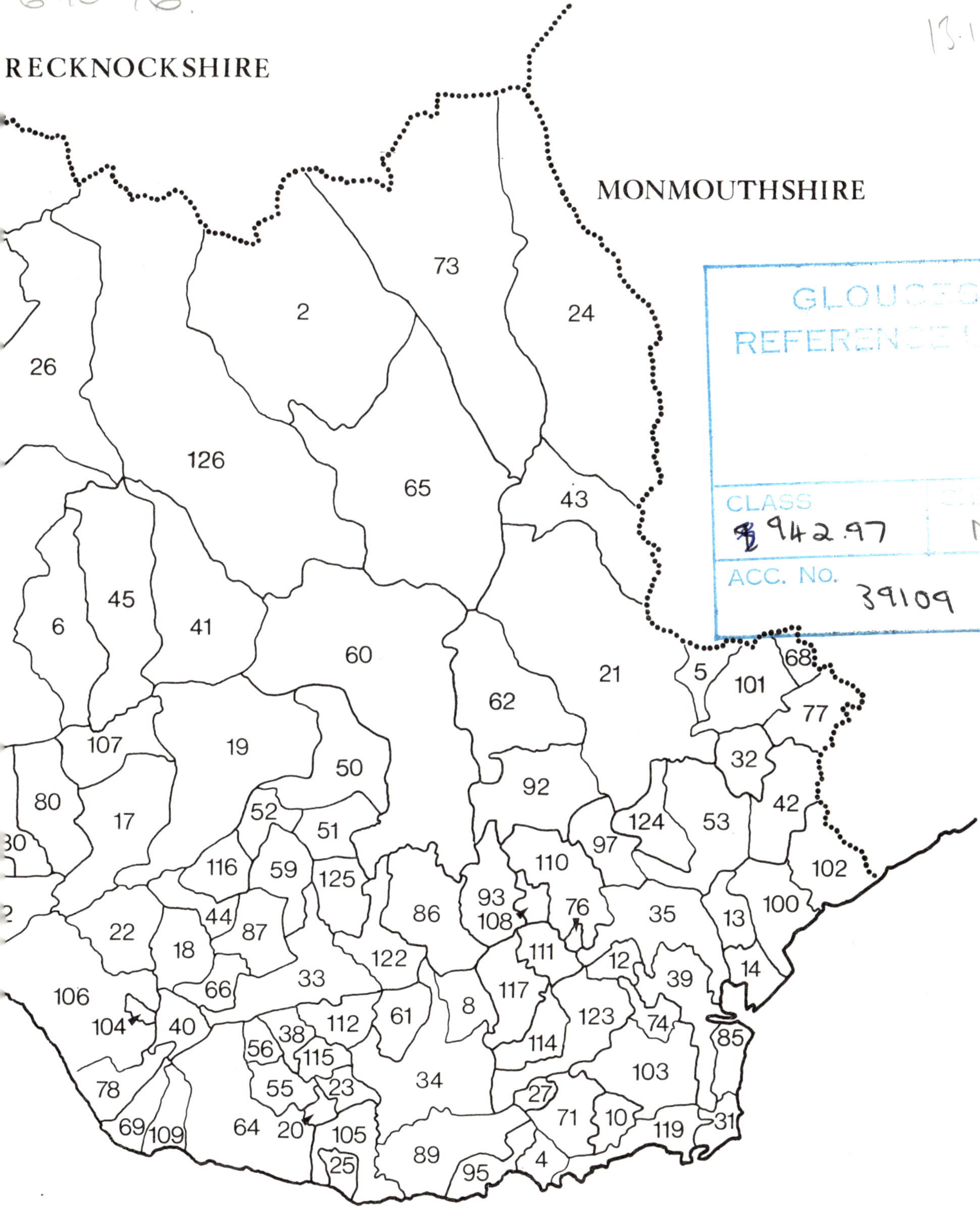

The numbering of parishes on this map corresponds to that in the List of Ecclesiastical Parishes on p. xvii.

Caer Dynnaf, from W. (670, p. 40b).

THE ROYAL COMMISSION
ON ANCIENT AND HISTORICAL MONUMENTS
IN WALES

AN INVENTORY OF THE ANCIENT MONUMENTS IN GLAMORGAN

VOLUME I: PRE-NORMAN

PART II
THE IRON AGE AND THE ROMAN OCCUPATION

CARDIFF
HER MAJESTY'S STATIONERY OFFICE

First published 1976

ISBN 0 11 700589 4

TABLE OF CONTENTS

SUMMARY OF CONTENTS OF PARTS i AND iii OF VOLUME I

Introductory material, lists and indexes are similar in all three parts.

LIST OF PLATES

With the exception of 4, lower, and 15, all Plates have been supplied by Dr. J. K. S. St. Joseph, and are reproduced by permission of the Committee for Aerial Photography, Cambridge University. Plate 15, top is reproduced by permission of the National Museum of Wales.

LIST OF FIGURES

The following Figures are based on Ordnance Survey maps, with additions: 1, 46–50, 52–6, and end-papers.

CHAIRMAN'S PREFACE

IN this volume, the first of those for Glamorgan, the Commission has dealt with the pre-Norman remains of the county; the accepted monuments total some 800, and the staff concerned have examined 1030 sites during the course of the work. At the same time, the investigation of later remains has proceeded.

There are three major changes in this Inventory as compared with those for Caernarvonshire and Anglesey. The first is the arrangement of entries according to types of monument instead of by parishes. It is recognised that the user who is interested in the complete history of a limited area will find this a disadvantage, but the older system was excessively inconvenient for the growing number of students who are concerned with the study of particular periods. The new arrangement also makes it possible to place the entries for individual monuments in close conjunction with the relevant general discussion. Further, since the division of material by volumes corresponds roughly to the division of expert knowledge among the investigating staff, publication of one section does not need to await completion of another.

This arrangement makes a second change possible. The Commissioners have long been concerned that the high and increasing cost of printing has made the price of the Inventories almost prohibitive for many people. They have therefore arranged, with the cooperation of Her Majesty's Stationery Office, to publish the material in separate sections. The details of the arrangements which result are described in the note on the Presentation of Material.

The third major change is the omission of the lists of 'finds'. The grounds for this decision, which was reached with considerable regret, were three-fold. First, this branch of the work for Caernarvonshire absorbed a disproportionately large part of the time of the investigating staff, especially of those concerned with the earlier monuments. Secondly, by the nature of the problem, the results could not even approach finality, for portable objects are continually being recovered from the soil, as demonstrated by the five pages of addenda given in the last volume of the Caernarvonshire Inventory; by contrast the list of surviving monuments can be completed at least in principle, although in practice a few escape record. Finally, it seems questionable whether small portable objects can be defined as 'monuments and constructions', and the preparation of such lists might therefore be regarded as outside the scope of the Commission's Warrant. Taking into consideration the great number of monuments requiring record, the rapidity with which specimens of many classes are destroyed, and the very limited number of staff available for the work it seems right in future to omit lists of finds.

Nevertheless there can be no question that such work is a very necessary contribution to archaeology, especially the accurate description of objects in private hands and the maintenance of a continuous record of new discoveries, and it is highly desirable that some organisation should be set up to continue it, whether by an extension of the field covered by the Commission or by some other means.

In view of some recent misunderstanding it seems desirable to explain that inclusion of a monument in the list of those recommended as 'most worthy of preservation' indicates that in the view of the Commissioners it is of quite exceptional importance. There are many other monuments which are of considerable interest and which should be preserved if at all possible.

Corrections or criticisms of the contents of this volume will be welcomed with a view to their possible inclusion in some future edition; they should be sent to the Secretary. Properly accredited persons may consult the records of the Commission at the headquarters at Edleston House, Queen's Road, Aberystwyth, Dyfed.

The contents of the volume are Crown Copyright, including most of the illustrations. Copies of these can be purchased through the Secretary of the Commission.

August 1973 — W. F. Grimes

REPORT

TO THE QUEEN'S MOST EXCELLENT MAJESTY

MAY IT PLEASE YOUR MAJESTY

We, the undersigned Commissioners, appointed to make an *Inventory of the Ancient and Historical Monuments and constructions connected with or illustrative of the contemporary culture, civilisation and conditions of life of the people in Wales from the earliest times, and to specify those which seem most worthy of preservation*, humbly submit to Your Majesty the following Report, being the fourteenth on the work of the Commission since its first appointment. This Report will accompany the first volume of the Inventory of Monuments in the County of Glamorgan.

2. It is with deep regret that we record the deaths of our former Commissioners Sir Cyril Fox and Sir Ifor Williams.

3. We have also to record the loss by retirement, on expiry of term of office, of our former Chairman Sir John Goronwy Edwards and of Professor Arthur Herbert Dodd.

4. We have to thank Your Majesty for the issue of a Commission under Your Majesty's Royal Sign Manual dated 28 September, 1963, revoking former Warrants but repeating the terms of reference given therein, and further empowering us to assume the general control and management of that part of the collection of the National Buildings Record which relates to Wales, and to make arrangements for the creation of a wider record concerning important sites and buildings throughout Wales.

5. We have to thank Your Majesty for the appointment of Professor William Francis Grimes to be Chairman of this Commission in succession to Sir John Goronwy Edwards for a period of ten years from January 1967, under Your Majesty's Royal Sign Manual dated 31 March, 1967.

6. We have also to thank Your Majesty for the appointment or re-appointment under Your Majesty's Royal Sign Manual of the following Commissioners: on 28 September, 1963, Professor Richard John Copland Atkinson, Professor Glanmor Williams and Dr. Raymond Bernard Wood-Jones, for nine years from 1963; on 31 March, 1967, Dr. John Davies Knatchbull Lloyd for seven years from 1967 and Professor John Gwynn Williams for ten years from 1967; and on 15 June, 1970, Professor Idris Llewelyn Foster, Professor Edward Martyn Jope, Dr. Arnold Joseph Taylor, Professor Dewi-Prys Thomas, and Dr. Hubert Newman Savory, for ten years from 1970, the first three being re-appointments. Tenure in each case is from 1 January.

7. We have pleasure in reporting the completion of our enquiries into the pre-Norman remains of the County of Glamorgan, in which we have recorded 803 Monuments. Rather more than 1000 sites were visited.

8. We have prepared a full Inventory of these Monuments, which will be issued as a non-Parliamentary publication.

9. We have considered the arrangement of the Inventory, and have concluded that for most users it will be more convenient to group the monuments by types rather than according to parishes. We are therefore adopting this system. We have also concluded that it will be an advantage to reduce the size of individual publications, and we have therefore arranged for this volume to be issued as three parts.

10. We desire to record our special thanks for valuable assistance from the owners and occupants of land where monuments exist; also from Professor L. Alcock, M.A., F.S.A.; Mr. G. C. Boon, B.A., F.S.A.; Mr. D. Q. Bowen, B.Sc., Ph.D.; Mr. J. B. Campbell, B.A.; Mr. C. B. Crampton, M.A., Ph.D.; Mr. J. L. Davies, B.A., F.S.A.; Mrs. B. Heywood, B.A., Ph.D., F.S.A.; Mr. M. G. Jarrett, B.A., Ph.D., F.S.A.; Mr. J. M. Lewis, M.A., F.S.A.; Mr. C. B. M. McBurney, M.A., Ph.D., F.B.A., F.S.A.; Mr. T. K. Penniman, M.A., F.S.A.; Professor J. K. S. St. Joseph, O.B.E., M.A., Ph.D., F.S.A.; Mr. G. de G. Sieveking, M.A., F.S.A.; Mrs. V. G. Swan, B.A.; Mr. R. J. Thomas, M.A.; Mr. D. P. Webley, B.Sc., D.I.C.; Sir Mortimer Wheeler, C.H.; Mr. D. R. Wilson, M.A., F.S.A.

11. We desire to express our acknowledgement of the good work of our executive staff; their names, and indications of their particular contributions, are included in the Inventory volumes.

12. We humbly recommend to Your Majesty's notice the following Monuments as most worthy of preservation:

CAVES

5. Goat's Hole.
8. Long Hole.
12. Minchin Hole.
16. Tooth Cave.
17. Cat Hole.

MESOLITHIC OPEN SITES

26. Burry Holms.

MEGALITHIC CHAMBERED TOMBS

33. Maen Ceti (Arthur's Stone).
36. Long Cairn, Parc Cwm.
40. Long Cairn, Tinkinswood.
42. Long Cairn, Maesyfelin.

CUP-MARKED STONES

49. Maen Catwg.

ROUND CAIRNS

57. Ring near Graig Fawr.
60. Ring on Tor Clawdd.
66. Carn Llechart.
111. Ring-cairn on Carn Caca.
153. Ring-cairn S.W. of Pen Garnbugail.
156. Carn Bugail.
173. Cairn on Rhosili Down.
262. Cairn S.E. of Mynyddherbert.
290. Cairn near Llyndwr Fawr.
348. Pebyll.
349. Crug yr Afan.
378–9. The Beacons.

GROUPS OF SMALL CAIRNS

482. Group on Mynydd Carnllechart.
484. Group on Mynydd y Capel.
490. Group near Tir-lan.

STANDING STONES

543. Stone N. of Knelston.
548. Mansel Jack (Sampson's Jack).
553. Carreg Bica.
554. Carreg Hir.

COOKING MOUNDS

586. Mound on Druids Moor.

HILL-FORTS AND RELATED STRUCTURES

In all these it is important that the interior should be protected as well as the ramparts.

613. Mynydd y Castell.
615. Castle Ditches, Llancarfan.
619. Gwersyll.
637. Coedcae Gaer.
646. Hardings Down, N. enclosure.
657. Caer Blaen-y-cwm.
665. Cil Ifor Top.
666. Dunraven.
667. Nash Point.
668. Castle Ditches, Llantwit Major.
669. Summerhouse Camp.
670. Caer Dynnaf.
671. Porthkerry Bulwarks.
673. Caerau, Ely.
678. Fort at Craig Tŷ-isaf.
681. Fort on Mynydd Bychan.
687–8. Hardings Down, W. and E. enclosures.
689. The Bulwark, Llanmadog.
690. Gaer Fawr.
693. Y Bwlwarcau.
698. Fort on Thurba Head.
699. Fort on The Knave.
700. Fort on Yellow Top.
705. Burry Holms Church site.

UNENCLOSED HUT SETTLEMENTS

711. Huts and enclosures above Garreg Lwyd.
715. Huts and enclosures, Buarth Maen.

ROMAN FORTS

731. Fort at Coelbren.
735. Fort at Cardiff.
737. Forts and annexe at Gelli-gaer.

OTHER ROMAN MILITARY WORKS

739. Marching camp, Blaen-cwm Bach.
741. Marching camp, Twyn y Briddallt.
743. W. Practice camp, Mynydd Carn-goch.
747 and 749. Practice camps, Fforest Gwladys.
751. Signal station on Hirfynydd.

ROMAN CIVIL SITES

758. Villa at Cae'r-mead.
762. Villa at Ely.

EARLY CHRISTIAN MONUMENTS

In most cases these are already in museums or churches.

841. Vicuritinus stone, Clwydi Banwen.
843. Tegernacus stone, Gelli-gaer.
844. Inscribed stone, Llanmadog.
846. Cantusus stone, Port Talbot.
847. Paulus stone, Merthyr Mawr.
848. Bodvocus stone, Mynydd Margam.
849. Pumpeius stone, Eglwys Nynnid.
850. Vendumaglus stone, Capel Llanilltern.
902. Carved slab, Nash.
907. Conbelin stone, Margam.
908. Enniaun stone, Margam.
911. Houelt stone, Llantwit Major.
912. Samson stone, Llantwit Major.
933. Ithel stone, Llantwit Major.
938. Irbicus stone, Llandough.
951. Carved slab, Llanrhidian.

The Monuments in this list have been selected solely with regard to their archaeological or historical importance. We consider that these are outstanding from that point of view; there are many other Monuments which are of considerable interest and which deserve protection.

All of which we submit with our humble duty to Your Majesty.

(Signed) W. F. GRIMES *(Chairman)*
R. J. C. ATKINSON
I. LL. FOSTER
E. M. JOPE
J. D. K. LLOYD
H. N. SAVORY
A. J. TAYLOR
D.-P. THOMAS
G. WILLIAMS
J. G. WILLIAMS
R. B. WOOD-JONES
A. H. A. HOGG *(Secretary)*

COMMISSIONERS AND STAFF

During the preparation of this volume (1963–72), the following Members, appointed by Royal Warrant, have served on the Commission:

Sir (John) Goronwy Edwards, M.A., D.Litt.(Oxon), F.B.A., F.S.A., Emeritus Professor of History in the University of London. (Chairman, retired 1967.)

William Francis Grimes, C.B.E., M.A., D.Litt., F.S.A., F.M.A., Professor of Archaeology in the University of London and Director of the Institute of Archaeology. (Appointed Chairman 1967 for ten years.)

Richard John Copland Atkinson, M.A., F.S.A., Professor of Archaeology in the University College of South Wales and Monmouthshire. (Appointed 1963 for nine years.)

Arthur Herbert Dodd, M.A., D.Litt., F.R.Hist.S., Emeritus Professor of History in the University College of North Wales. (Re-appointed 1963, retired 1966.)

Idris Llewelyn Foster, M.A., F.S.A., Jesus Professor of Celtic in the University of Oxford. (Re-appointed 1970 for ten years.)

Edward Martyn Jope, M.A., B.Sc., F.B.A., F.S.A., Professor of Archaeology in The Queen's University, Belfast. (Re-appointed 1970 for ten years.)

John Davies Knatchbull Lloyd, O.B.E., D.L., J.P., M.A., LL.D., F.S.A., Chairman of the Ancient Monuments Board for Wales. (Appointed 1967 for seven years.)

Hubert Newman Savory, M.A., D.Phil., F.S.A., Keeper of Archaeology in the National Museum of Wales. (Appointed 1970 for ten years.)

Arnold Joseph Taylor, C.B.E., M.A., D.Litt., F.B.A., Dir.S.A., F.R.Hist.S., Chief Inspector of Ancient Monuments and Historic Buildings. (Re-appointed 1970 for ten years.)

Dewi-Prys Thomas, B.Arch., F.R.I.B.A., M.R.T.P.I., Professor of Architecture and Head of the Welsh School of Architecture. (Appointed 1970 for ten years.)

Glanmor Williams, M.A., D.Litt., F.R.Hist. S., Professor of History in the University College of Swansea. (Appointed 1963 for nine years.)

John Gwynn Williams, M.A., Professor of Welsh History in the University College of North Wales. (Appointed 1967 for ten years.)

Raymond Bernard Wood-Jones, M.A., B.Arch., Ph.D., F.S.A., A.R.I.B.A., Architect, and Senior Lecturer in the School of Architecture of the University of Manchester. (Appointed 1963 for nine years.)

STAFF

DURING the preparation of this volume (1963–72) the following have served as Staff of the Commission:

Investigating Staff

Secretary	Mr. A. H. A. Hogg, C.B.E., M.A., F.S.A.
Investigators	Mr. H. Brooksby (from 1969).
	Mr. L. A. S. Butler, Ph.D., F.S.A. (to 1965).
	Mr. W. E. Griffiths, M.A., F.S.A.
	Mr. D. B. Hague, A.R.I.B.A., F.S.A.
	Mr. C. H. Houlder, M.A., F.S.A.
	Mr. C. N. Johns, M.A., F.S.A. (to 1969).
	Mrs. B. A. Morris, B.A. (1966 to 1967).
	Mr. A. J. Parkinson, B.A. (from 1970).
	Mr. P. Smith, B.A., F.S.A.
	Mr. C. J. Spurgeon, B.A., F.S.A.
	Mr. H. J. Thomas, B.A. (from 1969).
	Mr. W. G. Thomas, M.A., F.S.A.

Ancillary Staff

Executive Officer	Mr. E. Whatmore (from 1965).
Research Assistants	Mrs. E. T. Richards, B.Sc. (from 1970).
	Mr. J. F. O'N. Russell, M.A. (1968 to 1970).
Illustrating Staff	Mr. C. Baker (from 1971).
	Mr. D. J. Roberts (from 1966).
Photographic Staff	Mr. H. Brooksby (to 1969).
	Mr. R. G. Nicol (from 1970).
	Mr. C. J. Parrott (from 1970).
	Miss J. R. Rogers (1968 to 1970).
Audio Typist	Miss D. M. Ward.
Clerical Staff	Miss B. M. Davies (from 1970).
	Miss G. M. Davies (1966 to 1967).
	Miss C. A. Griffiths (from 1969).
	Miss P. A. Lawden (to 1966).
	Miss A. R. Williams (1967 to 1969).

Authorship and compilation of sections of this Volume were allocated as follows:

Part i. Caves; Neolithic Burial and Ritual Structures—C. H. Houlder.
Bronze Age Burial and Ritual Structures; Cooking Mounds—W. E. Griffiths.

Part ii. Hill-forts and Related Structures; Hut Settlements—A. H. A. Hogg.
Roman Remains—W. E. Griffiths.

Part iii. Dykes—A. H. A. Hogg.
Monastic Sites—D. B. Hague and W. G. Thomas.
Inscribed and Sculptured Stones—W. G. Thomas.

All Parts. Physical Background—C. H. Houlder.
Communications—A. H. A. Hogg.

LIST OF ECCLESIASTICAL PARISHES

WITH INCIDENCE OF MONUMENTS

THIS list corresponds with the map forming the end-paper at the front of the book, and indicates the ecclesiastical subdivision of Glamorgan into parishes as it stood *ca.* 1850, before any of the changes of names and boundaries which have taken place for administrative purposes (*cf.* back end-paper and list on p.xxi).

Ecclesiastical parishes are noted at the end of Inventory entries, distinguished by the letter (E) when the monument concerned stands in a civil parish of a different name (C). Spellings used are as shown on the left, generally agreeing with those used on O.S. maps current in 1970. The only departures from this practice (other than cases simply involving hyphens or capitals) are indicated by the addition of the map spellings in square brackets. The Welsh forms, which follow the recommendations of the Board of Celtic Studies, are given on the right only when they differ from those already adopted for use in this Inventory.

Nos. 5, 68 and 77 are parts of parishes which straddle the Monmouthshire border. No. 102 is included as a result of the expansion of Cardiff.

No.	*Parish name used*	*Correct Welsh form*	*Monument Nos.*
1	Aberavon	Aberafan	———
2	Aberdâr [Aberdare]		619 713–715 741
3	Baglan		652 678
4	Barry	Y Barri	766 767
5	Bedwas (Van hamlet)		———
6	Betws [Bettws]		———
7	Bishopston	Llandeilo Ferwallt	677 703
8	Bonvilston	Tresimwn	696
9	Briton Ferry	Llansawel	628 690
10	Cadoxton-juxta-Barry	Tregatwg	———
11	Cadoxton-juxta-Neath	Llangatwg Nedd	617 731 734 738 751 752
12	Caerau		———
13	Cardiff St. John	Caerdydd ———	735
14	Cardiff St. Mary	Caerdydd ———	———
15	Cheriton	———	622a 689
16	Cilybebyll		———
17	Coety [Coity]		635 636 745
18	Colwinston	Tregolwyn	———
19	Coychurch	Llangrallo	614 634 637
20	Eglwys Brewys [Eglwysbrewis]		———
21	Eglwysilan		736
22	Ewenni [Ewenny]		———
23	Flemingston	Trefflemin	———

No.	*Parish name used*	*Correct Welsh form*	*Monument Nos.*
24	Gelli-gaer		737 746–750
25	Gileston	Silstwn	———
26	Glyncorrwg		———
27	Highlight	Uchelola	———
28	Ilston	Llanilltud Gŵyr	676
29	Knelston	Llan-y-tair-mair	———
30	Laleston	Trelales	———
31	Lavernock	Larnog	———
32	Lisvane	Llys-faen	———
33	Llanblethian	Llanfleiddan	670 695
34	Llancarfan		615 638 683 759 760
35	Llandaf [Llandaff]		762
36	Llanddewi		643 686
37	Llandeilo Tal-y-bont		616
38	Llandough (near Cowbridge)	Llandochau	———
39	Llandough, Cogan and Leckwith	Llandochau, Cogan a Lecwydd	———
40	Llandŵ [Llandow]		———
41	Llandyfodwg		———
42	Llanedern [Llanedeyrn]		685
43	Llanfabon		———
44	Llan-gan		———
45	Llangeinwyr [Llangeinor]		———
46	Llangennith	Llangynydd	612 646 647 687–689 705 706
47	Llanguicke	Llan-giwg	———
48	Llangyfelach		642
49	Llangynwyd		657–659 693
50	Llanharan		———
51	Llanhari [Llanharry]		———
52	Llanilid		———
53	Llanisien [Llanishen]		———
54	Llanmadog [Llanmadoc]		689
55	Llanmaes	Llan-faes	———
56	Llanmihangel	Llanfihangel y Bont-faen	763
57	Llanrhidian		623 624 648 649 665 674
58	Llansamlet		650 651
59	Llansanwyr [Llansannor]		———
60	Llantrisant		639 672
61	Llantrithyd	Llantriddyd	682
62	Llantwit Fardre	Llanilltud Faerdref	740
63	Llantwit-juxta-Neath	Llanilltud Nedd	618 627 629 739
64	Llantwit Major	Llanilltud Fawr	668 669 758
65	Llanwynno [Llanwonno]		741
66	Llyswyrny [Llsworney]		———
67	Loughor	Casllwchwr	733 742–744
68	Machen (Rhyd-y-gwern hamlet)		———
69	Marcroes [Marcross]		667

No.	*Parish name used*	*Correct Welsh form*	*Monument Nos.*
70	Margam		613 625 653–656 679 692
71	Merthyr Dyfan		———
72	Merthyr Mawr		630 691
73	Merthyr Tudful [Merthyr Tydfil]		611 732
74	Michaelston-le-Pit	Llanfihangel-y-pwll	673
75	Michaelston-super-Avon	Llanfihangel-ynys-Afan	———
76	Michaelston-super-Ely	Llanfihangel-ar-Elái	———
77	Michaelston-y-Vedw (Llanfedw hamlet)	Llanfihangel-y-fedw	———
78	Monknash	Yr As Fawr	———
79	Neath	Castell-nedd	626
80	Newcastle	Y Castellnewydd	———
81	Newton Nottage	Drenewydd yn Notais	632 657
82	Nicholaston	———	675
83	Oxwich	———	701
84	Oystermouth	Ystumllwynarth	756
85	Penarth		———
86	Pendeulwyn [Pendoylan]		———
87	Pen-llin [Penllyn]		681
88	Pen-maen		———
89	Pen-marc [Penmark]		764 765
90	Pennard		702
91	Penrice	Pen-rhys	645
92	Pen-tyrch		684
93	Peterston-super-Ely	Llanbedr-y-fro	662
94	Port Einon [Porteynon]		———
95	Porthkerry	Porthceri	671
96	Pyle and Kenfig	Y Pîl a Chynffig	632
97	Radur [Radyr]		———
98	Reynoldston	———	644
99	Rhosili		620–622 697–700 707
100	Roath	Y Rhath	———
101	Rudry	Rhydri	———
102	Rumney (formerly in Monmouthshire)	Tredelerch	———
103	St. Andrews	Saint Andras	768 769
104	St. Andrews Minor	———	———
105	St. Athan	Sain Tathan	———
106	St. Brides Major and Wick	Saint-y-brid ac Y Wig	630a 631 666 708 709
107	St. Brides Minor	Llansanffraid-ar-Ogwr	———
108	St. Brides-super-Ely	Llansanffraid-ar-Elái	———
109	St. Donats	Sain Dunwyd	———
110	St. Fagans with Llanilterne	Sain Ffagan gyda Llanilltern	640
111	St. George	Sain Siorys	———
112	St. Hilary	Saint Hilari	———
113	St. John-juxta-Swansea	———	———
114	St. Lythans	Llwyneliddon	761

No.	*Parish name used*	*Correct Welsh form*	*Monument Nos.*
115	St. Mary Church	Llan-fair	———
116	St. Mary Hill	Eglwys Fair y Mynydd	633 660
117	St. Nicholas	Sain Nicolas	———
118	Sker (extra-parochial)	Y Sgêr	———
119	Sully	Sili	704
120	Swansea	Abertawe	———
121	Tythegston	Llandudwg	680
122	Welsh St. Donats	Llanddunwyd	———
123	Wenvoe	Gwenfô	641
124	Whitchurch	Yr Eglwys Newydd	663
125	Ystradowen		661
126	Ystradyfodwg		694 711 712 716
127	Land common to five parishes: Llanrhidian, Nicholaston, Pen-maen, Penrice, Reynoldston		———

LIST OF CIVIL PARISHES

WITH INCIDENCE OF MONUMENTS

This list corresponds with the map forming the end-paper at the back of the book, and indicates the civil subdivision of Glamorgan into parishes as it stood at the end of 1970. The boundaries and the names have undergone many changes since the original adoption of the ecclesiastical pattern for secular administrative purposes (*cf.* front end-paper and list on p. xvii), and modifications will continue to be made.

Civil parishes are noted at the end of Inventory entries, distinguished by the letter (C) when the monument concerned stands in an ecclesiastical parish of a different name (E). Spellings used are as shown on the left, in general agreeing with those used on the O.S. 1:100,000 Administrative Areas map, 1970. The only departures from this practice (other than cases simply involving hyphens or capitals) are indicated by the addition of the O.S. spelling in square brackets. The Welsh forms, which follow the recommendations of the Board of Celtic Studies, are given on the right only when they differ from those already adopted for use in this Inventory.

No.	*Parish name used*	*Correct Welsh form*	*Monument Nos.*
1	Aberdâr [Aberdare]		619 713–715 741
2	Baglan Higher		652
3	Barry	Y Barri	766 767
4	Betws [Bettws]		———
5	Bishopston	Llandeilo Ferwallt	677 703
6	Blaen-gwrach		———
7	Blaenhonddan		———
8	Bonvilston	Tresimwn	696
9	Bridgend	Pen-y-bont ar Ogwr	———
10	Cardiff	Caerdydd	664 735 762
11	Cheriton	———	622a 689
12	Cilybebyll		———
13	Clyne	Y Clun	618
14	Coed-ffranc		———
15	Coety Higher [Coity H.]	Coety Uchaf	635 636 745
16	Colwinston	Tregolwyn	———
17	Cowbridge	Y Bont-faen	———
18	Coychurch Higher	Llangrallo Uchaf	634 637
19	Coychurch Lower	Llangrallo Isaf	614
20	Cwm-du		———
21	Dulais Higher [Dylais H.]	Dulais Uchaf	731 751
22	Dulais Lower [Dylais L.]	Dulais Isaf	752
23	Dyffryn Clydach		———
24	Eglwys Brewys [Eglwysbrewis]		———

No.	*Parish name used*	*Correct Welsh form*	*Monument Nos.*
25	Eglwysilan		736
26	Ewenni [Ewenny]		———
27	Flemingston	Trefflemin	———
28	Gelli-gaer		737 746–750
29	Gileston	Silstwn	———
30	Glyncorrwg		658
31	Gowerton	Tre-gŵyr	742–744
32	Ilston	Llanilltud Gŵyr	676
33	Kenfig	Cynffig	———
34	Knelston	Llan-y-tair-mair	———
35	Laleston	Trelales	———
36	Lavernock	Larnog	———
37	Leckwith	Lecwydd	———
38	Lisvane	Llys-faen	———
39	Llanblethian	Llanfleiddan	670 695
40	Llancarfan		615 638 759 760
41	Llanddewi		643 686
42	Llandeilo Tal-y-bont		616
43	Llandŵ [Llandow]		———
44	Llandyfodwg		———
45	Llanedern [Llanedeyrn]		685
46	Llanfabon		———
47	Llan-fair		———
48	Llanfedw		———
49	Llanfythin	Llanfeuthin	683
50	Llan-gan		———
51	Llangeinwyr [Llangeinor]		———
52	Llangennith	Llangynydd	612 646 647 687–689 705 706
53	Llanguicke	Llan-giwg	———
54	Llangyfelach		642
55	Llangynwyd Higher	Llangynwyd Uchaf	659
56	Llangynwyd Lower	Llangynwyd Isaf	———
57	Llangynwyd Middle	Llangynwyd Ganol	657 693
58	Llanharan		———
59	Llanhari [Llanharry]		———
60	Llanilid		———
61	Llanillter [Llanilterne]		640
62	Llanmadog [Llanmadoc]		689
63	Llanmaes	Llan-faes	———
64	Llanmihangel	Llanfihangel y Bont-faen	763
65	Llanrhidian Higher	Llanrhidian Uchaf	623 624 648 649
66	Llanrhidian Lower	Llanrhidian Isaf	665 674
67	Llansanwyr [Llansannor]		———
68	Llantrisant		639 672
69	Llantrithyd	Llantriddyd	682
70	Llantwit Fardre	Llanilltud Faerdref	———

No.	*Parish name used*	*Correct Welsh form*	*Monument Nos.*
71	Llantwit Major	Llanilltud Fawr	668 669 758
—	Llanvithyn (*see* Llanfythin)		
72	Llanwynno [Llanwonno]		———
73	Llyswyrny [Llysworney]		———
74	Loughor Borough	Casllwchwr	733
75	Marcroes [Marcross]		667
76	Mawr		———
77	Merthyr Mawr		630 691
78	Merthyr Tudful [Merthyr Tydfil]		611 732
79	Michaelston Higher	Llanfihangel-ynys-Afan	———
80	Michaelston-le-Pit	Llanfihangel-y-pwll	673
81	Monknash	Yr As Fawr	———
82	Nash	Yr As Fach	———
83	Neath	Castell-nedd	626 628 690 734
84	Neath Higher	Castell-nedd Uchaf	617 738
85	Neath Lower	Castell-nedd Isaf	———
86	Newcastle Higher	Castellnewydd Uchaf	———
87	Newton Nottage	Drenewydd yn Notais	632 657
88	Nicholaston	———	675
89	Oxwich	———	701
90	Oystermouth	Ystumllwynarth	756
91	Penarth		———
92	Pen-coed		———
93	Pendeulwyn [Pendoylan]		———
94	Pen-llin [Penllyn]		681
95	Pen-maen		———
96	Pen-marc [Penmark]		764 765
97	Pennard		702
98	Penrice	Pen-rhys	645
99	Pen-tyrch		684
100	Peterston-super-Ely	Llanbedr-y-fro	662
101	Peterston-super-montem	Llanbedr-ar-fynydd	———
102	Pontypridd		740
103	Port Einon [Porteynon]		———
104	Porthkerry[1]	Porthceri	671
105	Port Talbot		613 625 653–656 678 679 692
106	Pyle	Y Pîl	632
107	Radur [Radyr]		———
108	Resolfen [Resolven]		———
109	Reynoldston	———	644
110	Rhigos	Rugos	712
111	Rhondda		694 711 716 741
112	Rhosili [Rhossili]		620–622 697–700 707
113	Rhyd-y-gwern		———

[1] The unnumbered area on the back end-paper map between 96 and 3 is a detached portion of Porthkerry.

No.	*Parish name used*	*Correct Welsh form*	*Monument Nos.*
114	Rhyndwyglydach [Rhyndwyclydach]		———
115	Rudry	Rhydri	———
116	St. Andrews Major	Saint Andras	768 769
117	St. Andrews Minor	———	———
118	St. Athan	Sain Tathan	———
119	St. Brides Major	Saint-y-brid	630a 631 666 708 709
120	St. Brides Minor	Llansanffraid-ar-Ogwr	———
121	St. Brides-super-Ely	Llansanffraid-ar-Elái	———
122	St. Donats	Sain Dunwyd	———
123	St. Fagans	Sain Ffagan	———
124	St. George	Sain Siorys	———
125	St. Hilary	Saint Hilari	———
126	St. Lythans	Llwyneliddon	761
127	St. Mary Hill	Eglwys Fair y Mynydd	633 660
128	St. Nicholas	Sain Nicolas	———
129	Sker	Y Sgêr	———
130	Stembridge	———	———
131	Sully	Sili	704
132	Swansea	Abertawe	650 651
133	Tongwynlais		———
134	Tonna		627 629 739
135	Tythegston Higher	Llandudwg Uchaf	680
136	Tythegston Lower	Llandudwg Isaf	———
137	Van	Y Fan	———
138	Welsh St. Donats	Llanddunwyd	———
139	Wenvoe	Gwenfô	641
140	Wick	Y Wig	———
141	Ynysawdre		———
142	Ynysymwn [Ynysymond]		———
143	Ystradowen		661
144	Land common to six parishes: Llanrhidian Higher & Lower, Nicholaston, Pen-maen, Penrice, Reynoldston		———

ABBREVIATED TITLES OF REFERENCES

Ann. Camb. . . . . . . *Annales Cambriae*, ed. J. Williams 'ab Ithel', Rolls Series (London, 1860).

A.P. . . . . Aerial photographs, indicating sortie, date, and frame no., refer to the national air cover available at higher planning authorities. See also C.U.A.P.

Arch. Camb. . . . . . . *Archaeologia Cambrensis.* The Cambrian Archaeological Association.

Arch. in Wales . . . . . *Archaeology in Wales.* Council for British Archaeology, Group 2.

Arch. Journ. . . . . . . *The Archaeological Journal.* The Royal Archaeological Institute.

Arch. Roman Britain . . . . R. G. Collingwood and I. A. Richmond, *The Archaeology of Roman Britain* (London, 1969).

B.B.C.S. . . . . . . *Bulletin of the Board of Celtic Studies.* University of Wales.

B.M. . . . . British Museum, London.

Brut . . . . T. Jones (ed.), *Brut y Tywysogyon*, Peniarth MS. 20 version (1952); Red Book of Hergest version (1955). Board of Celtic Studies, History and Law Series, Nos. 11 and 16, Cardiff.

Carlisle, *Top. Dict.*. . . . . N. Carlisle, *A Topographical Dictionary of Wales* (London, 1811).

Clark, *Cartae* . . . . . G. T. Clark, *Cartae et alia munimenta quae ad dominium de Glamorgan pertinent* (6 vols., 2nd edn., Cardiff, 1910).

C.U.A.P. . . . . . . Cambridge University Collection of Aerial Photographs.

Davies, *W. Gower* . . . . . J. D. Davies, *The History of West Gower* (4 vols., Swansea, 1877, 1879, 1885, 1894).

Frere, *Britannia* . . . . . S. S. Frere, *Britannia. A History of Roman Britain* (London, 1967).

Grimes, *Prehist. Wales* . . . . W. F. Grimes, *The Prehistory of Wales* (Cardiff, 1951).

Haverfield, 'Military Aspects' . . F. Haverfield, 'Military aspects of Roman Wales', *Trans. Cymmr.*, 1908–9.

H.M.S.O. . . . . . . Her Majesty's Stationery Office, London/Edinburgh.

I.A. Map . . . . . . *Map of Southern Britain in the Iron Age* (Ordnance Survey, 1962).

Inv. Caerns. . . . . . . R.C.A.M. (Wales), *An Inventory of the Ancient Monuments in Caernarvonshire* (3 vols., 1956, 1960, 1964, H.M.S.O.).

Lewis, *Top. Dict.* . . . . . S. Lewis, *A Topographical Dictionary of Wales* (2 vols., London, 1833).

Lhuyd, *Parochialia* . . . . . E. Lhuyd, *Parochialia* (3 parts, *Arch. Camb.* supplements, 1909–11, ed. R. H. Morris).

Lib. Land. . . . . . . J. G. Evans and J. Rhys (eds.), *Liber Landavensis. The text of the Book of Llan Dav* (Oxford, 1893).

Margary, *Roman Roads* . . . . I. D. Margary, *Roman Roads in Britain* (2nd edn., London, 1967).

Morgan, *E. Gower*	W. Ll. Morgan, *An Antiquarian Survey of East Gower* (London, 1899).
M.P.B.W.	Ministry of Public Building and Works, now Department of the Environment.
N.L.W.	National Library of Wales, Aberystwyth.
N.M.W.	National Museum of Wales, Cardiff.
O.D.	Ordnance Datum.
O.S.	Ordnance Survey.
R.C.A.M.	The Royal Commission on Ancient and Historical Monuments in Wales.
R.I.S.W.	The Royal Institution of South Wales, Swansea.
Roman Frontier	V. E. Nash-Williams, *The Roman Frontier in Wales* (2nd edn., revised M. G. Jarrett, Cardiff, 1969).
Roman Inscriptions	R. G. Collingwood and R. P. Wright, *The Roman Inscriptions of Britain: I, Inscriptions on Stone* (Oxford, 1965).
Roman Villa	A. L. F. Rivet (ed.), *The Roman Villa in Britain* (London, 1969).
Rutter, *P. Gower*	J. G. Rutter, *Prehistoric Gower. The Early Archaeology of West Glamorgan* (Swansea, 1948).
S.	In 'Hillforts and Related Structures' (Nos. 611–709), indicates number in H. N. Savory, 'List of hillforts . . . in Glamorgan', *B.B.C.S.*, XIII, iii (Nov. 1949), pp. 152–61; supplement, *ibid.*, XV, iii (Nov. 1953), pp. 228–9.
Simpson, *Britons*	G. Simpson, *Britons and the Roman Army* (London, 1964).
Trans. Cymmr.	*Transactions of the Honourable Society of Cymmrodorion.*
Vitae sanct.	A. W. Wade-Evans (ed.), *Vitae sanctorum Britanniae et genealogiae* (Cardiff, 1944). Board of Celtic Studies, History and Law Series, No. 9.
Wheeler, *P. and R. Wales* . .	R. E. M. Wheeler, *Prehistoric and Roman Wales* (Oxford, 1925).

PRESENTATION OF MATERIAL

General Arrangement. The entries in the Inventory are now arranged by types of structure, instead of by grouping together items of all periods which happen to lie within the boundaries of a given parish. The general discussion of each type of monument can therefore be accompanied by the complete set of relevant entries, and the material can be published in smaller sections which are individually less costly and easier to handle.

Volume I is concerned with those types of monument which seem generally to be earlier than the arrival of Norman influences. The remaining volumes will be as follows: II. Ecclesiastical Buildings; III. Castles and other defensive works; IV. Domestic Buildings (including those associated with farms); and V. Industrial and other late structures. Volume IV is likely to appear next, for the extremely rapid destruction of early houses has made it necessary to concentrate work on them. Detailed decisions as to possible arrangement and subdivision can only be decided after the material has been collected.

This first volume has been divided into three parts. *Part i* deals mainly with cairns and burial mounds, *Part ii* with hill-forts and with structures of Roman date, and *Part iii* with inscribed stones assigned to the Early Christian Period. The classification by types of structure corresponds fairly closely to a proper chronological sequence in terms of the classic Three-Age system, for which there is no satisfactory alternative, in the absence of precise dating.

Since the range of interest of the individual reader may lie within a single part of this Volume, the introductory material and indexes are repeated, modified in each part as necessary.

Monuments Included. Some structures cannot be classified satisfactorily by surface investigation, either because of their condition or because they present unusual features. The decision whether to include such marginal cases in the Inventory can only be based on a subjective judgement as to whether they are more likely than not to be genuine; any uncertainty is indicated in the descriptive entry, and rejected sites are listed at the ends of sections.

Form of Entries. These give a detailed description, illustrated where necessary. This is followed by the name of the parish; where the present civil parish differs from the original ecclesiastical parish both are named and indicated by (C) and (E) respectively. The last line gives the sheet number of the current 1/10,000 or 1/10,560 O.S. map; the National Grid reference, to eight figures, of the approximate centre of the monument or group; the date of survey, or of the most recent visit if no plan is given; and the sheet number of the obsolescent county series of 6″-to-one-mile O.S. maps. The note on condition given in former Inventories has been omitted; the information it conveyed is implicit in the entries themselves.

For the monuments described in this volume, the structural materials used were almost invariably obtained in the vicinity and are only specified when this is known not to be the case.

Numbering of Entries. Entries are numbered consecutively throughout each volume, save that gaps have been left to allow for future discoveries. Within each section, the entries are normally arranged in order of 1/10,000 or 1/10,560 map sheets, that is by the N.W., N.E., S.W., and S.E. quarters of 10 km grid squares. Where this scheme would break up an assemblage of monuments (such as cairns) which seem to form a group, the separate items of the group are enumerated and described in succession after the first relevant entry; cross-references are given in the appropriate positions to any entries displaced by this arrangement.

A few structures found after the text had been completed have been recorded in their correct places with numbers such as 240a.

Names. Most early structures are anonymous, and are indicated on the map merely in descriptive terms. Where a traditional name is known, or a specific modern name is well established, this heads the entry. In other cases, the name of an adjacent farm, village, or natural feature is used for convenience of reference, even though its correct application may be to some other object; thus 'Fforest-newydd' heads an entry describing a small earthwork which lies some distance N.W. of the farm of that name. Unless there is a good reason for a change the names used by previous writers are retained.

Distribution Maps. The maps which accompany each section are intended primarily to show the distribution of the monuments. The background gives a generalised representation of the suitability of different areas for settlement, distinguishing by tints between the permeable and impermeable soils and by shading between the higher and lower ground. The most favourable territories, with permeable soils and at a low level, thus appear white, while the least favourable have the darkest colouring. The distributions of the different types of monument are shown by overprints.

Location of Monuments. The individual monuments shown on these maps are not numbered, since to do so would obscure the distribution pattern at the scale used (1/250,000, about ¼-inch to a mile. Even one inch to a mile is not a large enough scale to permit the exact location of small sites). The position of any particular monument, however, can be precisely fixed by its grid reference. Conversely, if the six-figure reference of a monument of a particular type is already known, it can be identified by use of the Index of Grid References (pp. 127–9); some structures will have escaped record, and information as to these would be appreciated (see p. x).

Parishes. The numbers of the monuments within each parish are given on pp. xvii–xxiv. Separate lists are given for Civil and Ecclesiastical parishes; the end-papers show maps of their boundaries. The Civil parishes are taken as in 1971. The boundaries of the Ecclesiastical parishes are those shown by the Tithe Award Surveys of *ca.* 1850; no attempt has been made to separate those which, like Kenfig and Pyle, are combined in a single survey.

Superimposed Structures of Different Periods. Occasionally structures of widely different date are superimposed. In such cases, the structure relevant to the present volume is described in detail, and a fairly full summary description is given of the other remains. Thus at Caerau, Ely (I ii 673) this volume contains a full account of the hill-fort, with a brief description of the medieval ringwork superimposed upon it; in Volume III the ringwork will be described in detail, with a note on the hill-fort.

Metric Measurements. In view of the forthcoming national adoption of the metric system, it has been used throughout; a conversion table to imperial units is given on pp. xxix–xxx. For the same reason, the system of scales used for the Caernarvonshire Inventory has been replaced by a sequence with the reduction factors 1:10,000, 5,000, 2,500, 1,000 and so on throughout the range required.

Most of the fieldwork had been completed before the Government's decision was made known, and as a result conversion has not always been possible without implying a decree of accuracy which would be unrealistic for the type of monument described; it is hoped that this will not prove misleading. Contours on plans have been left in feet, since in many cases to convert them satisfactorily would have required a fresh survey.

Authorship. The final form of the Inventory is the result of detailed discussion between the Commissioners and their staff; the Secretary acts as Editor. The authorship and compilation of the initial drafts are indicated at the end of the List of Staff (p. xvi).

CONVERSION TABLES

METRIC TO IMPERIAL

For fairly accurate conversion without reference to the tables, the following good approximate correspondences may be useful. More precise values are given in parenthesis.

0·3 m ≏ 1 ft. (0·984 ft.)
5 m ≏ 1 rod, pole, or perch of 16½ ft. (16·40 ft.)
20 m ≏ 1 chain of 66 ft. (0·994 chain or 65·62 ft.)
200 m ≏ 1 furlong (0·994 furlong)
1 hectare ≏ 2·5 acres (2·471 acres)

If the objective is merely to obtain a general mental impression of size, a metre may be looked upon as a long pace.

The linear tables are given to the nearest inch so that they can be used in combination if desired, but in applying them regard must be had to the degree of accuracy appropriate to the type of site; measurements of earthworks, for example, can seldom be determined more precisely than the nearest 0·3 m (1 ft.).

AREA—to the nearest 0·1 acre

Hectares by tenths

Ha	·0	·1	·2	·3	·4	·5	·6	·7	·8	·9
0	acres	0·2	0·5	0·7	1·0	1·2	1·5	1·7	2·0	2·2
1	2·5	2·7	3·0	3·2	3·5	3·7	4·0	4·2	4·4	4·7
2	4·9	5·2	5·4	5·7	5·9	6·2	6·4	6·7	6·9	7·2
3	7·4	7·7	7·9	8·2	8·4	8·6	8·9	9·1	9·4	9·6
4	9·9	10·1	10·4	10·6	10·9	11·1	11·4	11·6	11·9	12·1
5	12·4	12·6	12·8	13·1	13·3	13·6	13·8	14·1	14·3	14·6
6	14·8	15·1	15·3	15·6	15·8	16·1	16·3	16·6	16·8	17·1
7	17·3	17·5	17·8	18·0	18·3	18·5	18·8	19·0	19·3	19·5
8	19·8	20·0	20·3	20·5	20·8	21·0	21·3	21·5	21·7	22·0
9	22·2	22·5	22·7	23·0	23·2	23·5	23·7	24·0	24·2	24·5
10	24·7	25·0	25·2	25·5	25·7	25·9	26·2	26·4	26·7	26·9
11	27·2	27·4	27·7	27·9	28·2	28·4	28·7	28·9	29·2	29·4
12	29·7	29·9	30·1	30·4	30·6	30·9	31·1	31·4	31·6	31·9
13	32·1	32·4	32·6	32·9	33·1	33·4	33·6	33·9	34·1	34·3
14	34·6	34·8	35·1	35·3	35·6	35·8	36·1	36·3	36·6	36·8
15	37·1	37·3	37·6	37·8	38·1	38·3	38·5	38·8	39·0	39·3
16	39·5	39·8	40·0	40·3	40·5	40·8	41·0	41·3	41·5	41·8
17	42·0	42·3	42·5	42·7	43·0	43·2	43·5	43·7	44·0	44·2
18	44·5	44·7	45·0	45·2	45·5	45·7	46·0	46·2	46·5	46·7
19	47·0	47·2	47·4	47·7	47·9	48·2	48·4	48·7	48·9	49·2
20	49·4	49·7	49·9	50·2	50·4	50·7	50·9	51·2	51·4	51·6

LINEAR—to nearest inch

0–10·9 metres by decimetres

m	·0	·1	·2	·3	·4	·5	·6	·7	·8	·9
0	ft./ins.	0′4″	0′8″	1′0″	1′4″	1′8″	2′0″	2′4″	2′7″	2′11″
1	3′3″	3′7″	3′11″	4′3″	4′7″	4′11″	5′3″	5′7″	5′11″	6′3″
2	6′7″	6′11″	7′3″	7′7″	7′10″	8′2″	8′6″	8′10″	9′2″	9′6″
3	9′10″	10′2″	10′6″	10′10″	11′2″	11′6″	11′10″	12′2″	12′6″	12′10″
4	13′1″	13′5″	13′9″	14′1″	14′5″	14′9″	15′1″	15′5″	15′9″	16′1″
5	16′5″	16′9″	17′1″	17′5″	17′9″	18′1″	18′4″	18′8″	19′0″	19′4″
6	19′8″	20′0″	20′4″	20′8″	21′0″	21′4″	21′8″	22′0″	22′4″	22′8″
7	23′0″	23′4″	23′7″	23′11″	24′3″	24′7″	24′11″	25′3″	25′7″	25′11″
8	26′3″	26′7″	26′11″	27′3″	27′7″	27′11″	28′3″	28′7″	28′10″	29′2″
9	29′6″	29′10″	30′2″	30′6″	30′10″	31′2″	31′6″	31′10″	32′2″	32′6″
10	32′10″	33′2″	33′6″	33′10″	34′1″	34′5″	34′9″	35′1″	35′5″	35′9″

0–109 m by metres

m	0	1	2	3	4	5	6	7	8	9
0	ft./ins.	3′3″	6′7″	9′10″	13′1″	16′5″	19′8″	23′0″	26′3″	29′6″
10	32′10″	36′1″	39′4″	42′8″	45′11″	49′3″	52′6″	55′9″	59′1″	62′4″
20	65′7″	68′11″	72′2″	75′6″	78′4″	82′0″	85′4″	88′7″	91′10″	95′2″
30	98′5″	101′8″	105′0″	108′3″	111′7″	114′10″	118′1″	121′5″	124′8″	127′11″
40	131′3″	134′6″	137′10″	141′1″	144′4″	147′8″	150′11″	154′2″	157′6″	160′9″
50	164′1″	167′4″	170′7″	173′11″	177′2″	180′5″	183′9″	187′0″	190′3″	193′7″
60	196′10″	200′2″	203′5″	206′8″	210′0″	213′3″	216′6″	219′10″	223′1″	226′5″
70	229′8″	232′11″	236′3″	239′6″	242′9″	246′1″	249′4″	252′7″	255′11″	259′2″
80	262′6″	265′9″	269′0″	272′4″	275′7″	278′10″	282′2″	285′5″	288′9″	292′0″
90	295′3″	298′7″	301′10″	305′1″	308′5″	311′8″	315′0″	318′3″	321′6″	324′10″
100	328′1″	331′4″	334′8″	337′11″	341′2″	344′6″	347′9″	351′1″	354′4″	357′7″

0–1090 m by decametres

m	0	10	20	30	40	50	60	70	80	90
0	ft./ins.	32′10″	65′7″	98′5″	131′3″	164′1″	196′10″	229′8″	262′6″	295′3″
100	328′1″	360′11″	393′8″	426′6″	459′4″	492′2″	524′11″	557′9″	590′7″	623′4″
200	656′2″	689′0″	721′9″	754′7″	787′5″	820′3″	853′0″	885′10″	918′8″	951′5″
300	984′3″	1017′1″	1049′10″	1082′8″	1115′6″	1148′4″	1181′1″	1213′11″	1246′9″	1279′6″
400	1312′4″	1345′2″	1377′11″	1410′9″	1443′7″	1476′5″	1509′2″	1542′0″	1574′10″	1607′7″
500	1640′5″	1673′3″	1706′0″	1738′10″	1771′8″	1804′6″	1837′3″	1870′1″	1902′11″	1935′8″
600	1968′6″	2001′4″	2034′1″	2066′11″	2099′9″	2132′7″	2165′4″	2198′2″	2231′0″	2263′9″
700	2296′7″	2329′5″	2362′2″	2395′0″	2427′10″	2460′8″	2493′5″	2526′3″	2559′1″	2591′10″
800	2624′8″	2657′6″	2690′3″	2723′1″	2755′11″	2788′9″	2821′6″	2854′4″	2887′2″	2919′11″
900	2952′9″	2985′7″	3018′5″	3051′2″	3084′0″	3116′10″	3149′7″	3182′5″	3215′3″	3248′0″
1000	3280′10″	3313′8″	3346′6″	3379′3″	3412′1″	3444′11″	3477′8″	3510′6″	3543′4″	3576′1″

INVENTORY

PART II: THE IRON AGE AND THE ROMAN OCCUPATION

INTRODUCTORY NOTE

THE arrangement of an Inventory, whether by types of monument or topographically, necessarily conflicts with an ordered discussion of the material. Further, concentration on a single county and on structural remains alone leaves out some important parts of the evidence. The summary given in this introduction is a consecutive historical and archaeological account, in the course of which the more important monuments are indicated. A fuller account is given in the sectional introductions to the Inventory entries, but since these are arranged by type no given section necessarily corresponds to a particular range of dates; but just as the majority of the round cairns belong to some phase of the Bronze Age, so hill-forts and related structures, as well as groups of round huts, are typical of the Iron Age. For the most part there is little doubt about the correct attribution of Roman structures. This second part, of the three which form Volume I of the Inventory, can therefore be regarded as covering the Roman period and the preceding Iron Age, though some of the groups of small cairns, dealt with in the first part, may in fact be Iron Age or later; there was also some native use of caves in the Roman period and later.

The Iron Age contrasts strongly with the earlier periods in two ways. First, little or no use seems to have been made of the mountain ridges, which played such an important part in the burial of the earlier inhabitants, and by inference in their life; as a result there is no evidence on which to base even a hypothetical discussion of communications during the Iron Age. Second, the period is represented almost entirely by settlement-sites. The earliest of these, as at Merthyr Mawr or Dinas Powys (p. 7), seem to have been unfortified, but very few forts have been excavated, and of these two produced evidence for occupation which must have been fairly early, though undated. Apart from these, the relics found all belong to the culture which developed out of the second wave of cultural influences, perhaps of about 250 B.C. initially. Unfortunately, the material is not distinctive enough to permit a detailed chronological classification of the fortified sites, though these can be classified by type into several different groups (p. 12). It must be realised that there is a risk that the nature and settlement patterns of this period appear distorted because the fortified sites mostly survive whereas unfortified settlements are lost. Hut groups, probably of the Iron Age but not accurately dated, occur in the mountains; a well preserved and accessible example is that above Garreg Lwyd (711).

Many of the fortified sites are well preserved and interesting, and most are fairly easily accessible, so no attempt will be made here to indicate particular examples.

The Silures, who inhabited Glamorgan and adjacent areas at the time of the Roman invasion, were subject to intermittent attack for more than twenty years before their final subjection in A.D. 74. It is to be expected that further excavation in their hill-forts will produce evidence of destruction in the course of this prolonged warfare, but nothing is certainly identifiable at present. Roman military activity, however, has left many traces.

Four temporary marching camps are known, thrown up by the army in the field as protection for a short period. Those at Twyn y Briddallt (741) and at Blaen-cwm Bach (739) are well preserved; the latter is large enough to accommodate three legions. All but one of the eight permanent forts built to consolidate the conquest have been located, and two, at Coelbren (731) and Gelli-gaer (737), remain visible. At Gelli-gaer a later fort was built on a new site close by, instead of being superimposed on the earlier fort. To this phase of consolidation, also, must be attributed the road network; much of the structure of 'Sarn Helen' is still visible (p. 109). There are also several examples of the small 'practice camps' built as exercises by the troops. A well preserved and accessible example is on Gelli-gaer Common (747).

The most striking relic of Roman military activity is the late fort at Cardiff (735). This has been extensively restored, and the walls are now probably nearly twice their original height, but nevertheless the rebuilt wall and north gateway give a good general impression of the appearance of a complete masonry fort during the latter part of the Roman period.

Despite their prolonged resistance the Silures do not seem to have been severely penalised by the Romans. Evidence for resumed or continued occupation has been found at several forts, notably the 'village' within Caer Dynnaf (670); and remains of huts of pre-Roman type have been found beneath typically Romanised buildings, as at Whitton Lodge (761) and perhaps also Moulton (759). By the latter half of the period substantial and luxurious 'villas' had been built. The best known is that excavated at Llantwit Major (758).

THE PHYSICAL BACKGROUND

By the beginning of the Iron Age, the general topography of the region approximated to its present form, so it is unnecessary to repeat here the discussion of the physiographical evolution and surface geology which was presented in Volume I, Part i. Nevertheless, despite man's steadily growing control over his environment, the soil pattern continued to influence settlement, so that some repetition on that topic is desirable.

SOIL TYPOLOGY

A classic pattern for regional archaeological studies, with due regard to ecological factors, was set by Fox in his 1923 study of the Cambridge region,[1] and was given wider application in his *Personality of Britain* in 1932.[2] In these studies the interpretation of settlement distribution was firmly based on the distinction between soils which are light, permeable, and hence easily cleared and cultivated, and those heavy, poorly

[1] C. Fox, *The Archaeology of the Cambridge Region* (Cambridge, 1923)
[2] C. Fox, *The Personality of Britain* (1st edn. Cardiff, 1932).

drained soils which would naturally support an intractable 'damp oak forest'. The distinction was for the most part a simple one, depending more on observation of surviving vegetation than on direct soil survey, which had not at that time reached the point of being uniformly reliable or available. Attention was soon drawn by Wooldridge and Linton[3] to the need to recognise a class of intermediate loams, distinguishable from either of the types defined by permeability alone. In reply, Fox[4] admitted the need, but advised the inclusion of some of these loams with his basic types, leaving 'an important residue which requires special consideration'; at the same time he doubted 'whether on small-scale maps . . . the plotting of an intermediary soil group is desirable'.

For the study of a county area however, Grimes[5] clearly indicated the desirability of detailed soil mapping in the case of Anglesey. There the almost total cover of boulder clay shown on the drift map conflicts with the apparent attraction of the terrain for neolithic and bronze-age settlers, until the evidence of the soil map is used to show a strong preference for the light and well drained soils derived from the drift. The parent material of developed soils can thus be a misleading indicator of their true character, as also can the present vegetation, so that only a pedological field survey can provide the necessary basis for the study of archaeological settlement patterns.

It is fortunate for the purpose of the present survey that detailed soil mapping of Glamorgan has been completed, and has already been studied by Crampton and Webley in terms of prehistoric settlement. In the Vale of Glamorgan[6], where the solid geology is mostly freely draining limestone, a basic distinction was made between soils developed directly on the rock and those on superimposed glacial drift. From these two categories certain soil areas were separated analytically on the basis of relatively impeded drainage, and were included in a third category with impervious clays of fluvial or glacial origin, as well as with soils overlying the marls of the eastern end of the Vale. In this way the lighter, sandy loams on the drift were retained as potentially habitable areas along with those of coastal dunes. The distribution of prehistoric sites was used to indicate a secondary colonising movement into these areas during the Iron Age, for the primary choice during the Neolithic and Bronze Age had been the more fertile soils on the limestone, freely drained but of less sandy texture.

In order to simplify the representation of soils on the base map for distributions in the present volume, both classes of loams noted in the Vale of Glamorgan have been indicated as *permeable soils*, thus following Crampton and Webley in their study of the remainder of the county,[7] where the term 'sols bruns acides' is used. Soils of impeded drainage are grouped by them as 'gleyed soils', without reference to solid geology or mode of formation, and are indicated on the base map here as *impermeable soils*. A more important distinction is made in the recognition of *semi-permeable soils* or 'podzols', used as an intermediate mapping unit which was not discernible in the Vale.

In the mountain zone of Glamorgan (Blaenau Morgannwg) podzols occur on the lower ridges and slopes radiating from the Craig y Llyn area, generally providing good grazing or a typical growth of bilberry in remote places. With decreasing altitude along the ridges there is an increasing proportion of permeable soils, typically covered by bracken growth where not cultivated, and virtually dominating the foothills which overlook the Vale. The gleyed, impermeable soils, carrying coarse moor grass or bog vegetation, occupy the higher, central core of the mountains and the radiating valley bottoms.

[3] *Antiquity*, VII (1933), pp. 297–310.
[4] *Antiquity*, VII (1933), pp. 473–5 and Appendix IV of *Archaeology of the Cambridge Region* (1948 edn.).
[5] *Antiquity*, XIX (1945), pp. 169–74.
[6] *B.B.C.S.*, XVIII, iv (May 1960), pp. 387–96.
[7] *B.B.C.S.*, XX, iii (Nov. 1963), pp. 326–37.

In Gower the podzols are limited to four isolated areas of the highest hills. The permeable, most fertile soils occupy much of the south and west of the peninsula on limestone formations, with a parallel band further to the north-east connecting Swansea and Carmarthen Bays. The poorer, gleyed soils form an intervening band over the millstone grit of the northern part of Gower, and occupy islands of drift-covered common land in the south-west, as well as the greater part of the eastern flank of the Llwchwr estuary.

The particular significance of the semi-permeable podzols appears to be that, when present, they were preferred for the siting of bronze-age cairns, even when better drained, more fertile loams lay adjacent. The latter, however, were preferred in the siting of most iron-age hill-forts, but only partly because of the supposed tendency towards a farming economy in which tillage ranked at least equally with pastoralism.

CLIMATE AND VEGETATION

On the uplands a series of changes of precipitation,[8] covering the Bronze Age as a whole between about 2000 and 500 B.C., led to a final increase of rainfall and a return to a cold, oceanic regime (sub-Atlantic), which encouraged the formation of blanket peat in iron-age and Roman times, with a renewal of heathland. The climatic change which thus encouraged an overall preference for lowland situations would also have improved the quality of the sandy, glacial loams which had been too well drained in drier conditions. The eventual intake of some of the heavier soil areas, with a consequent further reduction of forest, awaited the introduction of the heavier plough of Roman times.

[8] Evidence from dated buried soils is noted by Crampton and Webley, *B.B.C.S.*, XX, iv (May 1964), pp. 440–9.

COMMUNICATIONS

IRON AGE AND ROMAN

THE possibility that some hill-forts or hut-groups are contemporary with some round cairns cannot be disproved, but their distribution patterns are very different, and it is convenient to regard them as representative of the Iron Age and Bronze Age respectively. Using this criterion, the mountain ridges were extensively used for burial during the Bronze Age, and by inference for grazing, and probably in some cases for trackways. Conditions during the Iron Age form a complete contrast. Hill-forts lie mostly in the lowland areas, and those few which are built on mountain spurs almost always have their entrances downhill, away from the trackways. Y Bwlwarcau on Mynydd Margam (693) is a particularly significant example, in view of its proximity to 'Ffordd y Gyfraith', which was certainly used in the Early Christian period, and perhaps earlier (see below, p. 105). Similarly, the siting of hut-groups (711–15), though on high ground, shows no relation to the trackways. The only exceptions to this generalisation are three small ringworks: Carn Caca (618) and near Blaen-cwm Bach (627), both near the track which follows Cefn Mawr, and Gwersyll (619), on the Mynydd Merthyr ridge; the last two are unfinished. These are assigned to the Iron Age merely by analogy; they have not been dated by excavation, and have no very distinctive characteristics, so they may be later.

Whatever the condition of the ridges during the Iron Age, it is certain that they provided good natural lines of communication at the beginning of the Roman period, for three marching camps have been identified on them: Blaen-cwm Bach (739); Penycoedcae (740); and Twyn y Briddallt (741). All visible trails at these sites are later than the ramparts. These camps are unrelated to the network of engineered and metalled roads built primarily for military use (Fig. 46).

Three of these roads are known in Glamorgan. One (753), for much of its length, still forms the main route through Cardiff westwards to Carmarthen, leaving the present county at Loughor. The other two branched off at Cardiff (754) and Neath (755), leading northwards to meet at Brecon Gaer. These are discussed in detail in those entries. In addition, there must have been many roads, some probably metalled, connecting the settlements in the coastal regions (pp. 105–6 below); their routes in relation to modern roads and parish boundaries offer almost unlimited scope for conjecture, but evidence is lacking. Two possibilities deserve mention. Ffordd y Gyfraith (see also I iii, pp. 2–5), running northwards from near Laleston, is ancient, and seems to have been set out in the characteristically Roman fashion of straight alignments between sighting points. The presence of a bridge at Tal-y-bont near Pontarddulais (SN 585 031) as early as the 12th century also suggests that a Roman road may have crossed the river here, and indeed it has been suggested that the Roman site of *Leucarum* should be sought at this crossing (p. 121 below). At present there is no relic of the right period to support these hypotheses.

HILL-FORTS AND SETTLEMENTS

IRON AGE

By contrast with earlier periods, the Iron Age is represented more by sites of human occupation than of burial. Hill-forts,[1] and structures related to them, can thus be taken for convenience as corresponding to this period, just as round cairns correspond to the Bronze Age, though the possibility of some overlap cannot be disproved. The actual range of date covered by the use of hill-forts in this area is uncertain, for although casual finds are relatively common in comparison to other parts of Wales, they are only rarely found in association with structures or with other objects.

The earliest evidence of iron-using is given by a remarkable discovery in the small mountain tarn of Llyn Fawr, near Hirwaun.[2] During the construction of a reservoir, removal of peat exposed a collection of twenty-four objects, mostly of bronze but including three of iron; all are broadly of the same date, conventionally about 600 B.C. Their origins are diverse. The iron sword and harness seem to have come from the Continent. By contrast the two cauldrons seem of Irish making. The two bronze sickles and razor could have been made in Glamorgan, as could the socketed axes, though most of these last are of a type more commonly found in East Anglia. The sickles are the most instructive part of the group. All are of a type which seems to be restricted to Ireland and South Wales, but whereas two have been fabricated in the normal way, as bronze castings, the third is a copy of the same form in iron, showing that that metal was

---

[1] There are objections to the term 'hill-fort', but all suggested alternatives have as many, and moreover lack the advantages of brevity and established use.

[2] *Archaeologia*, LXXI (1921), pp. 133–7 (R. E. M. Wheeler; discovery and description); *Antiq. Journ.*, XIX (1939), pp. 367–404 (C. Fox; further details of discovery, description of second cauldron and iron sword); *Proc. Prehist. Soc.*, V (1939), pp. 223–39 (C. Fox; typology of sickles); *Arch. Camb.*, CVII (1958), pp. 38–40 (H. N. Savory; further comments on date and origins); Grimes, *Prehist. Wales*, pp. 221–3, Nos. 690–3 (summary description of all objects).

being made and worked in the area where sickles of this type were used. Fox considered 'the blacksmiths . . . knew no better than laboriously to copy in wrought iron socketed tools of cast bronze', but it seems more likely that the form was adopted to satisfy the requirements of their customers, and the skill with which this has been done indicates the smith's mastery of his material.

Any extended discussion of the implications of this discovery must depend almost entirely on conjecture. There is no hill-fort near the lake, and although three groups of stone-built huts (711–13) occur not far away they do not give the impression that they are likely to have housed anyone prosperous enough to be the owner of so much valuable metal-work; they are roughly built, and excavations at Garreg Lwyd (711) discovered nothing but a little iron, iron slag, and leather. It will be sufficient to comment briefly on the various hypotheses which have been put forward to account for the discovery.

The reason for its occurrence in the lake could be as a votive deposit, as relics from a dwelling, or as material concealed to await recovery. Fox rejected the first, as a sacred lake might be expected to contain objects covering a long period; but a single sacrifice is not impossible. Some support is given to the idea of a dwelling by the recorded presence of cut timbers, but as Fox noted, the site—'the most sunless and cold in the uplands'—is highly unsuitable for a dwelling. The third possibility, of concealment intended to be temporary, is incapable of proof.

The assemblage as a whole would be explicable as the personal accoutrements of a warrior of some rank, together with the equipment of his immediate household; or possibly it could have been the stock of a travelling metal-worker. The deposition could have been made by the original owner, or by a thief.

The hypothesis that the objects belonged to a warrior and his household requires that his main establishment was elsewhere; for if the sickles are taken to imply cereal-growing, the region round Llyn Fawr is unsuitable. Items similar to some of those in the collection have been found in the Vale,[3] in particular in a hoard from Cardiff,[4] which contained a similar sickle, a razor typologically related to that from the lake, and an axe decorated with ribs and pellets. The most likely location for this establishment, if it existed, is therefore in the coastal plain of Glamorgan, though the other side of the Bristol Channel cannot be excluded.

Another important accidental discovery was of one of the rare burial sites of the Iron Age. In 1818, during excavation for stone on the east side of Ogmore Down, several graves were revealed. The contents were subsequently lost, but notes and drawings were made at the time, and an intelligible description with engravings based on these has been published.[5] The principal objects were two helmets ornamented with silver and with red enamel; each contained a skull. The details shown in the engravings are consistent with Italo-Celtic work of the 4th–3rd centuries B.C., but the accompanying description explicitly records a band of blue enamel at the rim, which would imply a date well into the 1st century A.D. It is therefore necessary either to accept the helmets as relatively late copies of earlier work or to dismiss the 'blue enamel' as vivianite or some product of corrosion.[5a] The other objects recorded are two 'brass' skull-caps, a few pieces of chain, and several curious pointed iron objects described as daggers, the blades being furnished with a number of small barbs. No parallel to these last is known.

Apart from the arrival of these isolated imports or of occasional metal-workers, the earliest influences from the continental Iron Age probably arrived in Britain a little before 500 B.C. By the time the effects

[3] See *Arch. Camb.*, CVII (1958), maps 8 and 9.
[4] *Antiq. Journ.*, XIII (1933), pp. 299–300.
[5] *Archaeologia*, XLIII (1872), pp. 553–6. The field-name, Castell Lligiad, is lost, but must have been near SS 905 753.
[5a] J. N. G. Ritchie in 'Celtic Defensive Weaponry in Britain' (Thesis, Edinburgh University, 1968) has now given additional reasons for regarding a date in the 1st century A.D. as probable.

reached Wales, they were represented mainly by the appearance of a rather coarse pottery, generally of rounded situlate form where this can be recognised, but of too simple character and of too wide chronological range to justify any sort of close dating on typological evidence.

Settlements with pottery of this type have been found at Dinas Powys[6] and at Merthyr Mawr Warren.[7] At the former the finds, with no structures, were sealed beneath post-Roman defences. At Merthyr Mawr they were associated with post-holes, but the full plan was not exposed. The latter site is on a besanded area where objects of many periods have been found, including brooches of La Tène I type, which on continental parallels could be dated to the 4th century B.C.; the pottery from either site might occur at such a date.

Both these settlements were unfortified, and no similarly early relics have as yet been discovered in a defended site in this area. This however, may well be merely from the accident of discovery, for elsewhere in Britain univallate defences often belong to this phase.[8] If Hardings Down West (687) is correctly regarded as of two periods, the original univallate enclosure may perhaps be as early as this, for the levelled platform near the centre had carried a round hut, the roof of which was supported on four large posts set in a square. This arrangement is rare, and the best parallel is found in a more elaborate building at Little Woodbury[9], Wiltshire, where much of the associated pottery was a developed form related to the coarse ware already mentioned; yet in the absence of any relics associated with the house at Hardings Down the link must be regarded as tenuous, for house typology alone cannot yet be used as a reliable indication of date or cultural associations. Similarly, although the stone forts at Thurba Head (698) and Castle Ditches (615) may also belong to the earliest phases of the Iron Age in the county, the hypothesis rests merely on the evidence of the structural sequence.

Most of the pottery found in south Wales forts is plain ware of rather better quality, with a fairly good, smooth, dark finish. A few finer and more ornate sherds occur. All this is generally regarded as having developed owing to the arrival of further continental influences, perhaps (very roughly) during the 3rd century B.C. The most common form is a deep, wide-mouthed bowl with a plain bead or out-turned rim; decoration is rare and simple. The finer ornamental pottery has been shown to be the product of localised workshops, mostly south of the Bristol Channel.[10] Its distribution apparently corresponds to the range over which it was traded, and does not necessarily indicate cultural unity. The mass of the pottery is not distinctive enough to permit any chronological arrangement.

No large multivallate fort has been excavated in Glamorgan, but closely similar settlements in Monmouthshire have produced assemblages of pottery which do not differ significantly from those found at the large univallate fort of Castle Ditches, Llancarfan (615) or the small bivallate enclosure at Mynydd Bychan (681).

Towards the end of the pre-Roman period, a new type of pottery came into use, similar to that found in areas known to have been occupied by the Belgae. Generally there seems to be no interruption of the occupation, but at Mynydd Bychan this ware first appears in the undefended homestead which was built over the ruins of the fortified enclosure, apparently after an interval of abandonment. Roman pottery was also found.

---

[6] L. Alcock, *Dinas Powis* (Cardifi, 1963), pp. 16–19, 123–4.

[7] *Arch. Camb.*, LXXXII (1927), pp. 44–111; LXXXIV (1929), pp. 146–7; Grimes, *Prehist. Wales*, pp. 227–9, Nos. 710–7, 721–3; *Trans. Cardiff Nat. Soc.*, LXXXII (1952–3), p. 43.

[8] See, for example, L. V. Grinsell, *The Archaeology of Wessex* (London, 1958), p. 156.

[9] *Proc, Prehist. Soc..*, VI (1940), pp. 30–111.

[10] *Antiq. Journ.*, XLIX (1969), pp. 41–61 (D. P. S. Peacock).

At the time of the Roman conquest, the Silures inhabited the area. They offered strong resistance, but no evidence has been found for deliberate slighting of any forts. This may be the result of insufficient excavation, but on the other hand Roman pottery has been found in several. At Llwynheiernin (650) it was actually incorporated in the rampart, while at two sites in Gower (677, 702) it was apparently in primary deposits. These three are all small, but forts of all sizes have yielded surface finds of sherds (612, 615, 670, 671, 673, 682, 691) and rotary querns (670, 695). At Moulton (762) a Roman farmhouse was built over earlier remains, while at Whitton Cross (764) a ditched enclosure containing round huts preceded an elaborate group of Roman buildings. It would seem that the smaller defended enclosures were allowed to continue in use, and may even have been built, during the full Roman occupation. The position as to the larger forts is not so clear. At Caer Dynnaf (670) part of the actual settlement of the Roman period remains visible. Its arrangement suggests a village of perhaps half a dozen contiguous farmsteads defined by their enclosing walls, whereas the normal arrangement of dwellings in a hill-fort in this region seems always to have been an almost random scatter of round huts. It is difficult to see how such a radical change could result from unbroken evolution, and destruction followed by re-settlement must be postulated, though not necessarily with any very long interval. Re-occupation after clearance could be accounted for on the assumption that the larger forts retained some legal importance in connection with land-tenure.

There is no evidence in Glamorgan for continued use of the forts into the Early Christian period or later. The presence of castle rings at Cil Ifor Top (665) and at Caerau, Ely (673) can be attributed to the defensive advantage of the sites, and the age of the concrete found on the rampart of Dunraven (666) is quite uncertain.

SOCIAL ORGANISATION

Here again, the surface character of the hill-forts provides almost all the available evidence for any attempt to reconstruct the social organisation of the iron-age inhabitants of Glamorgan. The undefended hut-groups (711–15) imply that pastoralists eked out a rather poor existence in the mountains, but even allowing for further discoveries which are being made in Brecknock these are far too few to suggest any considerable practice of transhumance by the occupants of the forts.

On the lower ground there is a little evidence for open settlements, as at Moulton (762), or in the farm built over the ruins of the earlier Mynydd Bychan enclosure (681), but neither fieldwork nor aerial photography indicates any very large number of such sites. The character of the remarkable group of round houses at Whitton Cross (761) is not yet completely clear, but originally it was protected by a ditch. So far as present evidence goes, therefore, it would seem that most of the iron-age population lived in defended settlements. Although the univallate and multivallate forts may be of different dates and origins they can be discussed together, for there is too little information available to distinguish any difference in the character of their occupation.

There has been too little excavation to demonstrate the main basis of subsistence, but in view of the type of ground occupied it seems safe to postulate general mixed farming for most sites, with a greater reliance on cattle on the higher ground. There are no convincing examples of early field-systems. A little evidence for metal-working was found at Castle Ditches (615). The big multivallate forts remain unexamined.

Few of the houses in the forts have been excavated. Unlike those of the unenclosed settlements, they seem generally to have been of wood, almost always round, ranging from 6 to 10 m in diameter with the roof supported on a ring of posts. Before excavation, when traces survive, they appear either as low earthen rings or more usually as platforms cut into the hill-slope. These are easily destroyed by cultivation. In addition, huts were often built in the quarry-scoops behind the ramparts, and these are generally obscured by natural silting. It is therefore seldom possible to make any estimate of the total number of huts in an enclosure, and even when one can be made the result is subject to much uncertainty; but it is worth while to make the attempt, for the intensity of occupation is obviously one of the most important factors in considering the function of the enclosure.

House-platforms are visible in ten forts, but these are not all of the same value as indicating the probable original intensity of occupation. In Gower, at Bishopston Valley (677), The Knave (699) and High Pennard (702), excavation has probably revealed all the dwellings within the enclosed area. At Hardings Down North (646) the interior slopes so steeply that it is practically certain that the one visible house-platform represents the only dwelling in the enclosure. On Thurba Head (698) the soil cover is thin, and a total of five possible house-sites can be traced; only two are certain. At Mynydd Bychan (681) in the first period, remains probably representing three dwellings were exposed by excavation; two or at most three more could have existed in the unexcavated parts. In these six enclosures, therefore, the totals are fairly reliable within the limits indicated; and with the possible exception of Thurba Head there is no evidence for work of more than one period at any given site. Llanmadog Bulwark (689) and Hardings Down West (687) contain one and three visible house-platforms respectively. In both, most of the enclosed area slopes steeply, but there are fairly large areas where buildings could have stood without the need for levelled platforms, so the estimates of the probable numbers for these may well be too low. This may also be the case at Dunraven, where twenty-one house-sites can be traced. These last three hill-forts introduce a further uncertainty, for it is likely that their defences do incorporate work of more than one period. Details for these nine forts are tabulated below, with estimates in parenthesis of the number of houses likely to have existed besides those now visible. The tenth fort, Cil Ifor Top (665), still retains three house-platforms, but most of the enclosure has been ploughed; their spacing is consistent with an intensity of occupation of the same order as at the others.

No.	Name	Area (ha)	Hut-platforms
646	Hardings Down North	0·2	1 (+0)
666	Dunraven	6·5	21 (+8)
677	Bishopston Valley	0·1	1 (+0)
681	Mynydd Bychan	0·3	3 (+2)
687	Hardings Down West	0·6	3 (+2)
689	Llanmadog Bulwark	0·9	1 (+3)
698	Thurba Head	0·3	2 (+3)
699	The Knave	0·1	1 (+0)
702	High Pennard	0·4	3 (+0)

These estimates are necessarily very much less reliable than for regions where stone was used for walling and, as noted, forts such as Dunraven may well have contained many buildings which have left no surface traces. Nevertheless, having regard to these uncertainties, the figures are remarkably consistent, and suggest that *in this region* most forts, of whatever size, would contain five to ten dwellings per hectare.

It would appear to follow that the fort-builders were concerned rather with the area to be enclosed than with the number of people needed to defend the ramparts. Hardings Down North, for example, has a perimeter of about 140 m, but contained only one house. Only in the largest forts would the normal population be able to resist anything more than casual raids, though the defences would offer a considerable advantage against an attack even by slightly superior numbers. A possible explanation of the low intensity of occupation indicated by the few hut-emplacements visible on undisturbed sites is to assume that the forts were primarily places of refuge, and that the only buildings substantial enough to leave surface traces belonged to a restricted class of permanent inhabitants; the evidence at present does not permit a firm decision, but the scarcity of traces of settlements of any kind outside the forts tends rather against this theory.

Subject to this possibility, the evidence from surface features and from the few sites excavated suggests that the smaller forts, below 1·2 or more probably 0·7 ha, correspond generally to farms held by a single family with dependents, whereas the larger enclosures are villages; there is no doubt some overlap. Even the biggest, such as Dunraven or Caerau, Ely (673), are not likely to have contained more than fifty or sixty dwellings, so with permanent populations of no more than 300 or so they can hardly qualify as towns in any modern sense. On the assumption that the innermost enclosure of a wide-spaced multivallate fort corresponds to the main inhabited area, these also fall into the 'single-family farm' group.

GENERAL DISTRIBUTION AND COMMUNICATIONS

The general distribution of hill-forts (Fig. 1), considered as a whole, contrasts strongly with that for round cairns. Even when allowance is made for the fact that one pattern is of habitations and the other of burials, it seems almost certain that the change in the distribution corresponds to an actual shift of population, and to a decrease in the importance of the high ground. With few exceptions, hill-forts stand in the lowland areas. Even those which are built on mountain spurs generally have their entrances facing towards low ground. Y Bwlwarcau on Mynydd Margam (693) is a particularly significant example; the entrance points directly away from the important trackway Ffordd y Gyfraith (pp. 4–5), which runs within sight only half a kilometre to the west. Three small ringworks offer the only exceptions to the generalisation that hill-forts are located without regard to the ridgeways. These are at Carn Caca (618) and Blaen-cwm Bach (627) both near the track which follows Cefn Mawr N.E. of Neath, and Gwersyll (619) on the Mynydd Merthyr ridge; the last two are unfinished. These are assigned to the Iron Age merely by analogy. They have not been dated by excavation and have no very distinctive characteristics, so they may be later.

From another point of view, the change in distribution corresponds broadly to movement from semi-permeable to permeable soils. All large hill-forts, whether univallate or multivallate, stand on freely drained ground,[11] and so do most of the others. As a class, the only exception is the *inland* 'wide-spaced multivallate' type.

Trackways connecting settlements no doubt existed, and some probably survive in part as modern roads, but they cannot be identified. The mountain ridges, as noted, seem to have been of very little importance. That they were not completely deserted is demonstrated by hut-groups (711–15), and the presence of Roman marching-camps (p. 98) suggests that in the 1st century A.D. they provided relatively easy lines of communication. The hut-groups do not seem to be located with any regard to existing trackways, and the hollow trails which can be traced across the marching-camps are all later than their ramparts.

It seems reasonable to link the apparent movement of population away from the mountains with the

---

[11] Caerau, Ely (673) occupies a small platform of freely drained soil. *B.B.C.S.*, XVIII, iv (May 1960), p. 392 note.

deterioration of climate which took place about the middle of the first millennium B.C. (I i p. 8). Some indication of the effect which this had on the upland vegetation is given by the buried soil beneath the rampart of a marching-camp at Ystradfellte.[12] The pollen indicated that the vegetation when the camp was built was oak forest, with some birch. It does not necessarily follow that forests extended over all the Glamorgan ridges. In view of the archaeological evidence the woodland was probably patchy; for example, it seems unlikely that the Romans would have cleared 27 ha of oak-wood to construct their temporary camp at Blaen-cwm Bach (739).

HILL-FORTS AND RELATED STRUCTURES

DOCUMENTARY MATERIAL

Before dealing with the classification of the hill-forts it will be convenient to summarise the more important published information. There are very few early references. The *Life* of St. Cadog mentions *Cestilldincat* near Llancarfan, and refers to an *oppidum* within which he built his church,[13] probably at Cadoxton-juxta-Neath (SS 756 985). The name *Cestilldincat* seems likely to refer to Castle Ditches (615), though the identification is not absolutely secure. The *oppidum* has left no visible trace. Similarly, nothing can be seen of 'Dinas Cynllyfan' near Pontarddulais,[14] though its position is fairly certain. A confused account of an attack on St. Illtud's monastery in the time of the Normans mentions a defensive rampart being built above the sea-shore,[15] and if not taken literally this may indicate temporary re-use of Castle Ditches near Llantwit Major (668) at that time. Modern names seem almost invariably to be simply descriptive. Field names Rath Fawr and Rath Isaf[16] may imply the former existence of earthworks of which no trace remains, but the positions are not especially suitable.

In modern times more or less full descriptions have been published for most of the sites, but these rarely add anything to details now visible. Reports on excavations remain useful and are noted under individual entries; the earliest seems to have been the section cut by Edward Williams (Iolo Morganwg) at Dunraven (666). General field studies have been published by Sir Cyril and Lady Fox and by Dr. H. N. Savory,[17] and are accompanied by valuable introductory discussions. The reference numbers for Savory's lists are given at the end of each entry (*e.g.* S 8a for Mynydd y Castell, 613).

CLASSIFICATION OF HILL-FORTS

Three main classes can be recognised unambiguously, and these can be subdivided, using siting and size as criteria. The distinction between small and large enclosures has been taken at an enclosed area of 1·2 hectares (3 acres) to agree with that used on the O.S. *Map of Southern Britain in the Iron Age*; recent work[18] suggests that for Wales 0·7 ha is a more significant point of division, but the difference only affects the attribution of eight enclosures, all univallate. On this basis, the hill-forts would fall into seven classes;

---

[12] Breck. SN 924 163. *B.B.C.S.*, XX, iv (May 1964), p. 445 (C. B. Crampton and D. P. Webley).

[13] *Vita Sancti Cadoci* in *Vitae Sanct.*, p. 120 (*Cestilldincat*), p. 68 (*oppidum*).

[14] In boundaries of Llandeilo Tal-y-bont, *Lib. Land.*, pp. 140, 368. The survey seems to imply a point near SN 6040 0355; but note Tan-y-cynllwyn at 5957 0572.

[15] *Vita Sancti Iltuti* in *Vitae Sanct.*, pp. 232–3.

[16] At SN 8145 0870 and 7975 0665 (Dylais Higher Tithe Award schedule, 3775 and 3293). For the distribution and significance of 'Rath' in Wales, see W. F. Grimes in D. Moore (ed.), *The Land of Dyfed in Early Times* (Cambrian Arch. Ass., 1964), pp. 17–22.

[17] H. N. Savory, 'List of hill-forts . . . in Glamorgan', *B.B.C.S.*, XIII, iii (Nov. 1949), pp. 152–61; supplement, XV, iii (Nov. 1953), pp. 228–9. (This list superseded that by V. E. Nash-Williams, *Arch. Camb.*, LXXXVIII (1933), pp. 339–42). C. Fox, *B.B.C.S.*, VIII, iv (May 1937), pp. 364–370. C. and A. Fox, 'Forts and Farms on Margam Mountain', *Antiquity*, VIII (1934), pp. 395–413.

[18] A. H. A. Hogg in *Prehistoric Man in Wales and the West* (Bath, 1972), p. 295.

the reasons for separating inland sites with multiple wide-spaced ramparts from those standing on the coast are explained subsequently. An eighth group, containing only three items, has been included in this section for convenience. The resulting classification is:

Univallate hill-forts exceeding 1·2 ha in enclosed area.
Smaller univallate enclosures in positions which are naturally strong.
Smaller univallate enclosures in positions unsuited to defence.
Multivallate hill-forts with close-set ramparts enclosing more than 1·2 ha.
Smaller multivallate hill-forts with close-set ramparts.
Multivallate enclosures with wide-spaced ramparts, on inland sites.
Multivallate enclosures with wide-spaced ramparts, on coastal sites.
Small stone-walled enclosures resembling Irish *cashels*.

The Larger Univallate Forts (*over 1·2 ha, 611–615*)

A single rampart, with or without a ditch, is the simplest form of permanent defence, and when eroded can seldom display any distinctive features. The fort beneath Castell Morlais (611) stands well outside the main distribution of all Glamorgan hill-forts, and so far as can be judged in its damaged state appears to have been the only one without a ditch. Burry Holms (612) differs from the rest in being on a promontory. At Coedymwstwr near Coychurch (614) the ramparts are almost destroyed, but as at Mynydd y Castell (613) and Llancarfan (615) they are of the simple contour type. The earliest defences at Cil Ifor Top (665) and Caer Dynnaf (670) seem also to have been of this kind originally, later incorporated in a system of multiple ramparts.

If 0·7 ha had been used as the value at which to separate the larger enclosures from the smaller, eight more hill-forts would have been included in the 'larger' group. Among these, the ramparts at Cwm Bach (631) and Coedcae Gaer (637) are comparable to those of the larger forts, and they seem to have been equally large at Warren Hill (628), Mynydd Twmpathyddaear (632), Craig Tan-y-lan (633), and Castell Moel (638), though now worn down. The Mynydd Twmpathyddaear enclosure is only marginally below 1·2 ha, and the estimate of 1·0 ha as the original area at Cwm Bach may make too little allowance for erosion. At the other two sites, Pen y Gaer at Pen-clawdd (623) and Buarth y Gaer (629), the defences seem always to have been on an appreciably smaller scale.

The Smaller Univallate Forts (*1·2 ha and less, 616–641*)

A small univallate enclosure is almost the simplest type of defensive structure. Most are probably of the Iron Age, but one dating from the 5th century A.D. was incorporated within the 12th-century defences at Dinas Powys (I iii p. 11). At present the only useful subdivision would seem to be by siting, whether the position chosen is or is not naturally defensible; further excavation may make a more satisfactory classification possible.

There are six places where a small univallate enclosure has almost certainly been superseded by multiple defences. These are: Dinas Powys, already mentioned; Summerhouse Camp (669); Hardings Down West (687); Llanmadog Bulwark (689); Thurba Head (698); and Castle Ditches, Llancarfan (615); others may remain unrecognised. At the last two named the earlier structure was protected by a dry-built stone wall, with no ditch. Another stone-walled fort exists unaltered at Worms Head (620).

All the others were protected by a ditch with an accompanying bank, probably once revetted. Without excavation, the entrances appear merely as gaps, with no accompanying elaboration of the ramparts.

Most are simple ringworks, though the plan is occasionally modified to suit the shape of the ground, and they are generally sited on hill-tops. Four examples, however, are placed so that, although they are on steeply sloping ground, the circuit follows a good defensive line, while the upper edge crosses a small subsidiary crest which gives effective command over the saddle beyond. Summerhouse Camp and two on Hardings Down have been enlarged and altered (669, 687, 688) and the fourth, Coed y Cymdda (641), is unfinished. Carn Caca (618), Half Moon Camp (625) and Blaen-cwm Bach (627, unfinished), all very small, have taken advantage of a steep natural scarp to provide protection on one side. Rather surprisingly, promontories have seldom been chosen, only Old Castle (621), Horse Cliff (622) and Cwm Bach (631) being known on the coast, and inland Gron Gaer (624), Flemings-down (630a), Craig Tan-y-lan (633) and the fort beneath the later works at Dinas Powys (I iii p. 11). As at Thurba Head earlier works may have been incorporated in later multiple ramparts.

There are four examples of unfinished enclosures, at Gwersyll (619), Gron Gaer (624), Blaen-cwm Bach (627), and Coed y Cymdda (641).

Univallate Enclosures in Positions Unsuited to Defence (642–663)

These are distinguished from the last group merely by the choice of situations such as hill slopes, which offer few or no natural advantages for defence. All are small, ranging from a little over 0·2 ha in area down to about 0·05 ha. Most were probably farmsteads, but again the group as a whole may well include structures covering a wide range of functions and date. For at least half of them the enclosing bank is very slight, but excavation at Llwynheiernin (650) has shown that a rampart which now looks insignificant could have been quite effective in its original state. Hardings Down North (646) and Hen Gastell, Pen-clawdd (648), among others, still have strong defences relative to their size.

In most, the interior is featureless, but hut-platforms exist at Hardings Down North and probably at Wenallt (663). (See also pp. 8–10 above.)

The only direct evidence for date comes from the excavation at Llwynheiernin (650) where a fragment of mid-2nd-century pottery was found sealed beneath the bank. At Dinas Powys (I iii p. 11) an unfinished earthwork on a hill-slope (not the 5th-century enclosure) was later than the Iron Age A occupation and apparently earlier than the medieval remains; its function and intended plan are uncertain.

Three enclosures which stand close to dykes are described in detail elsewhere (I i 60; I iii 806, 812) but are also mentioned in their correct positions in this section of the Inventory; they are not shown on the accompanying map.

The Larger Multivallate Forts with Close-set Defences (over 1·2 ha, 665–673)

These comprise some of the most impressive earthworks in the county. They have a markedly coastal distribution, and the profiles of their defences are almost all strongly similar, although at least Cil Ifor Top 665) and Caer Dynnaf (670) seem to have developed out of earlier univallate enclosures. In spite of this similarity, the areas range from as much as 6·5 ha down to about 1·2 ha. For the coastal forts exact comparative figures are unobtainable, as there has been heavy erosion. At Nash Point (667), for example, the cliff edge seems, on average, to have receded by more than 3 m between the survey for the 1919 edition of the 1/2500 O.S. map and 1965, when the plan of the fort was made. On the admittedly questionable assumption that the rate has been constant, this would imply that the cliff edge has receded by at least 120 m since the construction of the fort. Allowance has been made for these effects in classifying the forts by size.

Ditch-sections are exposed in the cliff faces at three sites. At Nash Point they are flat-bottomed, as found by excavation at Cil Ifor Top, but at Castle Ditches, Llantwit (668) and Dunraven (666) they seem to have been V-shaped. The bank sections are less well exposed, but no clear evidence of stone revetment is visible. Except at Dunraven, there are three banks and ditches for most of the circuit of the defences.

The discovery by Iolo Morganwg of a mass of concrete capping the rampart at Dunraven is remarkable. His description is clear, indicating that it was apparently not a faced wall, and the fact that he noted the use of sand seems to imply that it was a deliberate construction, not the result of burning timber reinforcement in a mass of limestone rubble. It suggests that there may have been some post-Roman re-fortification at this site.

Where entrances survive, they generally seem to have been protected by fairly long inturns, as at Caer Dynnaf or at Caerau, Llantrisant (672) where the ramparts separate to give extra cover; or by the use of naturally eroded approaches to give the same effect, as at Caerau, Ely (673); or by adaptation of the defences to give extra command, as at Cil Ifor Top or Nash Point. Dunraven seems to have had particularly elaborate entrance-works, but the details are obscured by erosion.

Dwellings probably attributable to the original construction of the fort remain visible only at Cil Ifor Top and Dunraven, though at Caer Dynnaf a few may survive among the confused enclosures representing farmsteads of the Roman period.

The Small Forts with Close-set Multiple Defences (under 1·2 ha, 674–685)

For the multivallate enclosures, division by size does seem to separate out two genuinely distinct groups. The large forts as noted all enclose at least 1·2 ha when not eroded, and nearly all have three ramparts. None of these small forts much exceeds 0·4 ha, and ten out of the twelve are bivallate. One of the remaining two, Craig Tŷ-isaf (678), seems to have been bivallate originally, but it is possible that with Crawley Rocks (675) and Parkmill (676) it should be classed with the 12th-century fort at Dinas Powys (I iii p. 11); the third of these, especially, is unusually small relative to the width of its defences.

The distribution of these small forts bears no obvious relation to the other types of enclosure, apart from that imposed by the nature of the ground. Generally, except for Llantrithyd House (682) and Llanfythin (683), they are fairly evenly spaced, as though each may have exercised control over a compact block of territory. The objects and structures belonging to the first phase at Mynydd Bychan (681) would not be inconsistent with such an interpretation, but those at Bishopston Valley (677) imply a very poor standard of living.

These are the only two excavated sites. The first occupation at Mynydd Bychan was dated as roughly 50 B.C. to A.D. 50, while the meagre finds at Bishopston Valley suggest that its use both started and ended about half a century later.

Multivallate Enclosures with Wide-spaced Ramparts, on Inland Sites (686–696)

Apart from their distinctive plan, these enclosures differ from others in their choice of location; seven out of the eleven stand on semi-permeable soil, as against ten at most out of forty-three inland hill-forts of other types; despite the small numbers involved, the difference is probably significant.[19]

These forts have been studied in considerable detail by Lady Fox[20] for S.W. Britain as a whole. Their basic characteristic is a main enclosure, generally quite small and bounded by a single rampart, accompanied

---

[19] P is about 1·3% by Fisher's Test.

[20] See especially: 'Hill-slope Forts and Related Earthworks in S.W. England and S. Wales', *Arch. Journ.*, CIX (1952), pp. 1–22; 'South-Western Hill-Forts', in S. S. Frere (ed.), *Problems of the Iron Age in Southern Britain* (Institute of Archaeology, London, 1958), pp. 35–60.

by outer ramparts widely separated over some or all of the circuit; these additional banks do not always form complete enclosures. The sites chosen are not necessarily defensible. For most of these structures, it seems a convincing hypothesis that the wide spaces within the outer banks were intended to provide protection for cattle; their location on semi-permeable soil may be relevant. To account for examples where the outer banks do not form complete enclosures, as at Hardings Down West in this county (687), it is necessary to suppose either that the work was never finished or that the circuit was completed by a perishable boundary, perhaps of hurdling.

The earliest pottery recorded in association belongs to the second main phase of the Iron Age; the period for which they remained in use is uncertain. In S. Britain they have a well-marked south-western distribution. Glamorgan lies across the zone of transition in which this type of multivallate enclosure ceases to be predominant and gives way to forts with close-set ramparts.

At least four distinct varieties can be recognised within the main class, but the nature of the arrangement, with several lines of rampart which do not overlap, leaves the classification of some forts open to argument. For example, the replacement of a small univallate enclosure by a larger one could result in a plan indistinguishable from a type of wide-spaced multivallate fort, and excavation would be needed to discover whether the inner enclosure and the outer were in use at the same time;[21] there are examples where it is certain, or nearly so, that the final plan results from the deliberate modification of an originally simpler enclosure. Similar problems arise when multiple ramparts, mainly close-set, diverge for part of the circuit. Of the four main types only two seem to be represented in Glamorgan.

(*a*) *Concentric Enclosures*. Eight seem to fall into this class. These can again be subdivided. In their simplest form the inner and outer enclosures are not linked in any way (and are thus not certainly contemporary). These are Berry Wood (686); Moel Ton-mawr (692); Bonvilston Gaer (696) and probably also Llanquian Wood (695). All these sites have only one outer rampart besides the central enclosure; Cae Summerhouse (691) is too damaged for certainty. It may be relevant that these five enclosures include the four believed to be of this type which stand on permeable soil; Moel Ton-mawr is the exception.

The remaining three, Gaer Fawr (690), Y Bwlwarcau (693) and Maendy Camp (694) all have multiple ramparts, the outer generally very slight and connected to the inner enclosure by slight banks lining the entrance approach. Maendy Camp has suffered damage by robbing of the ramparts, which were mainly of stone, so its plan is not entirely clear, but it seems to be rather different in detail from the others; it is also exceptional in that it is sited in a position suitable for defence, though its ramparts are not strong. Gaer Fawr and Y Bwlwarcau, however, are both so placed that the central enclosure, though quite strongly embanked, has no command over much of the surrounding area; the slight, outermost bank does overlook the dead ground. In both there is a multiplication of very slight outer ramparts, the function of which is obscure. At Y Bwlwarcau surface evidence suggests two periods of construction in the central enclosure.

Although Summerhouse Camp (669) has an independent inner enclosure, the strength of the outer defences suggests a two-period structure rather than one of this type.

(*b*) *Dependent Enclosures*, in which two close-set ramparts diverge for part of the circuit, and

(*c*) *Annexed Enclosures*, in which a rampart forming an outer enclosure is added for part of the circuit, usually on the entrance side, have not been certainly identified in Glamorgan. The trivallate forts at Caerau, Llantrisant (672), Cil Ifor Top (665) and Caer Dynnaf (670) might perhaps be included in one or

[21] E.g. at Warren Hill (628), the recent discovery of an inner enclosure does not occasion transfer to this class, for which its siting would also be atypical.

other of these classes, but at the first the space seems rather to be an additional entrance-defence, while at the other two surface appearances suggest that the present plan is the result of modifying an earlier univallate fort to give stronger defences.

(*d*) *Cross-bank Enclosures* are represented by three sites, forming a compact group in western Gower. Characteristically they occupy a ridge or promontory, the outer ramparts being limited to the ridge top, and not continuing along the sides. In two sites (687 and 689) the approach through the outer enclosures runs between banks, as in the more elaborate of the Concentric Enclosures. At Hardings Down East (688), which is unfinished, the remains suggest that a similar arrangement was intended.

Each of the first two forts seems to have been formed by the elaboration of an original simple univallate enclosure. Only Llanmadog Bulwark (689) was completed, resulting in a complicated plan, the evolution of which cannot be satisfactorily worked out from surface evidence; it probably comprises work of more than two periods. At Hardings Down West (687) the two additional banks now end 'in the air', on no natural obstruction, and excavation has shown that there was no palisade or other structure to continue the line. Within the enclosure a large round house with no associated relics stood near the centre, and a smaller dwelling against the rampart on the W. side. Near this is a third hut-platform. These three buildings may be of different dates.

Multivallate Enclosures with Wide-spaced Ramparts, on Coastal Sites (697–704)

All these, except that on Sully Island, are in Gower. Their plan suggests that they were designed to serve the same function as those inland, with a space, presumably for cattle, between the inner and outer ramparts; but they differ in details. The positions chosen are usually well suited to defence and the outer enclosures are much smaller than at the inland sites, both absolutely and relative to the inner enclosures. They are on permeable soil, but the choice of a coastal position makes that inevitable.

The Knave (699) and High Pennard (702) have been excavated. The former produced iron-age pottery, but at the latter the few datable relics found were all Roman, probably 1st- to early 2nd-century. At Thurba Head (698), as noted above, an earlier fort defended by a single stone wall has been incorporated in the work.

Small Stone-walled Enclosures resembling Cashels (705–707)

Excavations at Burry Holms (705) showed that the earliest structure beneath the medieval ruins was a timber church within a small stone-walled enclosure resembling an Irish *cashel*. Two other sites in west Gower are generally similar and have therefore been included here as a separate class.

Later Earthworks

Castles and the banks which protected medieval dwellings will be described in detail in later volumes, but working from surface evidence alone it is not always possible to be certain that a simple earthwork enclosure has been correctly interpreted. For completeness, therefore, a list is given here of structures believed to belong to these classes; but typical 'pudding-basin' castle mounds, with or without baileys, are excluded, as also are homestead-moats, since there is rarely any uncertainty about their attribution.

In Glamorgan the enclosures which have been proved medieval are all small, seldom as much as 0·2 ha in enclosed area; they seem to fall into three distinct groups. In date, they can be attributed broadly to the 12th century.

The arrangement adopted here is to describe the present appearance of representative excavated sites, and then to list those which although unexcavated can probably be assigned to the same group on surface evidence. The object of these notes is merely to account for earthworks some of which could perhaps have been included in this volume of the Inventory. The descriptions of the excavated sites aim at indicating the surface features which may imply a similar date for unexcavated enclosures, so the remains uncovered are not discussed. The other sites are usually listed with no details.

Multivallate Enclosures

The type site for medieval multivallate enclosures in this area is the small earthwork at Dinas Powys.[22] Before excavation, it was generally accepted as pre-Roman, being exceptional only because of the small area enclosed relative to the width of the defences and because its entrance was from the end of the spur; the absence of any access through the main defences could be accounted for by assuming that erosion had destroyed a track past the end of the ramparts. Excavation[23] has shown that the visible defences are all work of the 11th or 12th century. The occupation of the site commenced in the Iron Age, but it does not seem to have been fortified until the 5th century A.D., when a bank and ditch were formed across the base of the promontory, protecting a settlement which (for this region) was remarkably rich in small finds. The natural advantages of the site for defence led to its medieval re-occupation; it had then been abandoned for 400 or 500 years. Initially a single large bank and ditch were added behind the earlier barrier, but after an uncertain but not necessarily long interval two more ramparts were added. In its final form, a system of four ramparts, 43 m across, defended an enclosure of 0·1 ha. The entrance was by a steep track leading to the apex of the promontory; there was no gap in the main defences.

Features which might be taken as diagnostic are the small internal area and the disproportionate width and multiplication of defences across one side of a site naturally protected on others, together with the absence of any entrance through the main ramparts. Three other Glamorgan forts satisfy these requirements. They are at Crawley Rocks (675), Parkmill (676) and Craig Tŷ-isaf (678). Any or all of these may well be post-Roman, but a sherd of iron-age pottery has been picked up at Crawley Rocks. This casts some doubt on how far the evidence from Dinas Powys is generally applicable, so these three forts have been included in this volume.

Strong Univallate Enclosures

Typically, these are defended by single ramparts which seem unusually massive for the area enclosed. The sites chosen generally have some natural strength, even though they are often on quite low ground and near water. These last three characteristics are not invariable. The absence of an entrance seems to be reliable evidence for a medieval date, but the presence of one does not necessarily imply that the structure is early.

Two sites have been excavated: Old Castle, Bishopston[24] is oval, 21 m by 15 m, bounded on the N. by the steep bank of a ravine and on the other three sides by a bank and ditch now about 12 m wide by 3 m high overall; a slight gap may represent the original entrance. Castle Tower, Pen-maen[25] is also oval, 36 m by 27 m, on a rocky promontory cut off on the landward side by a bank and ditch 13 m wide and about 5 m high originally which continues as a scarp round part of the circumference; the entrance is

---

[22] ST 17 S.W. (1482 7225); XLVII N.W. For the early medieval remains see I iii p. 11.
[23] L. Alcock, *Dinas Powis* (Cardiff, 1963).
[24] W. Morgan, *Arch. Camb.*, 1899, pp. 249–58.
[25] L. Alcock, *Antiq. Journ.*, XLVI (1966), pp. 178–210.

represented by a gap in the main bank. Pennard and Ogmore Castles have also been excavated, but the later stonework at those two sites makes them less useful for determining the characteristics which may distinguish medieval from prehistoric enclosures.

Fifteen earthworks seem to fall into this group. They are listed in order of grid-reference, including those mentioned above. At four of them, stone castles have been built over earlier earthworks:

Cae Castell, W. of Pontardawe (perhaps an aberrant motte-and-bailey castle)	SN 60 S.E. (6942 0474); VIII S.W.
Norton Camp, Oxwich	SS 48 N.E. (4915 8677); XXXI N.W.
Penrice Ring	SS 48 N.E. (4923 8786); XXXI N.W.
North Hill Tor, Cheriton	SS 49 S.E. (4530 9381); XXI N.E.
Castle Tower, Pen-maen (see above)	SS 58 N.W. (5340 8804); XXXI N.E.
Pennard Castle (beneath later stonework)	SS 58 N.W. (5441 8850); XXXI N.E.
Cil Ifor Top (see No. 665)	SS 59 S.W. (5069 9222); XXII S.E.
Old Castle, Bishopston (see above)	SS 59 S.E. (5819 9000); XXIII S.W.
Ogmore Castle (beneath later stonework)	SS 87 N.E. (8818 7697); XL S.W.
Llangynwyd Castle (beneath later stonework)	SS 88 N.E. (8517 8866); XXXIV N.W.
Bedford Castle, N.E. of Llantwit Major (perhaps with motte now almost destroyed. This enclosure is slighter than others in this group.)	SS 96 N.E. (9799 6930); XLV S.E.
Coety Castle (beneath later stonework)	SS 98 S.W. (9230 8149); XL N.E.
Llanilid	SS 98 S.E. (9777 8132); XLI N.W.
St. Nicholas Gaer	ST 07 S.E. (0845 7475); XLVI N.E.
Caerau, Ely (see No. 673)	ST 17 N.W. (1354 7509); XLVII N.W.

Weaker Medieval Ringworks

These are on average rather larger in area, in situations which give little advantage for defence, and with ramparts which in their present form seem of no great strength. Two have been excavated. At Coed y Cwm,[26] S.W. of St. Nicholas, the enclosure stands on level ground, but with a ravine on one side; it is about 26 m in diameter, with defences measuring about 12 m overall, now very slight. The ring at Llantrithyd,[27] on a low hillock east of the church, is oval, 55 by 40 m, with a bank now about 5·5 m wide and 0·9 m high.

Eight enclosures seem to belong to this group:

Castell Nôs near the head of the Rhondda Fach (the classification of this structure is uncertain)	SN 90 S.E. (9650 0017); XVIII N.W.
Horgrove, N.W. of Laleston	SS 88 S.E. (8558 8150); XL N.W.
Gelli Garn, N. of Llan-gan	SS 97 N.E. (9603 7879); XLI S.W.
Howe Mill, S. of Cowbridge	ST 07 S.W. (0049 7211); XLV S.E.
Llantrithyd	ST 07 S.W. (0455 7271); XLVI N.W.
Walterston, N.E. of Llancarfan	ST 07 S.E. (0679 7122); XLVI S.W.
S.E. of Bonvilston	ST 07 S.E. (0706 7335); XLVI N.W.
Coed-y-cwm, S.W. of St. Nicholas	ST 07 S.E. (0828 7366); XLVI N.E.

[26] *Morgannwg*, VIII (1964), p. 69; IX (1965), p. 95.
[27] *Morgannwg*, V (1961), p. 82; VII (1963), p. 126; VIII (1964), p. 70.

611–615. *THE LARGER UNIVALLATE FORTS* (*over 1·2 ha*)

(611) At CASTELL MORLAIS the ruins of the medieval castle occupy the sharp N. end of a limestone ridge at about 370 m above O.D. The axis of the ridge lies roughly N.W. to S.E. On the N.E. there is a short but steep fall to a saddle, and the height increases round the N. end to what must originally have been a very steep or precipitous natural scarp on the S.W., now replaced by a modern quarry face. To the S.E. the slope is more gentle, and the remains of a hill-fort extend outside the castle ditch.

In plan, the remains form an almost rectangular enclosure about 70 m wide from N.E. to S.W., with a slighter extension about 25 m wide for a further 45 m to the S.E.; both are cut by the quarry on the S.W. The main enclosure now extends 55 m beyond the castle ditch, but can be traced for another 30 or 40 m within it before being obscured by the medieval ruins. The surviving area is 0·8 ha, but originally it probably enclosed about twice that amount.

The N.E. rampart of the main enclosure is a massive bank of limestone rubble, 17 m wide at the base, nearly a metre high internally and 4 m externally; the section remaining within the castle ditch is rather slighter. At the E. corner, which is slightly rounded, there is a modern gap. Continuing along the S.E. side of the main enclosure, the width of the bank decreases to about 9 m and its exterior height to 2 m; in front it is separated by a berm 3 m wide from a scarp about 1 m high, and 12 m beyond this are traces of a ditch 4·5 m wide and about 0·7 m deep. This is only visible for about 10 m, and towards the junction with the extension the scarp merges with the rampart to give an outer height of about 5 m. The remaining banks are slighter, about 7 to 9 m wide and 1 m high.

Just S.W. of this junction there is a gap, beyond which the bank continues in the same direction but slightly N. of its previous line. The bank forming the extension is very slight, especially on the N.E. though it is there reinforced externally by a natural hollow. Just W. of the angle is a gap about 3 m wide, probably original. The banks of the main enclosure and of the extension both turn slightly northwards, suggesting that little has been destroyed along this side.

Merthyr Tudful.

SO 00 N.W., N.E. (0500 0950) 3 viii 65 VI S.W.

(612) BURRY HOLMS PROMONTORY FORT. At the N. end of Rhosili Bay the inclined beds of carboniferous limestone form a tidal island. The low plateau on the sheltered E. side is occupied by the remains of a small ecclesiastical settlement, but the W. end rises to about 30 m above O.D. with cliffs 15 m high, and has been fortified by a rampart about 100 m long running almost straight across the island from N. to S., the ditch following the line of a fault. The area enclosed is about 1·2 ha. The entrance, a little S. of the centre, is a simple gap approached by a causeway across the ditch. The defence consists of a bank, ditch and counterscarp bank now measuring about 15 m wide by 4·5 m high overall N. of the entrance, but only about 12 m wide to S. with no counterscarp bank. In

1965, during excavations on the ecclesiastical site, a section was cut across the rampart just N. of the entrance.[1] The causeway proved to be solid rock, and the ditch was of blunt V section, about 0·7 m deeper than the present bottom. No indication of a revetment was found, the bank being composed of material thrown up from the ditch. In the section opened this had apparently been re-cut and the material used to heighten the bank and to form the counterscarp bank.

In a 3 m square opened in the interior, about 30 m S. of the entrance, one large shallow post-hole was found, but no other sign of occupation outside the fort. Beneath the ecclesiastical remains there was an extensive layer of discoloured soil with calcined stones; this may represent the dwelling-place of the occupants of the fort, but no pottery was found.

A fragment of grey Roman pottery was found on the bottom of the ditch, and another, of the 2nd century or later, is recorded as having come from the filling of the ditch at its S. end.[2]

S 16c. Rutter, *P. Gower*, p. 66. *Trans. Swansea Sci. Soc.*, 1909–10, pp. 109 ff.

[1] By D. B. Hague, on behalf of the Commission. *Gower*, XVII (1966).

[2] *Arch. Camb.*, XCIV (1939), p. 29.

Llangennith.

SS 39 S.E. (3988 9258) 1965 XXI S.W.

(613) MYNYDD Y CASTELL (Fig. 2) in Margam Park. An isolated hill has been fortified by a single rampart. The enclosed area, 2·7 ha, is roughly D-shaped with the E. side straight, and measures 260 m N. to S. by 135 m wide. The level above O.D. within falls fairly evenly from about 120 m at the S.E. apex to 90 m on the N. side. Outside the rampart the ground falls away steeply.

The defences consisted of a massive bank or scarp accompanied by a ditch with a counterscarp bank. There is no indication of a revetment.

The *main bank* is best preserved along the E. side where it is 8·5–15 m wide, up to 1 m high internally and from 4 to 8·5 m high externally. Along the N. and W. sides it forms a scarp 7 to 12 m wide and of similar external height. The *ditch*, 3 to 4·5 m wide, is only visible as such along the E. side and on the N.W. and S.W.; elsewhere it forms a terrace 5 to 6 m wide. The *counterscarp bank* is only evident as such in those places where the ditch remains visible; its inner side is about 0·7 m high. On the N., and again on the W., its outer toe is faintly visible, indicating a width of 6 to 9 m, but in most places its outer scarp merges without a break into the steep natural slope. At the S. end of the fort natural crags are incorporated in the defensive lines.

There is some evidence that the enclosure was originally intended to be smaller than the existing fort. In the E. side, about 160 m N. of the S. angle, a change in the line of the defences coincides with a steepening of the natural slope, and at this point a northward-facing scarp is traceable well into the interior of the fort. Moreover, the commencement of the original turn of the outer rampart can be recognised. The scarp is 4 to 6 m wide and about 1·3 m high; it is traceable for about 60 m and ends in a sharp southward inturn as if for the

E. side of an entrance. There is even a suggestion of a similar break in the defences at the corresponding point on the W. side of the fort, but no connection can be traced between these features and it is possible that this earlier layout was abandoned before completion.

One *entrance* is on the S.W., where a ramp 4 to 5·5 m wide cuts through the outer scarp from the S. and enters a natural hollow between the slightly inturned ends of the inner scarp. At the N.E. angle of the hill-fort modern quarrying has confused the layout of the defences, but it seems likely that an original entrance existed here also. The modern track on to the hill approaches from the S.E. and bends sharply southward as it enters the interior. The S. side of the turn is commanded by a high scarp that appears to be a continuation of the inner rampart of the fort, and there is even a suggestion of a guard-chamber in the extreme angle of the defences on the N. side of the track; but it is not clear whether these features are preserved from an original layout or are due to modern disturbance.

The interior does not seem to have been ploughed, but there are no certain traces of early habitation. A round levelled area at the S. end resembles a hut-platform, but in view of the absence of platforms from the rest of the site it may well be modern, to be associated either with the construction of the adjacent reservoir or with the small ruined masonry building 'Hen Gastell', probably the summer-house mentioned in 1811.[1]

S 8a. *Trans. Cardiff Nat. Soc.*, XXVII (1894–5), p. 81 ff. (plan).
[1] Carlisle, *Top. Dict.*, *s.v.* Margam.

Margam (E), Port Talbot (C).
SS 88 N.W. (8061 8655) 1967 XXXIII N.E.

(614) COEDYMWSTWR hill-fort crowns an isolated rounded hill N. of Coychurch, at 110 m above O.D. Pasture fields on the N. half of the hilltop contain the much reduced remnant of an earthen rampart occupying the brow of the hill. Where best preserved it is 9 m wide and about 0·8 m high. In the S. half of the hilltop the ground has been more intensively cultivated, and the only probable section of the outline there is retained in the line of a field bank. The whole enclosure measured about 180 m E.–W. by 170 m, area about 2·5 ha. The position of the entrance is uncertain.

Coychurch (E), C. Lower (C).
SS 98 S.W. (9434 8099) 20 v 63 XLI N.W.

(615) CASTLE DITCHES, E. of Llancarfan (Fig. 3, Plate 1), occupies the western end of a ridge which rises gently towards the east. On other sides the ground falls away steeply and on the north it is almost precipitous. A single strong bank and ditch enclose an area of about 4·2 ha, now mostly under plough. Selective excavations by the staff of the Commission in 1963 and 1964, intended primarily to determine the cultural associations of the site, showed that the visible defences had been preceded by a smaller enclosure of different plan protected by a strong stone wall.[1]

The eastern end is protected by a strong rampart and ditch, but round the western half of the enclosure the defence consists of a bank which only rises slightly above the interior but is steep externally, and the ditch is accompanied by a counterscarp bank. Excavation showed that the ditch was flat-bottomed, shallow south of the entrance but much deeper to the east; the presence of much fallen stone in the filling indicated that the bank had formerly been revetted, but no walling remained in position. The difference in construction between the east and west ends suggested that the fort might have developed from a smaller western enclosure but neither excavation, nor air nor ground observation produced any evidence for this.

The only original entrance seems to have been that in the south side. Its form has been obscured by cultivation and by modern use, but in 1965 evidence was found for a slight inturn on its eastern side. This had apparently been altered or rebuilt twice, but a detailed investigation did not fall within the programme of work as planned. Outside the entrance two banks and ditches are built out from the main enclosure as if to protect the approach, and a slighter bank continues downhill to a stream; the remains south of the modern road have been almost obliterated by cultivation so the details of these arrangements are not clear.

Throughout most of the enclosure ploughing has apparently broken up all layers above the rock surface, but a greater depth of soil remains S.W. of the entrance. Excavations here showed a depth behind the rampart of nearly 0·6 m of dark soil containing pottery and organic remains, with traces of iron and copper working at the lowest levels. The pottery was almost all of plain Iron Age B character, but there were a few scraps with decoration similar to that found in the Somerset lake villages.[2] Foundations of a round hut 5·5 m in diameter were found at the highest level; these consisted of a single ring of flat stones sloping slightly inwards as though to take the thrust of the roof supports. A few scraps of Roman pottery were found unstratified in these excavations, and about a dozen more have been picked up in the ploughed interior; all were of the 2nd–4th centuries A.D.[3]

During the excavations evidence was found for the existence of an earlier enclosure protected by a strong stone wall 5 m thick without any accompanying ditch. This was traced from a point close to the later entrance, running in a quadrant to disappear under the modern road near the present gateway into the field. The wall faced S.W., but its northern extension had been destroyed by ploughing, so the area enclosed is unknown. One side of the entrance was uncovered near the field gateway. The rampart did not seem to have been thickened, and a single large post-hole was found, with indications that the post had been renewed at least once. The cobbling of the entrance passage was traced for a short distance towards the interior, and on it was found a small plain terret-ring; no other relics were associated with this enclosure.

S 4a. *Arch. Camb.*, 1913, p. 100 (small plan).
[1] Report forthcoming.
[2] D. P. S. Peacock, 'A Contribution to the Study of Glastonbury Ware . . .', *Antiq. Journ.*, XLIX (1969), Figs. 1, 2 and p. 48. The sherd belongs to his Group 3, probably manufactured in the Mendip area.
[3] *B.B.C.S.*, XVI, iv (May 1956), pp. 299–300.

Llancarfan.
ST 07 S.E. (0590 7002) 1964–5 XLVI S.W.

PROFILE A-B
A
B
Profile to twice Scale
CONTOURS IN FEET
280
270
300
290
Break
probably
modern
320
330
340
350
310
300
Old
field bank
60
Modern track
possibly through
original entrance
330
320
310
300

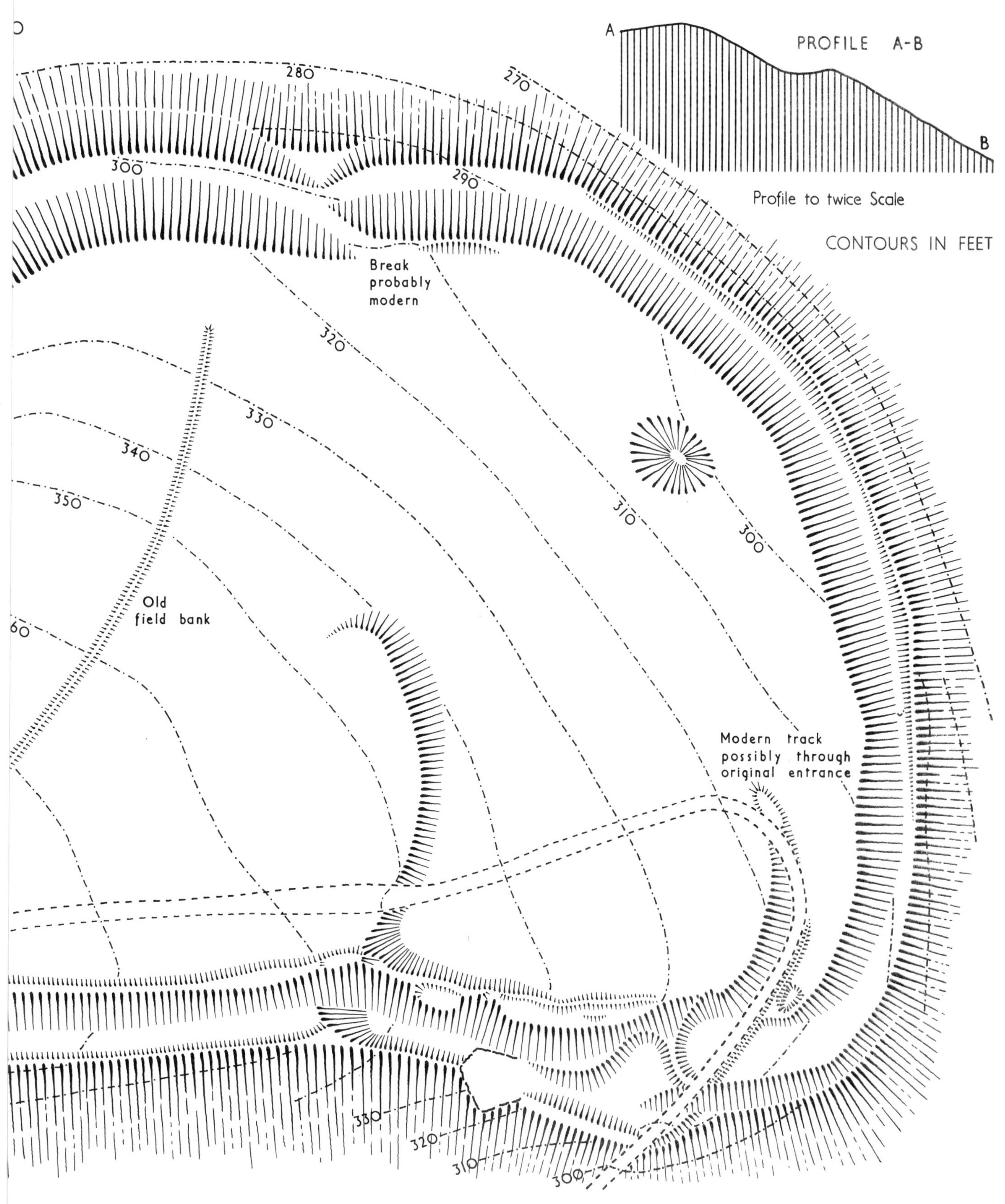

No. 613.

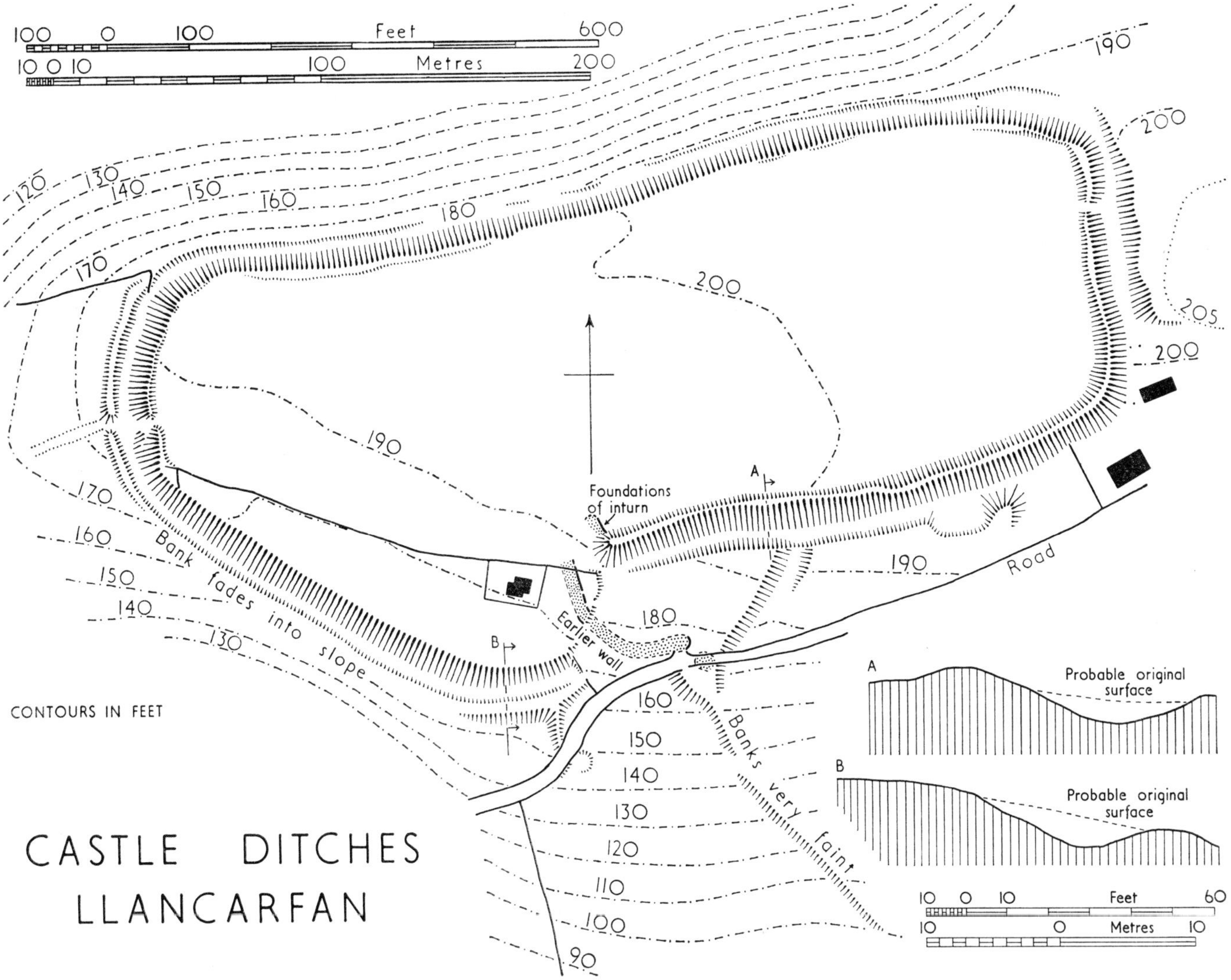

CASTLE DITCHES
LLANCARFAN

CONTOURS IN FEET

FIG. 3. No. 615.

616–641. THE SMALLER UNIVALLATE FORTS
(1·2 ha and less)

(616) Graig Fawr, about 4 km N.E. of Pontarddulais. The summit, 270 m above O.D., is occupied by a fortified enclosure. It is D-shaped, measuring about 90 m from S.W. to N.E. by 65 m, the area being 0·5 ha. Along the straight N.W. side the ground falls away steeply and there is no artificial protection. In other directions the ground is at first level and then curves away into a gentle slope, and there are traces of a slight enclosing bank 3 m wide, though it is generally reduced to a scarp *ca.* 0·5 m high. It is best preserved on the S. and S.E. where some loose stones are visible in the face.

A slight bank runs straight from SN 6187 0687 within the enclosure to 6193 0681. Where it crosses the enclosure bank on the N.E. it appears to be later; it should probably be associated with adjacent platform-house sites.[1]

[1] *Gower*, VII (1954), p. 40; XIV (1961), p. 82.

Llandeilo Tal-y-bont.
SN 60 N.W. (6185 0685) 27 vi 61 VII N.E.

On Tor Clawdd, N. of Clydach, near the Causeway and about 180 m S. of the Dyke (I iii 801), is a small ringwork. Its appearance suggests a cairn and it has been described as such (I i 60), but it may be a small, weakly defended enclosure. Rings similarly placed relative to dykes occur on Cefn Morfudd and Mynydd Eglwysilan (I iii 806, 812). It is almost circular, 16 m in diameter within a bank about 3 m wide and 0·3 m high, with traces of an external ditch. There is an entrance 2 m wide towards the S.E.

SN 60 N.E. (6703 0630) VIII N.W.

(617) GLYN-NEATH. The probable remains of a small fort occupy the summit of a hillock 75 m above O.D. which forms the S.W. end of a hill rising from the floor of the Vale of Neath, and commanding an extensive view S.W. down the valley. The hillock is roughly circular, with a rounded summit, falling steeply on the N.W. and S.W., but only gently on the S.E., while on the N.E. a pronounced dip separates the knoll from the rest of the hill.

The defences are partly natural. Earthworks are visible on the N.E. and S.E., forming two sides of a square with a rounded E. angle between them. The N.E. side, preserved for a length of 22 m, is a straight terrace above a scarp 1·3 m high. At the E. angle and along most of the N.E. side is also the suggestion of an outer ditch about 4·5 m wide with a very faint counterscarp bank. The S.E. side consists of a spread bank about 3 m wide and 0·3 m high, traceable in a straight line for 33 m from the E. angle.

The N.W. and S.W. sides appear to be entirely natural, and in any case modern gardens would have destroyed any artificial works that may have existed along the S.W. side. The area enclosed by the artificial defences and the natural slopes is about 36 m in each direction, roughly 0·1 ha.

From the N. angle a slight scarp runs N.E. along the crest of a natural fall to the N.W. This could be the last remains of the bank of a 'bailey', but might be nothing more than an old hedge line. Certainly the remainder of the hill, to the N.E. of the camp, appears to be undefended.

Cadoxton-juxta-Neath (E), Neath Higher (C).

SN 80 N.E. (8852 0680) 29 x 63 X N.W.

(618) CARN CACA, S. of Resolfen (Fig. 4). The enclosure stands on more or less level ground at 300 m above O.D. on the edge of a steep fall to the N.E. into the valley of the Melin Court Brook. It is oval, about 0·1 ha in area. The N.E. defence is provided by the natural slopes, down which the N.W. and S.W. defences are carried some way before fading out.

The defended area measures about 44 m long from N.W. to S.W. by 37 m wide. The defences consist of an inner bank from 3 to 3·5 m wide, separated by a ditch from an outer bank 3 to 5 m wide, the overall width ranging from 16 to 18 m. The defences are best preserved on the N.W. where the maximum height of the inner bank above the bottom of the ditch is nearly a metre, of the outer bank slightly less. On the W. the outer bank and ditch are interrupted by a causeway and the inner bank is inturned sharply to form an entrance 3 m wide. On the S.W. the outer bank has been destroyed by a hollow trail.

In the interior on the E., a scarped hollow and the footings of a stone wall 1·3 m thick appear to mark the site of a large circular hut about 10 m in diameter. There was possibly another hut about 6 m in diameter within the curve of the defences on the N.W.

Llantwit-juxta-Neath (E), Clyne (C).

SN 80 S.W. (8385 0004) 24 x 62 XVI N.E.

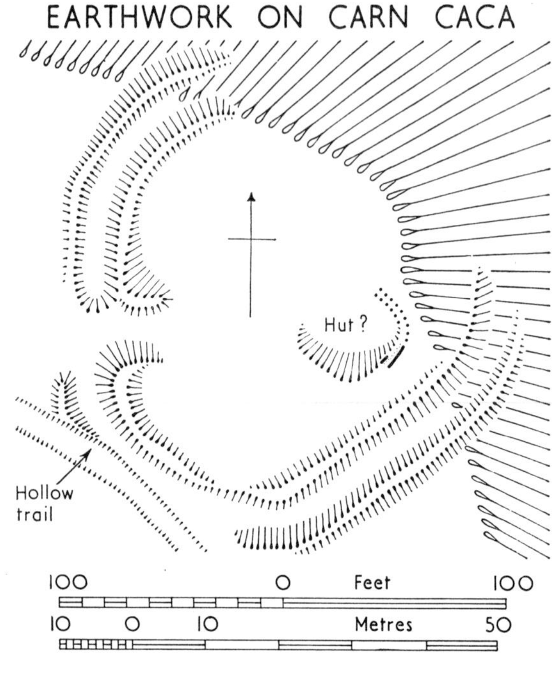

FIG. 4. No. 618.

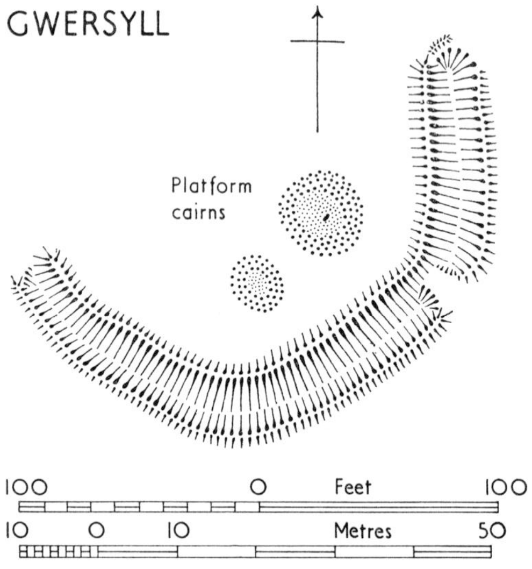

FIG. 5. No. 619.

(619) GWERSYLL, on the ridge between Aberdâr and Merthyr Tudful (Fig. 5, Plate 2), is a rampart, roughly semi-circular in plan, standing at about 410 m above O.D. on a broad ridge, in enclosed but uncultivated pasture. It appears to

be an unfinished ringwork; no trace of a marking-out ditch appears on the ground, but on an aerial photograph[1] a very slight mark completes the circuit. The diameter is about 52 m, and the enclosed area, if completed, would have been about 0·2 ha. The defences measure 11 m wide by nearly 2 m high overall, and comprise a bank, ditch and counterscarp bank. The intended entrance was probably at the E. end of the rampart, where a slight bank curves round the end of the ditch. There is a causeway across the ditch on the S.E., but no corresponding gap in the bank.

Two cairns (I i 135–6) stand within the semicircle, but the association is almost certainly fortuitous.

[1] C.U.A.P., No. AFS 47.

Aberdâr.
SO 00 S.W. (0271 0405) 11 x 60 XI S.E.

(620) Worms Head. The inner summit of Worms Head is protected by a stone rampart following approximately the line of the 30 m contour. The enclosure forms a segment of a circle, the straight N.E. side, about 190 m long, being formed by the steep natural scarp without any artificial defence. The greatest width is 45 m, the enclosed area being about 0·6 ha. The entrance, about 3 m wide, was 65 m from the S.E. end. The S.E. jamb of the opening is visible, and to the N.W. two courses of rampart facing survive for about 13 m. The wall seems to have been at least 1·5 m thick, but its inner face is not clear.

Rhosili.
SS 38 N.E. (3935 8755) 23 ii 67 XXX N.W.

(621) Old Castle, a promontory fort on the cliffs W. of Rhosili, about 50 m above O.D. The N. side of the enclosure is formed by the cliff edge which here turns outward to form a blunt promontory with sides of about 90 m (to N.W.) and 50 m. The base of this, 100 m long, forms the diameter of a rampart of semicircular plan, which thus encloses about 0·7 ha. The defences are best preserved for about 50 m on the E. and 30 m on the S., where they consist of a bank with external ditch measuring nearly 10 m wide and 2 m high overall. Another short length, now only 6 m wide and less than 1 m high but damaged, remains on the S.W. The whole site has been much disturbed by quarrying, so no house platform can be identified; the position of the entrance is also uncertain, but was probably on the S.W. where there is a gap nearly 20 m wide.

S 15c. Mentioned in *B.B.C.S.*, VIII, iv (May 1937), p. 366; Rutter, *P. Gower*, p. 66.

Rhosili.
SS 48 N.W. (4093 8798) 1 x 59 XXX N.E.

(622) Horse Cliff, about 3 km W. of Port Einon (Fig. 6). The promontory is aligned E.–W.; the N. side falls steeply to a bay, while the W. and S. sides are formed by sheer and indeed spectacular cliffs 60 m high. The site is well chosen though rather exposed; the defences occupy the E. end of the narrow headland and entailed a minimum of constructional effort.

The defended area is 65 m long and varies in width from 18 m to about 40 m enclosing about 0·4 ha. The defences consist of a single grass-grown bank of limestone rubble, running in a curve convex to the E., fronted on the landward side by a ditch. The bank is 5·5–6·5 m wide, 0·5 m high internally and nearly 2 m externally; its inner scarp has a stepped appearance, perhaps the remains of a rampart walk though a similar feature at The Knave (699) is almost certainly due to stone-robbing. On the N. the bank is eroded, though enough remains to allow its curve to be traced right to the cliff edge. On the S. it ends abruptly 5 m short of the edge, the gap clearly indicating that it was the entrance. The termination is inturned and there is a suggestion of a guard-chamber within the turn.

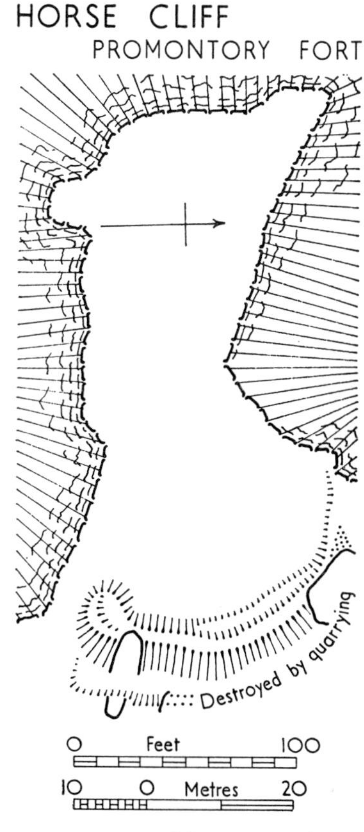

FIG. 6. No. 622.

The ditch is only preserved at the S. end, where it seems to have been fairly wide (5 m) and shallow. Elsewhere it is destroyed by quarry hollows. There are no signs of structures in the interior.

S 12c. Mentioned in *B.B.C.S.*, VIII, iv (May 1937), p. 365; Rutter, *P. Gower*, p. 65.

Rhosili.
SS 48 N.W. (4349 8604) 22 ix 65 XXX S.E.

(622a) Tor-gro, N.E. of Cheriton. At the highest point on this ridge, near the E. end and 80 m above O.D., a modern field-boundary follows the crest of an earlier bank, about 6 m wide and nearly 2 m high on its S.W. side. This seems to have been the rampart of a small enclosure, half oval in plan, bounded on the N. by the cliff with no other protection. Its width was about 40 m and its length along the cliff would probably have been about 120 m, corresponding to an enclosed area of 0·4 ha, but the S.E. side cannot be traced. The work may have been unfinished.

Ex. inf. H. R. Jenkins.

Cheriton.
SS 49 S.E. (4610 9355) 14 iv 71 XXII N.W.

(623) Pen y Gaer stands on sloping ground between 75 and 90 m above O.D. at the W. end of the ridge to the S. of Pen-clawdd. The fort is oval in plan, about 0·9 ha in area, 160 m long from E. to W. by 95 m wide. Its S. side follows the crest of the ridge and is visible as a high scarp crowned by a modern field bank. The ground within the fort falls steeply from S. to N., and the N. side is formed by a very steep natural scarp. The E. and W. sides are defined by an earthen rampart, that on the E. being better preserved, 8 m wide at the base and 3 m high, its crest occupied by a modern field bank. The W. rampart is slighter, 6 m wide and 1 m high. At the N.W. and N.E. the bank fades gradually into the northern scarp.

A gap on the E. appears to be a modern break. The only original entrance seems to be at the S.W., where there is a gap of 4 m between the tail of the W. rampart and the southern scarp. There is no sign of internal structures.

S 3g. Mentioned in *B.B.C.S.*, VIII, iv (May 1937), p. 366; Rutter, *P. Gower*, p. 66.

Llanrhidian (E), Ll. Higher (C).
SS 59 N.W. (5365 9552) 28 vi 61 XXII N.E.

(624) Gron Gaer stands at about 70 m above O.D. about a kilometre S. of Pen-clawdd on a spur defended naturally on the W. by a sharp fall into a ravine, and to a less extent on the N. by a re-entrant valley. There is no defence on the S., where the ground falls gently, but the E. side, where the ground rises very gently, is defended by a bank running in a curve slightly convex to the E. and traceable for 37 m; the area enclosed is about 0·1 ha. The bank is 10 m wide at the base, nearly 2 m high internally and 1 m externally. There is a suggestion of a turn towards the W. at its N. end. The bank has a curiously isolated air and the defences appear to be unfinished.

S 7f. Mentioned in *B.B.C.S.*, VIII, iv (May 1937), p. 368; Rutter, *P. Gower*, p. 66.

Llanrhidian (E), Ll. Higher (C).
SS 59 S.E. (5504 9476) 24 ix 64 XXII N.E.

(625) Half Moon Camp (Fig. 7) is an oval enclosure on the S. edge of a spur overlooking Margam Abbey, at a little over 150 m above O.D. The ground falls sharply from the S.W. edge of the earthwork. The enclosure measures about 53 m long from N.W. to S.E. by 37 m wide, but has been destroyed on the N.W. and S.W.; the area is about 0·2 ha. A detached length of bank on the W. is somewhat out of line with the rest of the earthwork but probably belongs to it. The defences consist of a single rampart, best preserved on the N.E. where it is 9 m wide, 0·3 m high internally and nearly 1 m externally. The bank on the W. is similar but only 7 m wide. The rampart is almost ploughed out in the adjoining field on the N., and on the S. survives only as a scarp; this fades out about the middle of the S. side, perhaps indicating the position of the entrance. An outer ditch is preserved only on the N.E., where it is 5 m wide and 0·3 m deep.

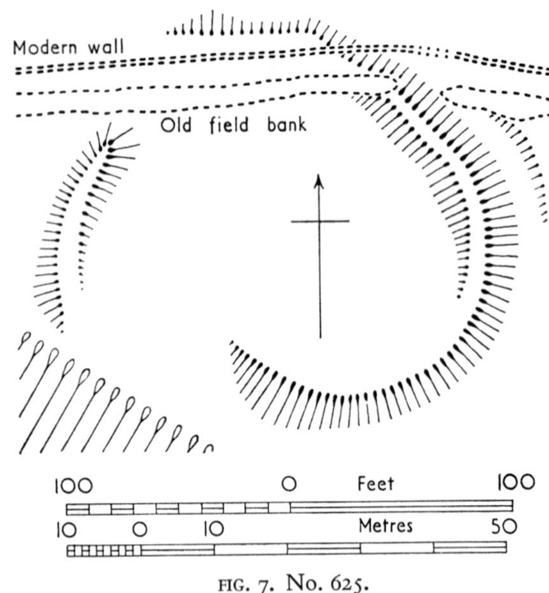

FIG. 7. No. 625.

The N. part of the camp is crossed from E. to W. by an old field bank and a modern stone wall.

S 5g (Graig Fawr).

Margam (E), Port Talbot (C).
SS 78 N.E. (7996 8673) 17 iv 66 XXXIII N.E.

(626) Pencaerau, at 75 m above O.D., stands at the N. end of the level summit of an isolated hill about 2 km S. of Neath. The S. end of the fort is indicated by a much spread bank, 6 m wide and half a metre high. The vague remnant of a similar bank follows the W. edge of the hill, and on the N.W. a natural gully breaking through this may mark the site of an entrance. On the N. and E. the bank is practically non-existent but presumably followed the natural edge. This would make the enclosure oval in plan, 45 m long from N. to S. by 35 m wide enclosing 0·1 ha.

Two small hollows among rock outcrops near the N. end

of the fort are probably quarries rather than huts, but there is a possible round hut about 7 m in diameter at the E. side.

Neath.

SS 79 N.W. (7484 9549) 23 vi 64 XVI S.W., XXV N.W.

(627) Blaen-cwm Bach. A small earthwork stands near the N.W. corner in the Roman marching camp on the ridge E. of Tonna (No. 739) at about 250 m above O.D. A bank with a ditch on the S.E., about 9 m wide and 1·5 m high overall, forms in plan the S.E. quadrant of a ciicle of about 50 m radius, with centre and N. end on the edge of a steep natural scarp. There is a gap about 7·5 m wide, with a corresponding causeway across the ditch, about 30 m from the N. end. The bank is of earth with much rubble, but no revetment is visible. There is no indication that the rampart ever extended further; the structure is probably an unfinished ringwork. If completed, it would have enclosed about 0·1 ha.

Llantwit-juxta-Neath (E), Tonna (C).

SS 79 N.E. (7935 9884) 9 x 58 XVI N.E.

(628) Warren Hill stands isolated immediately E. of the River Neath near its mouth, overlooking the site of the old ferry. The summit, just over 30 m above O.D., is encircled by the remains of a strong bank and ditch, now reduced to a scarp with a terrace below. There seem also to be traces of a counter-scarp bank. The surface of the hill has been much disturbed by industrial activities, but the defences are well preserved round the S. and E. sides, where they now measure about 15 m wide

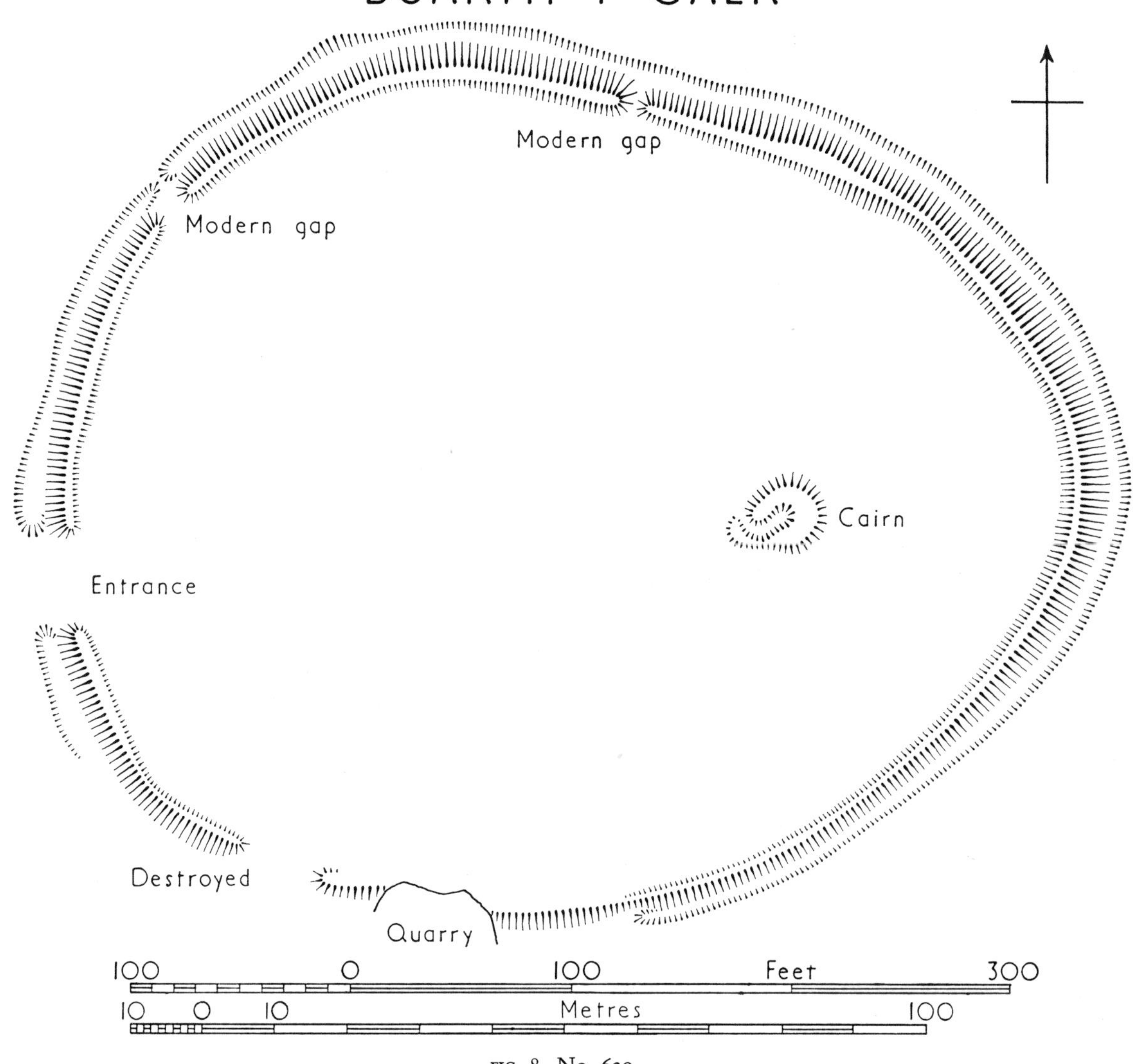

FIG. 8. No. 629.

overall and about 5 m high. The N. quadrant has been destroyed by the construction of a road. The position of the entrance is uncertain.

The enclosed area is oval, about 110 m N. to S. by 90 m (0·8 ha). Much of it has been disturbed by the construction of a reservoir, and no hut-sites can be identified. In 1971 a cutting for a water main provided a complete profile through the E. and W. defences, showing the visible rampart to have been about 6 m wide above a rock-cut slope 10 m long, falling to a ditch 1 m deep. Another ditch was also shown to have encircled a smaller area of the hilltop about 20 m inside the rampart terrace; it was about 6 m wide and 1·5 m deep, but its accompanying bank had been almost entirely obliterated. The two enclosures may be of different dates.

Briton Ferry (E), Neath (C).
SS 79 S.W. (7365 9410) 20 ii 67 XXIV N.E.

(629) BUARTH Y GAER (Fig. 8) is a simple contour fort at 300 m above O.D. on the summit of Mynydd y Gaer, 3 km E. of Briton Ferry. It is oval in plan and measures 135 m long from E. to W. by 107 m wide enclosing 1·1 ha, defended by a single bank with external ditch, of average overall width about 10 m. The defences are best preserved on the E. and N.E. where the bank is about 0·7 m high internally, and nearly 2 m externally above the bottom of the ditch. At the W. end is a simple entrance 12 m wide. Narrow gaps in the bank on the N. appear to be modern. The defences have been partly destroyed on the S. by modern quarrying.

Within the enclosure, on the highest point of the hill, is a cairn (I i 249), presumably earlier than the hill-fort.

S 9b (Mynydd Gaer).

Llantwit-juxta-Neath (E), Neath (C).
SS 79 S.E. (7655 9360) 22 X 64 XXV N.W.

(630) CHAPEL HILL N.E. of Merthyr Mawr is a summit rising to about 30 m above O.D. at the end of a spur projecting S.E. towards the valley of the Ogmore. An earth bank about 1·3 m high where best preserved and 6 m wide encloses a fairly level oval area of 0·4 ha about 75 m E.–W. by 70 m. An ill-defined gap about 3 m wide on the W. was probably the entrance. There is no visible ditch, but occasional slight indications of a counterscarp bank suggest that one may have existed. The remains are overgrown, and damaged by footpaths and tree-planting.

The ruins of the 12th-century chapel of St. Roque stand within the enclosure, and just outside on the W. is a large natural pothole.

Merthyr Mawr.
SS 87 N.E. (8887 7806) 23 ii 66 XL S.E.

(630a) PROMONTORY FORT, Flemings-down, on the N. edge of Ogmore Down, at about 60 m above O.D. A well-defined promontory, bounded on the N. by the scarp forming the edge of the Down and on the S.W. by a cwm, has been fortified by a substantial bank and ditch about 90 m long built across its E. side; the defences are slightly convex towards the E. They measure 20 m wide overall, and the crest of the bank generally stands about 3 m above the bottom of the ditch. The material of the bank is rocky, but no revetment is visible. The entrance was between the N. end of the rampart and the steep hillside; it has been damaged by later traffic and the construction of a field-wall, and its original width is uncertain.

The other two sides of the enclosure, about 100 m long on the N. and 140 m on the S.W., are followed by modern field-walls which have obscured any early features; the ground outside is very steep, and may have been artificially scarped. The interior of 0·45 ha is pasture; the cross-bank and ditch are wooded.

St. Brides Major and Wick (E), St. Brides Major (C).
SS 87 N.E. (8895 7680) 25 i 72 XL S.E.

(631) CWM BACH (Plate 3). The fort, at about 60 m above O.D., occupies the angle between a cliff to the S.W. and a steep-sided valley to the N. about 1·5 km S.E. of Dunraven. There has been considerable erosion on the S.W., so that the enclosure is now triangular, measuring 60 m in depth from its N.W. apex to the bank which defends it on the S.E. from the level ground beyond. The present area is about 0·3 ha but was probably at least 1 ha originally. The rampart has an external ditch and traces of a counterscarp bank. It is about 100 m long overall, in two slightly curving sections, with a gap near the middle. The N.E. section, with a width of 16·5 m and height of 2 m overall, is aligned forward of the S.W. section, which measures 15·5 m wide by 3 m high overall. The oblique entrance thus formed is 14 m wide. In the angle between the northern stretch of rampart and the edge of the cwm a very slight bank, about 2 m wide by 0·1 m high, forms a roughly rectangular enclosure with slightly rounded ends. This is some 33 m long and 7 m wide at its ends, widening to about 8 m in the middle. The side parallel to the rampart is straight, separated from the inner toe by about 10 m. The N. end is 6 m from the edge of the cwm. From the S.W. corner a similar bank runs for 20 m parallel to the other section of rampart, about 5 m from the line of its inner toe. The enclosure may correspond to a building, but may be no more than the last traces of the topsoil dumps formed when the defences were being built.

S 5c.

St. Brides Major and Wick (E), St. Brides Major (C).
SS 87 S.E. (8970 7173) 15 ii 61 XLIV S.E.

(632) MYNYDD TWMPATHYDDAEAR, 6 km W. of Bridgend, is a rounded hill rising to about 100 m above O.D. Owing to quarrying and other disturbances, very little is now visible of what was once a roughly circular enclosure, about 120 m in diameter surrounded by a single rampart and ditch. The area was about 1·2 ha. There was an entrance gap at the E. and a group of outworks, not certainly defensive, at the W. Human remains were found in the S. part of the fort in 1870. There are only two certain sectors of the defences remaining. (i) At the N.N.W. are two stretches 20 m and 10 m long, the bank being 5 m wide and 1·2 m high; a block of stone nearly 2 m long, 1 m high and 0·7 m thick at the S.W. end of the inner edge of this sector of bank may be part of an original

facing; the ditch is 4·5 m wide and 0·3 m deep, with a suggestion of an exterior bank. (ii) At the W.S.W. is a stretch 20 m long, the bank being 6 m wide and 0·7 m high, and the ditch 5·5 m wide and 0·7 m deep; it lies on the S.W. side of a fence which cuts off about one quarter of the original perimeter, and is grass-covered. The remainder of the area is covered with scrub and quarry dumps, and a limestone quarry has encroached on the area at the N.E.

S 1e (Stormy Down). *Trans. Cardiff Nat. Soc.*, XXVII (1894–5), p. 82 (plan).

Pyle and Kenfig/Newton Nottage (E),
Pyle/Newton Nottage (C).
SS 88 S.W. (8405 8037) 30 iv 61 XL N.W.

(633) CRAIG TAN-Y-LAN, 2 km E. of Coychurch. A spur at about 90 m above O.D. is fortified by a rampart about 110 m long and convex outwards, across its S. (accessible) end. Any defences which may have existed on the other sides have been destroyed by cultivation, but the enclosed area must have been about 0·9 ha. The entrance was probably at the W. end of the surviving rampart, but this is too damaged for certainty. Where best preserved, the defences consist of a ditch and a very stony bank measuring 14 m wide and about 2·5 m high overall, but for most of its length the ditch has been filled.

St. Mary Hill.
SS 97 N.E. (9585 7954) 23 ii 66 XLI N.W.

(634) TY'N-Y-WAUN, 7 km N.E. of Bridgend. A small spur, outlined by the contours and about 180 m above O.D. projects S. from higher ground. The end rises in a knoll which is naturally defensible, and this has been fortified by a single rampart to form a D-shaped enclosure measuring about 75 m N.–S. by 65 m, with a straight E. side, enclosing 0·4 ha. A terraced cart-track 15 m wide enters at the S.E. angle, possibly on the site of the original entrance. For most of the circuit the rampart appears as a scarp about 3 m high, but on the N. it forms a bank, of similar height externally, rising about 1 m above the interior and measuring about 12 m wide overall. It is composed of earth and rubble, with no revetment visible. There is no ditch.

Coychurch (E), C. Higher (C).
SS 98 N.W. (9485 8527) 15 vii 65 XXXV S.W.

(635) PANTYPYLLAU (Parcnewydd in *I.A. Map*). The remains of a D-shaped enclosure, about 87 m long from N. to S. by 57 m in maximum breadth enclosing about 0·4 ha, stand on level enclosed land at 90 m above O.D. on the S. side of Cefn Hirgoed. The straight E. side is defended by a scarp, mutilated towards the N., but on the S.E. falling into a vast ditch about 15 m wide and 4·5 m deep; this is probably partly or even wholly natural but has been incorporated in the defences. On the S. the surviving portion of the defences consists of a bank 7 m wide and 1·3 m high, with an external ditch 7 m wide and nearly 1 m deep, partly filled with rubbish. On the S.W. the defences have been partly, and on the N. completely, destroyed. The best preserved portion of the defences is on the W. and consists of a bank 8 m wide and 1·5 m high, with an external ditch 8 m wide and 1·3 m deep.

Coety (E), C. Higher (C).
SS 98 S.W. (9273 8245) 25 vi 63 XXXIV S.E.

(636) COED Y GAER, 1·5 km N. of Coychurch. The enclosure stands at about 80 m above O.D. on a small isolated hilltop bounded by low limestone cliffs on the W. It is roughly oval, measuring 75 m N.–S. by 55 m, area 0·3 ha, and is bounded on the N., W. and S. by a mutilated bank of earth and stone. Where best preserved, on the N., the bank has slight traces of a ditch outside it; the two features together measure 7·5 m wide by 0·6 m high overall. The whole of the E. side has been mutilated by quarrying. The entrance was probably at the S. end, where the bank is poorly preserved.

S 5b.

Coety (E), C. Higher (C).
SS 98 S.W. (9391 8139) 20 v 63 XLI N.W.

(637) COEDCAE GAER (Fig. 9, Plate 2). The earthwork stands at about 230 m above O.D., on the end of a spur projecting S.E. from Mynydd y Gaer. The ground falls away on all sides except the N.W., but not steeply, so that the position is not naturally strong although it commands an extensive view in all directions. The area is 1 ha, enclosed by a strong bank and ditch with a counterscarp bank, measuring about 20 m wide by 3 m high overall where best preserved. The bank seems to be mainly of earth, and no revetment is visible. It has been set out in straight sections, forming an irregular polygon, apparently of twelve sides though damage makes this uncertain. The entrance seems to have been on the S.; E. of this gap the rampart has an inturn of about 10 m, though it is very much worn down by cultivation. Although the wide gap on the E. shows no remaining trace of rampart or ditch, it seems likely that it is a modern break, rather than that the enclosure was unfinished. A gap of similar size has been partly levelled on the N.W., and there are other minor breaks, but the ramparts are generally well preserved. The interior is now pasture, but has been cultivated.

An exceptionally large field-bank runs S.W. from the fort, but it seems later, forming part of a group of abandoned field enclosures probably of no great age.

S 1g.

Coychurch (E), C. Higher (C).
SS 98 S.E. (9735 8495) 18 ix 65 XXXV S.W.

(638) CASTELL MOEL (LIEGE CASTLE) (Fig. 10) stands on a small hill the summit of which reaches 110 m above O.D. 6 km E. of Cowbridge. The principal remains consist of a strong bank and ditch, about 15 m wide by 3 m high with traces of a counterscarp bank in places, forming three sides of a rectangle about 25 m across. From the N.E. corner, a slightly larger rampart with its ditch almost silted up extends S.E. for about 30 m in a slight curve. Slighter banks extend all these features for about 18 m further S.

About 50 m W. of the rectangle, traces of a much eroded rampart cross the side of the hill from N. to S. in a gentle

THE COEDCAE GAER
Modern wall
A
B
Modern
field bank
100 0 Feet 100
10 0 10 Metres 50
Profile to twice scale
A
B

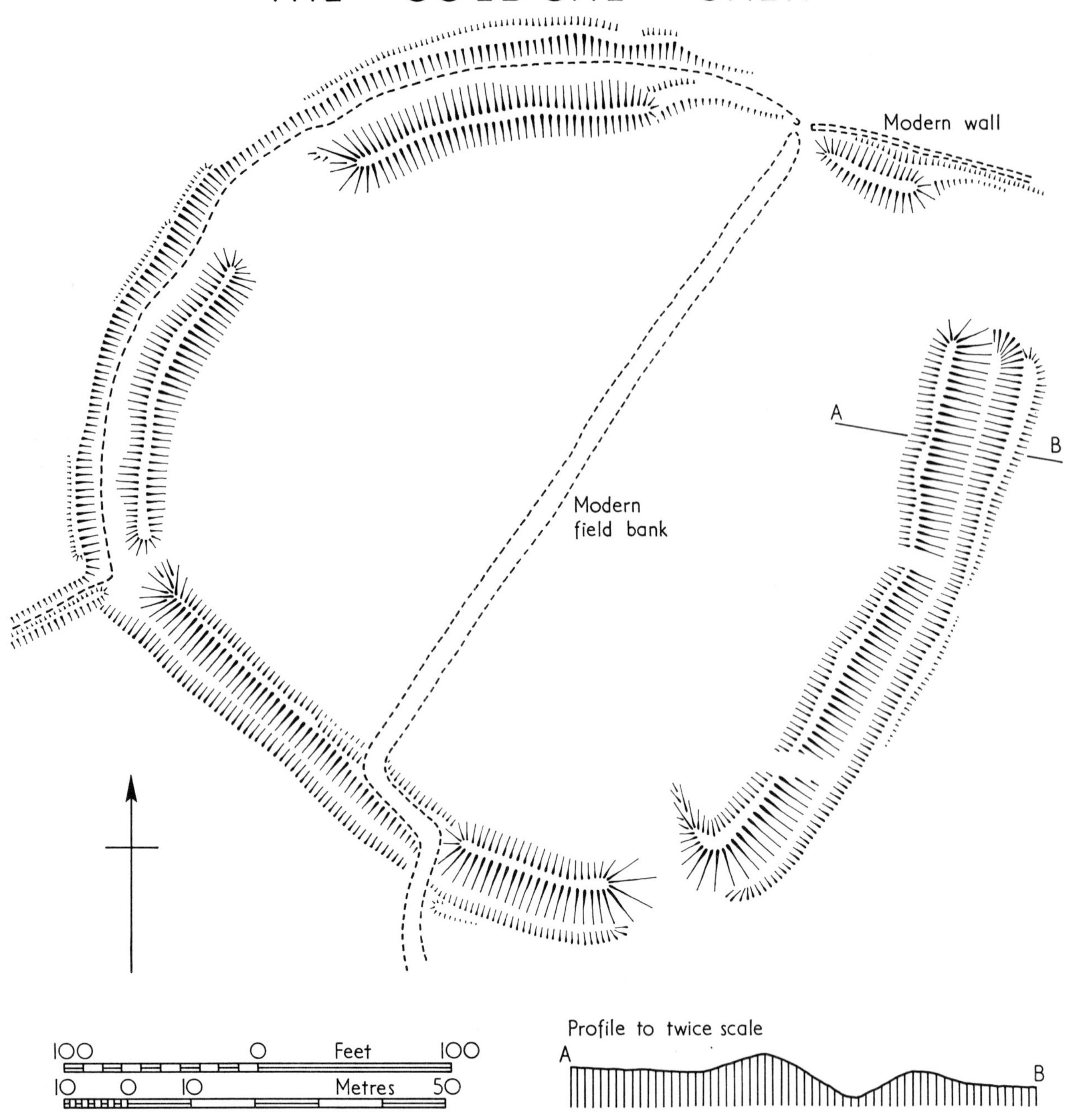

FIG. 9. No. 637.

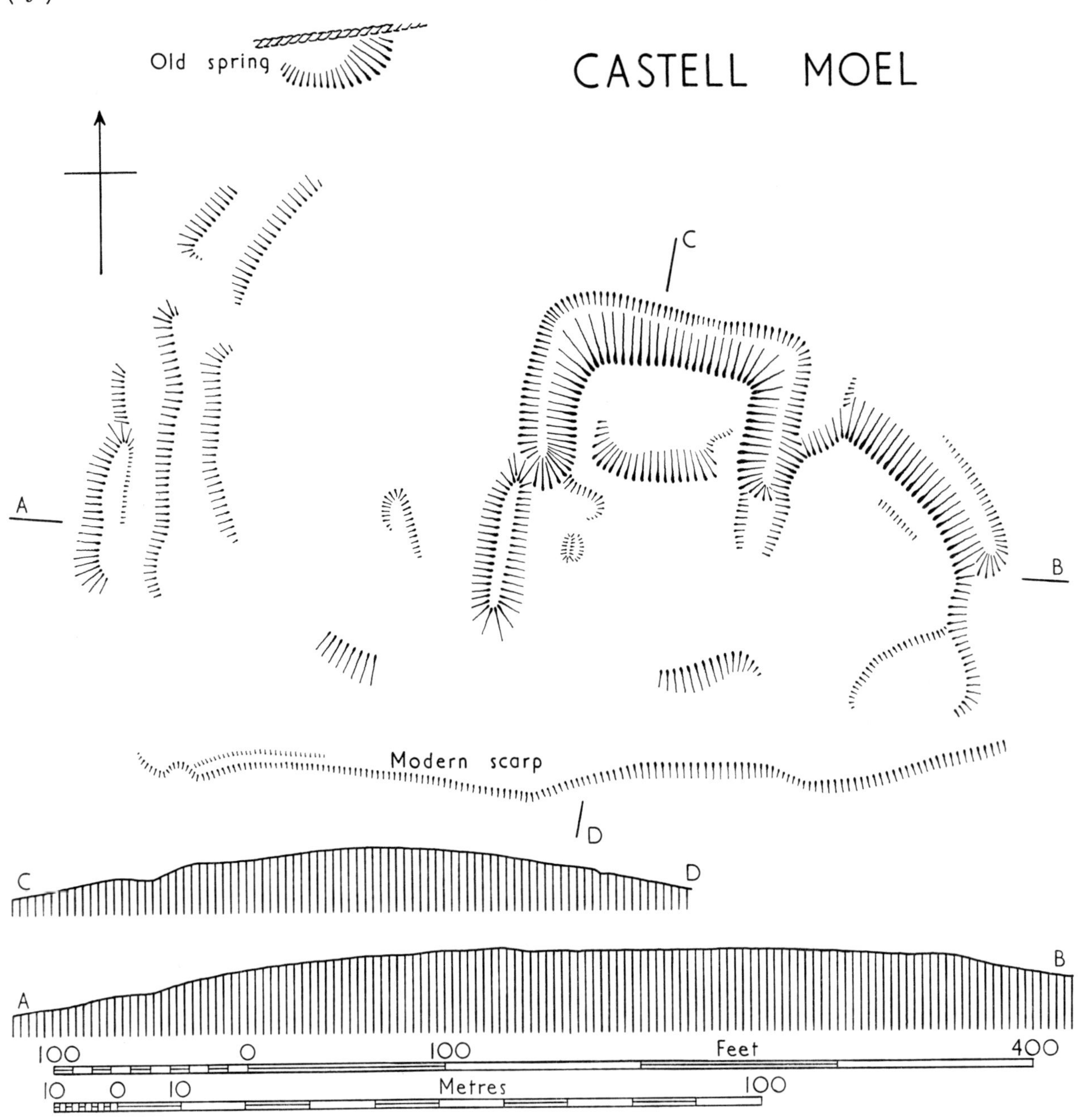

FIG. 10. No. 638.

curve. The remains now measure about 25 m overall, but it is not clear whether they consisted of two banks and ditches or of a single ditch and bank with a quarry-ditch at the back; the latter seems more likely. The N. end lies close to a hollow, now dry but formerly a spring, from which an old stream-bed runs N.

A description published a century ago[1] describes the quadrangular work as having an entrance in the S. side. It seems certain, therefore, that the present condition of the remains is the result of levelling, although superficially they give the impression of being unfinished.

The ditch of the rectangular structure is much sharper and better defined than that of the E. section of bank, which is nearly silted up; also, the crests of the rampart are not in alignment. A late 17th-century source states that 'the house place called castle moel in English lech castle . . . now beareth grass and corn'.[2] On present evidence, therefore, the most probable interpretation of the remains is that the rectangular work represents a small medieval defensive enclosure, which has been superimposed on a small univallate hill-fort, but a fully satisfactory explanation is impossible without excavation. The size of the hill-fort is uncertain, but it cannot have exceeded 115 m E. to W. by 85 m, enclosing 0·8 ha.

S 2d.

[1] *Arch. Camb.*, 1866, p. 14.
[2] Lhuyd, *Parochialia*, III, p. 137.

Llancarfan.
ST 07 S.E. (0540 7342) 7 vi 67 XLVI N.W.

(639) LLE'R GAER (Cwm Llwyd in *I.A. Map*), 4 km N. of Llantrisant, stands at a little over 180 m above O.D. with the ground falling away gently in all directions except to the north. A single bank much worn down by cultivation and now about 9 m wide by 1 m high encloses about 0·5 ha. Seen in plan it forms an irregular hexagon measuring about 90 m W.S.W. to E.N.E. by 80 m; it is symmetrical about the longer axis and the sides taken in order starting at the western end measure 23, 64, 30, 45, 30, 64 m. The only visible entrance is through the northern half of the W. end; it may be slightly inturned, but it has been damaged by use as a cart track and by the dumping of stones on the S. side of it.

S 3b.

Llantrisant.
ST 08 N.E. (0501 8703) 24 ii 67 XXXVI N.W.

(640) CRAIG Y PARC, 1·5 km S.W. of Pen-tyrch. On the W. end of a spur, just above the 90 m contour, with the ground falling away steeply on all sides except the E., a slight bank and ditch, about 7·5 m wide by 0·6 m high overall, encloses a space about 45 m in diameter; the area is about 0·2 ha. The site is in a wood with thick undergrowth, and details could not be followed, neither could the small ring said to be in this wood[1] be located.

[1] *Arch. Camb.*, 1918, p. 347.

St. Fagans with Llanilterne (E), Llanilltern (C).
ST 08 S.E. (0930 8082) 23 iv 64 XLII N.E.

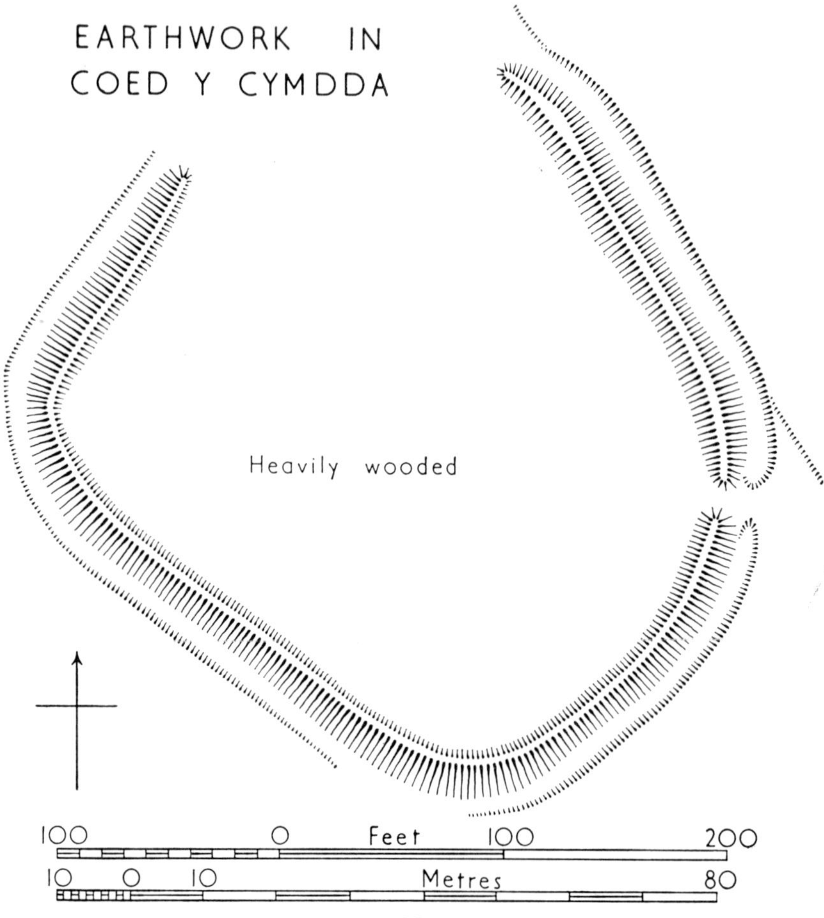

FIG. 11. No. 641.

(641) Coed y Cymdda (Fig. 11). The earthwork stands at about 105 m above O.D. on a broad ridge above ground falling gradually to the S.W. 1·5 km N.E. of Wenvoe. The enclosure is roughly quadrangular, 80 m long from N.W. to S.E., 50 m wide at the S.E. end, and about 75 m towards the N.W. end; its area is about 0·6 ha. It is defended by a slight but well preserved bank 5 to 7 m wide with a shallow external ditch 2·5 to 4·5 m wide. The entrance, on the W., is a gap 3 m wide in the bank, with a corresponding causeway over the ditch. On the N. the earthworks are missing for a space 43 m in width; the well defined ends of the surviving banks suggest that this portion was left unfinished.

S 9g.

Wenvoe.
ST 17 S.W. (1329 7398) 5 iii 63 XLVII N.W.

642–663. UNIVALLATE ENCLOSURES IN POSITIONS UNSUITED TO DEFENCE

(642) Fforestnewydd (N.W. of). Traces of an oval enclosure, 90 m N.E.–S.W. by 65 m, area 0·5 ha, stand at 90 m above O.D. on level ground above a sharp fall on the E. into the ravine of the Nant y Crimp, about 2 km N. of Llangyfelach. It is defined by a wide earthen bank, much spread, from 12 to 17 m wide and half a metre high, reaching nearly a metre in places. The S. side has been ploughed out in cultivated land. A gap at the N.E. end of the enclosure, 7 m wide, seems to represent an original entrance.

Llangyfelach.
SN 60 S.W. (6363 0155) 30 vi 61 XIV N.E.

(643) Llanddewi. The site is on level enclosed land at about 55 m above O.D. A much ploughed down oval enclosure measures, between the approximate crests of the bank, 44 m from E. to W. by 39 m, area about 0·1 ha. The defences comprise a bank with outer ditch but are much spread, varying in overall width from 15 to 25 m. They are best preserved on the W. and N.W., where the height of the bank above the bottom of the ditch is about 0·7 m; elsewhere they are very faint. There is a suggestion of an entrance some 10 m wide about the middle of the N. side. A hollow to the N.W. of the site appears to be an old pond, and there are several similar hollows in the field.

Llanddewi.
SS 48 N.E. (4557 8876) 12 i 67 XXXI N.W.

(644) Reynoldston. A round enclosure, about 55 m in diameter, stands at 100 m above O.D. on ground falling gently to the S.; the area is about 0·2 ha. It is defended by a spread bank with external ditch. The overall width of the defences is about 20 m; the bank rises 0·5 m above the interior and 1·4 m above the bottom of the ditch. On the S. are the remains of a damaged entrance about 5 m wide. The defences are mutilated by modern hedges and ditches on the N.W., W. and S.W., and are much ploughed out on the N.

S. Lewis in 1833 recorded the discovery of pottery,[1] said to be Roman, in the ditch. P. J. Williams in 1920 suggested[2] it was the site of the medieval house of the Lucases of Brynfield (the present Brynfield stands immediately to the N.), but the earthworks are more substantial than the known medieval domestic enclosures in Glamorgan.

S 2f (Brynsyfi). Rutter, *P. Gower*, p. 66; *B.B.C.S.*, VIII, iv (May 1937), p. 368.

[1] Lewis, *Top. Dict.*, *s.v.* 'Reynoldston'.

[2] *Arch. Camb.*, 1920, p. 341.

Reynoldston.
SS 48 N.E. (4834 8991) 9 vi 66 XXII S.W.

(645) Bryn-sil, about a kilometre S.W. of Penrice. An aerial photograph[1] indicates the presence of a ring at about 80 m above O.D. on ground rising very gently towards the S.W. and falling away more steeply on other sides. The markings indicate a ditch about 5 m wide forming a regular ring apparently about 55 m N.E. to S.W. by 50 m, enclosing 0·2 ha. Other fainter markings which appear on the photograph are probably due to recent agricultural operations. Nothing is visible on the surface. The siting, and oval plan, suggest a domestic rather than a religious function.

[1] Discovered by J. K. S. St. Joseph, C.U.A.P., No. AJB 61.

Penrice.
SS 48 N.E. (4850 8735) 22 ii 67 XXXI N.W.

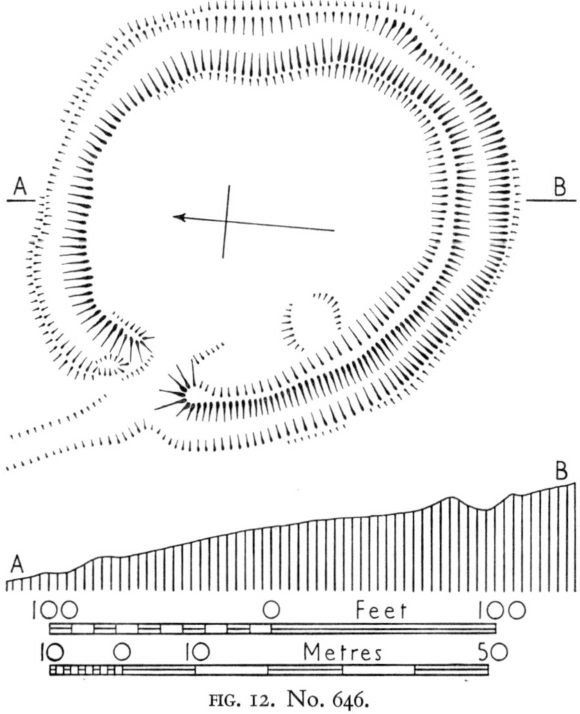

FIG. 12. No. 646.

(646) Hardings Down, N. Enclosure (Fig. 12, Plate 7). This stands on the N. slopes of the down, just above the 120 m

contour, on ground falling with a fairly uniform slope of about 1 in 6. The enclosed area is 0·2 ha. It is surrounded by a strong bank and ditch with counterscarp bank, apparently defensive in character in spite of the unsuitability of the position from that point of view. The entrance is on the N.W.; the ends of the rampart are slightly thickened. It is approached by a slightly hollowed trackway about 3 m wide, between low stony banks. On the W. side of the enclosure is a hut-platform, about 6 m in diameter.

S 3f. *Arch. Camb.*, 1920, p. 221 (plan) and p. 322; *B.B.C.S.*, VIII, iv (May 1937), p. 368; Rutter, *P. Gower*, p. 66.

Llangennith.
SS 49 S.W. (4366 9083) 20 iii 62 XXI S.E.

(647) Druids Moor on the S.E. of Hardings Down. An enclosure stands at about 75 m above O.D. on very water-logged ground falling gently (at 6°) to the S.E. It is oval, measuring 61 m N.N.E. to S.S.W. by 34 m between crests, and is bounded by a bank and external ditch; these measure 9 m wide by 1·3 m high overall where best preserved on the E., but round the upper, W. half they are much damaged and in places obliterated. The area is 0·2 ha. There is an entrance 3 m wide on the E.S.E.

S 8f.

Llangennith.
SS 49 S.W. (4416 9016) 11 v 62 XXI S.E.

(648) Hen Gastell, Pen-clawdd. The site, at 60 m above O.D., on ground falling rather steeply to the N., commands a magnificent view northwards over the estuary of the R. Loughor. The enclosure is oval in plan, about 50 m long from E. to W. by 30 m wide, area 0·1 ha. The N. side is formed by a natural edge where the ground falls away very steeply, The S. side is defended by a massive bank running in a curve. 12 m wide at the base, nearly 3 m high internally and 1·5 m externally; the impression of a wide shallow ditch outside the rampart is mainly caused by an increase in the angle of the natural slope. A slighter continuation of the bank can be traced round either end of the enclosure. The position of the entrance is uncertain.

Trans. Cardiff Nat. Soc., LXXXVII (1957–8), p. 23.

Llanrhidian (E), Ll. Higher (C).
SS 59 N.E. (5543 9577) 25 ix 64 XXIII N.W.

(649) Cilonnen, about 2 km S. of Pen-clawdd. A level, elongated oval area some 62 m long from E. to W. by 32 m wide, stands at 90 m above O.D. on the edge of a sharp fall northwards into the valley of the Afon Morlais; the area is about 0·2 ha. The only artificial defences are on the S., where the ground rises gently. Here the site is defended by a bank about 7 m wide and 0·7 m high, with an outer ditch now wooded; the overall width is 10 m and the height of the bank above the bottom of the ditch 1·3 m. At either end the ditch continues beyond the termination of the bank, curving round to the N. and deepening to act as modern drainage channels down the slope; this drainage function may perpetuate an original arrangement.

Gower, XIV (1961), p. 82.

Llanrhidian (E), Ll. Higher (C).
SS 59 S.W. (5464 9380) 23 ix 64 XXII N.E.

(650) Llwynheiernin. At 110 m above O.D. on the N. side of Kilvey Hill are traces of an oval enclosure, 63 m E. to W. by 50 m on almost level ground in a general fall to the N.; the area is 0·25 ha. It is best preserved on the W., where it is defined by a bank half a metre high, following a regular curve and fronted by a slight shallow ditch, the overall width of bank and ditch being 7 m. Along the N. side the bank has been obliterated by a later field boundary and it is hardly possible to tell if the existing section, which runs in a more or less straight line and reaches a height of 0·7 m, is fort bank or field bank, or a combination of both. On the S. the bank is very faint, no more than 0·2 m high and spread to something like 10 m in width; and on the E. it is absent altogether.

The foregoing describes the remains in 1961, but subsequent excavation by B. Morris on behalf of the Gower Society and the Royal Institution of S. Wales[1] has shown that there was a bank on each side of the ditch, which was originally 3 m wide and 1·5 m deep, with flat bottom and steep sides. A sherd of mid-2nd-century Samian ware was found sealed beneath the inner bank.

Gower, VII (1954), p. 16.
[1] *Arch. in Wales*, VIII (1968), No. 39 (interim report).

Llansamlet (E), Swansea (C).
SS 69 S.E. (6737 9472) 29 vi 61 XXIV N.W.

(651) Carnnicholas. The site lies at 150 m above O.D. on the N. side of Kilvey Hill. It forms a terrace in ground falling to the N., and consists of an oval enclosure 45 m long from W.N.W. to E.S.E. by 37 m wide, area 0·1 ha. The surrounding bank of earth and stones, grass- and heather-grown, is best preserved on the W. where it is 4 m wide at the base, 1·3 m high externally and 0·6 m internally. It decreases in width to 3 m along the S.W. side and gradually merges into the scarp on the S., where it is only 0·3 m high externally though 1·3 m high internally. On the E. it is ploughed out in an adjoining field, the boundary bank of which has curtailed the fort area slightly. Along the N. side the fort is bounded by a terrace nearly a metre high which continues in a straight line to E. and W. There is no evidence of a ditch except possibly a wide shallow one on the N.W., nor is there any clear sign of an entrance.

Inside the earthwork, 9 m from its W. end, is an oval disturbed area, 15 m long from N. to S. by 9 m wide, divided into two roughly circular hollows by a bank about a metre high running E.–W. across the middle. This may be the site of a hut or of two adjacent huts, but the MS. O.S. Map of *ca.* 1820 shows a building about here. The southern hollow contains a spring (dry when visited).

Llansamlet (E), Swansea (C).
SS 69 S.E. (6755 9434) 29 vi 61 XXIV N.W.

On Cefn Morfudd an oval enclosure stands 50 m S. of the dyke (I iii 806); it is described in detail under that entry. It measures 52 m from N.E. to S.W. by 40 m, with a bank and external ditch measuring about 10 m wide by 1 m high overall. It appears to be unfinished.

SS 79 N.E. (7682 9812) XVI S.W.

(652) Foel Fynyddau. Three oval enclosures stand at 240 m above O.D. on the N. slopes of the mountain, about 2 km N. of Cwmavon; they are almost though not quite conjoined, being separated in each case by a space of 5 m.

(i) The E. enclosure, centred at SS 7816 9443, is bounded on the E. by a bank with a wide shallow external ditch. The bank is 9 m wide, 0·6 m high internally and 1·3 to 1·8 m externally; the ditch is 6 m wide and 0·3 to 0·6 m deep. The N. boundary is traceable as a slight and rather ragged scarp; at its W. end it curves to the S. and here forms a well-marked scarp 6 m wide and 1·5 m high. The S. boundary is not preserved but if the enclosure were complete it would be practically circular and about 70 m in diameter, area nearly 0·4 ha.

(ii) The central enclosure, centred at SS 7799 9447, is bounded on the E. by a bank 9 m wide, nearly 2 m high internally and 1·3 m externally. On the N.E. the boundary is formed by a scarp 2 m high, traceable, though much fainter, along the N.W. side also. The W. side is bounded by a denuded bank 6·5 m wide and 0·3 m high, but reaching nearly a metre high on the S.W. The S. side is incorporated in a modern field bank, but on the S.E. the original bank reappears and attains an internal height of 2·5 m. The enclosed area measures 85 m long from E.N.E. to W.S.W. by 57 m wide, area as (i).

(iii) The W. enclosure, centred at SS 7792 9449, is bounded on the E. and S. by a bank 7·5 m wide, 1·4 m high internally and 0·7 m externally. Most of the N. and W. sides are absent but there is a faint trace of the bank at the N.W. The enclosure would have been 60 m long from E. to W. by 52 m wide, area about 0.2 ha.

Baglan (E), B. Higher (C).

SS 79 S.E. (see above) 24 vi 64 XXV N.W.

(653) Cwm Ffairty. A small enclosure stood at 150 m above O.D. on the E. end of a spur E. of Port Talbot, on ground falling very steeply to the E. O.S. records describe it (in 1956) as an oval platform, 35 m long from N.E. to S.W. by 25 m wide, area about 0·1 ha; on the downhill side it had a scarped edge 2·3 m high with another terrace edge some 4 m beyond it. It is now inaccessible in dense forest.

Margam (E), Port Talbot (C).

SS 79 S.E. (7850 9020) 25 vi 64 XXV S.W.

(654) Geulan-las, Mynydd Margam. The location is peculiar, even for a hillslope site. The enclosure stands at 270 m above O.D., filling the head of a narrow valley which opens above (*i.e.* to the N.) on to moorland and plunges below into a steep ravine. The ground rises steeply outside the bank on all sides except the S. In plan it is roughly quadrangular and measures about 72 m long from E. to W. by 48 m wide, area 0·4 ha. The E. side is straight, but the N. side runs in a wide curve along the steep hillside. Only the E. half of the S. side is preserved; and the course of the earthwork in the lowest part of the site and on the steep ground at the S.W. is obscure.

The enclosure is defined by a bank with external ditch. On the E. and S. the bank is 7 m wide and 0·6 m high, the ditch (missing on the S.) 4 m wide and about half a metre deep. The bank on the N. is nearly a metre high but has a much weaker ditch, and there are traces of a feeble bank on the W. About the middle of the N. side is a gap 3 m wide, probably the original entrance.

The site is certainly not defensive and was probably an enclosure for animals (wild or domestic?) driven down the funnel-like valley from the mountain above.

S 5h (rejected).

Margam (E), Port Talbot (C).

SS 88 N.W. (8129 8851) 28 v 63 XXXIII N.E.

(655) Cwm Philip West. The site lies at 220 m above O.D. on ground falling to the W., just outside the N.E. boundary wall of Margam Deer-park. The structure appears to have consisted of a simple oval enclosure, about 42 m long from N. to S. by 33 m wide, though the W. side is largely destroyed; the area is about 0·1 ha. It is defined by a single bank, best preserved on the E. where it is 3·5 m wide and 0·7 m high, an apparent external ditch probably being merely where material has been scooped out to form the bank. The position of the entrance is uncertain. The annexe shown on the S. on the 6-in. O.S. map is non-existent and is probably due to misinterpretation of the scarp of a hollow way that descends the slope some yards S.E. of the enclosure. The site is now in a forestry plantation though the enclosure itself is not planted.

S 6h (rejected).

Margam (E), Port Talbot (C).

SS 88 N.W. (8207 8707) 17 v 65 XXXIII N.E.

(656) Ton Mawr. The site lies at 240 m above O.D. on a broad spur W. of Cwm Kenfig, about 4 km N. of Pyle on ground falling gently to the S.E. A rather irregular ring varying from 60 to 70 m in diameter, area about 0·3 ha is defended by a single rampart which round the W. half consists of a bank 8·5 to 10 m wide, half a metre high internally and up to a metre externally, and elsewhere of a scarp 4 to 6·5 m wide and about 0·8 m high except on the S.E. where it reaches nearly 2 m in height owing to the fall of ground. Round the N.W. half there is also an outer ditch 8 to 12 m wide and about half a metre deep; the outward turn of its counterscarp on the S.W. suggests that it never extended round the remainder of the earthwork. The entrance is a simple gap on the S.W., now less than 2 m wide. There are no internal structures.

S 6g. *Antiquity*, VIII (1934), p. 398 and Fig. 2.

Margam (E), Port Talbot (C).

SS 88 N.W. (8310 8617) 25 viii 65 XXXIII N.E.

(657) Caer Blaen-y-cwm (Fig. 13, Plate 3) stands at 300 m above O.D. on a broad mountain spur falling gently to the S.,

CAER BLAEN-Y-CWM

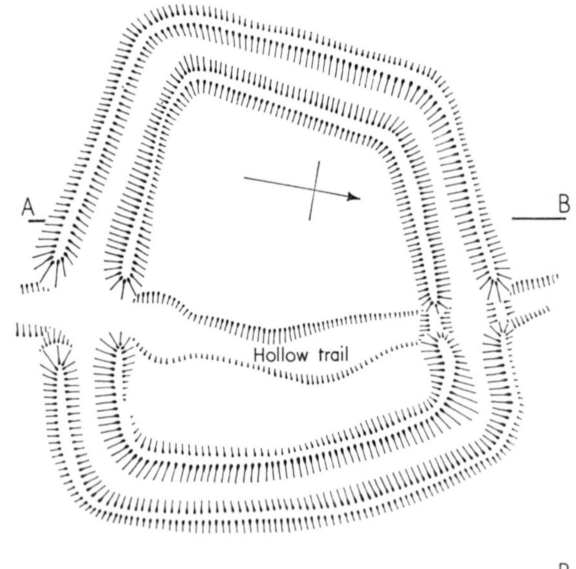

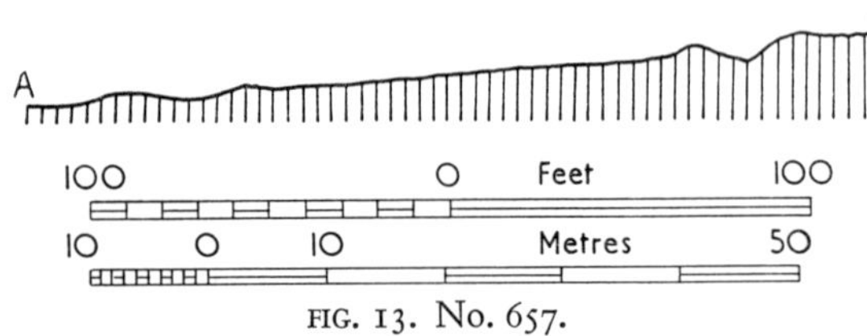

FIG. 13. No. 657.

about 4 km S.W. of Maesteg. The enclosure is quadrangular, the W. and N. sides straight, the E. and S. bowed outwards slightly and measuring respectively 25, 31, 39, 44 m; the area is 0·1 ha. It is defended by a ditch between two banks, both about 4 to 6 m wide, 1·5 m high above the ditch bottom and 0·7 m above the natural surface; the overall width is 11 to 15 m. A hollow trail cuts right through the fort from N. to S. On the N. it has breached the defences, but on the S. it appears to have utilised the original entrance, which survives as a gap 4·5 m wide through both banks.

The interpretation of the site published by Sir Cyril and Lady Fox in 1934 suggests that the fort lies at the centre of a much larger square enclosure about 210 m across; but reconsideration of the various earthworks suggests that they are not contemporary with the fort, or at any rate do not constitute an enclosure. The E. side is formed by the edge of the marshy hollow in which flows the Afon Kenfig, the W. side by a hollow trail that is merely an alternative to that which cuts through the fort, and the S. side by one of the branches of the well-marked medieval trail that crosses the hills from Llangynwyd in the N.E. to Margam in the S.W. Only the N. side of the supposed enclosure is a genuine earthwork that may be pre-medieval; this is a cross-ridge dyke that commences on the E. at the River Kenfig (SS 8337 8819), is breached by the first N.–S. hollow trail at 8331 8816, by the second at 8323 8802 (where the 'Tumulus' marked on the 6-in. O.S. map is merely the upcast from the breach), and is then traceable southwestwards to become lost in what is now a forestry plantation (about 8312 8800).

S 7d. *Antiquity*, VIII (1934), p. 400.

Llangynwyd (E), Ll. Middle (C).
SS 88 N.W. (8333 8807) 5 V 65 XXXIII N.E.

(658) MYNYDD PEN-HYDD, about 4 km N.W. of Maesteg. A small ringwork stands at 270 m above O.D. on ground falling gently to the N. It is 24 m in diameter, area about 0·05 ha, bounded around the S. half of its circumference by a bank 2·5 to 3 m wide and half a metre high, outside which is a shallow ditch 2 m wide. The ditch is more deeply cut on the W. and S.W. where the external height is nearly a metre. The bank and ditch are absent on the N. half of the circumference which, however, is traceable as a scarp 0·6 m high, though even this is lacking on the N.E. There is no sign of interior structures.

A modern stone wall bisects the site from E. to W. A sunken track follows its S. face and has cut a deep groove through the defences on both E. and W. The site is heavily overgrown with grass, bilberry and heather. Its character is not certain, and it should perhaps be regarded as a ring-cairn.

S 4f.

Llangynwyd (E), Glyncorrwg (C).
SS 89 S.W. (8200 9403) 31 V 63 XXV N.E.

(659) CEFN YR ARGOED (Fig. 14). The site is at 300 m above O.D. on ground falling to the S.W., about 3 km N.W. of Maesteg. An oval, or perhaps sub-rectangular, enclosure measuring about 45 m long from N.E. to S.W. by 33 m wide, area 0·1 ha, is bounded by a substantial bank with external ditch. The bank varies from 4·5 to 7·5 m in width, and from 0·7 to 1·3 m in internal and 1 to 1·5 m in external height. The ditch has a U profile, from 1·3 to 2 m wide at the bottom and 4·5 to 6 m wide at the top; it is well marked on the N.E. and S.E. but is slighter on the N.W. and is absent on the S.W. At the S. end of the fort a gap in the bank 4·5 m wide, coinciding with the termination of the S.E. ditch, indicates the position of the entrance. A modern stone wall crosses the site from N.W. to S.E. and has somewhat damaged the remains.

The defences are absent on the N.E. for a length of 12 m. That this gap is original seems certain from the fact that on its S.E. side the bank is inturned; moreover from the point of inturn a bank, with a hollow trail along its N.W. flank, runs N.E. up the hillside for about 32 m. It seems likely that the gap was used for driving in domestic animals from the slopes above the camp, and could be closed by thorns or fencing when necessary.

Some 20 m E.S.E. of the S. entrance is a bank about 15 m long with a ditch along its upper side, approximately in line with the S.W. end of the fort. The most likely explanation for this is that it was the commencement of the upper end of the site first chosen. The lower end would have been 55 m to the S.W., where there is a natural crest of steeply falling ground. The work had hardly begun, however, when the site was

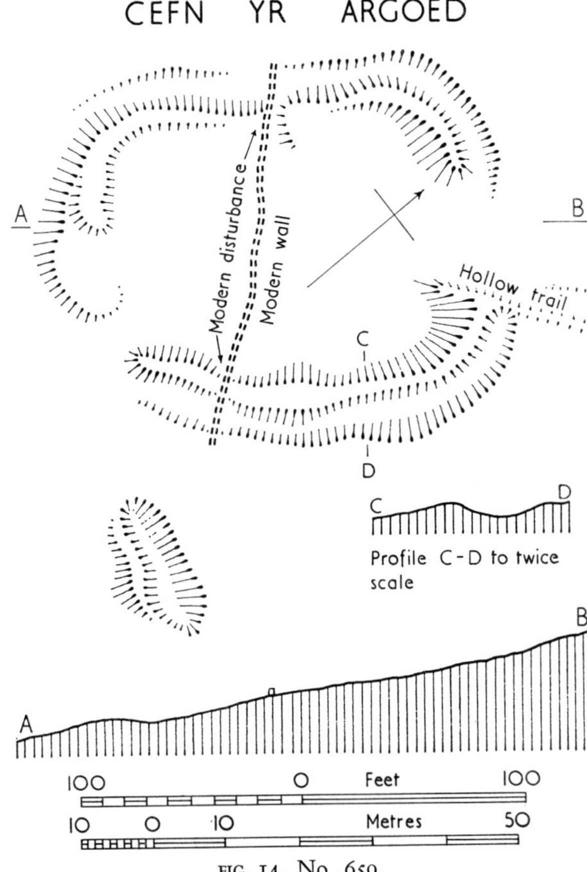

FIG. 14. No. 659.

abandoned, probably because the ground above it rose too steeply.

S 2g.

Llangynwyd (E), Ll. Higher (C).
SS 89 S.W. (8323 9406) 20 x 64 XXV N.E.

(660) ST. MARY HILL DOWN. The earthwork stands at about 90 m above O.D., on ground falling to the N.E. with a slope of about 1 in 12. The position is not naturally defensible. The enclosure, area 0·2 ha, is almost circular, 45 m in diameter, with a crescentic annexe on the S.W., about 55 m from N.W. to S.E. by 28 m. Both are protected by a bank and ditch measuring about 20 m wide by nearly a metre high overall where best preserved. There is an entrance to the annexe at its E. end, and immediately within this a simple gap leads into the round enclosure. The annexe bank is slightly inturned. There is another gap, probably also original, opposite this on the N.W. All gaps are about 3 m wide. The remains are now under pasture, but seem to have been worn down by cultivation.

St. Mary Hill.
SS 97 N.E. (9672 7905) 10 iii 66 XLI N.W.

(661) MYNYDD Y FFOREST. The earthwork stands at about 120 m above O.D., on a southward-facing slope of about 1 in 6 about a kilometre N.W. of Ystradowen. The position, which has a good view in all directions except to N., seems to have been chosen deliberately; there is no obvious reason for avoiding the summit of the hill, only a short distance to N.

The enclosure is nearly circular, about 60 m in diameter, area 0·3 ha, and is protected by a bank, ditch and counterscarp bank, measuring about 18 m wide by 0·6 m high overall where best preserved, on the E. side. The enclosure is bisected by a modern hedge-bank, and ploughing has almost obliterated the remains W. of this, including the probable site of the entrance on the S.W. On the S.E. there is a small semicircular projection from the inner bank, about 7·5 m in diameter; the ditch follows its outer edge. The remains are turf-covered, and no stonework is visible.

Ystradowen.
ST 07 N.W. (0074 7835) 10 iii 66 XLI S.E.

(662) Rectangular Enclosure W. of PARC COED MACHEN, and about 2 km N.W. of St. Brides-super-Ely, at about 60 m above O.D. on ground falling gently towards the N.E. The remains[1] have been almost obliterated by cultivation, though the field is now old pasture. The S.W. side is 75 m long, and the remaining parts of the N.W. and S.E. sides extend for about 55 and 80 m respectively, so the enclosed area was at least 0·6 ha, perhaps as much as 0·8. The W. and S. corners are almost true right-angles, and are not rounded as in most Roman military works. The bank and ditch now measure about 9 m wide by 0·3 m overall where best preserved. A slight scarp joins the visible ends of the N.W. and S.E. banks, but it is doubtful whether this corresponds to the original N.E. side.

[1] Visible on aerial photographs, CPE/UK 1871, Nos. 2094–5 and CPE/UK 2081, Nos. 3362–3.

Peterston-super-Ely.
ST 07 N.E. (0850 7910) 16 ix 64 XLII N.E.

(663) WENALLT. The enclosure stands just over 150 m above O.D., on ground falling towards the S. with a slope of about 1 in 4, about 3 km N. of Whitchurch. There is a good view in all directions except to the N. A bank and ditch about 12 m wide and 1·5 m high overall encloses a fairly regular oval, 60 m N. to S. by 38 m, area 0·2 ha. On the upper side the bank shows traces of an external revetment of large blocks. There may also have been a counterscarp bank, but this is more probably debris from an adjacent quarry. The entrance appears as a simple gap on the S.E. Near the middle of the enclosure is a slightly levelled terrace about 7·5 m in diameter, perhaps the site of a hut, and on the S.W. is a hollow, probably a quarry-scoop.

S 8g. *Arch. Journ.*, CIX (1952), p. 7 and plan, Fig. 5.

Whitchurch (E), Cardiff (C).
ST 18 S.E. (1522 8276) 7 vi 67 XXXVII S.W.

On MYNYDD EGLWYSILAN a small ringwork stands close to the dyke (I iii 812). It is described in detail under that entry. It measures 9 m in diameter within a bank and external ditch

4·6 m wide and 0·9 m high overall where best preserved. 40 m to the N.W. is a small enclosure 5 m square within a slight bank with an internal ditch.

ST 19 S.W. (1007 9014) XXVIII S.E.

665–673. THE LARGE MULTIVALLATE FORTS WITH CLOSE-SET DEFENCES (over 1·2 ha)

(665) CIL IFOR TOP (Fig. 15, Plate 4). This strongly defended hill-fort occupies the summit of an isolated ridge running N.W. to S.E. and rising nearly to 120 m above O.D. On the N.E. the ground falls very steeply to the flat-bottomed valley of a small stream and on the N.W. to the edge of the salt marshes which start about a quarter of a mile from the fort and now extend for about a mile even at high tide. Round the S.W. side the slope decreases and on the south the ridge is connected to an irregular plateau at rather over 90 m by a slightly lower col. The site commands an extensive view, particularly over the estuary to the north. The enclosure follows the outline of the ridge and is roughly oblong with rounded ends, measuring about 320 m N.W. to S.E. by 110 m, the area being 2·9 ha. A small ringwork inserted at the S.E. end measures about 40 m E. to W. by 30 m, enclosing nearly 0·1 ha.

The defences show no traces of built revetment although they are stony on the N.E. and N.W. A narrow section cut in 1910 by W. Ll. Morgan near the S. corner close to the profile CD[1] showed that the inner rampart had been built up to a depth of about 3 m with disintegrated shale, the top running almost level back to the slope of the hill. It incorporated a bank of yellow clay about 2 m high and 12 m wide, interpreted by the excavator as an earlier defence. The rampart was accompanied by a ditch 7·5 m wide and 2·5 m deep, with a flat bottom. The second bank was almost entirely levelled, but was also accompanied by a flat-bottomed ditch, 4 m wide and 1·5 m deep. No revetment-walling remained, but a layer of fallen stone was found in each ditch. It was at a high level in the filling, implying either that the revetment was embedded in the bank (as suggested by the excavator) or that it formed a breastwork. During the same excavation a trench was opened across the ringwork. No finds significant for dating were made in either cutting.

The innermost rampart is well preserved and can be traced throughout the whole circuit. Its upper side is level with the interior but its outer scarp has in places a vertical height of nearly 7·5 m in 15 m horizontal. Throughout the N.W. half of the enclosure it is accompanied by a wide internal quarry ditch; the continuation of this has probably been destroyed by cultivation. The rampart generally follows the natural slope of the hill but near the middle of the S.W. side, just S. of the entrance, it forms a bluntly rounded salient with a base of about 50 m and a projection of 10 m. The resulting platform commands both the approach to the gateway and the greater part of this side of the fort.

The outer defences have been badly damaged by cultivation except at the W. corner. A ditch probably accompanied the inner rampart throughout the S.W. and S.E. sides but not along the very steep slopes on the N.E. and N.W. Outside this ditch was a second substantial rampart. This was probably also continuous between its surviving ends, although the middle of the S.W. side has been almost obliterated, and it may also have been accompanied by a ditch along most of its length as in Morgan's section. This rampart ran roughly parallel to the inner rampart along the S.W. side but at the S.E. end it curved away to a distance of 50 m, apparently to command a steeper section of the hillside which is not visible from the main defences. From here the rampart converged on the inner bank and died out on the steep N.E. slope.

At the S. corner across the col a third rampart now very much worn down can be traced for 120 m. Its crest lies about 40 m outside that of the middle rampart, making the overall width of the defences on this side about 85 m. At the W. corner also the surviving section of ditch accompanying the middle rampart has a strong counterscarp bank, although the hillside here is very steep.

At the only entrance, in the S.W. side, the approach slopes up steeply to what is now a simple gap flanked on the S. by the salient platform mentioned above. At the second rampart, which here seems to turn in slightly, the track bends through a right-angle and continues towards the S. as a faint but definite terraced roadway. Another well defined terraced roadway, however, approaches from the N.W. and points directly towards the entrance gap. On the ground this trackway appears to have been blocked by the construction of the second rampart. If this interpretation is correct it implies that the outer defences and the southern terraced roadway are modifications of an original univallate fort; but excavation would be needed to confirm this as the relevant parts of the N.W. trackway and the second rampart are much damaged and eroded. Some support is given by the supposed earlier bank observed in the 1910 excavations.

The interior, now pasture, has almost all been cultivated, and there are some small quarry-pits at the N.W. end. In the undisturbed part three round hut-platforms 10–13 m in diameter survive, with indications of perhaps two or three more.

Outside the fort a low bank, much eroded and probably not defensive, runs downhill from near the entrance. Further S.E. near the line of the southern terraced trackway there is a strong spring rising in a deeply excavated hollow.

The ringwork inserted in the S.E. end of the enclosure is probably medieval. Its rampart has been disturbed by cultivation and in part almost obliterated, but where best preserved it stands to a height of about 1·5 m with a base width of about 7 m. A slight thickening of the grass suggests the presence of an external ditch.

S 9a, 5f. *Trans. Swansea Sci. Soc.*, 1910–11, p. 133; 1911–12, p. 92; *B.B.C.S.*, VIII, iv (May 1937), pp. 364, 369; Rutter, *P. Gower*, p. 65.

[1] *Arch. Camb.*, 1911, pp. 43–53. The position of the section is visible in a face exposed by sheep-rubbing.

Llanrhidian (E), Ll. Lower (C).

SS 59 S.W. (5055 9240) 23 xi 66 XXII S.E.

(666) DUNRAVEN (Fig. 16, Plate 5). The fort occupies a conspicuous headland, which rises to 60 m. South of this summit hard strata have resisted erosion, and form the nose

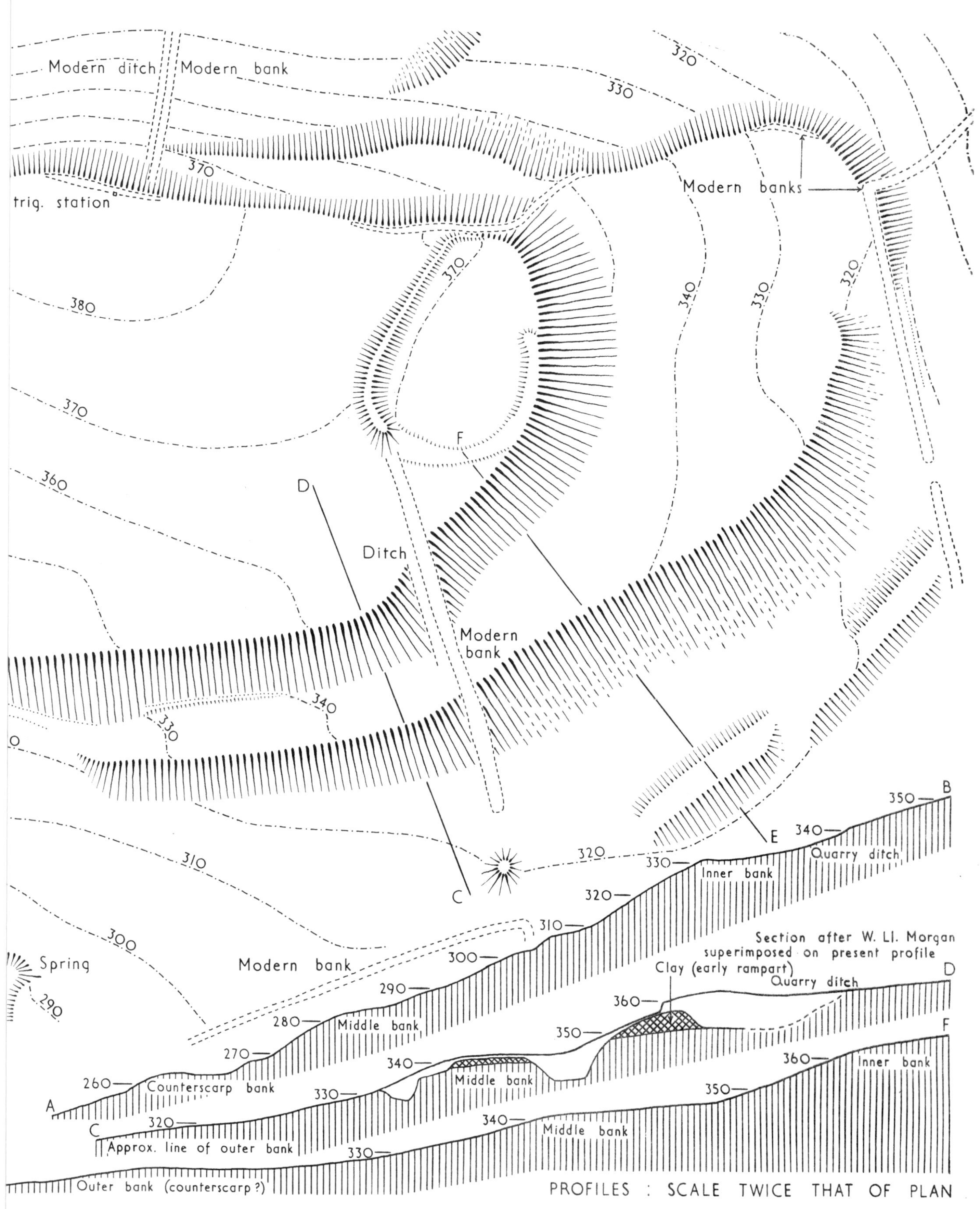

Modern ditch
Modern bank
320
330
370
trig. station
Modern banks
370
380
340
330
320
370
F
360
D
Ditch
Modern bank
340
330
E
320
310
C
300
Spring
290
Modern bank
350
B
340
Quarry ditch
330
Inner bank
320
310
Section after W. Ll. Morgan superimposed on present profile
300
Clay (early rampart)
D
Quarry ditch
290
360
280
Middle bank
350
F
270
340
Middle bank
360
Inner bank
260
Counterscarp bank
A
330
350
C
320
340
Middle bank
Approx. line of outer bank
330
Outer bank (counterscarp?)
PROFILES : SCALE TWICE THAT OF PLAN

DUNRAVEN HILLFORT
100 0 100 Feet 600
10 0 10 100 Metres 200
PLAN
CONTOURS IN FEET
Damaged; probable site of entrance
Approximate edge of cliff
Hut sites?
Disturbed area; site of Dunraven Castle
Possible hut sites
Modern field banks
Modern paths and fences omitted
Mounds
Trace of bank?
Summerhouse
Post pits
Hut sites?
10 0 Feet 100
10 0 Metres 20

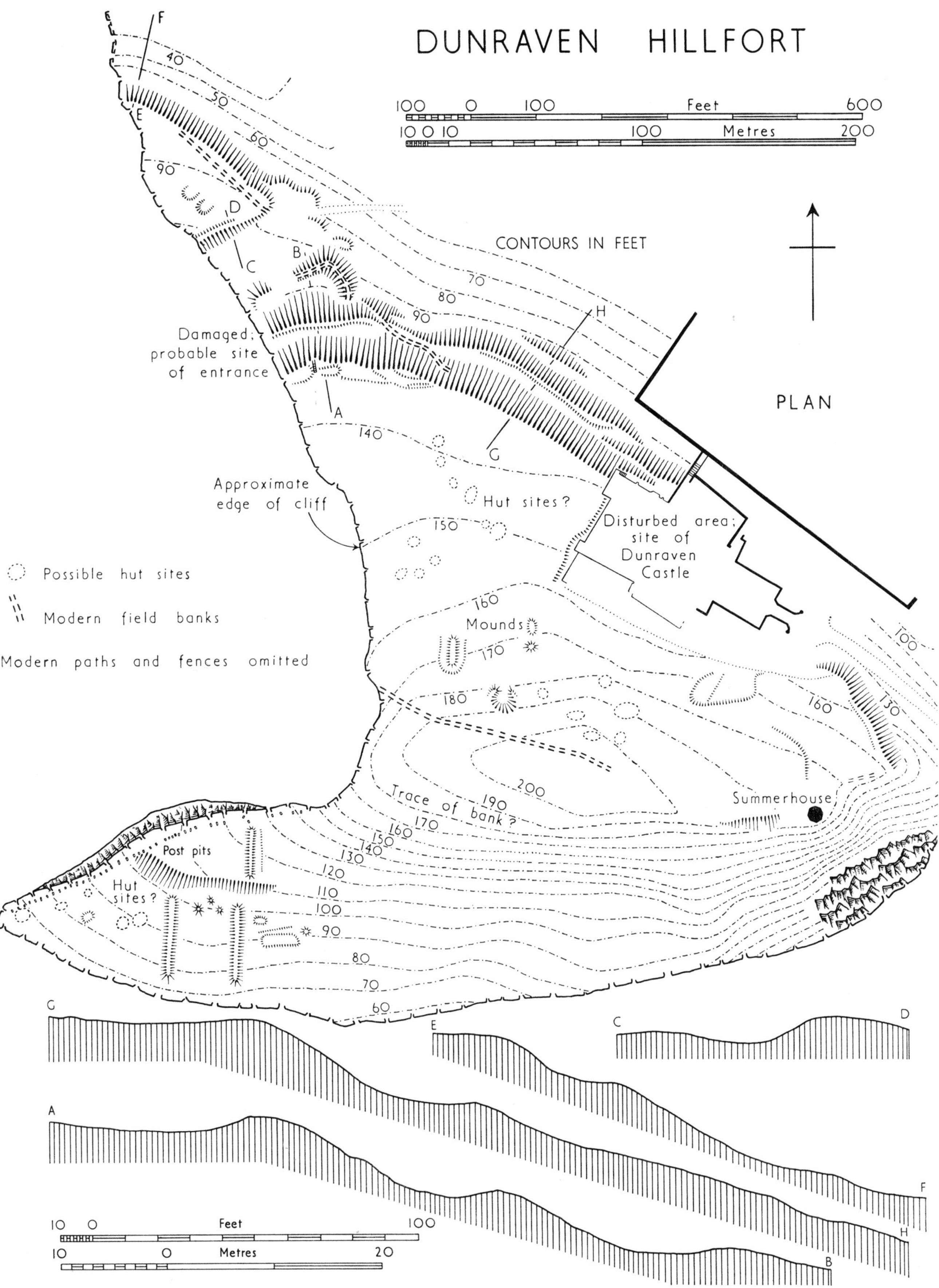

FIG. 16. No. 666.

Trwyn y Witch, but north of it the W. side of the promontory is being worn away, and presents a high vertical cliff. To the N.E. a steep-sided cwm cuts across the base of the headland. The area enclosed is now about 6·5 ha, but was probably at least half as much more originally.

The main defences follow the S.W. side of the cwm. Their S.E. half has been damaged and partly destroyed by Dunraven Castle and its approaches, but where best preserved they seem to have comprised two banks and ditches now measuring about 43 m wide and nearly 12 m high overall. These curve round to the present cliff, and where they cross the almost level ridge of the promontory they are reinforced by a small additional bank. The gateway was probably just W. of the present eroded end of these ramparts, as the additional bank curves round as though to flank an entrance passage, and rubble similar to that forming the ramparts is exposed in the cliff-top for some distance S. of the inner bank.

A fairly well-defined mark on some aerial photographs[1] suggests the presence of a filled ditch, 25 m behind the main rampart at the cliff edge and diverging to 35 m at the castle site; nothing is visible on the ground.

About 25 m N.W. of these defences the ridge is crossed by another bank, standing above a scarp facing S.E. but with no accompanying ditch. At the E. end this curves round sharply to the N.W. and becomes a single bank and ditch following the edge of the cwm, and continuing to the cliff edge. Owing to erosion, the relation of this rampart to the main enclosure is not clear, but it probably protected some form of annexe outside the entrance.

The space between this annexe and the main defences is partly obscured by blown sand, but its N.E. end seems to have been protected by a slight bank following the top of the steep natural scarp. From the middle of this bank a terraced trackway leads down to the bottom of the cwm, at a point where there are springs and where it is joined by another cwm in which a small stream flows.

There is no other clearly defined rampart on the headland, but just S. of the summit a faint trace of bank follows the 55 m contour; this could have been defensive, as its position at the top of a steep natural slope would make very little additional work necessary. On the N. side of Trwyn y Witch, also, where erosion is not active and the cliff is not unclimbable, there is a line of large rectangular post-sockets, generally about 0·3 m by 0·6 or 1·0 m. There is nothing to indicate the age of these, but their appearance has not changed during forty years.

Within the enclosure there are three groups of shallow hollows or hut platforms, generally 5 to 6 m in diameter; the majority are probably the sites of huts contemporary with the fort, but a few may be merely small quarries. The largest group, of nine or ten, lies on the gentle slope N. of the summit; in the most easterly of these the wall survives as a bank with its entrance to the S.W. Six further platforms occur just N. of the summit, and five, together with a small rectangular hut-foundation which is probably later, lie near the tip of the promontory. The character of the two hollows in the annexe is uncertain; they may be the result of wind- erosion.

The main enclosure also contains two groups of 'pillow-mounds' (I i p.41). A group near the tip of the promontory comprises four long mounds, one oval, and four round; and there are four round mounds and one long mound on the slope N. of the summit. Near these a round hollow, with banks on the lower side, has been cut into the hillside; it does not seem to be a hut, and may be a small quarry.

In 1813 Iolo Morganwg cut a section through one of the ramparts;[2] he describes the upper part as being formed by a rough mass of concrete, of lime and sand. The steps through the inner rampart may indicate the position of this cut.

S 7a.
[1] OS 1/2500 set, 67–090, No. 044.
[2] E. Waring, *Recollections and Anecdotes of Edward Williams* (1850), p. 175.

St. Brides Major and Wick (E), St. Brides Major (C).
SS 87 S.E. (8867 7279) 26 iv 63 XLIV N.E.

(667) NASH POINT (Fig. 17, Plate 5). The remains of this fort occupy what is now a narrow promontory between Cwm Marcroes and the sea cliffs, about 30 m high. The area is now only about 0·4 ha, but the cliff is being rapidly eroded, and at least another hectare must have been lost, more probably twice that amount. Along the edge of the steep slope into Cwm Marcroes the enclosure seems to have been protected by a slight bank of rubble, now mostly obscured but appearing in the cliff face as a dump of medium-sized stones about 4 m wide and 0·3 m thick in the centre. The main defences are on the N. Here a small cwm ascends W. from the main cwm, giving an easy approach to the top of the cliff; near the top it bifurcates, a smaller depression leading off to the N. These features were utilised in the defences and entrance arrangements.

The neck of the promontory was defended by four ramparts, measuring 60 m. overall; exposures in the cliff face show that the ditches were flat-bottomed and that the banks were mainly of rubble, though there is no certain evidence for revetting. The inner ramparts were close-set, the third from inside following the bottom of the small cwm. The fourth, outermost, rampart was built about 10 m from the edge of the third ditch, and extended E. as far as the depression; the two gaps in it seem modern. Anyone approaching from the N., therefore, was compelled to descend the depression to join the main approach which led up the small cwm. When it reached the end of the ramparts, the approach turned through a sharp angle and followed a terraced and revetted trackway, overlooked for most of its length from the innermost rampart. At the entrance this was thickened, or perhaps slightly inturned; it has been disturbed here by modern pits.

In the interior there are five modern pits, probably from military exercises, and some rounded hollows due to wind-erosion, but the only ancient feature is a pillow-mound. Although much of the cliff section is fairly clear, there is no sign of occupational material.

S 4c. Mentioned in *B.B.C.S.*, XIII, iii (Nov. 1949), pp. 153, 156; *Arch. Camb.*, LXXXIII (1928), p. 399.

Marcroes.
SS 96 N.W. (9148 6848) 14 ix 65 XLVIII N.E.

(668) CASTLE DITCHES, LLANTWIT MAJOR (Fig. 18, Plate 6),

NASH POINT
100 0 100 Feet 600
100 0 Metres 100
Low bank of rubble
Cliff edge
Pillow mound
Modern pits
A
B
Mod. gap
Mod.
50 0 Feet 50
10 0 10 Metres 20
Approx. form of ditches as exposed in cliff face
Approx. original surface
A
Mod. wall
B

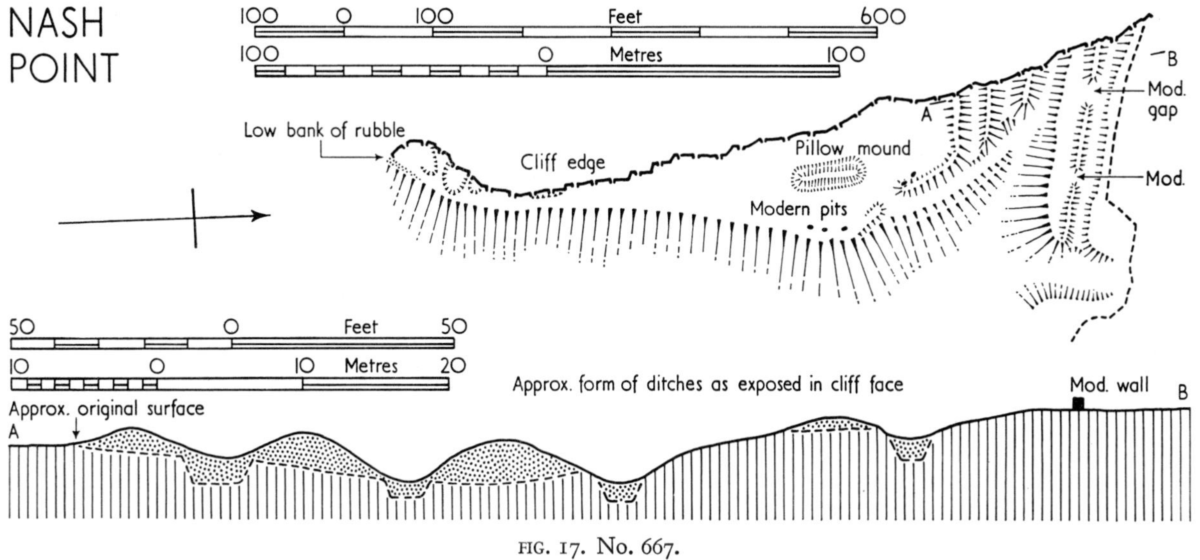

FIG. 17. No. 667.

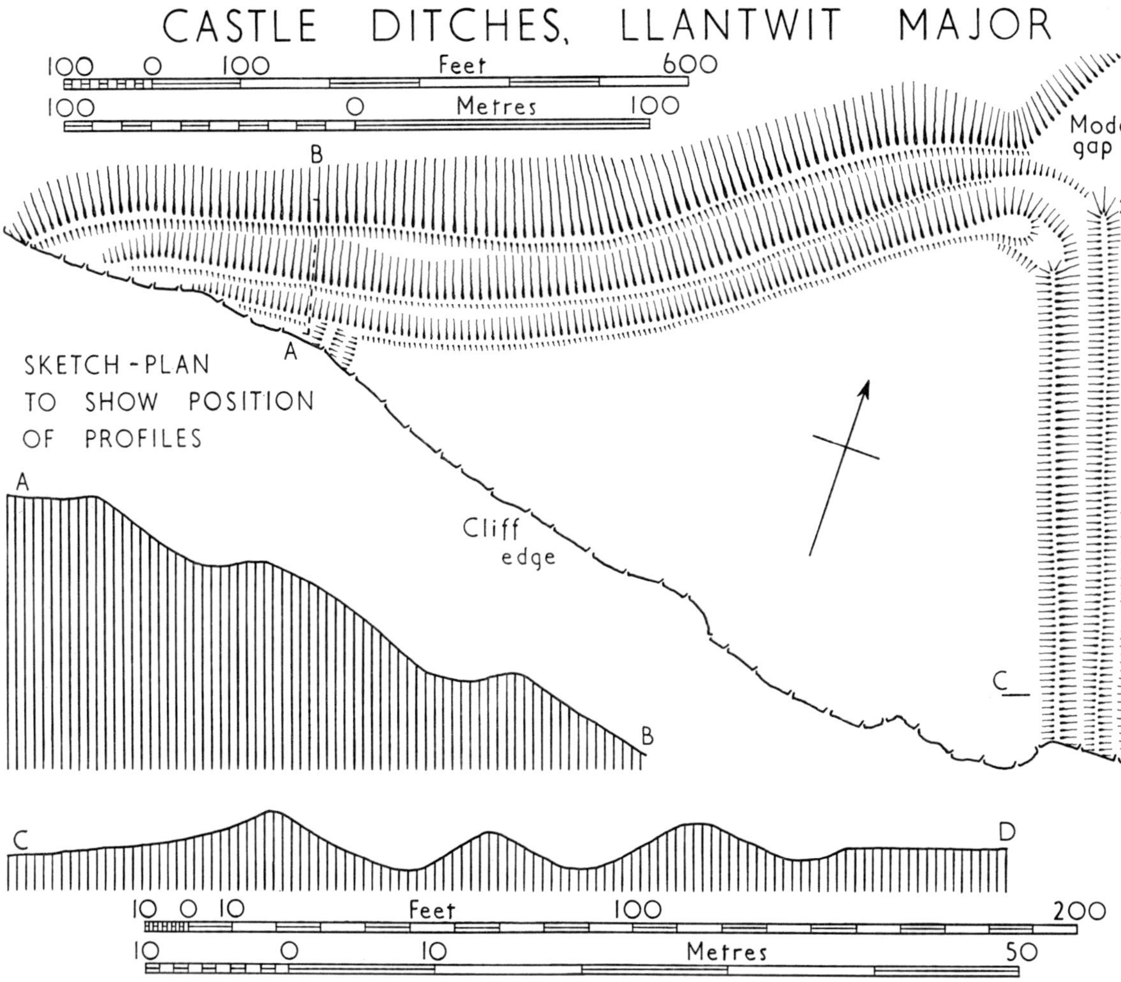

CASTLE DITCHES, LLANTWIT MAJOR
100 0 100 Feet 600
100 0 Metres 100
B
Modern gap
A
SKETCH-PLAN TO SHOW POSITION OF PROFILES
Cliff edge
C
D
A
B
C
D
10 0 10 Feet 100 200
10 0 10 Metres 50

FIG. 18. No. 668.

occupies the tip of an almost level promontory between the Colhugh Valley and the sea at about 40 m above O.D. On the N. the ground falls steeply to the Colhugh valley, and on the S. is the sea cliff, but the approach from the E. is almost level, and is barred by three massive banks and ditches, measuring about 45 m overall.[1] The cliff-face is partly overgrown, but the innermost bank, which now stands about 3·5 m above its ditch, seems to be almost entirely of rubble, whereas the other two contain much earth; the ditches are probably V-shaped. The middle bank is slightly smaller than the other two. The banks continue round the N. side of the promontory, but the outermost ditch is absent and the others are almost silted up to form terraces.

The present entrance is at the N. angle, but seems to be a later breach; the innermost bank can be traced across the gap, though much worn down.

Near the W. tip of the promontory about 10 m remain of a smaller rampart with a single ditch, much damaged but now measuring about 14 m wide by 2 m high overall. Its relation to the main defences is not clear, but it seems likely that it represents an earlier and smaller fort.

The interior has been cultivated, but is now pasture crossed by two old field-boundaries; other modern banks follow its edge. The present area is about 2·5 ha, but probably at least as much has been lost by erosion, which has also destroyed the original entrance. Coins of Carausius are said to have been found on the site.[2]

S 5a. Brief account in *Arch. Camb.*, LXXXIII (1928), p. 408.

[1] These main defences are almost all thickly overgrown, and the labour required for a fresh survey would be disproportionately large; the plan, given primarily to indicate the positions of the profiles, has therefore been based on the 1/2500 O.S. Map.

[2] M. Trevelyan, *Llantwit Major: its History and Antiquities* (1910), p. 16.

Llantwit Major.
SS 96 N.E. (9602 6742) 15 ix 65 XLIX N.W.

(669) SUMMERHOUSE CAMP (Fig. 19), occupies the E. end of a spur bounded on the N. by a shallow steep-sided valley and on the S. by cliffs. The appearance of the site suggests that the circuit of ramparts was originally complete, and that about a quarter of the total area has been destroyed by erosion. The ground occupied by the fort rises fairly uniformly from 10 m above O.D. at the E. end to nearly 30 m above O.D. just outside the W. defences; further W. the surface continues to rise, though less steeply. The main enclosure (probably originally about 1·3 hectares) is defended by three banks and accompanying ditches. On the W. these measure 50 m overall and comprise two large ramparts with accompanying ditches and a smaller inner rampart and ditch. On the N., where the natural slope is steep, the outer and middle ditches appear as terraces, and the outer bank merely as a scarp. At the E. end the outer ditch reappears faintly and turns E. to follow a scarp which seems to have formed part of the original defences. This encloses an annexe about 60 m long. The scarp is now followed by a hedge and in places has been disturbed by digging for stone; the gap on the N. is probably recent. The middle bank, accompanied by its ditch, continues S.; a slight counterscarp bank, with no outer ditch, continues the line of the outer rampart and forms the W. boundary of the annexe. The middle bank and ditch end about 20 m N. of the cliff, and it seems probable that there was an entrance here. Between this point and the cliff edge all features have been worn down by traffic, and are much overgrown, so the detailed arrangements are uncertain. A scarp continues the line of the inner rampart across the gap, which may indicate either that the entrance passage was sinuous or that the inner rampart corresponds to an earlier structure, which would account for its apparent uselessness as part of the W. defences.

Within the main defences there is a smaller enclosure, about 60 m in diameter (probably originally 0·4 hectares) defended by a single fairly strong bank and ditch. No entrance is visible. Although its banks appear rather sharper than those of the larger fort, its position suggests that it is likely to be earlier; the defences nowhere overlap.

All the ramparts are stony, and were probably revetted, but no masonry is visible and the cliff sections are overgrown. An 18th-century summerhouse (now ruinous) has been built on the site, but has not damaged the earthworks. There is a small modern drainage tank in the middle ditch.

S 3c.

Llantwit Major.
SS 96 N.E. (9945 6650) 22 ii 63 XLIX N.E.

(670) CAER DYNNAF (Fig. 20 and Frontispiece) occupies a ridge rising to 100 m above O.D., about a kilometre S.W. of Cowbridge. The ground falls away very steeply on the east and north, more gently on the south and west. The space within the main rampart measures 300 m E. to W. by 150 m, containing 3·8 ha; on the east there is a further space of about 1·1 ha between the inner and outer ramparts.

Except at the extreme western end the ramparts have been very badly damaged by field boundaries and modern cultivation, but they appear to have been double on the north and east and triple on the south and west. The inner rampart can be traced throughout the whole circuit. It is very stony and two short stretches of what may be original revetment occur near the eastern end of the north side. Except where it follows the edge of the steep northern scarp it is accompanied by a ditch. This has further a counterscarp bank round the eastern half of the circuit, and probably also south of the west entrance, but the arrangements there have been disturbed. An intermediate rampart existed along most of the west and south side. It is well preserved close to the entrance but the remainder has been almost obliterated by ploughing; its general line is just visible in suitable light. There is no sign of it beyond the north-west corner of the farm enclosure. The outer rampart is badly damaged but can be traced throughout the greater part of the circuit. It seems generally to have been accompanied by a ditch. At the east end it diverges from the line of the inner rampart so as to command a section of steep slope which would otherwise be dead ground. The enclosed annexe is subdivided by a cross-bank which is probably medieval and is discussed below. Outside the south-east corner the natural scarp has

SUMMERHOUSE CAMP
0
0
100
Feet
300
0
10
Metres
50
100
C
50
CONTOURS IN FEET
70
60
50
40
Edge of cliff
B
80 ft. O.D.
Bank of inner enclosure
D
Profiles to twice scale
50 ft. O.D.

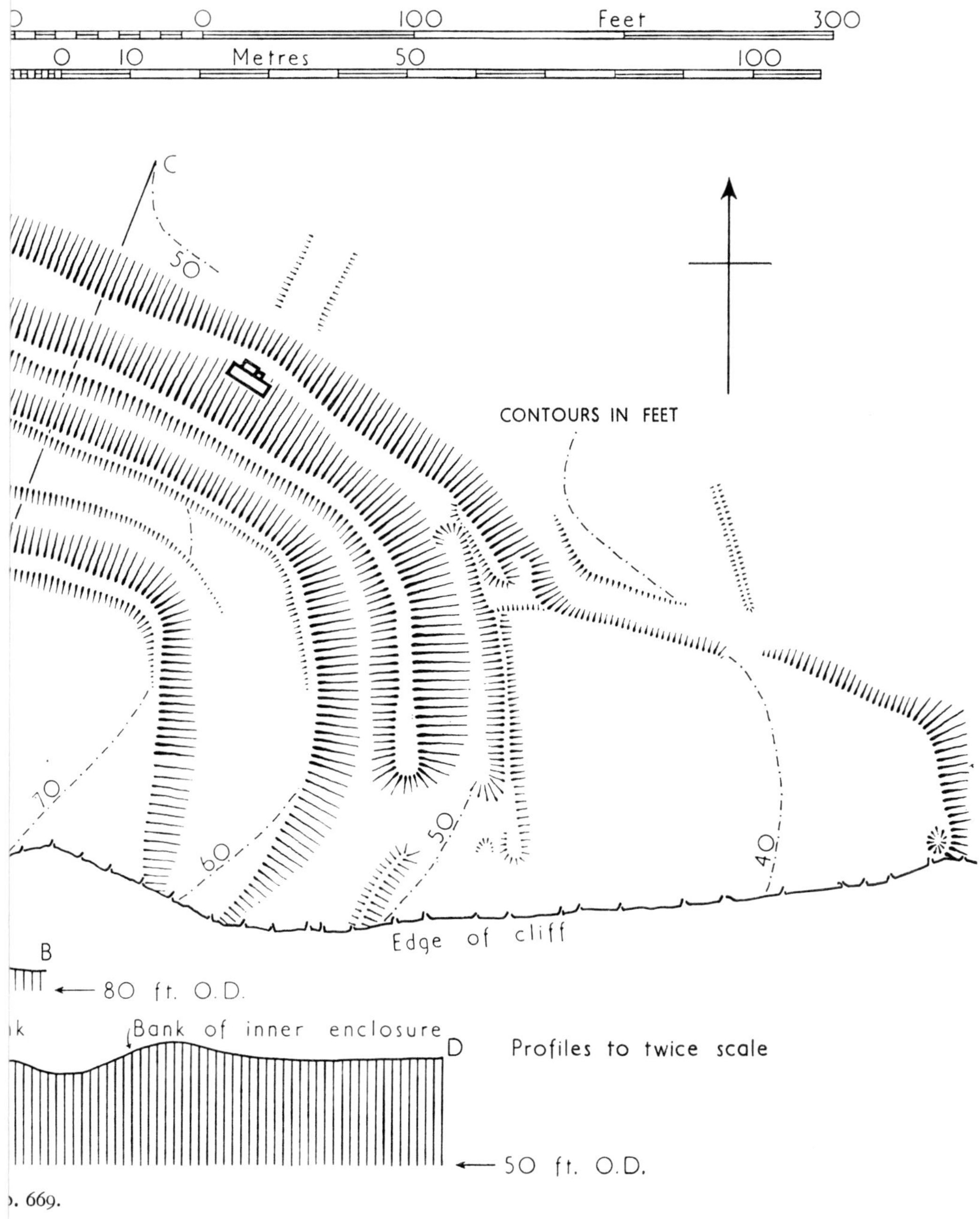

). 669.

been steepened artificially at the top for a length of 120 m to the south where there is an indication of a corner, but no return of this bank to the west can now be traced. Along the northern slope the outer bank is very ruined and overgrown in places. It seems to have continued along the top of the natural scarp as far as the corner of the inner rampart and there to have been interrupted by a cutting continuing the line of the inner rampart ditch. From there it seems to turn downhill and to be represented by a stony terrace running about 15 m below the top of the natural scarp.

North of the entrance at the western end the arrangement is puzzling. The outer rampart is clearly defined and runs north, curving round to the north-east for about 100 m to terminate on a small natural crag. A very slight bank which may represent the intermediate rampart runs parallel to it for the same distance. This end of the outermost rampart however lies about 55 m N.W. of the last trace of the stony terrace which follows the natural scarp, and although the two points are connected by steep natural slopes and small scarps facing N.E. these do not provide a barrier to access in their present form.

Only this entrance, at the W. end, is certain. Its defences are complicated and interpretation is rendered difficult by damage. The gap in the outer rampart close to the present hedge seems recent, and the original entrance probably lies about 30 m to the S.E. where the banks appear slightly thickened and inturned. Direct approach to this gap is prevented by a short length of the outer bank. This entrance leads to an irregular space which narrows to become an approach about 12 m wide bounded on the north by the top of the natural scarp and on the south by a long inturn of the innermost rampart. After about 50 m another bank runs south from the northern scarp towards the end of this inturn leaving a narrow gap which was presumably the site of the gate. There may have been another entrance near the middle of the S. side about 30 m W. of the modern cross-wall, where there is a slight lowering of the inner rampart, and the counterscarp bank of the accompanying ditch turns northwards to join it. If there was in fact an entrance here it presumably gave access from the main enclosure to the eastern annexe since there is no other break in the inner rampart.

Within the enclosure the ground is covered with low banks and hollows generally rather slight and ill-defined. North of the modern field-wall these are well preserved and to the S. they can still be traced though the ground has been improved by cultivation. The rectangle E. of the southern end of the wall appears to be sharper and more level than the other remains and is of a size appropriate for use as a tennis court. At the highest point on the hill is a low ring of stones about 1·5 m wide by 0·3 to 0·6 m high and 7·5 m in diameter; this may be a ruined ring-cairn (I i, p. 53a). The other banks seem to correspond to three or four roughly rectangular enclosures with irregular internal subdivisions and separated by narrow lanes. Their plan and superficial appearance suggest that they were a group of small farmsteads, which have been heavily robbed for stone and which have also suffered from surface quarrying. Excavations in 1965–7[1] at the lower end of a terrace on the S. side, which on this interpretation would represent a garden plot, showed that it was built up of rubble which incorporated much late 1st- to 4th-century Roman pottery and broken quern-stones. The S. wall of a rectangular Roman building, of unknown size or purpose, overlay a pit containing sherds of Belgic and Iron Age B pottery. A further fragment of rotary quern was found in a lane at the S.E. during survey in 1966.

The northern third of the annexe has been cut off by a strong bank to form a small medieval fortification.[2] In the S.W. corner of the resulting enclosure, on the outer lip of the main hill-fort ditch, are the ruins of a substantial building 16 m by 8 m externally, with walls 1·3 m thick. The structure is overlooked from the W., and forms a 'strong house' rather than a castle.

S 2a. C. Fox, *Arch. Camb.*, XCI (1936), pp. 20–4.
[1] By J. L. Davies, *Morgannwg*, XI (1967), pp. 77–8.
[2] Perhaps Llygod. Rice Merrick, *Morganiae Archaiographia, (1578)* . . . (2nd edn., J. A. Corbett, London, 1887), p. 112.

Llanblethian.
SS 97 S.E. (9835 7427) 1966 XLV N.E.

(671) PORTHKERRY BULWARKS (Fig. 21). The defences of this fort are now very thickly overgrown. This entry and the accompanying plan have therefore been based on the careful investigation published by Willoughby Gardner in 1935.[1] The fort occupies the end of a spur facing westwards and overlooking the now silted-up creek of Porthkerry. On the S.E. and on the N. the natural slopes are very steep but towards the W. the ground is almost level. The S. side is now formed by the cliff edge but it seems likely that the enclosure was originally complete. The enclosed area is trapezoidal and at present measures about 230 m from N. to S., 250 m along the N. side tapering to 120 m on the S.; the area is 4·1 ha. A strip about 120 m wide has probably been lost by erosion corresponding to a further 1 ha.

The defences were composed of three close-set banks and accompanying ditches, still well preserved on the W. where they measure about 50 m overall, but reduced to terraces on the other two sides.

The only entrance seems to have been in the middle of the W. side and is now represented by simple gaps in the ramparts and causeways across the ditches. The entrance passage is slightly oblique to the line of ramparts.

The interior is almost level at about 60 m above O.D. It is now cultivated.

Rescue excavation in 1968, by J. L. Davies on behalf of the Department of the Environment, found indications of three successive rectangular buildings behind the W. rampart; the earliest was undated, the others occupied during the first to second centuries A.D. and the third to fourth centuries respectively.[2]

S 3a.
[1] *Arch. Camb.*, XC (1935), pp. 135–40.
[2] *Arch. in Wales*, VIII (1968), No. 14.

Porthkerry.
ST 06 N.E. (0820 6630) 1966 L N.E.

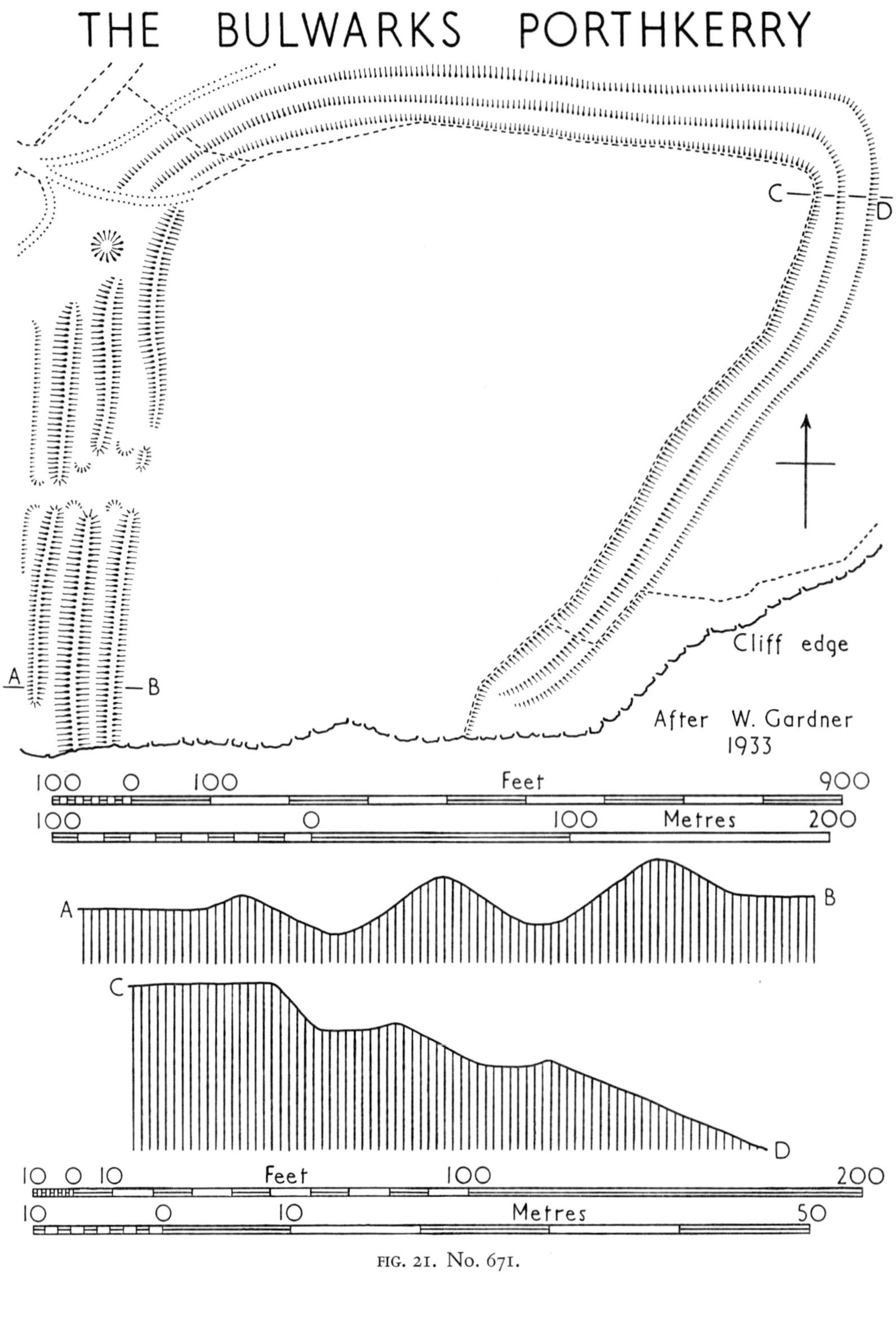
THE BULWARKS PORTHKERRY
C
D
A
B
Cliff edge
After W. Gardner
1933
100 0 100 Feet 900
100 0 100 Metres 200
A
B
C
D
10 0 10 Feet 100 200
10 0 10 Metres 50

FIG. 21. No. 671.

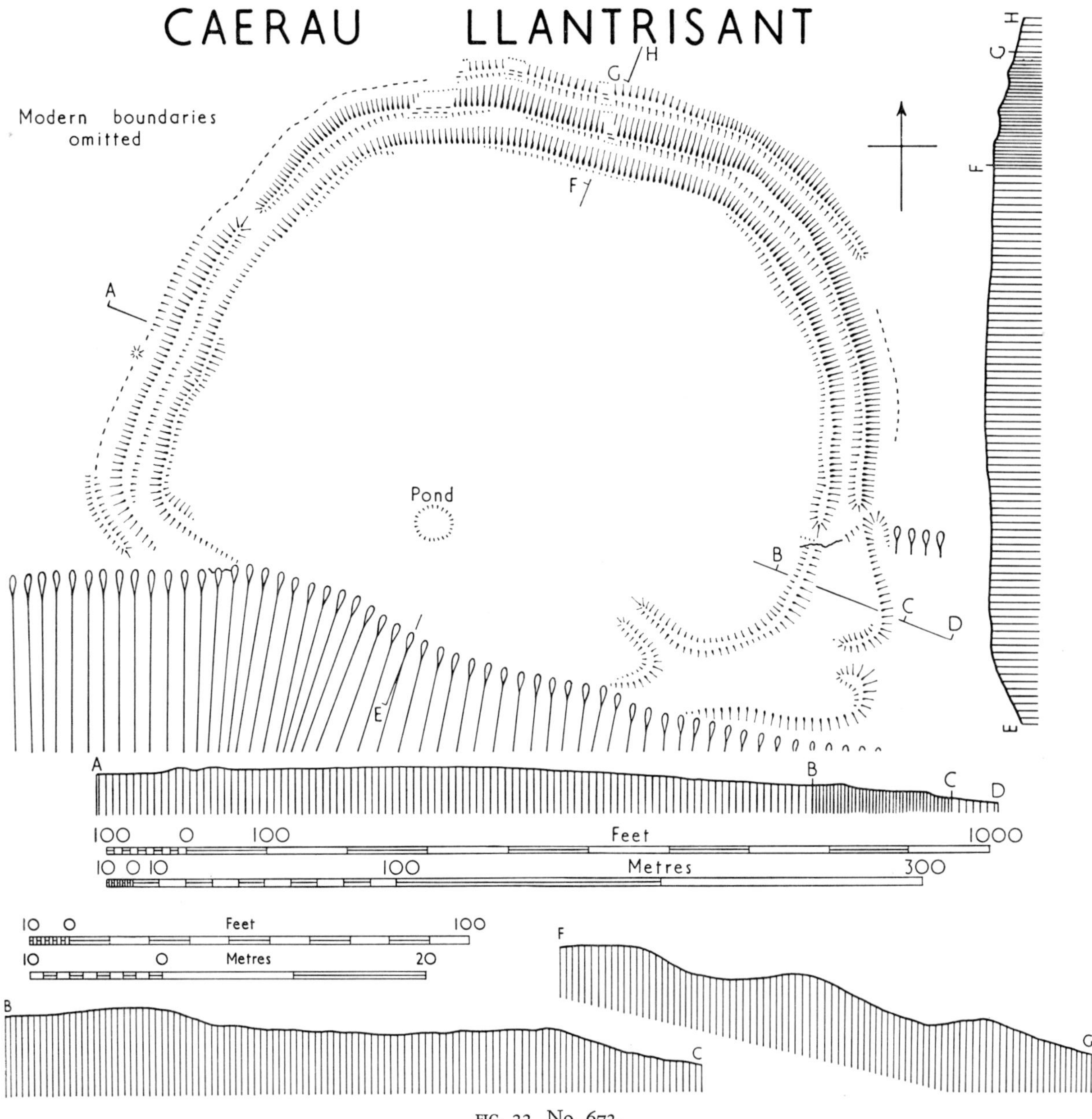

FIG. 22. No. 672.

(672) CAERAU, LLANTRISANT (Fig. 22, Plate 6) is 3·6 ha in area and occupies a smoothly rounded summit which rises to 165 m above O.D., about 2 km E. of the town. For most of the circuit the defences comprised two close-set banks and ditches and a counterscarp bank, though that and the outermost ditch have been destroyed except in the N.E. sextant and for a short length on the W. side. Where best preserved, a typical profile measures about 30 m horizontally and 7·5 m vertically overall. There is no sign of stone revetment. On the S., where the hillside is steeper than elsewhere, the outer defences were omitted, but the innermost rampart seems to have continued along the crest of the slope, though it has been levelled. The entrance was on the S.E. Here the inner and middle banks diverge, to leave between them an irregular space of about 0·3 ha. The entrance through each rampart was by a passage about 7·5 m wide between parallel, inturned banks now only about 0·6 m high, about 15 m long through the outer defences and about 28 m through the

inner. The ramparts near the entrance do not seem to have been accompanied by ditches or by the counterscarp bank.

The interior, now pasture, has been cultivated, and contains no feature except a small pond, probably modern. Shortly after the date of survey, most of the well-preserved stretch of defences on the N.E. was destroyed.

S 6a. *Arch. Camb.*, 1913, p. 112.

Llantrisant.
ST 08 S.E. (0645 8320) 14 V 65 XXXVI S.W.

(673) Caerau, Ely (Fig. 23). The fort occupies the western tip of a fairly extensive plateau rising to about 75 m above O.D. The old parish church stands within it. A small stream has cut back from the northern scarp of the hill and has reduced the connecting neck of high ground to a width of about 70 m. The enclosure is roughly triangular about 400 m from E. to W. and about 250 m across the base; the enclosed area is 5·1 ha. The N.E. corner is occupied by an oval ringwork 35 m by 20 m, which is almost certainly medieval. A little S.W. of this is the church. There is a permanent pool of water a little N.W. of the church and springs break out along the N. side of the promontory and its W. tip.

The steep N. side and S. slopes have been fortified by three massive ramparts, with accompanying ditches now largely silted up. These defences measure 30–40 m wide overall. Along the N. half of the E. side, where the ground still falls steeply to a small stream, these ramparts seem to have been reduced to two; they have suffered more than the rest from erosion and disturbance. Along the S. half of this side where the ground runs relatively level to connect with the rest of the plateau the multiple defences are replaced by a single very large bank and ditch, accompanied at its S. end by a counterscarp bank. Except along the N. half of the E. side the ramparts are thickly wooded, but are generally well preserved.

There seem to have been two entrances to the enclosure, one near the middle of the E. side, and one a little W. of the S. corner. In both the ground has been very much lowered by traffic and erosion, but it seems likely that they were originally natural hollows. On both sides of the E. entrance the ramparts curve round to command the approach. There is no corresponding inturn at the S. entrance but the approach there is flanked on one side by a continuation of the large E. rampart of the fort. There is now also a wide gap at the W. apex of the enclosure, but the arrangement of the ramparts seems to indicate that there was no entrance here and that the break has been caused by erosion from the spring which rises just within the defences.

The interior is now mainly pasture but seems at one time to have been cultivated; it is traversed by two old field boundaries. The curvilinear bank which follows much of the N. side of the fort and then turns S. to cross the enclosure is probably also the result of cultivation, in its present form. It may, however, follow the edge of a quarry ditch. It is unlikely to be the remains of an earlier rampart as it does not follow a good defensive line. Fragments of Roman pottery and some possibly of the Iron Age have been found within the enclosure.[1]

The ringwork at the N.E. corner, near the church, is protected by a strong bank and ditch 20 m wide by 3 m high overall with a gap for entrance towards the S.W. It is almost certainly a medieval castle site, but there is no historical record of it. A strong spring breaks out just below the junction of its ditch with the E. rampart of the fort and another rises in a rock-cut tank on its E. side.

Hollow trails later than the defences lead downhill outside the fort on the N. On the E. just S. of the entrance there is a short length of bank with a ditch on the uphill side and a terrace below it. Their function and date are uncertain; they may have formed part of the original entrance approach.

S 1a. *Arch. Camb.*, 1913, p. 103.
[1] *Arch. in Wales*, V (1965), No. 33.

Michaelston-le-Pit.
ST 17 N.W., S.W. (1335 7500) 1965 XLVII N.W.

674–685. *THE SMALL FORTS WITH CLOSE-SET MULTIPLE DEFENCES (under 1·2 ha)*

(674) Stembridge Promontory Fort occupies level ground at about 40 m above O.D., overlooking a steep-sided valley and lying in an angle which provides natural defence on two of its three sides. The W. and S.E. sides are roughly straight, measuring 55 and 51 m long respectively, with traces of a very slight bank, perhaps for a palisade, at the edge of the scarp. The N.E. side is 69 m long, defended by a strong bank and ditch with a smaller bank outside. These defences are bowed outwards so that the foot of the inner bank at the centre is 50 m from the apex of the promontory; the enclosed area is 0·2 ha. Recent quarrying has caused damage at both ends of the defences, particularly severe for 15 m at the N.W. end of the inner bank. The gap of about 3 m between the S.E. end of the latter and the natural scarp appears to be original, suggesting that the entrance lay at this side of the fort.

In a typical profile near the centre the inner bank and ditch measure 24 m overall, the bank being 2·5 m high and the ditch nearly 2 m deep from ground level, with no berm. The outer slope of the bank is steeper than the inner, presumably owing to its stone revetment, which is visible near the S.E. end. The outer bank is 7·5 m wide, separated from the ditch by a berm 9·5 m wide; it is 1·3 m high on the inner side, and its height of 2·5 m on the outer side, where no ditch is preserved, is probably partly due to its siting on the crest of a natural rise.

S 18c. *B.B.C.S.*, VIII, iv (May 1937), p. 364; Rutter, *P. Gower*, p. 66.

Llanrhidian (E), Ll. Lower (C).
SS 49 S.E. (4697 9145) 4 V 64 XXII S.W.

(675) Crawley Rocks Fort, above Nicholaston Burrows on the Gower coast, stands at just under 60 m above O.D., on a natural headland about 60 m long from N. to S. by 35 m seaward bank, about 8·5 m wide and 1 m high, is separated by a steep wooded slope on the E. The neck of the promontory, on the N., is defended by two banks and ditches. The inner or seaward bank, about 8·5 m wide and 1 m high, is separated by a ditch from the outer or landward bank, 7 m wide and 1·3 m high. Outside this is an outer ditch, preserved only on the N.W.

CAERAU ELY
Church
Pond
Vicarage site
Ring work
MODERN BOUNDARIES OMITTED
CONTOURS IN FEET
Feet
Metres

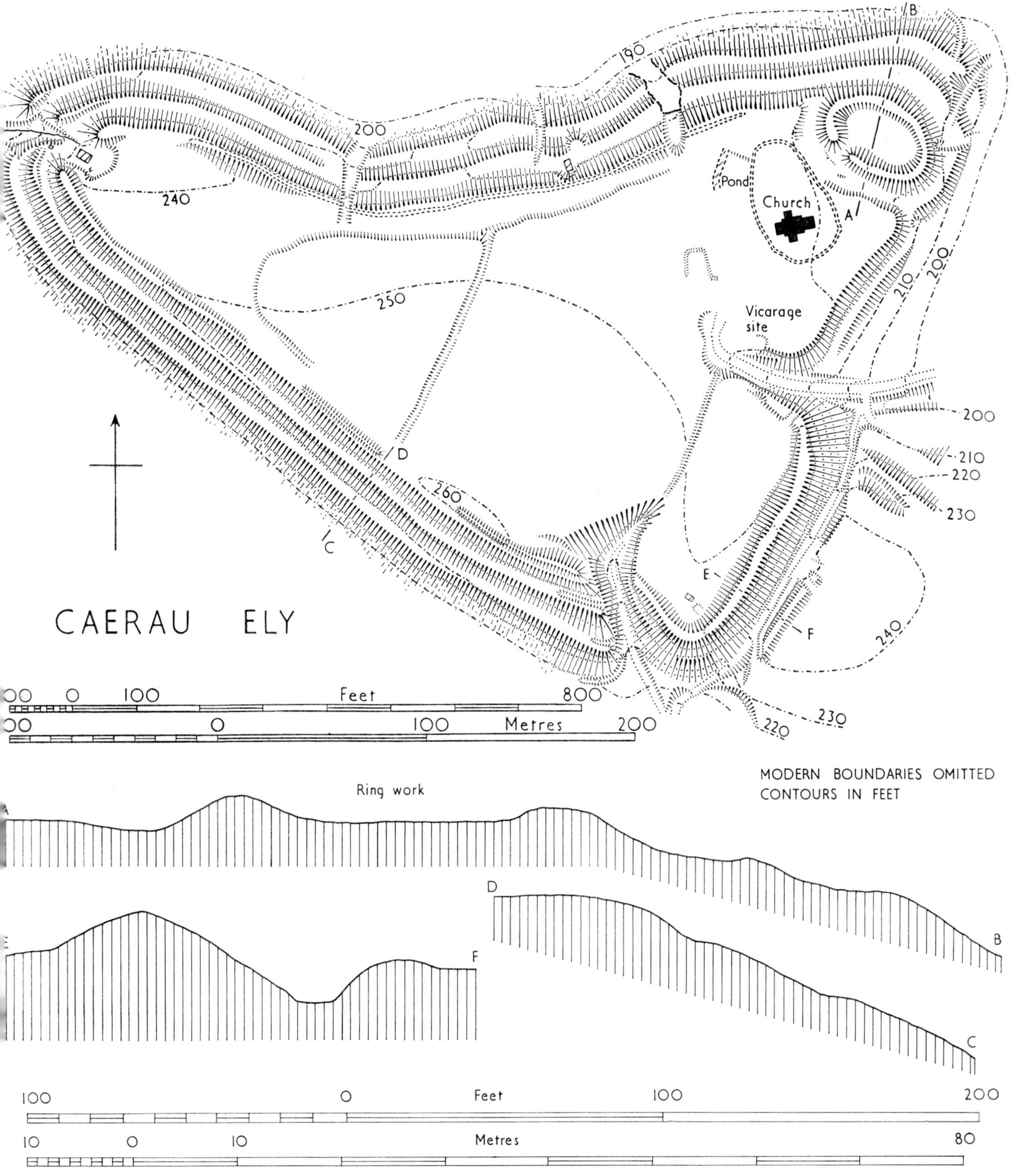

FIG. 23. No. 673.

The overall width of the defences is something like 22 m and the area enclosed about 0·1 ha. A depression in the outer bank towards its W. end may mark the site of an entrance, but is not matched by any break in the inner bank. The site is heavily overgrown with trees and brambles.

In 1949 the outer rampart yielded a small sherd of black pottery (pre-Roman), a flint flake and a pot-boiler.

The smallness of the enclosed area compared to the size of the defences, and the absence of any definite entrance, suggest that the site may be of the 12th century A.D. See p. 17.

S 19c. *Gower*, II (1949), p. 12.

Nicholaston.
SS 58 N.W. (5188 8796) 13 i 67 XXXI N.E.

(676) Fort E. of PARKMILL. Markings visible on an aerial photograph[1] indicate the former existence of a small fort, at about 40 m above O.D. The position is protected on the S. by the steep side of Parkmill Cwm, but to the N. the ground rises gently. Nothing is visible on the surface, but the markings imply ditches rather more than 3 m wide separated by spaces of about 6 m; on the assumption that there was an inner bank of similar width, the defences, except on the S., consisted of three close-set banks and ditches measuring about 30 m overall, enclosing an oval 40 m E. to W. by 20 m (0·05 ha). The position of the entrance is uncertain.

The very small area enclosed and the exceptional width and number of the defences suggest that the structure may be of the 12th-century A.D. See p. 17.

[1] Discovered by J. K. S. St. Joseph. C.U.A.P. AJH 10.

Ilston.
SS 58 N.W. (5488 8921) 23 ii 67 XXXI N.E.

(677). BISHOPSTON VALLEY. The fort stands at about 30 m above O.D. at the W. extremity of a narrow ridge within a loop of the Bishopston river about a kilometre S. of the village. Steep slopes, and in places cliffs, form natural defences on the N., W. and S.; the neck of the promontory, on the E., is defended by two banks with external ditches. The interior measures about 48 by 36 m, area 0·1 ha. The inner or western bank runs in a slight curve and is some 35 m long and 8·5 m wide, 1·3 m high internally and 3 m externally. The ditch separating it from the outer bank is about 4 m wide at the highest point of the neck, but widens greatly to the N. because of the curve of the inner rampart. The outer bank runs straight and is 28 m long and 8·5 m wide, 3 m high internally and 2 m externally. The outer ditch is about 4·5 m wide. The overall extent of the defences is about 26 m. The interior of the fort is hummocky and has no visible signs of occupation. It is now very thickly overgrown.

The site was excavated in 1939 by Audrey Williams (Mrs. W. F. Grimes). The inner rampart was found to be 6 m wide and 1·3 m high, roughly revetted with stones externally. On the N. it curved to the N.W. to merge with a natural rock face forming a scarp along the N. side of the fort. The inner ditch was V-shaped, 4·5 m wide and 1·5 m deep. The outer rampart was 6 m wide and 1 m high and had a berm 1·5 m wide on its inner side. The outer ditch utilised a fault in the underlying limestone rock, and was 3·5 m wide and nearly 2 m deep, with practically vertical sides. The entrance lay towards the N. end of the inner rampart and was approached by a track ascending from the E. past the N. end of the outer rampart; no details of construction were preserved. Against the inner face of the inner rampart S. of the entrance was a hut site marked by five postholes and a hearth, indicating an oval hut 4 m by 3 m. On the N.W. side of the entrance an oval hollow 3·5 m by 2·5 m., filled with dark soil, shells and bones, was thought to be a midden rather than a hut site. Small finds from various parts of the excavation included a bronze penannular brooch of Roman date; an iron finger-ring; two slingstones; bones of red deer, ox, pig and sheep (or goat); shells of dog-whelk, limpet, mussel, periwinkle and also of snails; charcoal (hawthorn, hazel and oak); a sherd of Iron Age B (?) pottery; and a fragment of plain Samian ware of the late 1st–2nd century.

S 9c. *B.B.C.S.*, VIII, iv (May 1937), p. 364; Rutter, *P. Gower*, p. 65; *Arch. Camb.*, XCV (1940), pp. 9–19 (excavation report with plan).

Bishopston.
SS 58 N.E. (5693 8780) 7 vi 65 XXXII N.W.

(678) Fort at CRAIG TŶ-ISAF (Fig. 24). At about 210 m above O.D., on the S.W. slopes of Mynydd y Gaer, overlooking Baglan, a steep-sided narrow spur has been utilised as the site of a small but strong fortification. The interior, which falls fairly steeply both towards the W. tip of the spur and from N. to S. has been protected by a rubble wall or bank, apparently following the complete circuit, to form an oval enclosure of about 65 m E. to W. by 40 m (0·2 ha). The only entrance, at least in the final form of the defences, was towards the tip of the spur, where there is a gap about 3 m wide and the ends of the rampart seem to have been thickened, but there is another gap at the E. end of the enclosure. The wall is much ruined and its original dimensions are uncertain. It is barely visible on the S. side, but on the N., where it follows the spine of the ridge, it appears as a belt of loose rubble up to 9 m wide, and 2·5 m high on the inner face where it has fallen down the slope.

At the E. end, across the easier approach, there are three ramparts, the innermost being the wall already mentioned. This is separated from the middle bank by a space 6 m wide at the S. end increasing to 20 at the N., where for about 10 m a shallow ditch runs parallel to the wall. The middle rampart is slightly curved and consists of a bank and ditch, about 10 m wide and in places nearly 2 m high overall. There is a gap a little N. of the centre. The outermost rampart is unbroken and is almost straight, comprising a bank and ditch 12 m wide and in places over 2 m high overall, with a short length of counterscarp bank at the N. end. What appears to be another ditch, unfinished, is almost certainly a mining trial-cut. There is another in the interior, which is otherwise featureless.

The plan suggests that the enclosure had originally two ramparts at the E. end, with an entrance through both where the present gaps occur; and that the outermost rampart which completely cuts off access from that end was a later

CRAIG TY - ISAF
Entrance
Mining trial
Mining trial?
A
B
C
D
10 0 10 100 Feet 200
10 0 10 Metres 50

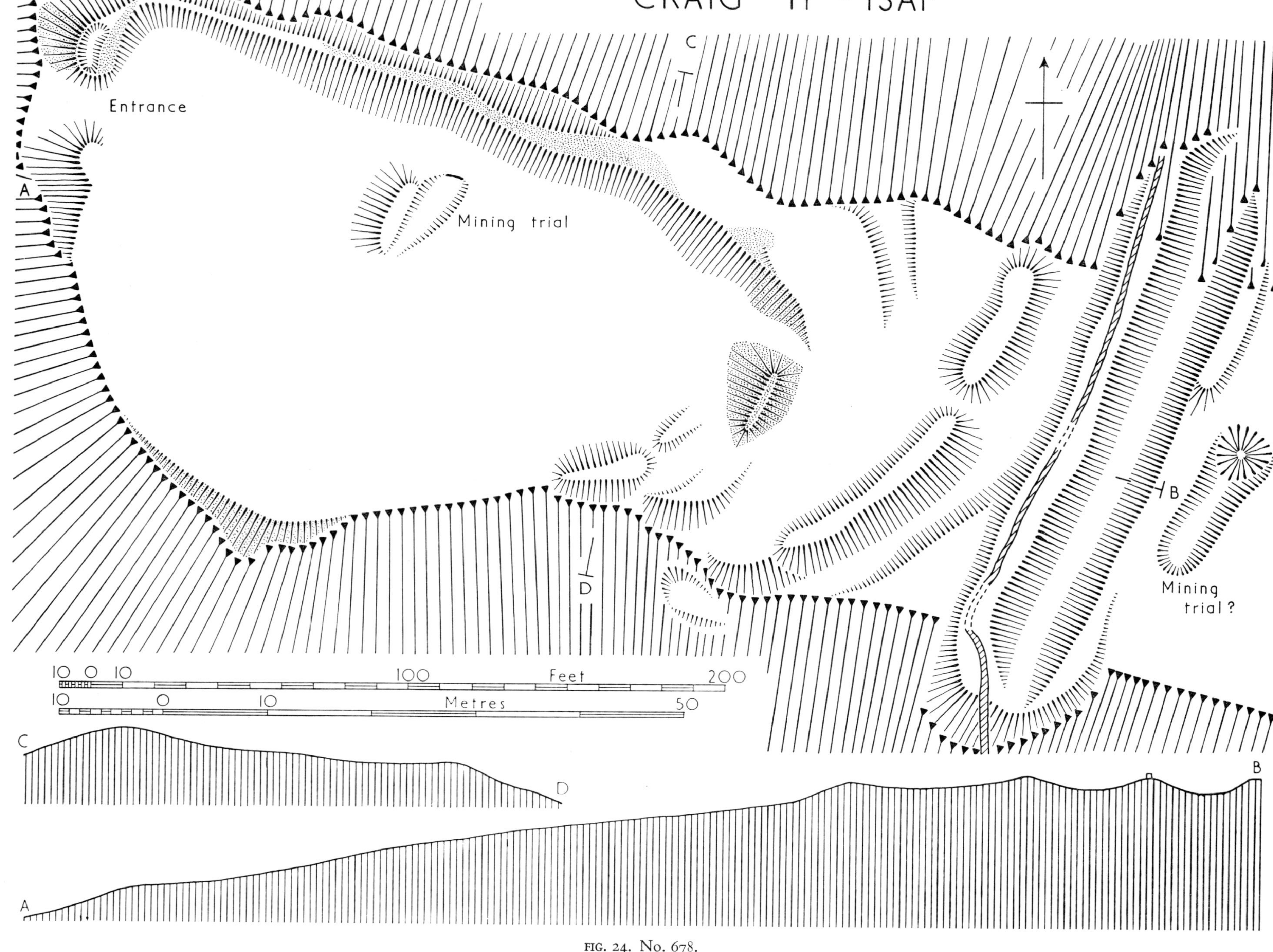

FIG. 24. No. 678.

addition. In its final form, with no entrance from the more accessible end and with a very wide band of defences relative to the area enclosed, the fort displays resemblances to the latest development, probably of the 12th century A.D., at Dinas Powys (see p. 17).

Baglan (E), Port Talbot (C).
SS 79 S.E. (7565 9338) 25 xi 64 XXV N.W.

(679) PEN Y CASTELL, CWMAVON, is an oval enclosure occupying the summit of a small steep-sided hill at 150 m above O.D. It measures 65 m long from E. to W. by 30 m wide enclosing 0·2 ha, and is defended by a bank following the contours, 0·3 m high internally but with an outer scarp nearly 3 m high. At the E. end is a simple entrance 4·5 m wide. Outside the bank is a berm 6–7 m wide, followed by a second rampart. This is missing on the N.E. and along the E. half of the N. side; along the W. half of the N. side it is visible as a bank 3 m wide and 0·6 m high. It is best preserved across the W. end where it is 6 m wide and nearly a metre high; along the S. side it forms a scarp fading into the natural slope. The entrance is again on the E. and is 14 m wide; outside it are traces of an approach road winding up the hill.

S 8b. *Trans. Cardiff Nat. Soc.*, XXVII (1894–5), p. 83.

Margam (E), Port Talbot (C).
SS 79 S.E. (7886 9175) 25 vi 64 XXV S.W.

(680) PEN Y CASTELL, KENFIG HILL, is a small fortified enclosure at the W. end of a low limestone ridge S.E. of Kenfig Hill village, at about 130 m above O.D. About 30 m of the interior has been removed by quarrying from the W. end, leaving the present maximum length as 110 m., the width across the ridge being 52 m; the area enclosed was slightly over 0·4 ha.

The enclosure was completely surrounded by two banks, each with its own ditch. The profile is best preserved on the S. side, where it has partly decayed into a strong terrace formation with an overall spread of 24 m, over a height of 6 m. On the N. side the surface profile is poorly preserved, but in the E. face of the quarry the section of defences can be clearly seen. The inner rampart contains a made-up height of 1 m, spread to 10 m wide, with a field bank and ditch at its centre; its own ditch is 3·5 m wide and at least 1·5 m deep. The second bank is 0·3 m high, spread to 5 m wide; its ditch is 3 m wide and 0·6 m deep. These dimensions would agree with the profile at the S. side.

At the E. end the inner bank survives, crossing the ridge, where it is 8 m wide and up to 1·7 m high. The outer bank has been destroyed, but the inner ditch is visible in the hedge line at the N.E. corner.

The entrance is probably represented by the simple gap 4 m wide in the inner rampart at the S.E. corner. Here the line of the outer bank from the S. side keeps well out as though to flank an entrance passage. There are no internal features.

The site has been identified with Kibor Castle,[1] but is more likely to be pre-Roman.

S 7b. *Trans. Cardiff Nat. Soc.*, XXVII, p. 82 (plan).

[1] W. Rees, *Map of S. Wales and the Border in the fourteenth century* (Ordnance Survey, 1933). The name *Castellum Kibur* appears in 1203 (Clark, *Cartae*, II, p. 276) but Clark considers (*ibid.*, I, p. 56) that the name probably refers to the motte at Whitchurch (ST 1560 8041, XLIII N.W.).

Tythegston (E), T. Higher (C).
SS 88 S.W. (8422 8270) 28 vi 67 XXXIV S.W.

(681) MYNYDD BYCHAN (Fig. 25). This small enclosure stands just S.W. of Pentre Meyrick at about 80 m above O.D., at the S. edge of a plateau where the ground begins to fall away rather more steeply. On the other sides there is no natural protection. It was investigated by Dr. H. N. Savory in 1949–50, and although the site remains in good condition it is now partly overgrown. This entry is therefore based on Dr. Savory's account. In the 18th century the site was known as Gwael Hilis, but the name is forgotten.

The excavations showed that the remains represented three phases of development. In the first (*ca.* 50 B.C. to A.D. 50) it was a small fortified settlement. In Phase II (*ca.* A.D. 50–120 or perhaps rather later), a group of dry-stone huts were built over the ruined defences; Iron Age C and Roman material was found. Finally, after a long interval, the enclosure was adopted for a peasant's croft, in the 11th to 13th centuries A.D. These phases have been separated on the plan, for clarity.

In Phase I the defences consisted of a bank 5·5 m wide and a ditch originally about 1·3 m deep and 3 to 4 m wide, with a flat bottom about 1·5 m wide; outside this was a small counterscarp bank. On the north side, where the ground is almost level, there was a second ditch. The enclosure was roughly shield-shaped, about 60 by 55 m (0·3 ha). Within were at least three, perhaps five, timber-framed round huts. The gateway was at the W. apex. The gates had been supported on four substantial posts set in line, and a massive bastion stood on the S. of the gate passage. Outside this the lines of wall and ditch continued to form a 'barbican' protecting the approach.

Phase I ended with decay or perhaps demolition, and the site was reoccupied by an undefended settlement comprising at least three round huts with wall footings dry-built of stone. Each stood in a lightly walled courtyard. Three burials, apparently of this phase, were found in the upper filling of the S. ditch outside the entrance to the original enclosure.

After the abandonment of the site early in the Roman period, it remained unoccupied until about the 11th or 12th century, when a roughly rectangular dwelling about 11 m by 3·5 m was built in the N.E. corner of the enclosure. This house was twice rebuilt and enlarged, reaching a size of 16 m by 5 m before the site was finally deserted, probably in the 13th century.

S 4b. *Arch. Camb.*, CIII (1954), pp. 85–108 (general discussion); CIV (1955), pp. 14–51 (detailed report and finds).

Pen-llin.
SS 97 N.E. (9630 7561) 3 vii 70 XLV N.W.

(682) LLANTRITHYD HOUSE. A bivallate enclosure stands about half a kilometre N.W. of the Church, on ground falling gently to S.E., at about 100 m above O.D. The area has been ploughed, and the remains are much worn down and obscured; in addition, the E. side has been damaged by an old quarry and a hedge-bank.

MYNYDD
BYCHAN
GENERAL PLAN
SHOWING AREAS EXCAVATED
Hearth
Pit
Oven
Hut site?
Defences destroyed by road
Palisade slot
PERIOD I
ca 50 BC - AD 50
Earlier
phases
After H. N. SAVORY
PERIOD II
ca AD 50 - 120
PERIOD III
XI-XIII CENT. AD
100
0
Feet
200
10
0
10
Metres
80

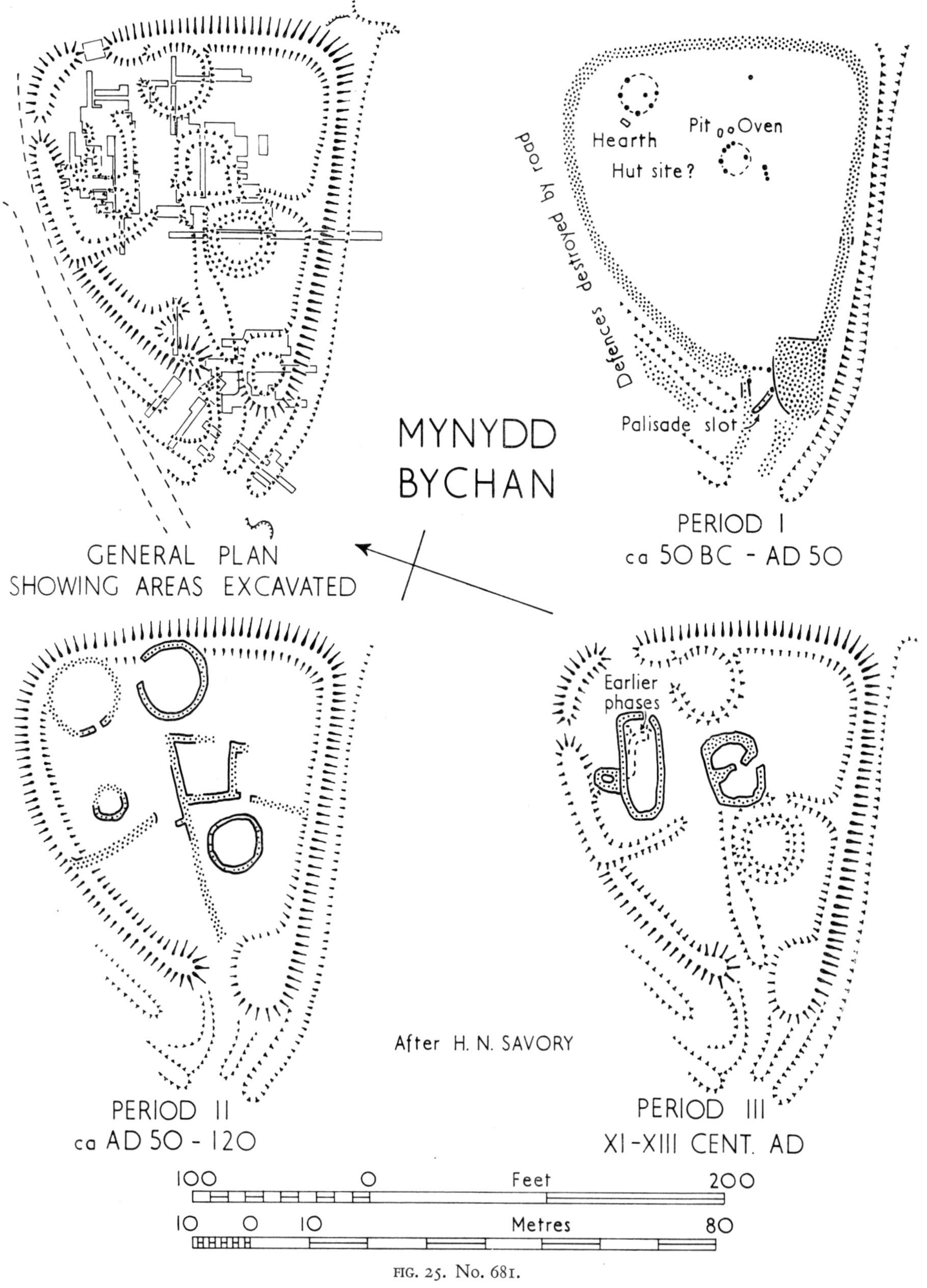

FIG. 25. No. 681.

The defences seem originally to have consisted of two banks and ditches, close-set and measuring about 20 m overall; the inner bank seems to have been lower than the outer, but of the same width. Where best preserved, they stand to heights of about 0·6 m and 0·9 m respectively. The entrance seems to have been a simple gap on the N.W., now about 10 m wide through the outer bank, and perhaps wider through the inner. Outside the entrance a bank with ditch on E. starts at the outer lip of the ditch and runs N. for 50 m to the field-boundary; the bank and ditch measure about 9 m wide overall, but are now almost obliterated by ploughing. S. of the entrance a similar bank runs W. for 40 m to the field-boundary. No ditch is visible, but N. of it, for a width of about 15 m, the ground surface is irregular as if disturbed by quarrying or by destroyed buildings. The banks are symmetrically placed relative to the entrance, with their ends 36 m apart; it is uncertain whether they are contemporary with the enclosure.

The enclosed area (0·4 ha) is oval, 67 m N.N.W. to S.S.E. by 80 m; the latter measurement is to the modern boundary, which seems to follow the line of the inner bank on the E. Low banks, now much disturbed, suggest the former presence of three or four buildings; their size and shape are uncertain, but they seem to have been oval or rectangular rather than circular, with smaller diameters of 6 to 9 m. Small stone slabs, probably from destroyed walling, are scattered over the area. Romano-British pottery of the 2nd to 4th centuries A.D., and a fragment of rotary quern, have been found on the site.[1]

Morgannwg, II (1958), p. 69.
[1] *Arch. in Wales*, VI (1966), No. 29.

Llantrithyd.
ST 07 S.W. (0386 7318) 5 vi 67 XLVI N.W.

(683) LLANVITHYN. The fort stands about half a kilometre N.E. of the house. A spur rising to about 60 m above O.D. and bounded on N. and S. by the fairly steep-sided valleys of two small streams which meet in marshy ground a short distance to E., has been fortified by two ramparts running N. and S. across its base. Each comprises a bank and ditch measuring about 18 m wide by a metre high overall, the outer bank being separated from the inner ditch by 9 m. The outer bank remains in good condition for about 65 m across the ridge and at its N. end shows the beginning of a turn to the E. before it is destroyed by cultivation; to the S. it can be traced, though much eroded, as far as the stream. The inner bank runs for 35 m across the ridge; the beginning of a turn can be seen at the S. end, and at the N. the line can be traced for about 18 m along the N. flank of the spur. The remaining defences have been destroyed by cultivation. The E. limit is probably indicated by a very slight scarp 45 m E. of the inner bank, but may be represented by a modern hedge-bank another 45 m to E., at the edge of the marshy ground; the corresponding areas would be about 0·1 or 0·2 ha. The position of the entrance is uncertain.

Attention was directed to this site by Dr. H. N. Savory and Mr H. J. Thomas.

Llancarfan (E), Llanfythin (C).
ST 07 S.E. (0548 7193) 24 ii 67 XLVI S.W.

(684) LLWYNDA'-DDU. The earthwork stands about 1 km south of Pen-tyrch on the W. end of a small hill, just above the 120 m contour, with ground falling away fairly steeply on all sides except the E. The defences are damaged and partly destroyed, but seem originally to have comprised two ramparts and ditches, enclosing an egg-shaped space 85 m N.E.–S.W. by 60 m, with the entrance at the smaller (S.W.) end; the area is 0·4 ha. The outer ditch has been obliterated round nearly all the circuit, the outer bank along most of the S. side, and the inner bank round the N. half; where best preserved, each bank stands about 2·5 m high above the bottom of the ditch, and just S. of the entrance the defences measure about 27 m wide overall. The entrance is straight, across a causeway which interrupts the outer ditch and between banks about 7·5 m apart joining the ends of the inner and outer ramparts. The interior has been cultivated.

S 2b.

Pen-tyrch.
ST 18 S.W. (1085 8100) 23 iv 64 XLII N.E.

(685) CASTLE FIELD, GRAIG-LLWYN (Fig. 26). The enclosure occupies the summit of a ridge about 2 km N. of Lisvane at about 100 m above O.D., with extensive views in all directions. It is trapezoidal in plan, 79 m from E. to W. and tapering from 52 m at the E. end to 47 m at the W., with an area of 0·4 ha; the N. and S. sides follow the crests of the steeper slopes on either side of the ridge.

The inner defence, where best preserved at the W. end, consists of a bank and ditch measuring nearly 20 m wide and 1·5 m high overall; slight recent disturbance in removing a superimposed hedge-bank suggests that the bank is mainly of earth, and shows no trace of a stone revetment. On the other sides the ditch is no longer visible, but the bank on the N. is represented by a scarp about 3 m high.

At the E. end there are traces of an outer bank, now very much eroded by former cultivation; the present overall width of the defences here is about 30 m. This bank curves round to continue along the sides, but has been destroyed on the N. by cultivation and on the S. by a modern road. It does not appear at the W. end.

The entrance was near the middle of the E. end; the suggestion of inturns is probably caused merely by the spread of the eroded ramparts.

The site is now pasture, but except at the W. end it has at some time been cultivated, and no traces of internal structures remain.

S 1b. *Trans. Cardiff Nat. Soc.*, XL (1907), pp. 26 ff.

Llanedern.
ST 28 S.W. (2045 8403) 8 vi 67 XXXVII S.E.

686–696. MULTIVALLATE ENCLOSURES WITH WIDE-SPACED RAMPARTS, ON INLAND SITES.

(686) BERRY WOOD. A double ringwork stands S. of Knelston at about 55 m above O.D. in enclosed land with a very

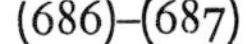

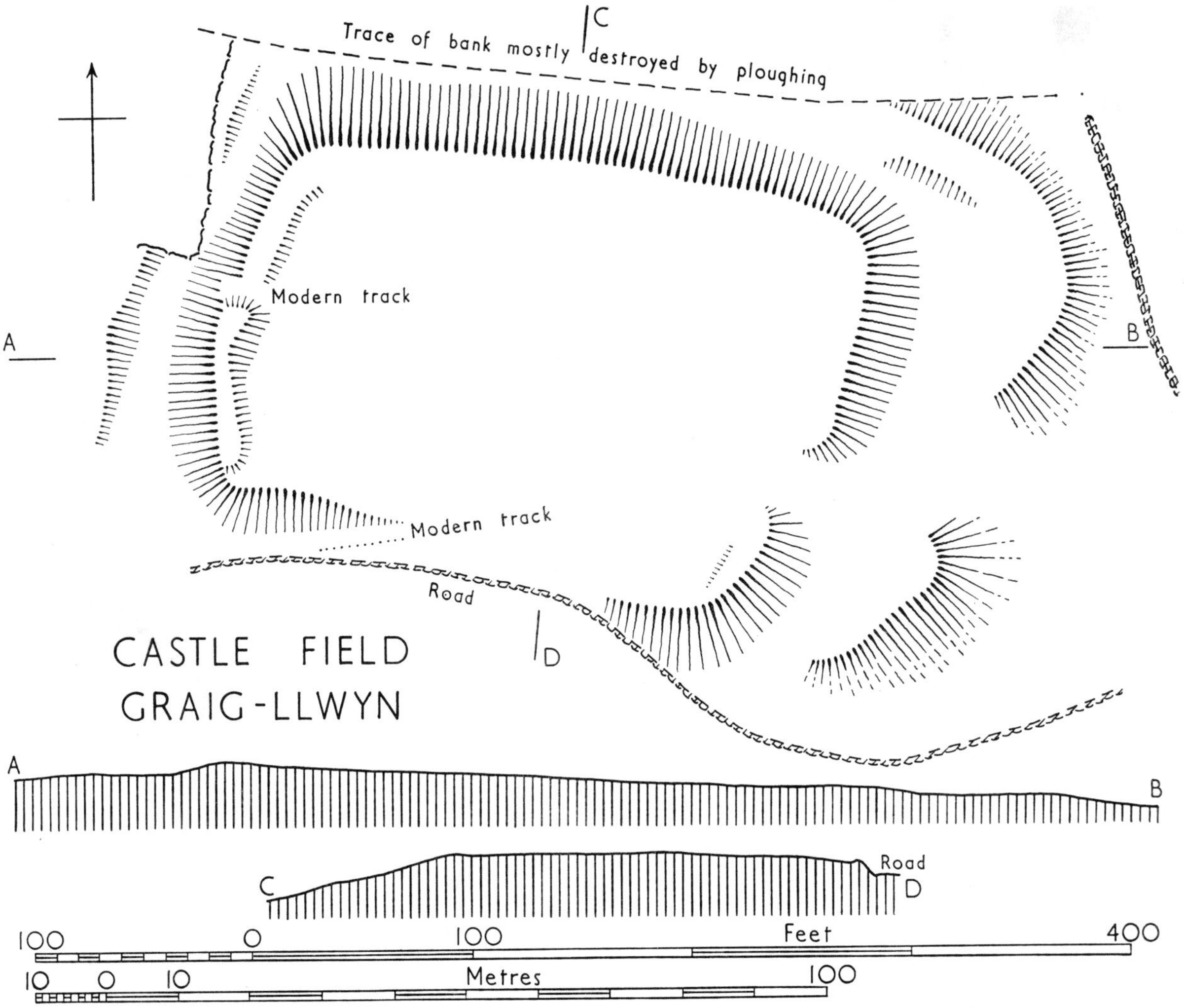

FIG. 26. No. 685.

slight fall to the N.E. The banks are roughly circular but not concentric since they are almost contiguous on the E. The dimensions given below are between the approximate crests; the remains have been eroded by ploughing.

The *inner enclosure* is about 33 m in diameter but the bank is almost destroyed on the N. and elsewhere and is much spread; it is best preserved on the S.W. where it reaches 15 m in width and stands more than a metre high above the marshy interior.

The *outer enclosure* is about 73 m in diameter. Its bank, 8·5 m wide, is best preserved on the E. and S.E. where it is nearly a metre high with a shallow outer ditch 3·5 m wide. On the S. the bank is faint and on the S.W. virtually absent, but it reappears on the W. where it is 0·6 m high but without a ditch. It is again absent on the N.W. and N., but a fragment survives sufficiently to show that the ring had an entrance some 9 m wide on the N.E. The areas of the inner and outer enclosures are about 0·1 and 0·4 ha.

The earthwork has been described as a triple ringwork, but no trace survives of the third ring, which was presumably a counterscarp bank. What appears to be a third bank outside the entrance on the N.E. is probably natural.

S 1f. Rutter, *P. Gower*, p. 66.

Llanddewi.
SS 48 N.E. (4723 8847) 12 i 67 XXXI N.W.

(687) HARDINGS DOWN WEST (Fig. 27, Plate 7) occupies the spur at the W. end of the isolated hill of that name, which rises to a height of about 150 m above O.D. about a kilometre S.E. of Llangennith. The summit also is partly enclosed by an unfinished fort (688), and small univallate enclosures (646, 647)

lie on the upper N. slope and lower S.E. slope respectively. This western fort consists of an oval enclosure about 110 m by 75 m, area 0·6 ha, protected by a substantial bank with ditch and counterscarp bank. The enclosure is arranged so that its upper end crosses a slight subsidiary summit at 140 m above O.D., beyond which the ground falls away very slightly to a saddle before rising again to the summit. Although it stands on a hill-slope, therefore, this rampart is sited so that it commands the ground on all sides; it is doubtful whether the hill provides any better defensive position for an enclosure of this size. Outside to the east, two additional slighter ramparts cross the saddle. These obstruct the view from the main rampart, and can be passed by without difficulty at their S. ends. The other end of the outermost rampart is continued northwards by a much slighter bank with a ditch on the side towards the main enclosure. This may be medieval or later, for a modern field-boundary only recently destroyed continued almost the same line to N., and was apparently linked with another which joined up with the ditch immediately S.W. of the modern quarry. This ditch forms the N.E. end of a small enclosure which is later than the fort and which seems to have belonged to a small cottage, the foundations of which are visible N.W. of the modern road.

The entrance to the fort now appears as a simple gap, approached by an artificially terraced roadway. Three hut-platforms are visible within the enclosure.

In 1962 excavations were undertaken[1] primarily to determine whether, like similar structures in Devon and Cornwall, the fort had Iron Age B associations; no fort of this type had been examined in Wales.

A section across the rampart on the N.E. showed that the ditch was V-shaped, containing 1·3 m of silting, giving an original overall height for the defence of at least 5 m. The rampart was a simple dump of earth and rubble but the presence of large blocks in the ditch-fill probably implies that its outer face was formed by revetment built up from near the lip of the ditch. All other banks were unrevetted. No palisade or other barrier continued the lines of those crossing the saddle, but it was not clear whether they should be regarded as unfinished.

The gateway was formed by four large posts set at the corner of a 2·7 m square, the toes of the bank being supported by kerbs of large blocks; those on the N.W. side had been removed. The entrance-passage had originally been surfaced with 0·2 m of cobbling, on which a second layer 0·1 m thick had been superimposed.

Two hut-platforms were cleared. That adjacent to the rampart on the N.W. had been occupied by a building about 7 m in diameter with low walls partly of earth and partly of scarped rock. The roof was supported on 6 or 7 posts set in an oval measuring 5·2 m by 3·3 m. A few scraps of plain Iron Age B pottery lay on the floor. The large platform near the middle of the enclosure produced no relics, but carried a number of post-holes. These seem to represent two periods of construction, the earlier being a round house 10 m in diameter, the rafters being supported at the centre on four massive posts set at the corners of a 2·4 m square, and resting at their outer ends on the upper side on the rock surface about half a metre above the levelled platform. Later, the platform seems to have carried other upright post-structures, including at least three settings in pairs, perhaps drying-racks.

S 9c. *Arch. Camb.*, 1920, p. 221; *B.B.C.S.*, VIII, iv (May 1937), p. 368; Rutter, *P. Gower*, p. 66.

[1] By the staff of the Commission. Report forthcoming.

Llangennith.
SS 49 S.W. (4343 9078) 1962 XXI S.E.

(688) Hardings Down East (Fig. 28, Plate 7). The summit of the Down is partly surrounded by the unfinished defences of a fort similar in general character to that 250 m to the W. (687) but larger; the area to be enclosed was about 0·9 ha. Present appearances suggest that the banks, where started, were carried up nearly to completion. There is no trace of a setting-out ditch where the banks are absent, but a short isolated stretch of rampart indicates approximately the position of the W. end. The main rampart, where complete, now generally appears as a turf-covered bank and ditch about 2·5 m high by 11 or 12 m overall, but the short isolated section at the W. end still retains about 3 m of an inner face formed by a single course of large blocks. A robber-trench following much of the S. side suggests that a similar inner facing has been removed. The outer rampart exists only on the east. Its remains are slighter, appearing as a grassy bank or scarp about 1 m high by 3 m wide, with no trace of a ditch except at its S. end. The slight low intermediate bank seems to be unconnected with the fort, and may be earlier. It can be traced in an irregular course down the hill to near the enclosure on the N. slopes (646). It is partly followed on its N.E. side by a hollow trail.

The entrance through the outer rampart is a simple gap. A barely perceptible hollowed track leads from it to the entrance through the main rampart. Here the end of the bank on the S. side is slightly thickened. There is a vague irregular levelled area behind it, but without excavation it is impossible to say whether this indicates a guard-chamber.

There is no recognisable hut-platform within the enclosure.

S 10c (Hardings Down Upper Camp). *Arch. Camb.*, 1920, p. 221; *B.B.C.S.*, VIII, iv (May 1937), p. 368; Rutter, *P. Gower*, p. 66.

Llangennith.
SS 49 S.W. (4370 9064) 20 iii 62 XXI S.E.

(689) The Bulwark (Fig. 29, Plate 8), a small hill-fort with elaborate multiple defences, occupies the E. end of Llanmadog Hill about a kilometre S.E. of the village. The hill forms a ridge about a mile long, mostly just under 180 m above O.D. but rising a little higher near each end. From the E. summit the ground falls gently to a slight saddle (176 m), which is crossed by a bank and ditch, and then rises to another low summit (177 m) which is crossed by the main defences (*cf.* Hardings Down West, 687). From here the ground falls away on all sides except the W.; the lowest part of the interior of the fort is just over 160 m above O.D.

The plan of the fort leaves little doubt that it incorporates work of more than one period, but several alternative interpretations are possible from the surface indications, and none is entirely satisfactory, so no attempt will be made to describe the evolution of the structure in detail.

HARDINGS DOWN
WEST CAMP
B
Outer
Rampart
470
Middle
Rampart
A
Main
Rampart
460
410
Road
400
390
430
Entrance
420
450
Middle
Hut
440
430
Modern
Quarry
Lower Hut
420
410
CONTOURS IN FEET
100
0
Feet
100
10
0
10
Metres
50
Profile to twice Scale
A
B

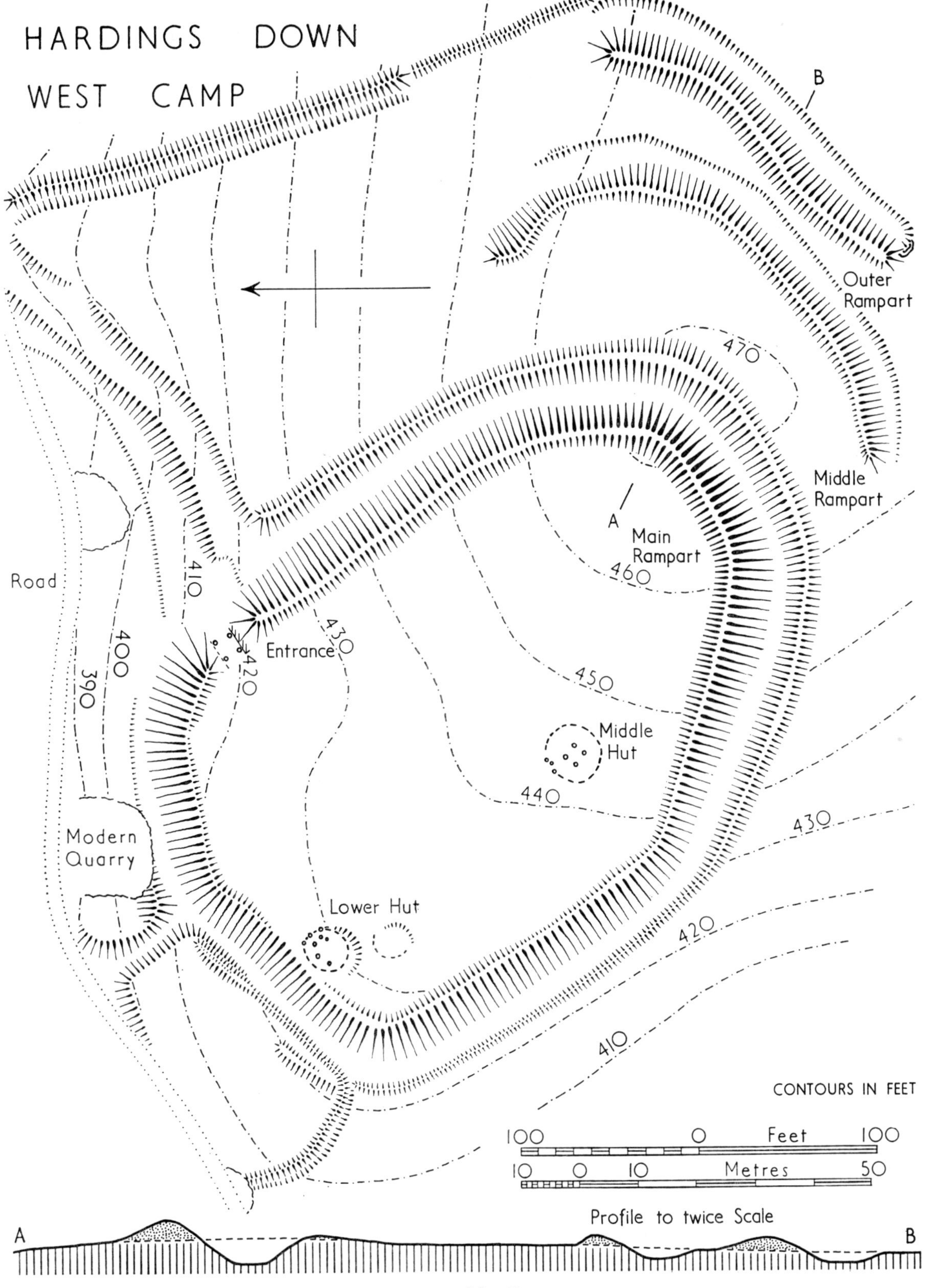

FIG. 27. No. 687.

HARDINGS DOWN
EAST CAMP
450
460
470
480
490
500
CONTOURS IN FEET
Modern pit
A
B
80
70
Profile to twice Scale
100
0
100
Feet
300
10
0
10
Metres
100

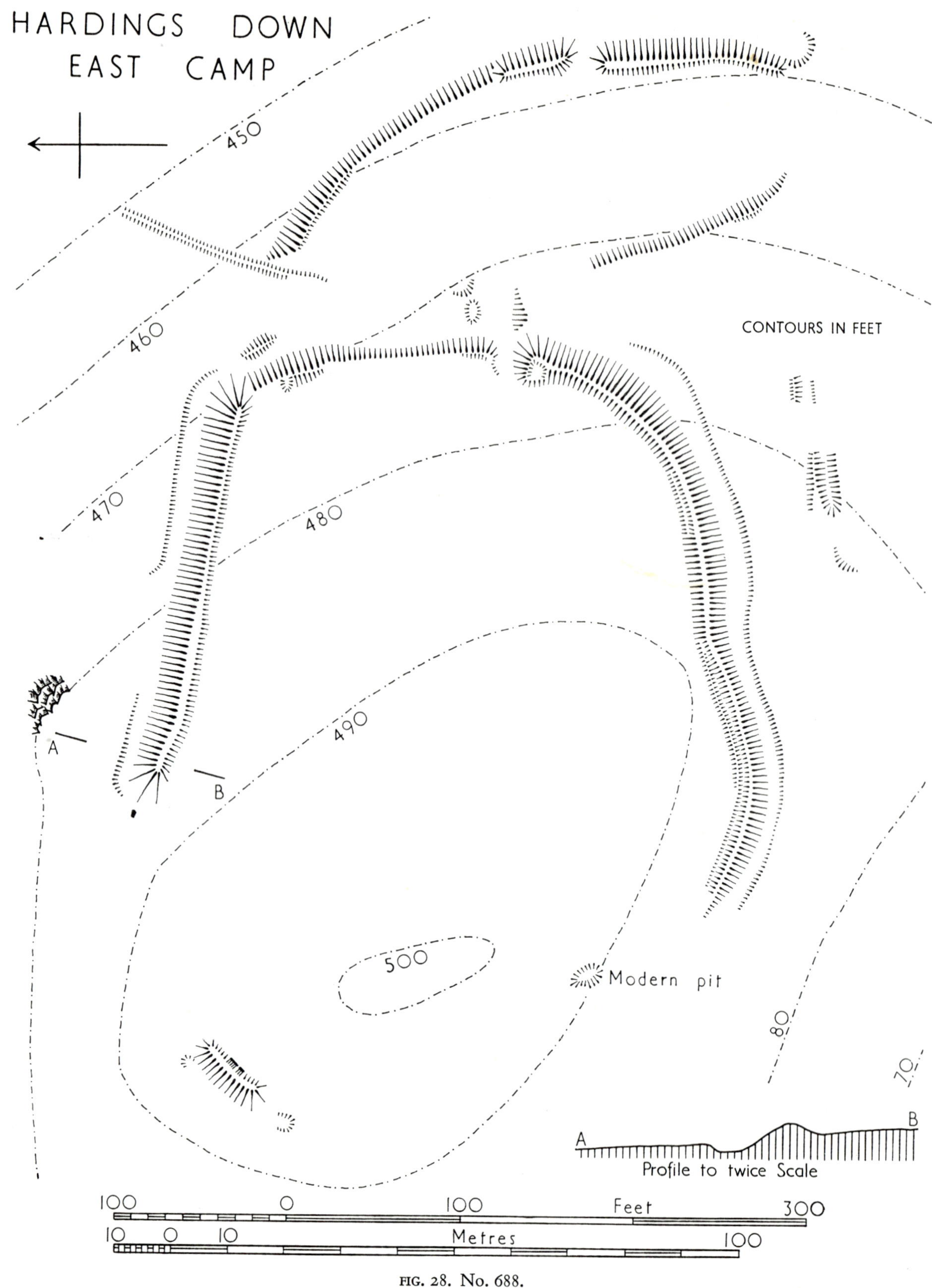

FIG. 28. No. 688.

The innermost defence is a bank and ditch, about 45 m wide overall with the top now rising 2·5 or 3 m above the ditch bottom in places. On the south it is accompanied by a counterscarp bank. This rampart, like all the others in this fort, is turf-covered and shows no sign now of any stone revetment. The area enclosed is 0·9 ha.

On the W., this rampart merges with another line of bank and ditch of similar size; towards the N. end the ditch dies out and the bank decreases in size and becomes a counterscarp bank to the inner rampart, continuing along a short length of ditch which runs N. from the N.W. corner of the enclosure to a point at which the hillside steepens. The plan suggests strongly that the inner rampart has cut into and modified an earlier dyke running across the ridge.[1] Near the point at which the two meet, the supposed earlier ditch is interrupted by a causeway, which suggests there may have been an entrance at this point; there is, however, no corresponding gap in the bank now.

A further line of defence protects the fort on three sides. It is separated from the inner rampart by an interval of varying width, and comprises a bank and ditch with a counterscarp bank for most of the circuit. Generally it is much slighter than the inner rampart, being about 5 to 6 m wide and 1·3 m high overall, but where it crosses the low summit which forms the end of the ridge its height increases to 2·5 m and it is accompanied by a further short length of bank and ditch, giving a total overall width of 26 m. Near the S.W. corner of the main enclosure, this bank and ditch are interrupted by a narrow gap and causeway, which may be original; the causeway dips slightly below the original surface, but this could be the result of erosion. This second defence terminates at the steep northern slope of the hill, but although there are some small crags and outcrops in the interval between the two ends they are slight and intermittent and would not form an effective barrier.

The outermost defence on the W. is formed by the bank and ditch already mentioned, running across the slight saddle at its lowest point. This is 45 m wide and nearly 3 m high overall. Its ditch has been deepened by use as a trackway across the hill, and this has developed as a ditch continuing in both directions, but the original defence ended where the hillside steepened; in the absence of any additional barrier the ends could have been passed without difficulty. At about 12 m from the S. end a gap and causeway about 6 m wide seem to be original. There is no further defence on the W. side.

On the E. the innermost and next lines of defence are slighter, and are not very widely separated. A third barrier, comprising a bank, ditch and counterscarp bank measuring about 12 m wide by 1·5 m high overall, crosses the end of the ridge and outside this is a short length of a fourth bank and ditch, only about 6 m wide and less than a metre high, This last only exists N. of the present approach track; there is nothing to indicate whether it extended further to the S., into an enclosed pasture field, or how it was related to the original entrance.

The surviving entrance arrangements start at the third barrier, which is interrupted by a simple gap about 3 m wide. From there a slightly sinuous entrance passage 12 m wide leads to the innermost defence; it is bounded by low banks which continue to the edge of the inner ditch, and maintains its width through the line of the second defences. The inner rampart shows a slight inward curve at the gateway, which is now about 6 m wide, but the ends seem to have been disturbed.

The chief feature visible inside the fort is a small bank and ditch cutting off a sub-rectangular enclosure in the S.E. corner, with an entrance on the N.E. A probable hut-platform, 9 m in diameter, is visible just W. of this enclosure, but the pit near its N.W. angle is probably a fairly recent quarry, as are some which occur among the W. defences. In the steeply sloping ground towards the N.W. corner of the fort some slight irregularities in the ground suggest the possible presence of further huts, but there is nothing which can be identified as certain.

A small excavation made by A. G. Davies during 1957 in the N.W. corner of the fort[1] suggested that there were two periods of construction in the rampart there. This would be consistent with the interpretation suggested above. In its later form, the inner face of the rampart had a stone revetment; the outer face was not examined.

S 8c. *B.B.C.S.*, VIII, iv (May 1937), pp. 366–8; *Arch. Journ.*, CIX (1952), pp. 1–22 and Fig. 4; Rutter, *P. Gower*, p. 66.
[1] *B.B.C.S.*, XXI, i (Nov. 1964), p. 100.

Llanmadog/Cheriton/Llangennith.
SS 49 S.W. (4430 9275) 11 v 62 XXI S.E.

(690) GAER FAWR (Fig. 30, Plate 8) stands about 4 km S. of Neath, and occupies a shelf on the N. slopes of Mynydd y Gaer, the summit of which, 700 m to S., is occupied by the univallate fort Buarth y Gaer (629). The shelf is outlined on the N. and W. by the 240 m contour, below which the ground falls away fairly steeply; it rises gently to the E. and S. The fort was probably roughly symmetrical originally, but the outer banks on the N. have been destroyed by cultivation; otherwise, the remains are well-preserved.

Near the centre of the shelf is an oval enclosure, 55 m by 30 m, area 0·1 ha. On the S., and probably originally throughout, it was defended by two banks and ditches, with a counterscarp bank, the total width being about 25 m. The main entrance was on the W., but on the S.E. a gap leads diagonally through the defences, which here show a break in direction; this is probably an original entrance to the central oval from the outer enclosures. Outside the central enclosure the ground rises gently to an intermediate bank which survives on the S. and E. and in a much damaged state on the W. Beyond this, on the S. and E. only, is an outer bank. The outer and intermediate banks are both slight. To the E., the ground between them is almost level, but to the S. it rises steeply, and the ground outside the outer bank is invisible from the central enclosure; it is, however, visible from the outer bank, which follows the upper edge of the shelf. Within the outer enclosures on the E. two further lengths of bank run parallel to the outer and intermediate banks. They are very slight indeed, and their function is obscure. On the S., also, a short length of bank, apparently original, curves away from the intermediate bank towards the central enclosure.

Along the W. side the outer and intermediate banks seem

GAER FAWR
D
Approx. limit
of enclosure
100
0
Feet
100
10
0
10
Metres
50
Intermediate
banks
Wall
Banks destroyed by cultivation
Inner
defences
Fence
A
Inner
bank
Outer
bank
B
Approx. limit
of enclosure
Wall
Field bank
C
Inner
Main
Intermediate
Outer
A

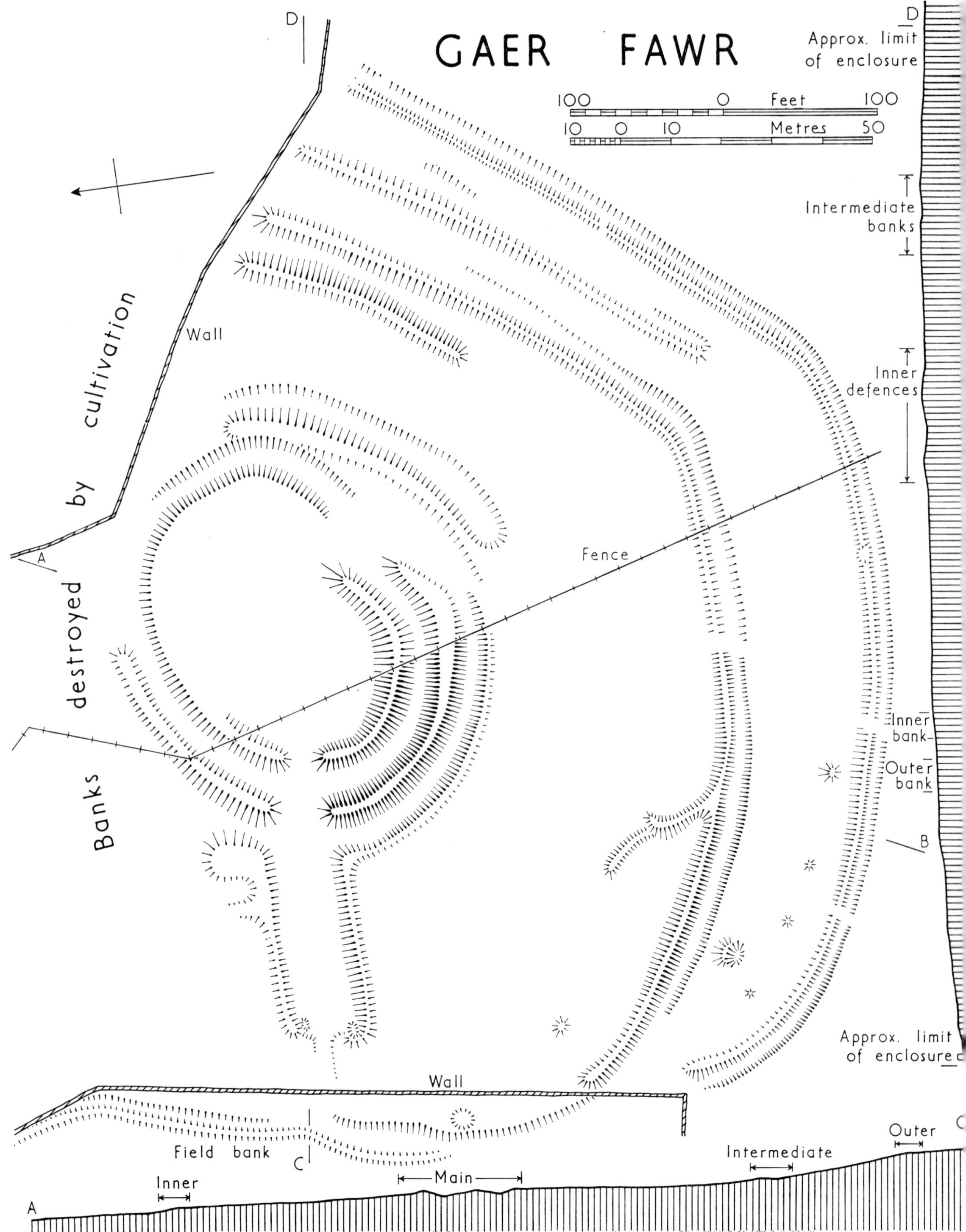

FIG. 30. No. 690.

to have coalesced, though their junction is damaged. From them, a slight hollow trail about 3 m wide leads inwards for 14 m, and passes between the inturned ends of two low parallel banks 12 m apart which form an approach to the W. entrance of the central enclosure, at which they join the counterscarp bank. Two small pits within the inturned ends seem to be original features.

No hut-platforms are visible. On the S.W. side there are five small cairns (I i 486), one within the intermediate bank and four between it and the outer bank. Their relation to the fort is uncertain (but *cf.* Maendy Camp, 694).

S 5d. *Arch. Journ.*, CIX (1952), pp. 1–22.

Briton Ferry (E), Neath (C).
SS 79 S.E. (7657 9425) 12 xi 64 XXV N.W.

(691) CAE SUMMERHOUSE (Fig. 31). The remains stand about 1 km S.E. of Tythegston, on an almost level summit at 75 m above O.D., with a good view in all directions, but with no natural advantages for defence. Parts have been almost obliterated by cultivation. The position of the entrance is uncertain.

The *inner enclosure* was almost square, area 0·2 ha. It was defended by a single bank and ditch, originally fairly strong. A slight stony bank projects inwards from the N. side, forming a yard or large building about 9 m by 30 m. This is joined to the E. wall of the enclosure by a similar bank.

The *outer enclosure* seems to have been roughly trapezoidal, the inner being set near its N. side; its rampart is almost obliterated. Its area was about 0·9 ha. From near the middle of the S. side a bank can just be traced for 52 m to S., when it turns E. until destroyed by a modern quarry. It may have been no more than a field boundary.

In 1966 J. L. Davies, on behalf of the Department of the Environment, began excavations on the site, which is being eroded by ploughing. A tentative interpretation of the results for 1966–7[1] indicates a complex sequence of three pre-Roman phases, commencing with an undefended settlement comprising at least one round timber house. This was followed by a settlement eventually protected by a bank and ditch. At least two further phases are represented, associated with 2nd- to 4th-century Roman pottery.

[1] *Morgannwg*, XI (1967), pp. 75–7.

Merthyr Mawr.
SS 87 N.E. (8639 7798) 21 ix 66 XL S.W.

(692) MOEL TON-MAWR (CAER CWMPHILIP) (Fig. 32, Plate 9). The site consists of two polygonal enclosures, the smaller asymmetrically placed within the larger. They lie about 2 km E.N.E. of Margam Abbey, mostly on level ground at about 270 m above O.D. to the S.W. of a stream flowing in a shallow ravine which both steepens and deepens to the N.W. The N.W. portion of the outer enclosure lies on ground falling towards this steeper section of the ravine.

The *inner enclosure* is placed near the S. side of the larger one and is trapezoidal in plan; its area is just over 0·4 ha. It is defended by a bank with external ditch which in places has a counterscarp bank. The main bank is 6 to 9 m wide and the ditch 4 to 6 m wide; the counterscarp bank, which is absent round the angles of the enclosure, is very faint and varies between 2·5 and 7·5 m in width. The overall extent of the defences ranges between 10 and 17 m. The original entrance seems to be a gap about 9 m wide in the broad N.E. angle of the enclosure; from it a faint track descends a slight slope north-eastwards to the stream. A gap in the S. defences has the appearance of an entrance but is probably a modern breach caused by a cartway that has also partly levelled the defences at a point on the W. side. The interior of the enclosure shows no signs of structures.

The *outer enclosure* is roughly pentagonal, about 2·7 ha in area. The N.E. side is formed by the stream; the other sides have artificial defences similar to those of the inner enclosure. They are best preserved on the E. and S.E., where the main bank is 6 to 8 m wide, 0·6 m high internally and 1·3 m externally, separated by a ditch from a counterscarp bank 5 to 8 m wide; the overall extent of the defences is 14 to 18 m. On the S. and W. the defences are much ploughed down and the counterscarp bank is absent except at the S.W. angle. The curving line of defences at the N.W. end of the site is better preserved though for the most part the main rampart consists of a scarp rather than a bank; it is 2 to 4 m wide and up to 1·5 m high. Outside it is a well defined flat-bottomed ditch, 1·5 to 2 m wide at the bottom and 5 to 6·5 m wide at the top, with (along the N. portion) a counterscarp bank 4 to 5 m wide and nearly a metre high.

The position of the entrance is uncertain. The most probable position would seem to be at the E. angle where the bank terminates on a knoll 12 m short of the edge of the ravine. A gap towards the E. end of the S. side might be an entrance but as in the case of the inner enclosure seems more likely to have been made by a cartway. Modern hedge-banks have broken through and partly destroyed the defences about the middle of the S. and W. sides. The annexe on the S. side of the site, shown on earlier plans including the 6-in. O.S. map, is now almost ploughed out, but seems to have been a natural feature.

S 6d (Caer Cwm–Philip). *Trans. Cardiff Nat. Soc.*, XXVII (1894–5), p. 81, plan (Ton Mawr); *Antiquity*, VIII (1934), p. 400 (Caer Cwm-Philip).

Margam (E), Port Talbot (C).
SS 88 N.W. (8255 8702) 24 viii 65 XXXIII N.E.

(693) Y BWLWARCAU (Fig. 33, Plate 9) is the most important of the forts discussed by Sir Cyril and Lady Fox in their study of the antiquities of this area[1] published in 1934. The 'yard' and 'annexe' mentioned below correspond to features described by them. The fort stands at about 300 m above O.D. on a broad spur of Mynydd Margam about 2 km W. of Llangynwyd. The axis of the spur lies just S. of the site, but the ground is nearly level from N. to S. across most of the area, until on the N. side it falls steeply to Cwm Cerdin; from W. to E. there is an almost uniform fall of about 8°. The remains comprise a small fairly strongly defended enclosure roughly concentric with slighter banks which protect a much larger area. The plan suggests that there were two main periods of

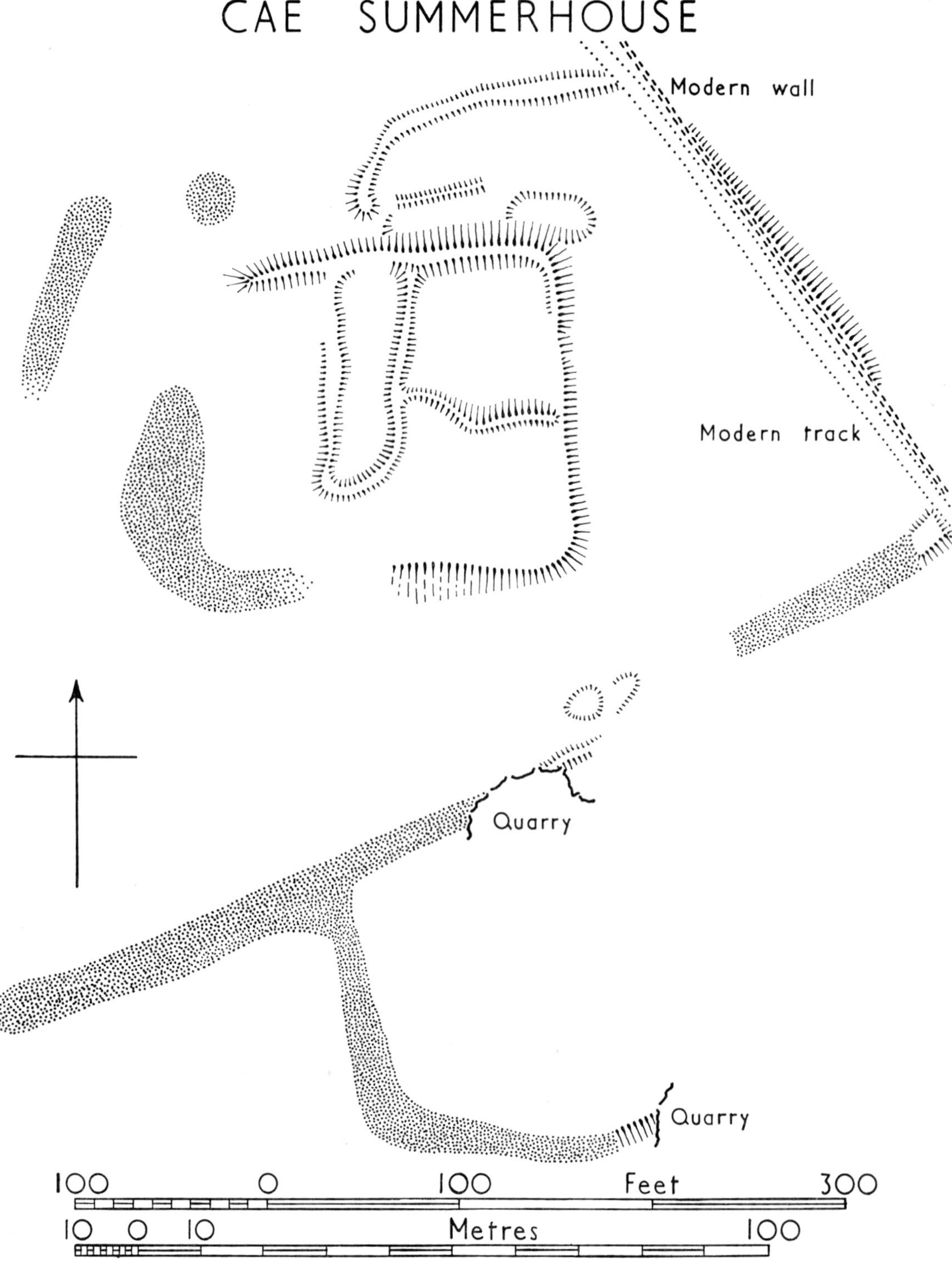

FIG. 31. No. 691.
Stipple represents traces of ploughed-down banks.

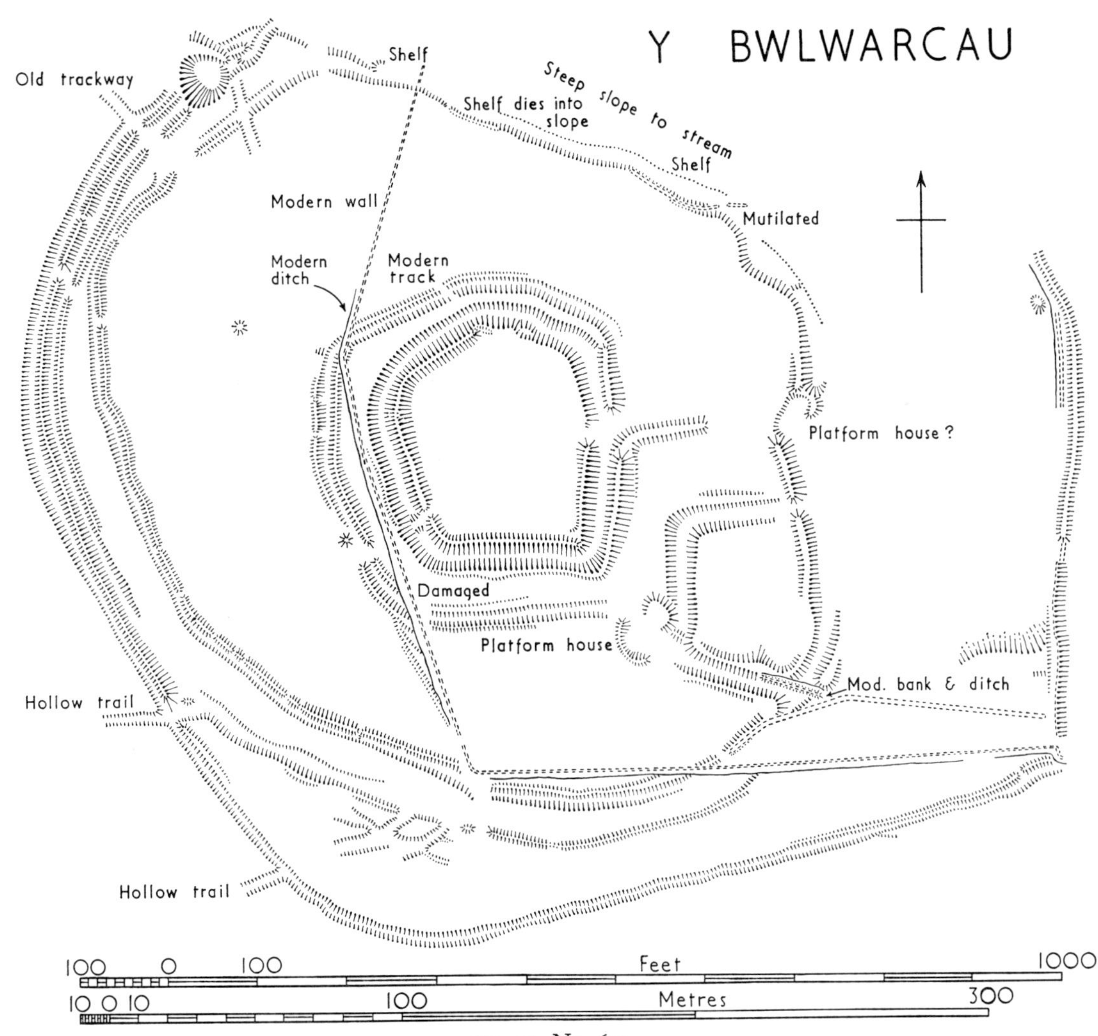

FIG. 33. No. 693.

construction as well as some later use, probably medieval. This analysis has been adopted as a convenient basis for the description of the structure, but it must be emphasised that lacking excavation it cannot be regarded as certain.

The innermost enclosure is pentagonal, area about 0·3 ha, protected by a substantial bank, ditch and counterscarp bank about 18 m wide overall; there is an entrance, apparently a simple gap, in the E. side.

The enclosure seems to have been superimposed on an earlier one of about twice the area, with similar but rather slighter defences. The gap on the S.W. seems to be original, but the main entrance probably coincided with that through the later rampart.

This earlier central defence may be associated with a pair of banks and ditches which enclose an area of about 4·4 ha. These seem to be little more than boundaries. The inner bank and ditch measure about 9 m wide, and rather more than 0·5 m high overall; the bank is interrupted by gaps generally about 1·5 m wide, which seem mostly to be original but which are not accompanied by causeways across the ditch. The second bank runs roughly parallel, with an intervening space from 6 to 15 m wide. It is very slight and much damaged, the ditch often being untraceable; on the E. it is absent, probably destroyed by ploughing.

There was an entrance through the surviving bank on the E., connected to the entrance to the central enclosure by a slightly hollowed track with a low bank on its S. side.

Further S., a quadrilateral 'yard' has been formed against the inner boundary-bank, surrounded by a broad shallow ditch in part accompanied by slight banks on each side. The ditch cuts the boundary-bank, and the 'yard' was regarded by Sir Cyril Fox as belonging to the adjacent platform-house; but the terracing for this seems to over-lie the ditch, so the 'yard' may belong to the second period of the earlier works. A slight bank

D
A
B
+ Site of 'cist'
PROFILES E-F AND G-H ENLARGED FROM A-B
E
F
G
H
10 0 10 Feet 40
5 0 5 Metres 10
C
MAENDY CAMP
A
Mound
Low bank
G
Rampart
H
Low bank
E
Bank
F
Bank
Bank
B
Bank
Bank
Bank
C
D
100 0 100 Feet 400
10 0 10 Metres 100 150

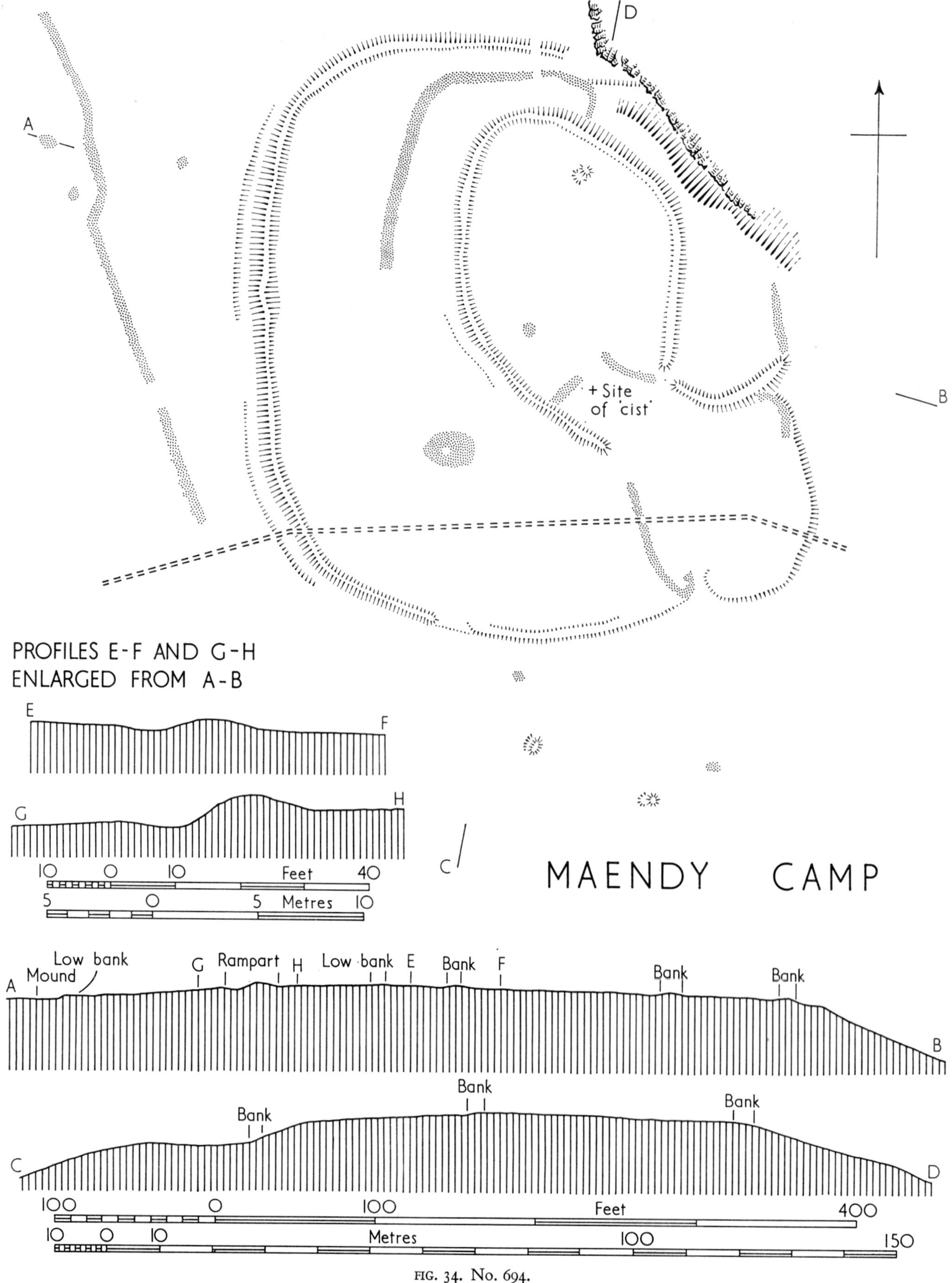

FIG. 34. No. 694.

with a ditch on the W. joined the earlier central enclosure to the inner boundary-bank, but this may be no more than the precursor of the modern stone wall and accompanying ditch, by which it has been damaged and largely destroyed. The age and nature of the small mound W. of the central enclosure are unknown.

This pair of boundary-banks seems to have been superseded by a slightly larger bank and ditch enclosing a D-shaped area of about 7·2 ha, bounded on N. by Cwm Cerdin. Where best preserved, the bank and ditch now measure about 6 m wide by 0·6 m high overall, but the ditch has in places been enlarged by use as a trackway or as a drainage ditch, and on the E. the bank has been built up and revetted to form a field-boundary. There is a gap, crossed by a modern bank, near the middle of this section.

A later house-platform, about 18 m N.E.–S.W. by 7·5 m, has been formed close to the S.W. corner of the 'yard', and what may be another smaller one occupies the site of the entrance through the inner of the pair of boundary-banks. Old straight field-banks form large polygonal enclosures W. of the site (the 'Annexe') and may be contemporary with the platform-houses, but their straightness suggests that they are probably quite recent.

The site has been crossed by several old trackways, which have worn down the banks in places and have converted the N. part of the inner boundary-bank and ditch into a terrace, and modern field boundaries have caused localised damage. On the S., also, the space between the inner and outermost boundary-banks has been cut up by irregular surface water-courses. In general, though, the remains are well preserved.

S 4b. *Trans. Cardiff Nat. Soc.*, XXVII (1894–5), p. 81 (plan); *Arch. Journ.*, CIX (1952), pp. 1–22.
[1] *Antiquity*, VIII (1934), pp. 395–413.

Llangynwyd (E), Ll. Middle (C).
SS 88 N.W. (8388 8855) 18 iv 67 XXXIV N.W.

(694) Maendy Camp (Fig. 34, Plate 10) stands at about 350 m above O.D. about 1·5 km S. of Treorci at the E. end of a spur overlooking the Rhondda valley, with ground falling away fairly steeply on all sides except the W. The total area is about 0·9 ha, that of the central enclosure about 0·2 ha. A low cairn (I i 350) and nine smaller mounds (I i 488) are scattered over the site, but there is no structural connection to indicate their age relative to the 'camp', (but *cf.* 690, Gaer Fawr).

The inner enclosure is formed by a stony bank with faint traces of an external ditch, measuring about 6 m wide and 0·6 m high overall where best preserved. On the S.E. this bank ends at a gap 15 m wide, partly closed by low ill-defined banks of stone. These leave an entrance about 7·5 m wide. Near this, excavation in 1901[1] revealed an empty 'cist, about a foot square',[2] now destroyed, though a hole indicates its site; its size and position suggest that it may have been a hole for a post forming part of a gateway.

The outer enclosing rampart is more substantial than the inner, and the ditch is clear on the W.; the dimensions overall are 9 m wide and 1·5 m high where best preserved, but the bank decreases in size on the S. and is barely perceptible on the N.E. where the ground begins to fall more steeply. On the S. the bank turns inwards to form an entrance passage about 4·5 m long and 2·5 m wide: details are obscured by a recent trench. The excavations of 1901 exposed a pavement of stones laid flat, 2·7 m wide and extending at least 11 m. Between this entrance and that to the inner enclosure two main ramparts are connected, on the W. by a low stony ridge and on the N. by a more substantial bank nearly 1 m high. Both are separated from the inner rampart by gaps, but that on the N. may not be original. On the N.W. a stony bank curves round in a quadrant midway between the inner and outer ramparts. There was probably an entrance on the N. between this and the outer rampart, but this area seems to have been damaged by stone robbing and quarrying.

Outside the enclosure, on the W., where the approach is almost level, a low bank of stones runs across the saddle.

No dwelling-sites are visible, but the report on the 1901 excavations records charcoal and two potsherds from a 'hut floor' between the inner and outer ramparts, about 20 m N.E. of the 'cist' in the inner entrance. Most of the relics found during those excavations, however, are probably to be associated with the cairn (350).

The remains have been extensively robbed of stone, and it seems likely that the low banks of rubble were originally much more substantial than their present appearance suggests. The structure is probably all of one period, but certainty is impossible without excavation.

S 11c.
[1] *Arch. Camb.*, 1902, pp. 252–60.
[2] *Ibid.*, 1913, p. 146.

Ystradyfodwg (E), Rhondda (C).
SS 99 N.E. (9573 9551) 16 vi 65 XVIII S.W.

(695) Llanquian Wood (Fig. 35). The fort stands in woodland about 2·5 km E. of Cowbridge at 90 m above O.D. on ground falling gently to the N.W., with a steeper fall into a small dry valley on the W., and a crag on the N.W. that has been incorporated in the outer defensive line. The defences consist of two widely spaced lines of bank and ditch, heavily overgrown on E. and S., and damaged by modern disturbance in places. The distance apart ranges from 15 m to 40 m.

The *inner enclosure* is oval in plan, 140 m long from N.E. to S.W. by 87 m wide, area about 1·0 ha. On the E. and S. it is defended by a bank varying between 5 and 11 m in width and up to 1·4 m high. On the S.E. only there is also an external ditch about 6 m wide and 0·5 m deep. On the N., W. and S.W. the bank is replaced by a scarp 4 to 8 m wide and up to 2·3 m high, and the ditch is absent. There are two possible entrances: a narrow gap on the S.W., and a wider break in the scarp on the N.W.

The *outer enclosure* is approximately circular and about 165 m in diameter, area 2·2 ha. It is defended on the E. and S. by a bank 6 to 11 m wide and 1·5 m high, with an external ditch 3 to 6 m wide and 0·5 m deep. On the N.E. and W. the bank is replaced by a scarp 3·5 to 6 m wide and up to 2 m high, that runs diagonally downhill across the contours; while on the N.W. the defence is mostly formed by a natural crag. There appear to be two entrances: a sunken gap 3·5 m wide on the

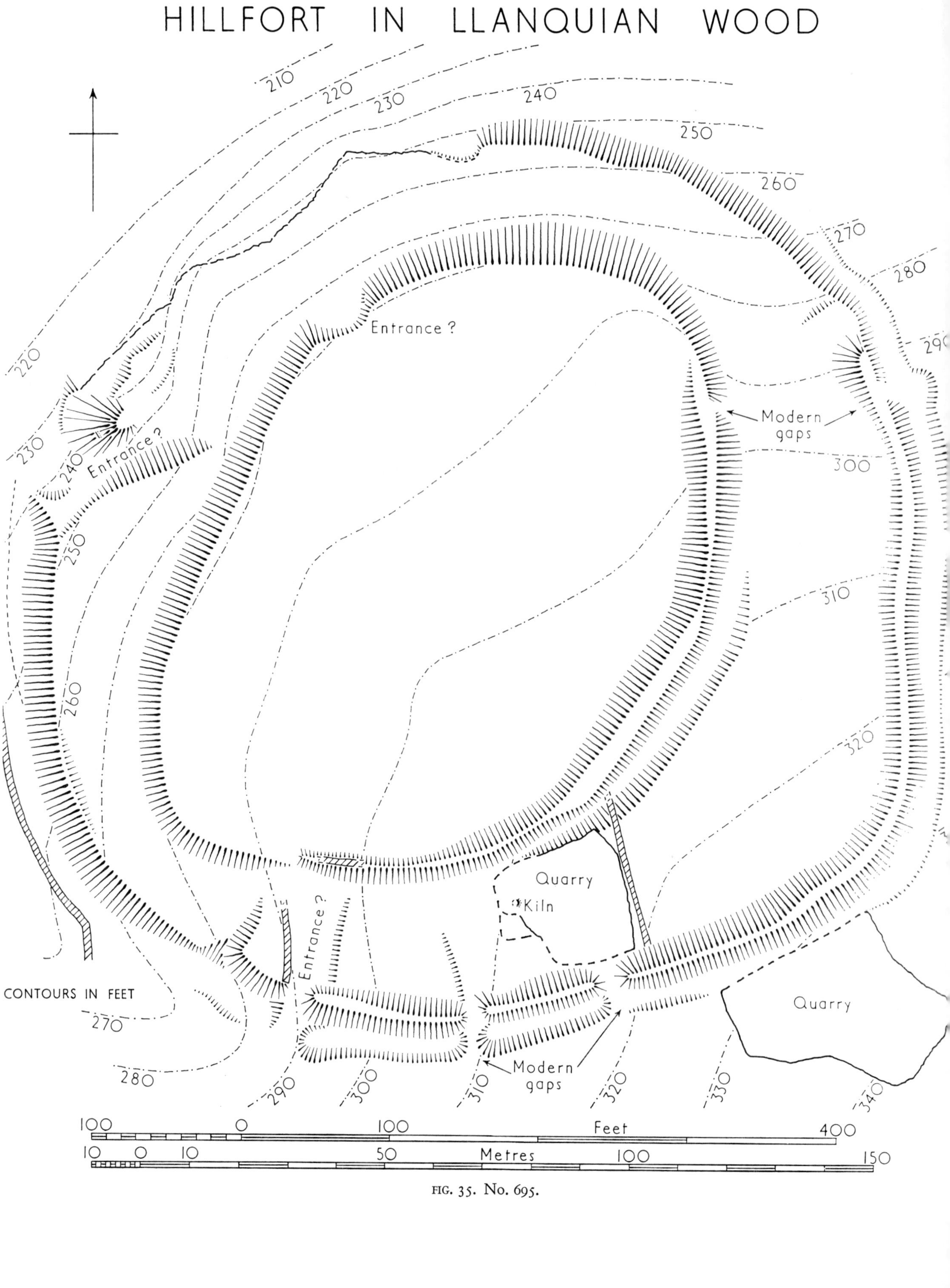

HILLFORT IN LLANQUIAN WOOD

Entrance ?

Entrance ?

Entrance ?

Modern gaps

Modern gaps

Quarry

Kiln

Quarry

CONTOURS IN FEET

210 220 230 240 250 260 270 280 290 300 310 320 330 340

100 0 100 Feet 400

10 0 10 50 Metres 100 150

FIG. 35. No. 695.

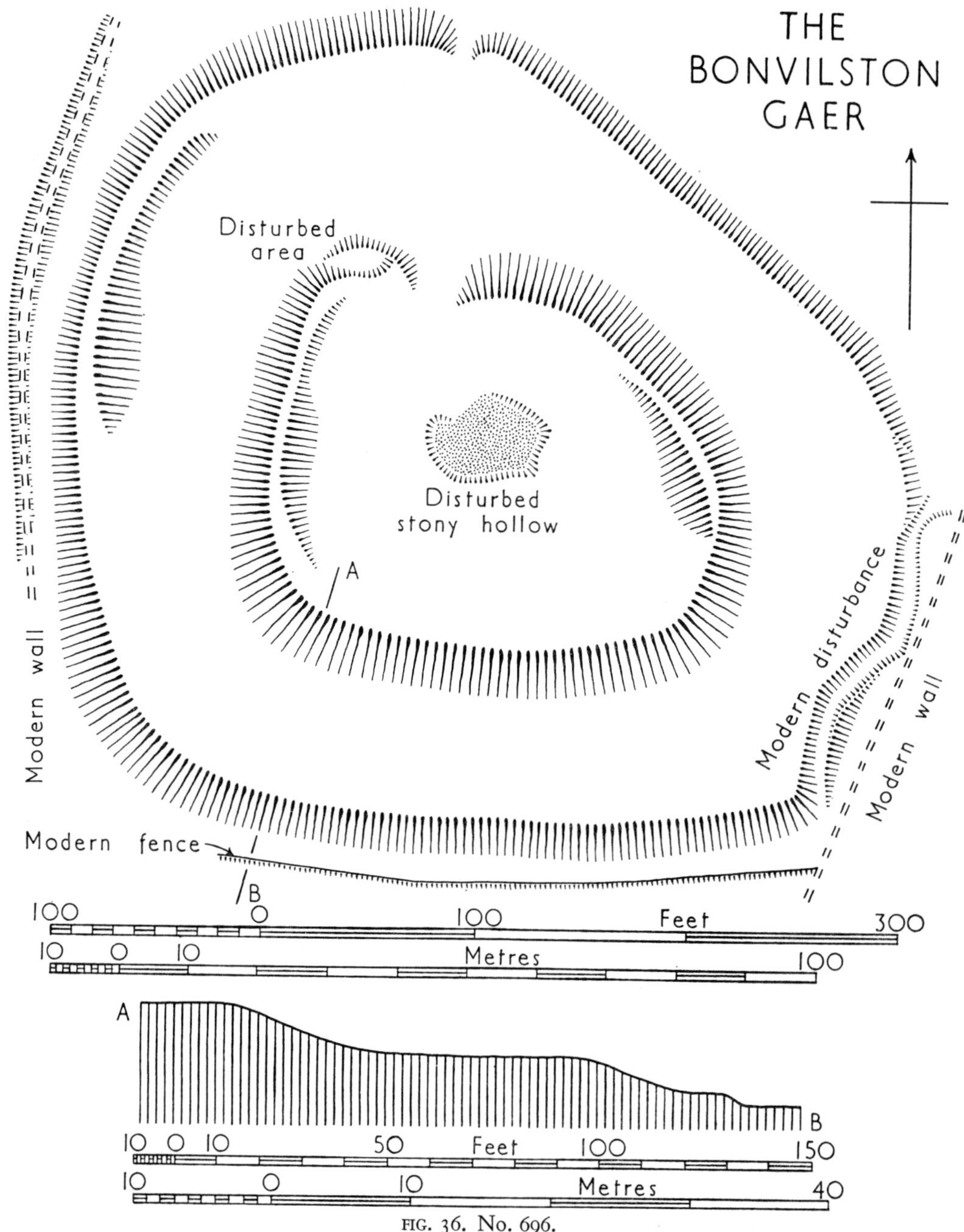

FIG. 36. No. 696.

S.W. opposite the corresponding gap in the inner bank; and on the W. a less certain opening, dominated by a high bank on its N.E. side, from which a trackway ascends the hill to the entrance through the inner scarp about 40 m further to the N.

There are no remains of internal structures. Gaps in the defences on the E. and S. are almost certainly modern. An old quarry has obliterated the counterscarp of the outer ditch on the S.E.; and between the two defensive lines on the S. is another quarry containing the remains of an old limekiln Part of the upper stone of a rotary quern was picked up outside the defences on the N.W. during the survey in 1963.

S 3d. *B.B.C.S.*, I, ii (May 1922), p. 171.

Llanblethian.

ST 07 S.W. (0214 7446) 25 vi 63 XLV N.E.

(696) BONVILSTON GAER (Fig. 36), on level ground at 120 m above O.D. about 0·75 km N. of the village. It consists of two approximately oval concentric enclosures, separated by a space of some 10 m. The inner measures 65 m long from E. to W. by 50 m, the outer 120 m long by about 105 m. Their areas are 0·2 and 1·0 ha. Each enclosure is defended by a single bank which has been reduced to a scarp except on the E. and W. of the inner circuit and on the N.W. of the outer circuit. The banks are 10·5 to 12 m wide, the scarps 3 to 7·5 m wide. The internal height of the banks is very slight except on the N.W. of the outer circuit where it reaches 1·5 m; the external height averages nearly 2·5 m. A shallow external ditch 6 to 9 m wide is visible along part of the W. side. The entrance through both ramparts is on the N.; the inner entrance appears to be slightly inturned but its W. side is disturbed. The S.E. portion of the outer defence has also been disturbed by a modern drainage ditch. A stony hollow at the centre of the enclosures is probably the site of a building which is shown here on the O.S. map of 1813.

The iron slag and Roman objects said to have come from here (*Arch. Camb.*, 1896, p. 167) were in fact found at Miskin (*Archaeologia*, II (1807), p. 14).
S 1d. *Arch. Camb.*, 1862, p. 100.

Bonvilston.
ST 07 S.E. (0635 7474) 26 iii 63 XLVI N.W.

697–704. *MULTIVALLATE ENCLOSURES WITH WIDE-SPACED RAMPARTS, ON COASTAL SITES*

(697) LEWES CASTLE occupies an irregular headland projecting towards the S., about 0·75 km S. of Rhosili. The ground falls gently towards the neck of the promontory and then rises more steeply to the cliff edge; the saddle is sheltered on the S. and W. It is crossed by two ramparts. The inner, formed by a small bank with a ditch on the N. measuring about 5·5 m wide and nearly 1 m high overall where best preserved, runs E.S.E. for about 50 m and then turns nearly through a right-angle to run 30 m further to some crags which continue to the cliff edge; the enclosed area is about 0·3 ha. The outer is formed by two banks of about equal size with a ditch between, measuring about 9 m wide by nearly 1 m high overall. This is separated from the inner rampart by a space about 12 m wide. Its line is generally curvilinear though apparently set out in short straight lengths. The entrance through both ramparts seems to have been simple gaps about 3·5 m wide and lying about 30 m from the W. cliff edge. The defences are much more angular and slighter in construction than in the other promontory forts on the Gower coast.

Rhosili.
SS 48 N.W. (4144 8734) 23 ii 67 XXX N.E.

(698) THURBA HEAD (Fig. 37). The headland, as outlined by high-water mark, measures about 250 m long from N.E. to S.W. and about 140 m broad, but the greater part of this is either bare rock or steep craggy slopes; apart from banks across possible lateral approaches, the fortified area covers 1·2 ha and is triangular, about 150 m long from N.E. to S.W. to the outermost rampart, and about 80 m across the base. The headland is very irregular. A section from N. to S. would appear as a series of steps of various sizes formed by shelves separated by vertical crags and ascending to the nearly flat top of the ridge; S. of this are one or two narrower 'steps' above a steep slope, ending at a vertical cliff. The shelves, however, are not level, but fall uniformly towards the N.E., and several of them, as well as the grassy slope on the S., provide relatively easy access to the seaward end of the promontory from points outside the defences. These approaches have been barred by ramparts. That on the N.W. now appears as a scarp, though a shelf at its toe suggests the presence of a ditch. That on the S. comprises a ditch, now very faint, backed by a bank of earth and rubble with remains of a stone revetment to front and rear.

The main defences are arranged to prevent approach along the nearly level ridge. Approaching from the N.E., the first barrier is a bank and ditch now about 15 m wide by 2 m high overall; the ditch is almost obliterated by cultivation and a modern field-wall follows the bank. At its N. end, now slightly damaged by a small quarry, this bank seems to have ended on a low crag, below which a slighter bank running E.–W. crosses the upper end of a grassy shelf. The S. end of the outer bank curves round to the S.W. and dies out close to the end of the second rampart. This is a bank and ditch now about 10·5 m wide and over 2 m high overall. It is separated from the first line of defence by a space averaging about 21 m wide, with no visible traces of occupation.

To the W. of the second rampart the ridge rises gently to form an oval plateau measuring about 50 m by 35 m; the summit is just over 54 m above O.D. Along the E. edge are traces of a wall of dry stone about 6 m wide with no accompanying ditch. This wall has been almost entirely robbed, probably for lime-making (see below), but about 10 m of the outer face still stands up to 0·5 m high; the rest can be traced by the low rims of small stones left after robbing. This defence seems to have continued round about half the circuit of the plateau; most of the remainder is precipitous. A short length of similar walling, only about 3 m thick, bars a possible approach from the S. just beyond the W. end of the summit plateau. A few stones of the outer face remain just below the summit, and after a gap 3 m wide the line is continued by a robber-trench and a further short length of facing. The whole is much ruined, but there seems to have been a gateway here. There is no trace of an entrance elsewhere.

The approach to this gate seems to have followed the ditch (perhaps a hollow trail) outside the S.W. extension of the first rampart, which leads to a terraced roadway following the foot of the crags where they join the grassy slope, but the W. end of this roadway is obliterated for about 35 m by quarrying and debris associated with an adjacent limekiln. Beyond this disturbance there is no roadway, but an easy slope leads up to the gateway.

Within the enclosure are shallow hollows with level floors, ranging from 3 to 6 m across. The two adjacent to the stone wall are almost certainly hut sites, and the other three shown on the plan are very probably so. Others, less regular and not indicated, are probably shallow surface quarries. No hut-sites

120
130
140
150
160
Hut?
Hut?
Entrance
Hut?
Hut
Hut
C
Robbed wall
Fallen rubble
180
170
160
150
140
130
120
110
100
90
80
A
B
Area obscured by quarrying
Old kiln
Track
Small quarry
D
E
2
CONTOURS IN FEET
SCALE OF PLAN 2
50 0 50 Feet 100
10 0 10 Metres 30
THURBA HEAD
1
Cliff
SCALE OF PLAN 1
100 0 100 Feet 300
0 Metres 100
Revetment
Robbed stone wall
C
D
Modern wall
E
10 0 10 Feet 100 200
10 0 10 Metres 50

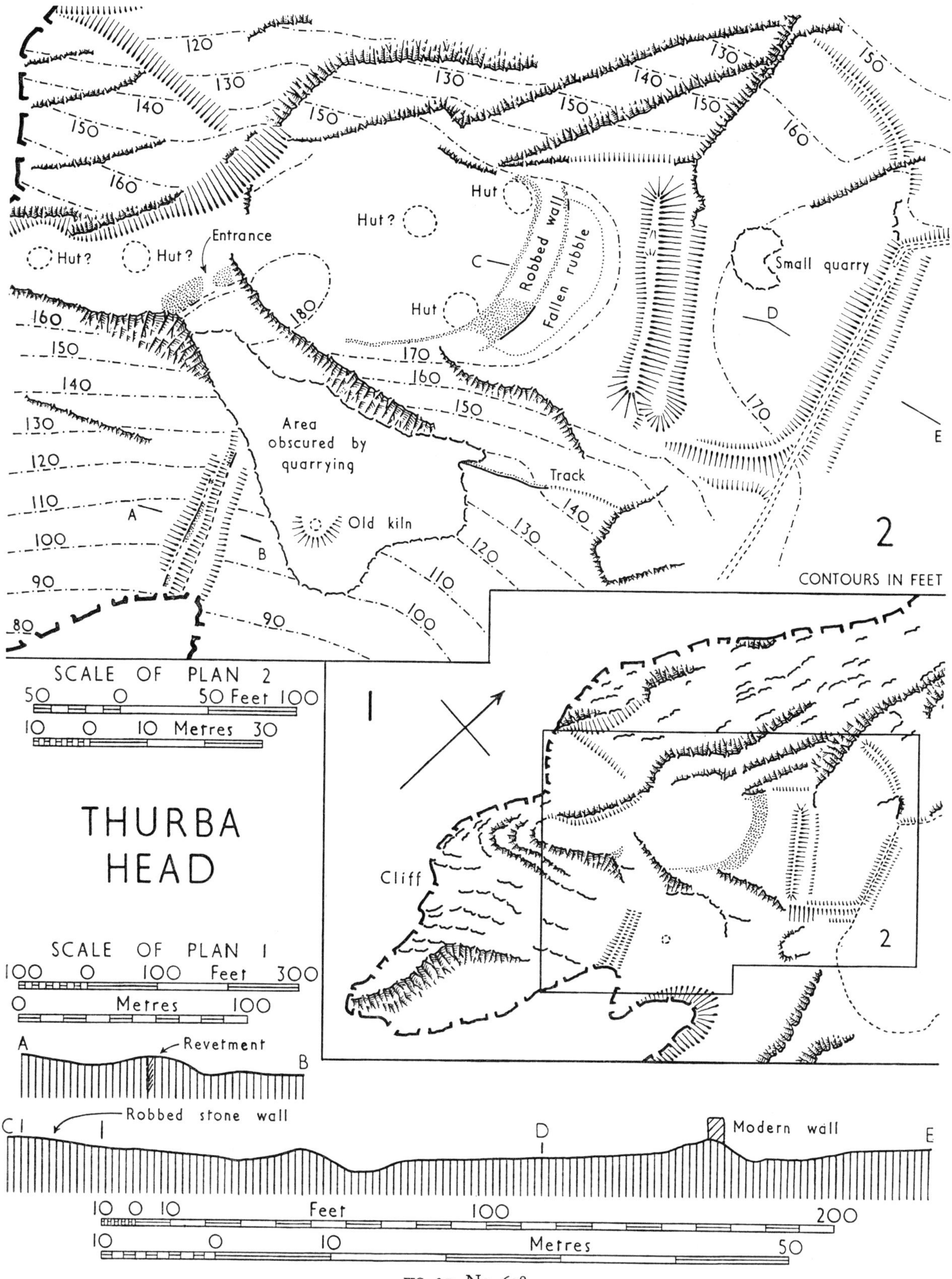

FIG. 37. No. 698.

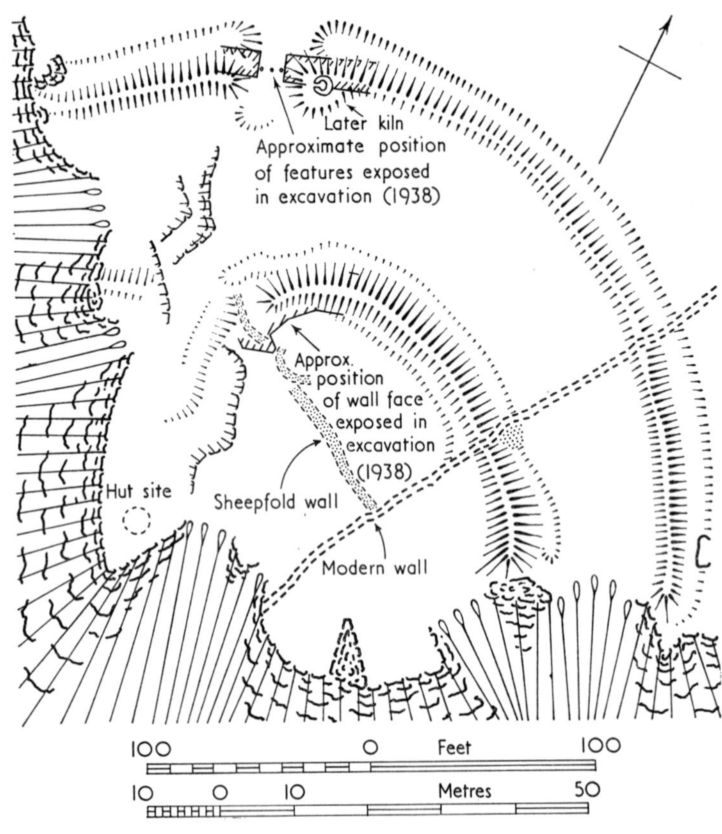

FIG. 38. No. 699.

were observed on the N. or S. slopes. The habitable area within the stone wall is about 0·3 ha.

Surface appearances suggest that the fortifications comprise work of two periods, the earlier being the stone wall round the summit, but this has not been verified by excavation.

S 14c. *B.B.C.S.*, VIII, iv (May 1937), p. 365; Rutter, *P. Gower*, p. 66.

Rhosili.
SS 48 N.W. (4220 8705) 7 v 64 XXX N.E.

(699) THE KNAVE (Fig. 38, Plate 11). The site is a blunt headland about 2·5 km S.E. of Rhosili, with a sheer cliff 60 m high on the S., and more broken cliffs on the S.W. and S.E. It has a very wide base in relation to its length, so that although the inner defended area of about 0·1 ha is only about 45 m by 30 m, the outer defences are 130 m long.

The defences form two more or less concentric arcs:

(i) The outer or landward defence consists of a grass- and gorse-grown bank, 3 to 5 m wide, about 0·6 m high internally and mostly nearly 1 m externally, though the portion S.W. of the entrance is 1·5 m high externally. Outside the bank is a ditch 3 to 4 m wide, for the most part densely overgrown with gorse. Towards the W. end is an entrance 4·5 m wide; on its E. side the bank terminates in a high mound with a hollow centre, which looks like a guard-chamber but which excavation (see below) proved to be an old lime kiln.

(ii) The inner line of defence, separated from the outer by a space of from 14 m to 20 m, consists for the E. two-thirds of its length of a grass-grown bank of limestone rubble, 5·5 to 7·5 m wide, nearly 1 m high internally and mostly 2 m externally, though reaching nearly 3 m at the E. end. The inner scarp has a stepped appearance, but this is probably due to stone robbery. Outside the bank is a ditch 1·5 to 2·5 m wide and up to about 1 m deep. Entrance arrangements, now obscured, were exposed by excavation (see below). After a gap of about 15 m, a straight length of bank with no ditch links a rock outcrop to the cliff. Very faint surface traces suggest a continuation of the rampart and ditch turning sharply to the S.W. from the entrance, but no ditch was found in excavation, and the features are probably natural, perhaps enhanced by quarrying. No hut platforms are visible in the interior. The faint footings of an old enclosure wall, probably for a sheepfold, are traceable in the inner enclosure, partly blocking the entrance. A modern stone wall crosses the E. part of the fort from N.E. to S.W.

The site was excavated by Audrey Williams (Mrs. W. F. Grimes) in 1938. The inner rampart was shown to be 4·9 m wide, revetted internally (and perhaps also externally) with at least two courses of limestone blocks. The ditch was 4·3 m wide and 1·1 m deep, with very gently sloping sides and a slight counterscarp bank. The bank near the cliff on the W. was only 3·7 m wide with no ditch, but with a substantial outer revetment, to accommodate which the rock had been scarped. The entrance was approached obliquely along a ridge of outcrop. On the S. it was protected by a natural scarp with no additions. The bank and ditch terminated on the N., the bank being slightly inturned. No post-holes for the gate were found.

The outer rampart was shown to be 3 to 4 m wide, with an inner kerb of boulders; the ditch was 3·7 to 4·3 m wide and 1·4 m deep, of blunt V-section. At the entrance, the roadway was 3 m wide between the squared ends of the rampart; a line of three post-holes across the middle of the gap indicated a pair of gates closing on a central upright.

Within the enclosure, an occupation layer was found within the inturn of the rampart at the entrance; all the pottery came from this. A natural hollow near the cliff edge on the S. had a hearth and a central post-hole suggesting a round hut 3·7 m in diameter. Small finds from various parts of the site included slingstones, pot-boilers, hammer-stones, part of a stone mace, pieces of clay daub, and sixteen sherds of Early Iron Age B pottery of Glastonbury type dated to the period 50 B.C.–A.D. 50.

S 13c (Deborah's Hole). *B.B.C.S.*, VIII, iv (May 1937), p. 365; Rutter, *P. Gower*, p. 66; *Arch. Camb.*, XCIV (1939), pp. 210–19 excavation report).

Rhosili.
SS 48 N.W. (4318 8637) 6 x 65 XXX S.E.

(700) YELLOW TOP, PAVILAND (Fig. 39). The fort occupies a long narrow headland aligned N.N.E.–S.S.W. between two deeply cut valleys. The seaward cliff, which contains the famous Paviland Cave (I i 5), is spectacularly sheer and almost 60 m in height. The lateral cliffs are less sheer and are broken by steep grass gullies that have determined the position of some of the ditches of the fort. Foxhole Slade, the ravine to the S.E. of the headland, extends far inland beyond the camp; the valley to the N.W. is shorter and ends about the line of the furthest landward defences.

The total length of the promontory from the landward commencement of the defences is about 145 m, but only 50 m lies within the most seaward of those defences, the inner area being about 0·1 ha. The headland varies greatly in width, from 10 m about the middle to 65 m at the landward end. There are four defensive lines which, commencing at the landward end, are as follows:

(i) A grass-grown bank of limestone rubble, 6 to 10 m wide, over 1 m high internally (*i.e.* on the seaward side) and 2 m externally, is fronted on the landward side by a ditch 3·5 to 5 m wide and 1 m deep. These defences end on the S.E. at the cliff edge; on the N.W. there seems to be room for an entrance between their termination and the fall into the lateral valley. Both bank and ditch curve seaward at either end; the ditch has been mutilated by quarry scrapings on the N. and apparently also at its S.E. end.

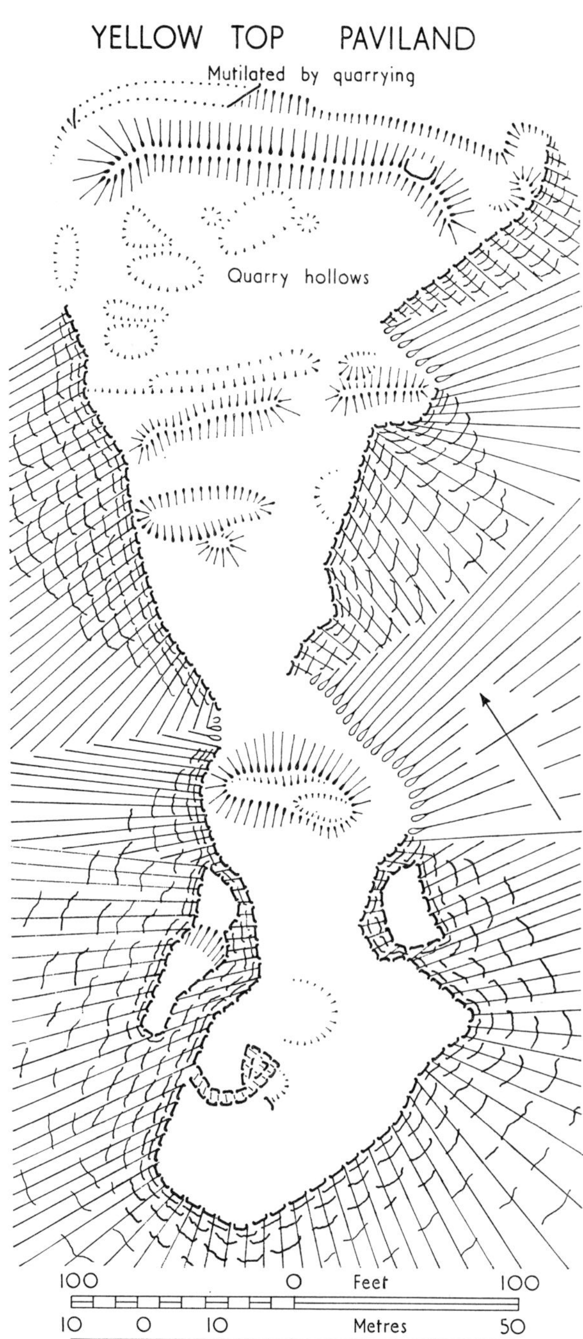

FIG. 39. No. 700.

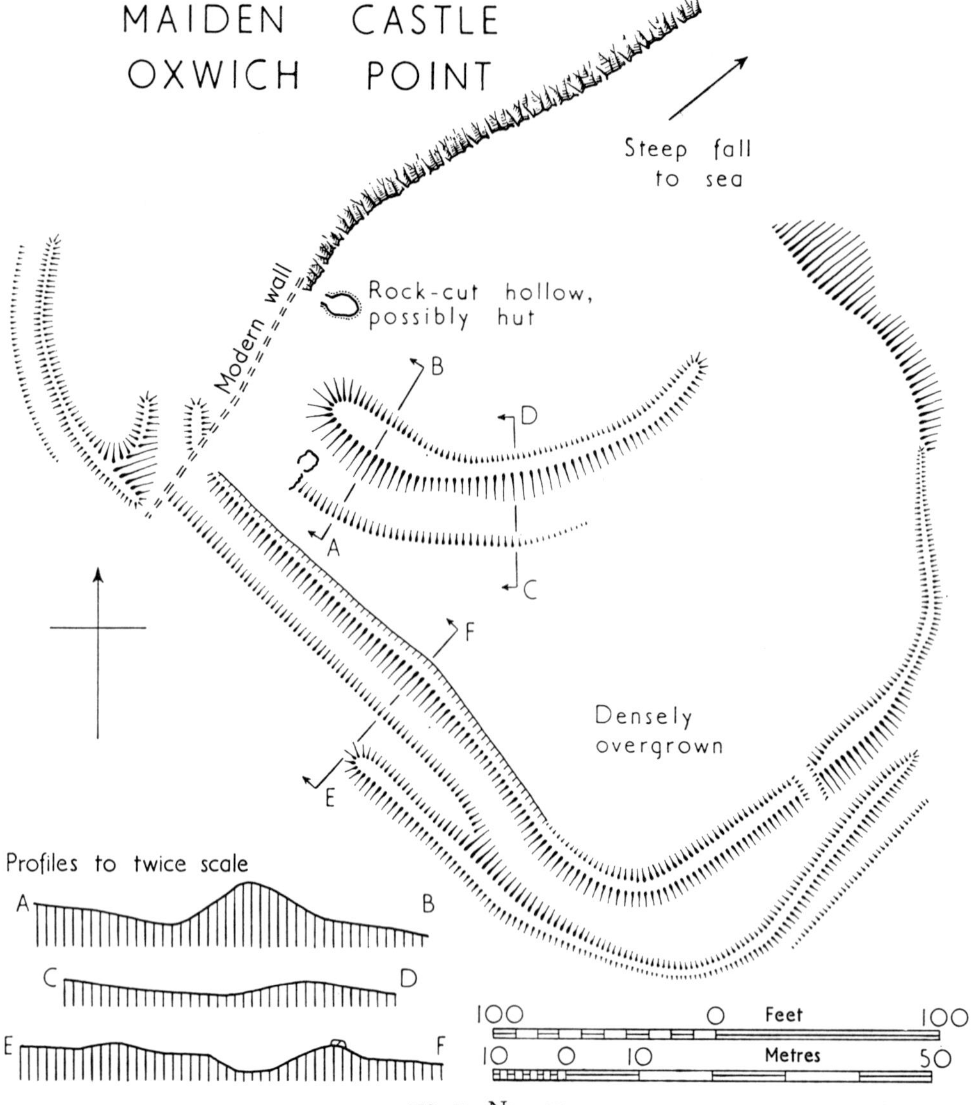

FIG. 40. No. 701.

(ii) The second line of defence commences 20 m further seaward and consists of a rock-cut ditch 2·5 to 3·5 m wide and nearly 1 m deep, across which is a causewayed entrance 2·5 m wide towards the S.W. end. On the seaward side of the ditch, and (at any rate along the portion N.W. of the entrance) separated from it by a narrow berm, is a grass-grown bank of limestone rubble, 3 to 6 m wide, 1·5 m high internally and 1·3 m externally. This contains an entrance 4 m wide opposite the causeway in the ditch. The bank is somewhat eroded towards its N.W. end, which again curves seaward.

(iii) The third line commences 6 m further seaward and consists of another rock-cut ditch, 4·5 to 7 m wide and 0·7 m deep, apparently unfinished. It terminated on the S.E. at a causewayed entrance some 5 m wide beyond which are faint traces of a continuation of the ditch at the edge of the cliff. On the seaward lip of the main portion of ditch is a fragment of bank about 7·5 m long and 4·3 m wide.

(iv) The fourth line lies 23 m further seaward and consists of a high bank of limestone rubble, 11 to 13 m wide, nearly 1 m high internally and 3 m externally, which on the landward side utilises a depression between the heads of two gullies as a ditch. The bank ends 2 m short of the cliff edge on the E., this being apparently the entrance. The summit of the bank is disturbed, perhaps by excavation.

Signs of occupation within the fort are exiguous and are confined to the area to seaward of the fourth line of defence. They consist of half a dozen vague platforms of various shapes, that may have been the sites of huts, some among the outcrops on the level summit of the headland, others on ledges in the lateral cliffs. The area between the first and second lines of defence contains a number of modern quarry hollows. Slingstones have been found in the camp.

S 11c. *B.B.C.S.*, VIII, iv (May 1937), p. 365; *Rep. R.I.S.W.*, 1920–1, p. 12; Rutter, *P. Gower*, p. 65.

Rhosili.

SS 48 N.W. (4370 8596) 23 ix 65 XXX S.E.

(701) MAIDEN CASTLE (Fig. 40). The fort, known locally by this name, lies a little N. of Oxwich Point between the 60 and 75 m contours above O.D., just above a hillside falling very steeply to the shore of Oxwich Bay. The greater part of the enclosed ground falls with a slope of about 1 in 4 towards the N.E. From about 30 m within the W. angle a line of cliff runs N.E. increasing in height; below this, to the N.W., the slope is steeper. The whole area is thickly covered with trees and undergrowth, and parts of it, particularly near the defences, are impenetrable even in winter. The outer defence seems to have enclosed a total of about 0·6 ha, the inner 0·2 ha, but neither terminates on a natural obstacle and the boundaries of the fort to the N. are uncertain.

The outer rampart first appears at its E. end as a low bank of rubble above a fairly steep natural scarp. The bank increases in size and on the S.E. side is accompanied by a slight outer bank with an outer ditch. As the defences round the S. corner, the stone in the main bank gives place to earth, and the space between this and the outer bank becomes a ditch. The outer bank loses its external ditch and becomes a counterscarp bank to the main ditch, from which it diverges soon after the S. corner, to die away about half-way along the S.W. side. The main bank and ditch, here nearly 2 m high overall, run straight to a modern wall, beyond which a bank starts on a different line and curves round northwards, dying away on a moderately steep hillside. The probable line of ditch accompanying the bank has been utilised to form a hollow track. The inner rampart forms a quadrant about 60 m long, dying away indefinitely at the E. end, but at the W. end standing about 3 m high, accompanied by a partly rock-cut ditch.

The entrance through the outer rampart seems to have been where it was crossed by the modern wall. The banks now turn inwards to form a parallel-sided passage about 9 m long. Unfortunately, not only is this area much overgrown, but the modern wall has caused some damage, so the arrangement cannot be fully worked out. From here, the inner enclosure was probably reached by passing between the W. end of the rampart and the end of the cliff. Just above the cliff at this point is a small oval hollow cut into the rock, with an entrance at the W. side. This gives the impression of a small hut, possibly a guard-chamber at the entrance; but without excavation it cannot be said for certain that it is not a quarry-pit, or perhaps even natural. No other hut-site was observed.

Oxwich.

SS 58 N.W. (5095 8546) 22 iii 62 XXXI S.E.

(702) HIGH PENNARD (Fig. 41). The headland, about 75 m above O.D., projects to the S.W. between two wide inlet valleys on the W. side of Pwll Du Head. It is defended on the S. and W. by sheer cliffs, but the slopes to N.W. and S.E. are less steep. The artificial defences lie to the N. and N.E. across the wide base of the headland, but the configuration of the ground is not straightforward and at first sight the layout of the defences seems confused. The dip of the limestone strata is to the S.E., and because of this the N.W. side of the promontory forms a broken series of short cliffs, enlarged in modern times by quarrying. The rock also outcrops on the summit of the headland, and in particular a pronounced cliff some 4 m in height runs N.E.–S.W. like a spine, separating the defended area into two parts, a larger one to the N.W. measuring about 85 m by 43 m, and a smaller to the S.E. about 25 m by 20 m. Modern quarrying along the base of this cliff has resulted in banks of upcast that must not be confused with the defensive earthworks. The total area is about 0·4 ha.

The inner or seaward defence runs in an arc some 80 m long across the whole base of the headland, but is divided into two halves by the above-mentioned cliff. The W. half where the ground falls fairly steeply to the N., consists of two scarps: an inner high scarp 4 to 6·5 m wide and 3 m high, with a suggestion of an outer ditch towards its E. end; and an outer scarp up to 4 m wide and 1·2 m high. The S.E. half of the inner defences consists for the most part of a rampart about 6 m wide, very slight internally but 1·5 m high externally, and a slight outer ditch 2·5 to 3·5 m wide. About midway along the rampart is an entrance 2 m wide approached by a causeway across the ditch; to the S. of the entrance the defences are incurved sharply to merge with the cliff edge, and here consist of a scarp 3 to 4 m wide with faint outer ditch.

The outer or landward defences are confined to the E. portion of the headland above the low cliff. They lie 18 m beyond the inner line and consist of a bank 40 m long and 5 to 7 m wide, 0·6 m high internally and nearly 2 m externally, with an outer ditch 3 to 5 m wide and nearly 1 m deep. A narrow break about the middle of the rampart is probably modern. The S.E. end of this defensive line ends 17 m short of the cliff edge and has an unfinished appearance.

Within the fort, platforms in the sloping ground on the N. side of the larger enclosure may have been used as habitation sites, but seem in the main natural and have been omitted from the plan.

The site was excavated by Audrey Williams (Mrs. W. F. Grimes) in 1939. The outer rampart was found to be 4 m wide and 0·8 m high, with a rough battered revetment externally; the ditch was 5 m wide and 0·9 m deep with gently-sloping sides on a flat bottom. Excavation indicated that the defences had at one time extended 7·6 m further to the S.E. than their present termination. The inner rampart was found to be 4·3 m wide and 1·1 m high, roughly revetted with boulders on both faces; the rock-cut ditch of blunt V-section was 3 m wide and 1·2 m deep. The entrance was 4·6 m wide with a row of three post-holes in the middle of the passage, indicating a pair of gates closing on a central upright; on the S.E. side the rampart was thickened to 7·6 m. North-west of the entrance a rock-cut gully, following the curve of the rampart 3 m from its inner face and debouching into a rectangular pit at the edge of the roadway, was thought to be for the collection and storage of

HIGH PENNARD PROMONTORY FORT

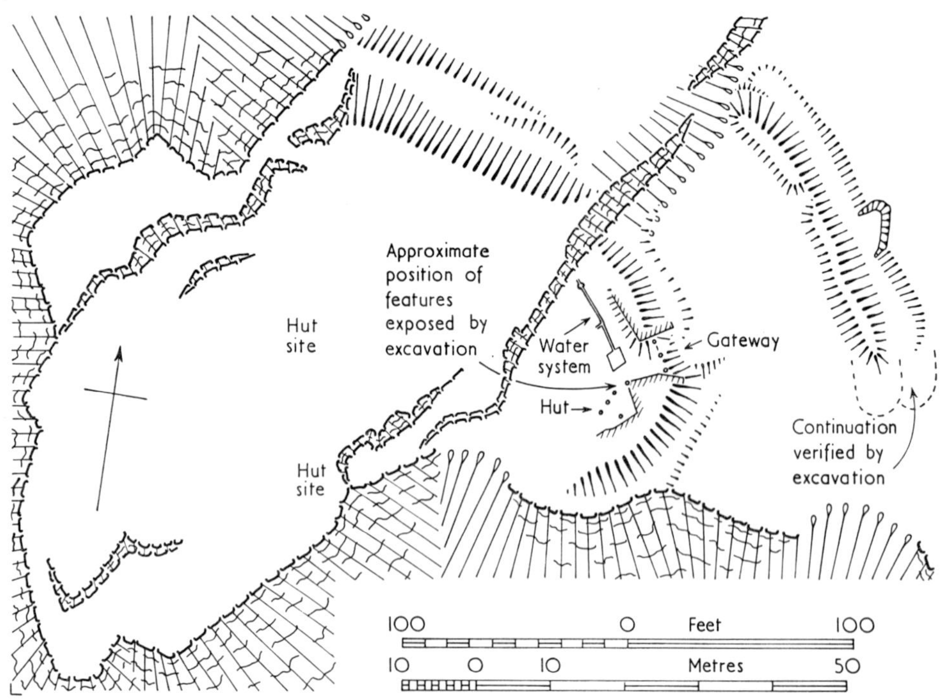

FIG. 41. No. 702.

surface water. In the W. portion of the fort, the main defensive scarp was found to have been surmounted by a stone rampart 3·4 m wide; at the foot of the scarp was a flat-bottomed rock-cut ditch 1·8 m wide and 0·9 m deep, with nearly vertical sides.

Three *huts* or occupation floors were discovered and excavated:

(i) Within the S.E. inturn of the entrance was a small triangular hut 4·6 m long, 3·7 m wide at the N. end and 1·8 m at the S. Its N. and E. walls were formed by the inner face of the rampart, its W. wall by a row of four posts. A fifth post-hole and a trench-like hearth occupied the middle of the hut floor.

(ii) At the S.W. end of the low cliff dividing the fort was an occupation layer 4 m by 3·7 m, with fragments of daub suggesting a wattle-and-daub framework grounded in fissures in the rock.

(iii) A hollow at the foot of an outcrop about the centre of the larger enclosure contained a similar floor about 4 m by 2·4 m.

Small finds included bones of ox, pig and sheep (or goat); shells of limpet, mussel, periwinkle, oyster and whelk; charcoal (ash, elm, hazel and oak); two slingstones; pot-boilers; fragments of clay daub; a piece of blue-green glass; a spindlewhorl of grey pottery; and a rim sherd of a *mortarium* of red ware, dated late 1st-2nd century A.D.

S 8c. *B.B.C.S.*, VIII, iv (May 1937), pp. 365–70; Rutter, *P. Gower*, p. 65; *Arch. Camb.*, XCVI (1941), pp. 23–30 (excavation report).

Pennard.

SS 58 N.E. (5677 8663) 20 x 65 XXXII N.W.

(703) REDLEY CLIFF. The site is densely overgrown, and its interpretation is therefore not completely certain. On a spur at about 45 m above O.D., projecting E. to Caswell Bay, two lines of defence about 45 m apart cut off the only easy approach, from the W. The outermost coincides with a modern field wall, built at the centre of a V-shaped ditch, which is distinguishable for a length of 20 m, with a width of 5·2 m and a depth of up to 2 m. The bank at its E. side is scarcely visible, but undoubtedly did exist. The inner defence has a similar ditch, the bank being better preserved and measuring up to 4·5 m wide and 0·6 m high. It can be traced for a distance of about 50 m across the promontory. At the S. end it continues over the brow of the slope to end at an outcrop. At the N. it ends at a crag forming a natural defence on the N.W. side of the area between the two banks.

The interior of the defended promontory is irregularly broken up by outcrops, but presents an inhabitable area of about 0·2 ha, measuring about 55 m E.–W. by 30 m, in which, however, no certain traces of huts can be made out. It is not certain whether the remaining perimeter of this area was defended by banks, since the whole hilltop is thickly overgrown with brambles and scrub; though the E. end would have been more or less impregnable without artificial defence, the N. and S. sides would have required some sort of fortification at the top of their steep slopes.

S 7c. *B.B.C.S.*, VIII, iv (May 1937), p. 365; Morgan, *E. Gower*, pp. 185–6; Rutter, *P. Gower*, p. 65.

Bishopston.
SS 58 N.E. (5880 8756) I x 59 XXXII N.W.

(704) SULLY ISLAND. The E. end of the island, rising to about 45 m above O.D. is defended by a succession of ramparts. There has been much erosion, particularly on the S., and the N. half is thickly overgrown; the present area of the main enclosure is about 0·4 ha, but it may originally have been twice as much.

The outermost rampart, on the W., now appears as a scarp about 1·5 m high with a slight external ditch; it runs N. to S. across the island which is here about 45 m wide. The cliff which forms the N. boundary of the enclosure ends just outside this defence. Fifteen metres further E. is the second bank, about 2·5 m high externally and nearly 1 m internally. It was accompanied by a ditch, now completely silted up but visible in the cliff face as 3·5 m wide and nearly 1 m deep, with rubble against its inner scarp from a fallen revetment; the overall width of this defence seems to have been about 7·5 or 9 m. The promontory continues at about the same width for another 80 m, and then contracts suddenly to about 25 m. This narrower projection is protected by a third rampart, appearing as a stony scarp nearly 2 m high with a slight ditch in front; there is a gap 3 m wide, perhaps an entrance, between its N. end and the cliff edge. The promontory continues for another 25 m, narrowing slightly and with a south-easterly inclination. At its end is a low mound, perhaps a barrow, about 4·5 m in diameter and nearly 1 m high (I i 401). It shows signs of disturbance at the centre.

S 2c.

Sully.
ST 16 N.E. (1685 6699) 26 x 66 LI N.W.

705–707. SMALL STONE-WALLED ENCLOSURES RESEMBLING CASHELS

(705) BURRY HOLMS CHURCH SITE. Beneath the visible medieval ruins, excavation[1] produced evidence for a small oval stone-walled enclosure, measuring 14 m by 15 m, enclosing 0·02 ha. The walls were of sand or turf filling between two lines of orthostats and varied from 1·2 m to 2·1 m in thickness. There was an entrance 1·2 m wide in the S. side. Near the centre of the enclosure four corner post-holes indicated an early church, about 3·7 m long and 3·3 m wide.

The remaining structures are all 12th-century or later and will be described in detail in subsequent sections. In brief, the timber church was succeeded, probably in the 11th or 12th century, by a stone church with an apse; this stood in a slightly larger cashel, built over the ruins of the earlier. Later, in the 14th century, the apse was replaced by a square-ended chancel. To the S., the remains of the associated dwelling are visible, consisting of a large 13th–14th-century hall 10 m by 5 m. To the W. of this a late medieval wall was found to be built over an earlier enclosure, connected with the church cashel, which contained the remains of a small wooden hut about 2·5 m in diameter and was clearly the site of earlier medieval dwellings. To the N. of the church another small building, with stepped seats at the W. end, was probably a school-room. The ruin N.E. of this, close to the cliff edge, is post-Reformation in date.

[1] During 1965–9 by D. B. Hague on behalf of the Commission. *Gower*, XVII (1966); *Arch. in Wales*, IX (1969), No. 52 (interim reports).

Llangennith.
SS 49 S.W. (4009 9258) 1965–7 XXI S.W.

(706) BLUEPOOL BAY. Near the N. coast about 1 km from Burry Holms, in two adjacent slacks scooped out by wind from the sand-dunes, here about 30 m above O.D., curved segments of wall are exposed. These are apparently part of an enclosure about 30 m in diameter, the centre of which remains buried; the area enclosed was about 0·07 ha. The wall is about 1·5 m thick, of rubble faced with medium-sized stones; it stands on the old ground surface and survives to a height of 0·8 m. The small amount of debris suggests that its original height did not much exceed a metre. A gap on the S., about 6 m wide, may have been an entrance. To E. of this the wall is separated by a berm 2 m wide from a ditch with a counterscarp bank which together measure about 5 m wide by 0·6 m high overall. A line of rubble, apparently a very ruinous wall, starts 15 m S. of the entrance and is exposed for 12 m to the S.E. A small trench has located a layer of cockle and mussel shells adjacent to this, and shells and burnt stones occur both within and near the enclosure.

Gower, XIV (1961), p. 14 (plan).

Llangennith.
SS 49 S.W. (4078 9288) 2 viii 65 XXI S.E.

(707) RHOSILI DOWN. On open ground falling gently to the E. at 120 m above O.D. is a roughly circular enclosure, 14 m in diameter, surrounded by a ruined wall originally 1·5 m thick but now forming a bank of stones and earth 2·5 m to 3·5 m wide. Its external height is 0·3 m, internal height almost 0·6 m; large facing slabs are visible in places on both sides of the wall. On the S. is an entrance 2 m wide. The area enclosed was about 0·02 ha.

Abutting on the E. and S.W. sides of the enclosure is a ruined stone wall, apparently the remains of the boundary wall of a large circular paddock lying to the S.E. of the enclosure. Its E. branch is visible for only a short distance before fading, but on the S.W. it can be traced in a wide curve for about 60 m.

Rhosili.
SS 48 N.W. (4228 8980) 6 vi 66 XXI S.E.

708–709. UNCLASSIFIED SITES, POSSIBLY DEFENSIVE

(708) BANK N.W. of CWM BACH, 2·5 km S. of St. Brides

Major. On the cliff edge there survives a short length of bank now 25 m long and 0·6 m high, with a shallow ditch 4·3 m wide and on the landward side. Too little remains to indicate its age or purpose; it seems too slight to be defensive.

St. Brides Major and Wick (E), St. Brides Major (C).
SS 87 S.E. (8958 7197) 15 ii 61 XLIV S.E.

(709) WHITMORE STAIRS, about 3·5 km S. of St. Brides Major. Only the E. corner remains of an enclosure of rectilinear outline, which has mostly been eroded by the sea. The N.E. and S.E. arms of the right-angle are about 200 m and 45 m long respectively, and consist of a bank with external ditch varying between 9 m and 17 m in overall width and between 1 m and 2 m in overall height where fully preserved at the cliff edge at the N. and S. extremities. In between, the ditch has been filled, and only a bank is visible, averaging 9 m in width and 0·5 m in height.

Faint traces of a bank continuing the alignment of the S.E. side north-eastwards, and of another parallel to it 230 m to the S.S.E., at SS 9005 7126, together with a third between these, only visible on air photographs,[1] formed part of an early agricultural system, perhaps associated with the promontory fort at Cwm Bach (631), 90 m further N.W. along the cliff. The banks forming the right angle, however, seem exceptionally strong for field-boundaries, and the enclosure may have been defensive.

A bank with a ditch at the W., of generally similar proportions, and with an additional outer bank 0·2 m high, runs along the W. edge of a patch of scrub S.E. of those described above, from SS 9018 7120 to SS 9028 7090, with remains of an entrance roadway running E. between slighter banks at SS 9021 7100. It may be of later date, since it ends on the S. at the boundary dyke, Clawdd y Mynach, which is almost certainly medieval.

S 6c. *Arch. Camb.*, LXXXVIII (1933), p. 341, No. R 59.
[1] CPE/UK 1871, 4/12/46, 2058–9.

St. Brides Major and Wick (E), St. Brides Major (C).
SS 87 S.E. (8988 7145) 15 ii 61 XLIV S.E.

Place-names including 'gaer'

There are three sites where the word 'gaer' almost certainly implies the former existence of a fort of some kind, but where nothing has been identified by examination of the ground.

(i) HEN-GAER about 2 km S.W. of Seven Sisters (Farm name). An aerial photograph (542/621, 12/10/51, 4060) suggests a vague oval about 110 m N. to S. by 90 m. just N.E. of the farm. The position seems unlikely for a normal hill-fort. SN 80 N.W. (8025 0815) IX N.E.

(ii) BRYN-Y-GAER (Farm name). Just S.W. of the ruined farm, about a kilometre N.W. of Hirwaun, a well-marked hillock rises to 220 m above O.D., about 20 m above the marshy surroundings. It would form an excellent position for a small fort, but though now under grass the ground has been cultivated and enclosed. SN 90 N.W. (9444 0645) XI N.W.

(iii) MYNYDD RUTHIN, 2 km S.E. of Pen-coed. The O.S. maps record a 'camp', and an adjacent farm is named Pen-y-gaer, but the only banks now visible seem to be the result of old quarrying activities. SS 97 N.E. (9710 7960) XLI N.W.

Omitted Sites

These have been suggested as defended sites, but their authenticity is very doubtful.

(i) KINGSLAND, 1·5 km S. of St. Hilary. A large oval enclosure on a hill-top is formed by field-banks which have been partly ploughed out since the Tithe Award survey. ST 07 S.W. (0220 7190) XLV S.E.

(ii) KENNEL GROVE, about 3 km N.E. of Ystradowen. A line of overgrown quarry-pits suggests on some aerial photographs the presence of a ploughed-out hill-fort. (C.U.A.P., No. ABZ 43). ST 07 N.W. (0395 7900) XLII N.W.

(iii) CAERGWNAF, 1 km S. of Miskin. This enclosure, shown as an antiquity on some O.S. maps, seems to be a recent landscape-feature associated with the layout of Hensol Park. ST 08 S.W. (0475 8004) XLII N.W.

(iv) PEN-MARC. The large oval field N.W. of the village is scarped round its edge, but this seems to be the result of its use as a cultivated field. ST 06 N.E. (0550 6890) L N.W.

(v) SWELDON, about 1 km N.N.E. from Wenvoe. The O.S. marks a 'fort' here. It is possible that the banks shown are ancient, but it seems much more likely that they are merely field-boundaries. The site is much overgrown. ST 17 N.W. (1278 7502) XLVII N.W.

(vi) PENCOEDTRE, BARRY. 'Banks and ditches suggesting a possible hill-fort' are said to have been observed at the grid-reference cited (*Arch. in Wales*, V (1965), no. 13). The position indicated lies on enclosed pasture with no trace of earthworks other than field-banks. Search at likely sites in Pencoedtre Wood (127 706) revealed no earthworks, but the undergrowth is very thick. There is a substantial modern bank in a plantation N. of the main road (120 705). ST 17 S.W. (121 702) XLVI S.E.

UNENCLOSED HUT SETTLEMENTS

IN contrast to the numerous hill-forts, unenclosed hut-settlements are rare in Glamorgan. On the uncultivated mountain pastures those now known are probably most, if not all, of those which ever existed. In the Vale of Glamorgan traces of what may have been an undefended dwelling were found beneath the Roman villa at Moulton (759), and others have probably been destroyed,[1] but no example has been revealed by aerial photography, nor have any survived on the downs or common lands. These are fairly extensive and have mostly never been tilled, so open settlements were probably relatively uncommon in the Vale also. On Ogmore Down much of what is now moorland is covered by abandoned fields, outlined by low banks and lynchets; but as these seem generally to continue the pattern of existing field boundaries, they can be regarded as probably medieval or later.

Platforms closely resembling hut emplacements were also made in large numbers during the early modern period. These carried hearths for charcoal-burning to provide fuel for iron-working, and the dust and fragments left on the platform make identification certain if the ground is disturbed. Known charcoal-hearths are not associated with enclosures and show a characteristic choice of position, in groups on the flanks of valleys, and in this region no certain hut-platforms have been found located in that way; but some genuine hut-sites may have been wrongly interpreted as hearths, and omitted from the Inventory. The risk is rather greater when dealing with isolated platforms, and some which are probably but not certainly hearths are therefore listed, without monument numbers.

Charcoal-burning platforms show no trace of walling. There are also some stone rings which superficially resemble huts but which seem more likely to be sepulchral or religious structures of the Bronze Age, and have therefore been classed as such. That at Graig Fawr near Pontarddulais (I i 57) requires mention here, for it could be regarded as a hut within a heavily robbed enclosure wall. The enclosure is almost perfectly circular, which is unusual for a dwelling site, and there is no modern work anywhere near which could account for the removal of stone; the 'hut' has no entrance. A ritual function seems therefore to be more probable than domestic use.

When all these structures have been eliminated, seven fairly certain hut-settlements remain (Fig. 1). One of these is the compact group of four or five dwellings superimposed on the ruins of the small fortified enclosure at Mynydd Bychan (681). This is the only surviving example in the Vale. It dates from the latter half of the 1st century A.D.

The Ring W. of Southerndown (SS 8777 7378, I iii 1002), if not a natural feature, may have been an enclosure containing huts, but its almost accurately circular plan (diameter 65 m) seems more in keeping with a ritual function.

The remainder lie in the uplands. All except that at Buarth Maen (715) are directly accessible along the ridges which fan out from Mynydd Beili-glas, about a kilometre S.E. of Llyn Fawr, and one of the largest, at Garreg Lwyd (711) is less than 2 kilometres from the lake; but there seems to be no other reason to associate these huts with the fine metal-work found there (p. 5). The walls and huts are for the most part poorly built, and excavations at the Garreg Lwyd group yielded nothing except a little iron and leather. Fieldwork in preparation for the Inventory for Brecknock has shown that similar groups occur there, so no reliable conclusions can be based on their distribution in Glamorgan only.

Characteristically these groups consist of irregular rounded enclosures, sometimes incomplete, associated with round huts. The enclosures may be anything from 10 or 20 m across up to 50 or 60 m, or sometimes more. The huts seldom exceed 6 m in diameter, and are often smaller. They may be free-standing, or incorporated in the lines of the enclosure walls. There is no regularity in the arrangement of any of the settlements.

---

[1] During 1940 evidence for a hut was found in the garden of Milva, Caswell Road, Newton, at SS 6018 8793. Five post-holes were located (out of seven or eight), in a ring of 2·5 or 3 m diameter, with rough, worn paving and a hearth just outside the ring. A saddle quern and a pounding stone lay on the floor. *Ex. inf.* L. E. Latchford, 19 iv 71.

As a group, they show some general resemblance to the 'Upland type of Huts associated with Enclosures' found in Caernarvonshire,[2] but so far as present investigation indicates the Brecknock–Glamorgan sites are smaller in extent, with fewer huts and few associated cairns, if any. The huts in these southern groups tend to be rather larger, and the masonry as a whole to be of better quality, though still very poor. In particular, the enclosing walls are built, and still display facing in some places, whereas those in Caernarvonshire could be accounted for merely as the incidental result of moving stones to the edge of a cleared area. There is no sign of lynchet formation at any of the Glamorgan sites.

All the remains have been affected to some extent by partial rebuilding for sheepfolds or small shelters. The two largest, at Garreg Lwyd (711) and Buarth Maen (715), have not been much altered. At Mynydd Cefnygyngon (714), which also seems to have been fairly large, only excavation could determine how many of the huts scattered near are likely to be contemporary with the enclosure in origin. The two small settlements at Padell y Bwlch (712) and Tarren y Bwlch (713) are less typical, and may not be of the same kind.

Hen Dre'r Gelli (716) is the only upland settlement which has produced evidence for date; the associated pottery was of the 2nd or 3rd centuries A.D. Its situation is similar to that of other upland groups, but whether it resembled them otherwise must remain uncertain, as the ground seems to have been cleared of stone.

[2] Class II(a), *Caerns. Inv.*, III, p. xcii.

(711) HUTS AND ENCLOSURES above Garreg Lwyd, overlooking the head of the Rhondda Fawr (Fig. 42, Plate 12) on unenclosed grassland with much outcrop and loose stone, at about 460 m above O.D. The ground falls fairly steeply to the cliff Garreg Lwyd which is about 180 m south of the site. The remains consist of two groups of irregular enclosures, associated with round huts most of which are between 2·5 m and 3·5 m in diameter. The larger (E.) group includes about 12 or 13 round huts, as well as two pairs of roughly rectangular enclosures whose character and age is uncertain. The walls, where best preserved, stand about a metre high and are about 1·2 m thick, of rubble faced partly with laid stones and partly with orthostats. Excavations in 1921 by the Rhondda Naturalists' Society found leather, iron and iron slag.[1]

Below Garreg Lwyd, 300 yds. S. of the larger group (SN 9224 0168) are some modern sheepfolds which may have been built over small ancient enclosures. The walls and enclosures close to the stream seem to be wholly recent.

[1] *B.B.C.S.*, I, i (Nov. 1921), p. 70. No full report has been published.

Ystradyfodwg (E), Rhondda (C).
SN 90 S.W. (9225 0187) 4 x 60 X S.E.

(712) HUTS AND ENCLOSURES, Padell y Bwlch (Fig. 43) at about 440 m above O.D. and 2 km S. of Hirwaun. The remains lie at the foot of a scree facing N.E. below the high cliff of Craig y Bwlch, on well drained ground at the top of a marshy slope. The walls are roughly built, those of the enclosures being mainly formed by a rough alignment of large blocks of stone, with rubble filling, while those of the huts contain smaller blocks showing some coursing. The material was evidently obtained in the clearance of the enclosed ground at the foot of the scree, which forms the S.W. boundary of the group. The whole is much ruined, and has been adapted in places to provide shelter for sheep. The enclosures resemble others of this group, but in view of the absence of round huts it is possible that they are more recent.

On a ridge of dry ground running N. into the marshy area, 204 m at 5° from the N.W. end of the group, are two poorly preserved huts, each measuring about 3·7 m square, having one common side, and their longer common axis at 50°. 30 m further to the N.E., on the same alignment, is the very ruined foundation of a rectangular building measuring 10·7 m long by 2·7 m.

At the foot of the scree 22 m at 307° beyond the N.W. end of the main group are the possible remains of a rectangular hut about 7·3 m long at 303° by 2·4 m. The S.W. side of the hut continues as a rough wall for 32 metres to the N.W.

Ystradyfodwg (E), Rhigos (C).
SN 90 S.W. (9445 0355) 11 x 60 XI S.W.

(713) HUTS, below Tarren y Bwlch, at *ca.* 460 m above O.D. on a steep north-facing slope, about 600 m E. of 712. Four huts lie on small shelves in very broken ground.

(i) Subrectangular with rounded ends, 5 m long at 166° by 3·3 m wide, slightly terraced into the hillside. The walls are of laid slabs, 1 m wide and half a metre high in places.

(ii) 20 m at 236° from (i), with (iii) adjacent at 301°. (iii) is

HUTS ABOVE GARREG LWYD
280ft
280ft
Modern track
Wall face (laid or orthostatic)
Inferred wall faces
Wall without face
Very slight wall
100
0
Feet
100
10
0
10
Metres
50

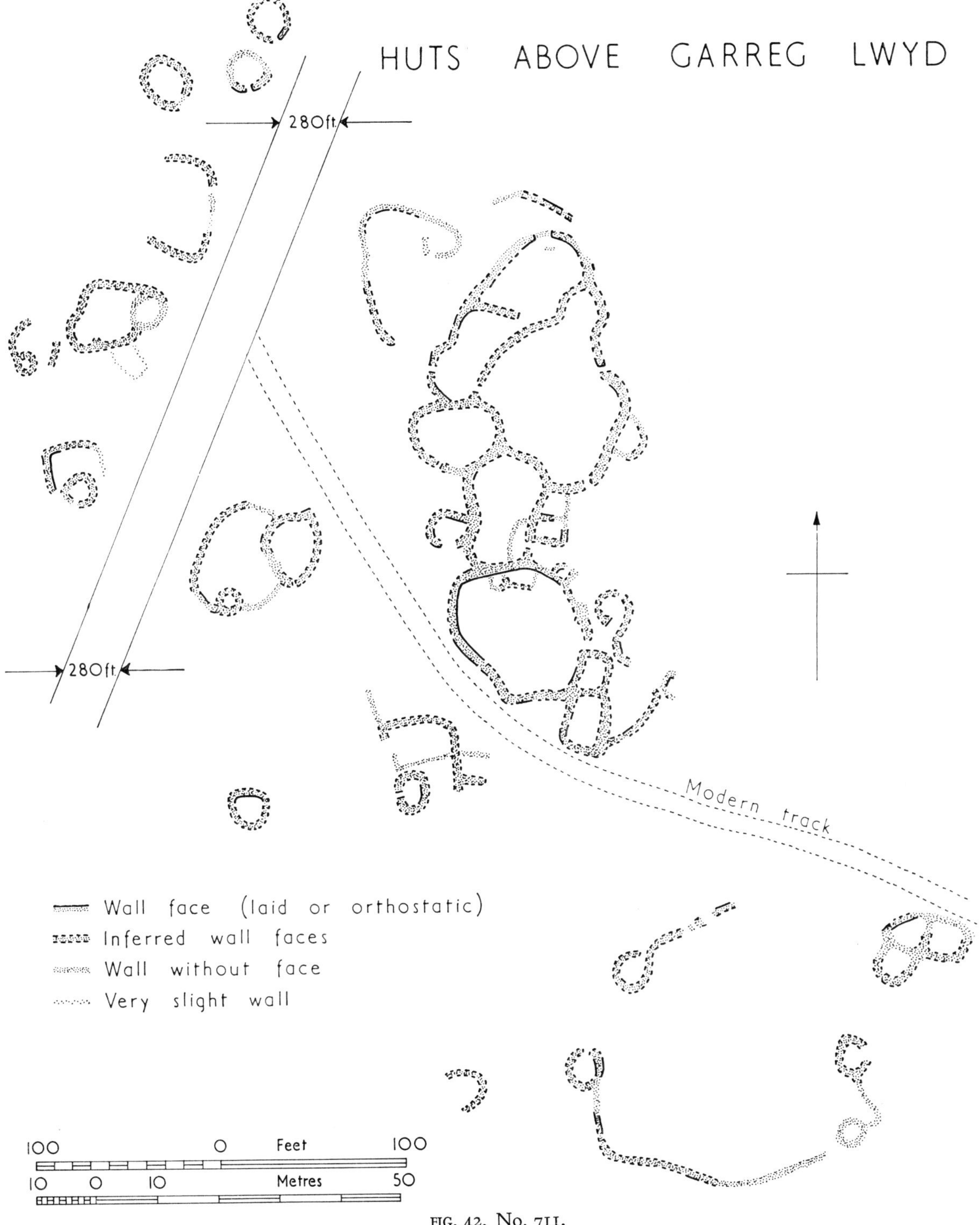

FIG. 42. No. 711.

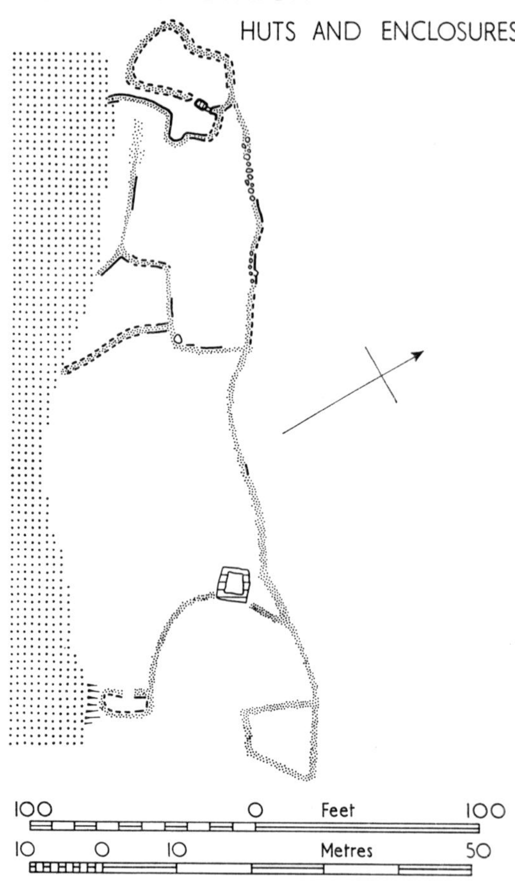

FIG. 43. No. 712.

the main structure, oval, 3·3 m wide, and 2·7 m long on the common axis; (ii) is built against it, being 3·7 m long by 3 m wide. The walls, of laid slabs, are much dilapidated.

(iv) 42 m at 216° from (ii). Subrectangular, 4·3 m long at 216° by 3·3 m wide; walls of angular rocks, about 1 m wide and up to half a metre high.

Aberdâr.

SN 90 S.E. (9511 0351) 11 x 60 XI S.W.

(714) HUTS AND ENCLOSURES, Mynydd Cefnygyngon, 2 km S. of Hirwaun (Fig. 44, Plate 12). The site lies between 400 and 430 m above O.D., on ground falling to the S.E. Ffynnon Rhiw-galch, the source of Nant Melyn, rises about 200 m to the S. The earliest remains resemble those at Buarth Maen (715), but seem never to have been so extensive, and apart from the main enclosure and the associated round hut (i) they are in poor condition. Later structures have obscured the original arrangement.

Where best preserved, the wall of the main enclosure is now a bank of piled stone, 3 m thick and up to 0·5 m high. The position of the entrance is uncertain, but was probably at the N. end. The hut lies at the S. end of the enclosure, on the line of the wall, which abuts against that of the hut. It is 3·7 m in diameter, with a wall over 2 m thick, and has an entrance 0·6 m wide opening to the W., outside the enclosure.

From the S. side of the hut, after a gap, another rubble bank about 3 m wide curves round south and then eastwards. Traces of other walls projecting from the east side of the main enclosure probably joined up with this, but have been robbed to build the modern fold. Only these enclosures and the hut can be confidently accepted as early.

Twenty metres S. of the fold a quadrilateral enclosure lies across the line of the annexe wall, which it has destroyed. Inside this enclosure, built out from the middle of its E. side, is an oblong hut, nearly 3 m E. to W. by 2 m. The hut walls are about 0·8 m thick, those of the enclosure 1·2 m, with facing exposed in places to a height of 0·5 m. This enclosure and hut are probably medieval or later.

The remaining structures are scattered at random to E. and N. of the main enclosure. They are ill-defined and ruinous, and most seem to have been re-used, or perhaps even built, as shepherds' shelters. Some may have been *hafotai*. Others, which are round, may have been contemporary with the early enclosures. Several are unusually small for early huts, and may have been no more than lambing pens.

These are listed below with brief descriptions. Unless otherwise noted all walls are about a metre thick, of thin laid slabs, and survive to a height of about 0·3 m or less. The small slabs set upright near the centres of (ii), (iv) and (ix) do not seem to have been burnt; they may have been packing for a central post.

(ii) Round, 4 to 5·5 m diameter, with small upright slabs near centre. Entrance 1·5 m wide on E.S.E.

(iii) Oblong, 4 m N.–S. by 2 m. Ill-defined entrance on E.

(iv) Oblong, 4·5 m N.N.W.–S.S.E., 2·5 m wide at the N. end narrowing to 2 m. Setting of small upright slabs near centre. Entrance in S. end wall. Wall 0·6 m high in places.

(v) Oblong, 6·5 m N.–S. by 2·5 m.

(vi) Oblong, 4·5 m E.N.E.–W.S.W. by 3 m.

(vii) Round, 2 m diameter. Ill-defined entrance to W.N.W.

(viii) Round, 3·5 m diameter. Entrance to S.E.

(ix) Oblong, 4.5 m E.N.E.–W.S.W. by 3·7 m, destroyed on S.E. Small upright slab near centre.

(x) Enclosure roughly 7·5 m square. The S.E. side is almost destroyed.

(xi) Waterhole (?) about 3 m square, with revetted sides on W. and N.

(xii) Oblong, 3·5 m N.N.W.–S.S.E. by 2 m. Ill-defined entrance to S.S.E.

(xiii) Round, 3 m diameter. Entrance to W.S.W.

(xiv) Round, 2·7 m diameter.

(xv) Oval, 4·3 m N.–S. by 3·7 m. Ill-defined entrance on S.

(xvi) Oval, 3 m N.–S. by 2·5 m. Entrance on S.

(xvii) Ring, on a small knoll, nearly 2 m diameter with wall 1 m thick. No entrance visible. Purpose uncertain.

Aberdâr.

SN 90 S.E. (9573 0340) 1971 XI S.W.

MYNYDD
CEFNYGYNGON
XIII.
XIV.
XV.
XVI.
Ring
XVII.
X.
XI.
XII.
VIII.
IX.
I.
II.
III.
IV.
V.
VII.
VI.
100 0 100 Feet 1000
100 0 Metres 100

Mod. fold
Hut
100 0 Feet 200
10 0 10 Metres 100

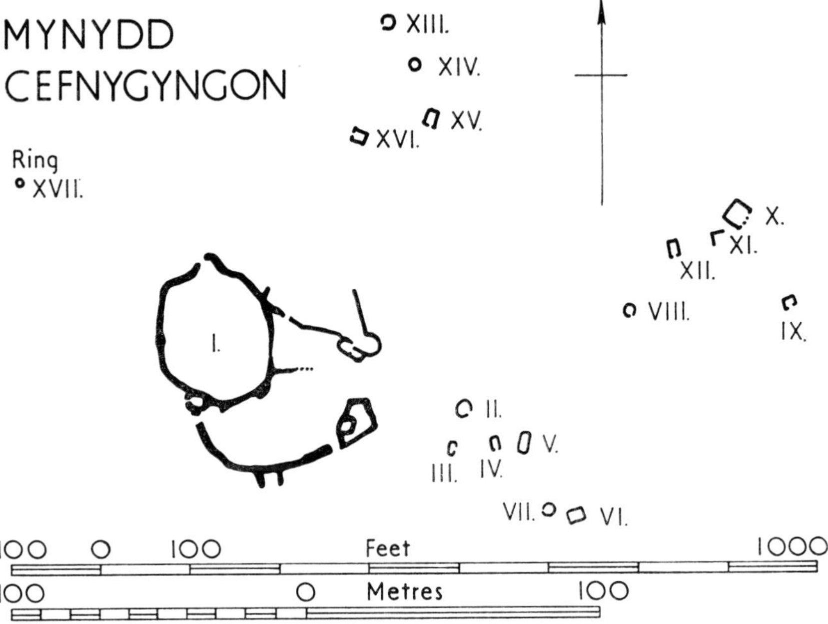

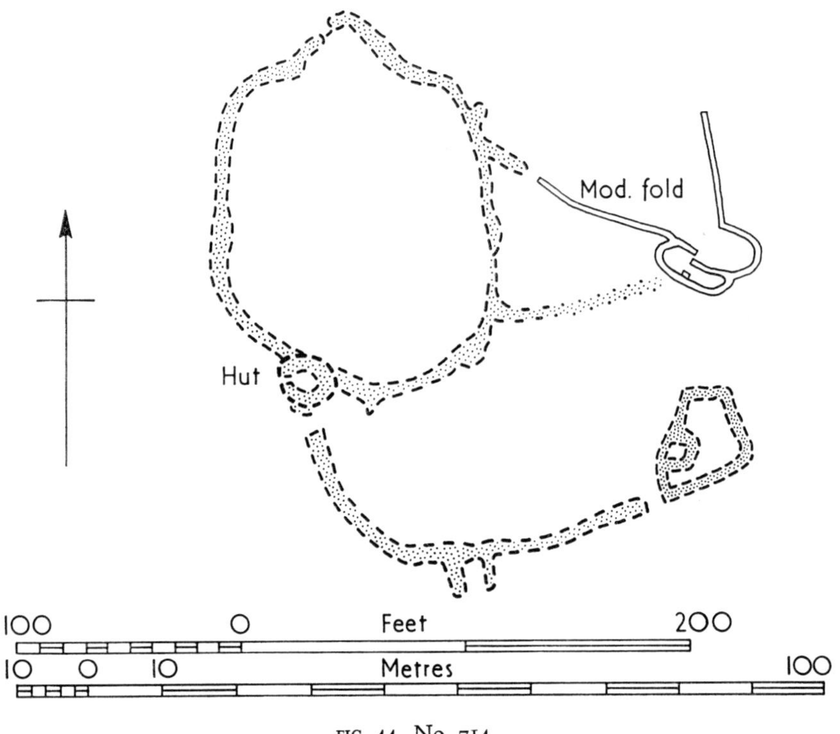

FIG. 44. No. 714.

(715) HUTS AND ENCLOSURES, Buarth Maen (Fig. 45, Plate 10) at about 400 m above O.D. on a shelf sloping gently towards the S. On the S.W. the ground falls away steeply towards the Afon Cynon, and on the N.E. it rises less abruptly towards the ridge of Mynydd Aberdâr. The site lies on unenclosed grassland, with large areas of outcrop, scree, and loose rock.

The remains, which are generally undisturbed, comprise three main enclosures, not all complete, and some short subsidiary lengths of walling, as well as some round huts and a few mounds of stone. The enclosure walls are mostly ruinous but where best preserved stand about 0·6 m high and 1·2 m to 1·8 m wide, of rubble faced with laid stones; the hut walls are similar but seldom remain as much as 0·3 m high. The huts range from about 2·5 m up to about 6 m in diameter.

The N. enclosure is incomplete and its walls are slight and very ruinous. The two huts to the E. are also in very poor condition; they seem to be oblong. On the W., the enclosure is bounded by a steep rocky slope which has been partly quarried, and on a shelf below this are two rocky mounds about a metre high and 3·7 m in diameter, and a third which is roughly rectangular, about 4 m by 2·4 m by 0·6 m high. These mounds are perhaps to be associated with the quarrying rather than with the earlier remains.

The central enclosure and associated huts are fairly well preserved at its W. end, but little facing remains and towards the E. the walls become very slight.

The S. enclosure is well preserved, particularly on the N.E. where part of the wall-face is still visible to a height of nearly a metre; the gaps in the E. and W. sides seem to be original. The associated huts are also mostly in good condition. Outside the enclosure to the W. is a cairn 8 m in diameter and nearly a metre high, probably ancient; to the E., two small mounds seem likely to be clearance-dumps.

Aberdâr.
SO 00 N.W. (0126 0530) 9 x 60 XI N.E.

(716) HEN DRE'R GELLI. This site stands at about 350 m above O.D., about a kilometre S. of Ystrad, on a spur projecting E. from Mynydd Bwllfa. The name is that given by J. Griffith who excavated here in 1903–6 on behalf of the Rhondda Naturalists' Society. His report[1] is obscure, and the excavations have been refilled but the principal features can still be identified.

He appears to have discovered the remains of a round house, just over 10 m in diameter with a wall 1·3 to 1·7 m thick, of laid slabs. There was an entrance on the S., and a crescentic annexe about 2·5 m wide outside the wall on the N. This seems now to be represented by a small cairn about 4 m in diameter and 0·5 m high, at 9766 9402. No pottery was found.

Eighty metres N.N.E. from this, in about the position indicated by J. Griffith, is a low bank nearly 2 m wide; two straight sections, 9 m at 46° and 22 m at 153°, meet in an angle at 9769 9409. The excavator found that this bank concealed the foundations of a massive wall. Within the angle 'six yards' from the W. wall, a round hut was cleared (diameter not given). Pottery was found on its floor, and within it, cut to a depth of 0·3 m, was a trench 2·3 m long by 0·6 m wide, the edges formed by upright slabs. More pottery was discovered in other excavations nearby. Some of the small cairns (I i p. 120, Rvi) were also examined, and are said to have covered hut-foundations.

The pottery found is now in the National Museum of Wales. It is coarse grey Romano-British ware, of 2nd- or 3rd-century date.

Two cairns (I i 368–9) stand a short distance to the W., and a beaker was found nearby (I i p. 97a).

[1] *Arch. Camb.*, 1906, pp. 293–302.

Ystradyfodwg (E), Rhondda (C).
SS 99 S.E. (9766 9402) 21 iv 67 XXVII N.W.

Omitted Sites

The following rings and platforms are almost certainly the results of fairly recent minor industrial activity, but there is a very slight possibility that some may be early huts. They are therefore listed for completeness. Those at Meiros may have been for burning lime, the others were probably charcoal-burning platforms.

(i) MOEL TROED-Y-RHIW, N. of Llangynwyd. Two oval terraced platforms on the N.E. slopes at 180 m above O.D. (a) at 8602 8945, nearly 10 m in diameter, with a very slight raised rim round most of its circumference. (b) at 8609 8938, 7·3 m N.E. to S.W. by 8·5 m, with no rim. There are traces of other smaller platforms in the same field, but they are now much ploughed down. SS 88 N.E. XXVI S.W.

(ii) MEIROS, N.E. of Llanharan. Two rings, close to the farmhouse, at 150 m above O.D., on a level rounded summit in enclosed land. (a) at ST 0069 8360, is 7·3 m in diameter, defined by a low grass-grown bank about 3 m wide and half a metre high; this is absent for about 6 m on the N. (b) 26 m to N., is similar, but only 3 m in diameter. ST 08 S.W. (0069 8360) XXXV S.E.

(iii) EAST OF TŶ-MAWR, about 1·5 km S.E. of Llantwit Fardre. A levelled platform nearly 5 m in diameter on ground falling slightly to N.W. towards a small stream. ST 08 S.E. (0886 8393) XXXVI S.E.

(iv) CRAIG YR EFAIL. Round platfoım at *ca.* 330 m above O.D. on the ridge between the Taf and Cynon valleys, in ground sharply falling to the E.S.E. A level space 5·5 m in diameter has been made by terracing out material excavated from above. The site measures about 9 m in diameter overall. There are no traces of superstructure, so that this may be an isolated charcoal-burning platform. ST 09 N.E. (0746 9751) XIX S.W.

BUARTH MAEN
Faced walling
Wall faces inferred
Wall without facing
Slight wall
Modern walling
Mound
Scree
100
0
Feet
100
10
0
10
Metres
50
Continues for 120 ft.
Continues for 100 ft.

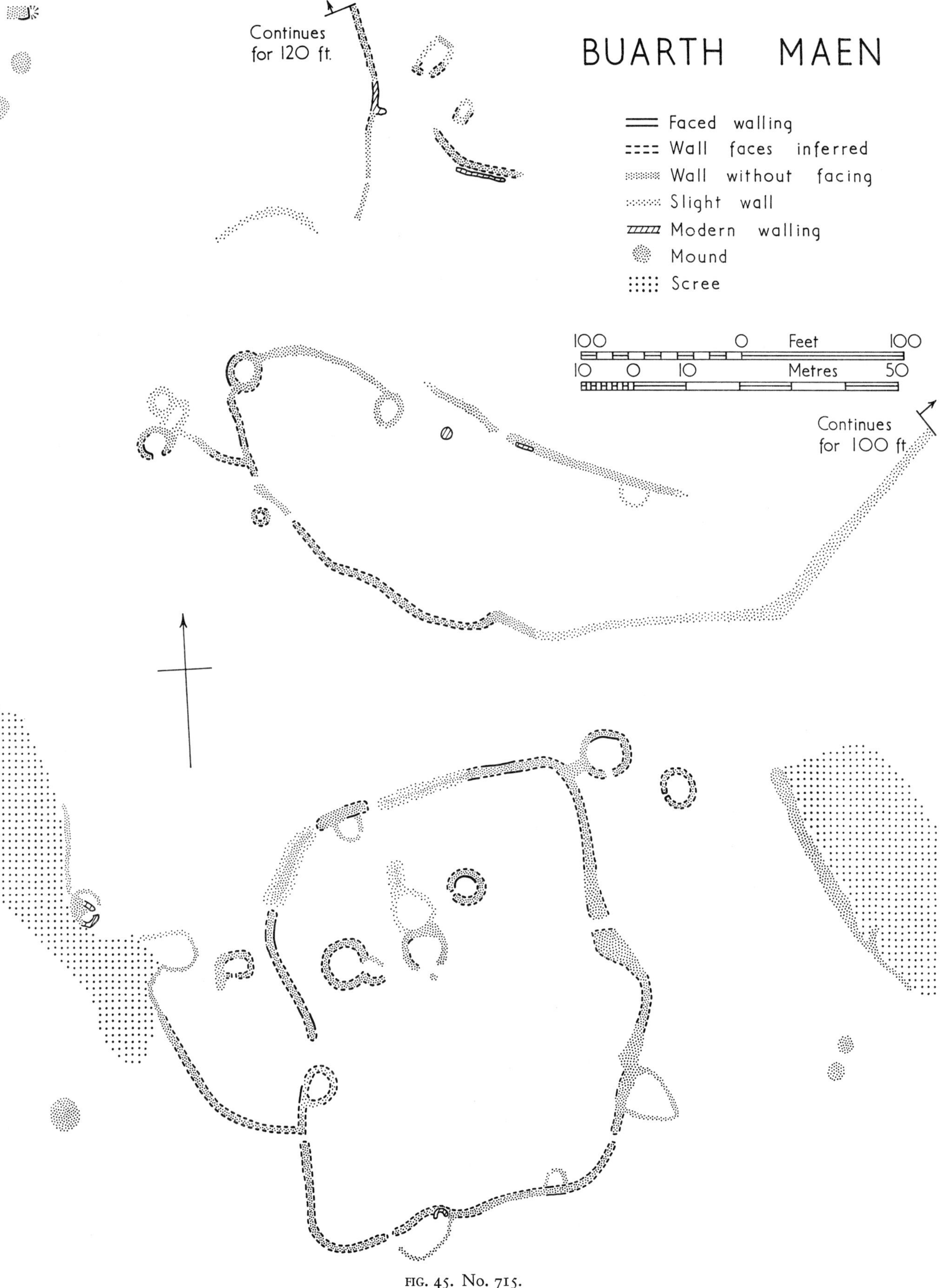

FIG. 45. No. 715.

ROMAN REMAINS

THE distribution of Roman sites in Glamorgan (Fig. 46) can only be studied satisfactorily against a much wider background; the irrelevance of the arbitrary boundary of a modern county becomes particularly obvious in dealing with this period. Even names such as Glamorgan, England or Wales, are anachronisms, since they relate to administrative systems which did not develop until many centuries later, but it is convenient to retain them purely as geographical terms.

The body of published material dealing with the history and archaeology of Roman Britain is considerable, and there is general agreement over the main points, though recent work has led to some modifications of older views. The principal sources on which this account is based are therefore listed in a bibliographical note,[1] and individual references are not generally given to the particular items.

At the time of the Roman invasion, the area was inhabited by the Silures; their territory seems to have covered Glamorgan and Monmouthshire, and probably extended some distance outside those counties. They were a warlike tribe who gave the Romans considerable trouble and withstood a long period of warfare before finally capitulating. After the Roman conquest of what is now southern England in the years following A.D. 43, they provided a refuge and base of operations for the principal British leader, Caratacus. It was probably at his instigation that they made their first recorded attack on the Romans in 49, during the governorship of Ostorius Scapula. As a result of this the Twentieth Legion was moved up from Colchester and established at Gloucester on the Severn. Caratacus then transferred his operations to the territory of the Ordovices in mid-Wales. In 51 he was defeated in battle and later handed over to the Romans by Cartimandua with whom he had sought refuge. The battle was followed by prolonged but indecisive warfare against the Silures, who succeeded in inflicting heavy casualties on the Romans.

In 52 Scapula died and was succeeded by Didius Gallus. He arrived in Britain to find that the Silures had defeated a legion and were raiding over a wide area. He managed to contain them but after 54 took no further action against them, probably on the Emperor Nero's instructions. His successor, Quintus Veranius (57–8), seems fairly certainly to have renewed the Roman offensive against the Silures, though no details are known. The first campaign by the next governor, Suetonius Paulinus, in 58 was also probably against the tribe, and seems sufficiently to have subdued them to enable him to transfer his attentions to northern Wales in 59–60. After that the Boudiccan rebellion and the reduction of Brigantia kept the Romans occupied for sixteen years, and it was not until the governorship of Julius Frontinus (74–8) that the attack on Wales was resumed. Tacitus, in a single sentence, records that he overcame the Silures, surmounting

[1] The conquest of Wales was recorded by Tacitus in *Annals*, XII, 31–40; XIV, 29–39; *Agricola*, 14–17. For modern accounts, see *Roman Frontier* ch. I; Frere, *Britannia*, ch. 5; M. G. Jarrett, 'Early Roman Campaigns in Wales', *Arch. Journ.*, CXXI (1964), pp. 23–39. On the Second Legion and the establishment of Caerleon, see G. C. Boon and C. Williams, *Plan of Caerleon* (N.M.W., 1967); M. G. Jarrett, 'Legio II Augusta in Britain', *Arch. Camb.*, CXIII (1964), pp. 47–63. For older summaries of military history, see F. Haverfield, 'Military Aspects', pp. 55–187; R. E. M. Wheeler, 'Segontium and the Roman Occupation of Wales', *Y Cymmrodor*, XXXIII (1924); Wheeler, *P. & R. Wales*, ch. VII. For more recent accounts of the military history of Roman Britain, see I. A. Richmond, *Roman Britain* (London, 1955), ch. I; Frere, *Britannia*, chs. 6–9, 16–17; and for Wales in particular, see M. G. Jarrett, 'The Military Occupation of Roman Wales', *B.B.C.S.*, XX, ii (May 1963), pp. 206–20; *Roman Frontier*, ch. III. For a survey including a detailed account of modern dating of Samian ware, see Simpson, *Britons*. For roads, see Margary, *Roman Roads*, ch. 8.

not only their valour but the physical difficulties of their land. The marching camps in Glamorgan (738–741), and those further north in Brecknock and Carmarthenshire (Ystradfellte, Y Pigwn, Arosfa Garreg) are probably memorials of his campaigns, though some could date from earlier wars. That near Neath (739) is very large, and could have accommodated three legions.

Archaeological evidence is sufficient to attest the importance of Frontinus' work in southern Wales. It led to the establishment of a network of auxiliary forts linked by roads and based on the legionary fortress of *Isca* at Caerleon-on-Usk near Newport. The Glamorgan forts were probably all founded at this time; the evidence is definite for Penydarren (732) and Neath (734). Although the exact position of *Bomium* (p. 121) is not certain, there is no doubt that it was somewhere roughly midway on the road between Cardiff and Neath, where a fort would seem strategically desirable, so it may well belong to the same system.

The arrangements made by Frontinus continued apparently unaltered for a full generation, but during the early part of the 2nd century several of the forts were abandoned. It used to be held that the military frontier in Wales was reorganised and stabilised under Trajan (98–117), that the garrisons of the forts were drastically reduced to help in the building of Hadrian's Wall (122–8), and that the forts were virtually abandoned at the time of the construction of the Antonine Wall (*ca.* 142). Some were later reoccupied in strength under Septimius Severus at the beginning of the 3rd century. This view is now regarded as an undue simplification of a complicated problem. The bold outlines of the earlier picture have become somewhat blurred, partly because of the re-interpretation of older evidence, especially the revised dating of 2nd-century Samian ware proposed by Dr Grace Simpson, and partly through the accumulation of new evidence from more recent excavations; but it still remains true that the bulk of the datable material from the Welsh forts is early, *i.e.* late 1st and early 2nd century. After that there is a marked falling-off in the quantity of datable finds even where continued occupation is not in doubt. The reasons for this are obscure and complicated, and may include among other factors: the decline and eventual extinction of the Samian industry; changes in supply and distribution methods in the Roman army; and the erosion or destruction of the later levels on Roman sites.

So far as Glamorgan is concerned, it would seem that while Gelli-gaer and perhaps Penydarren were rebuilt in stone during Trajan's reign, and then abandoned under Hadrian, the former fort was reoccupied in the reign of Antoninus (138–61). At the same time Neath and perhaps Coelbren and Caerffili were abandoned. Gelli-gaer may have survived in use into the reign of Marcus Aurelius (161–80) and perhaps even later, but by the end of the 2nd century no garrisons remained at any of the forts in Glamorgan, though civil settlements may have existed at some. Jarrett has suggested that this was due to the spread of Romanised life among the Silures and Demetae.

The events of the 3rd century and later remain obscure. Legionary quarters at Caerleon were rebuilt soon after 250, and milestones found near Port Talbot (753, i, ii, iv) indicate repairs to the road system at about that time, presumably by the military, though no auxiliary fort seems to have been garrisoned. Gelli-gaer is a possible exception, but the small quantity of relevant material could derive from occupation on a care-and-maintenance basis.

In 287 Carausius, Count of the Saxon Shore, proclaimed himself Emperor, and during the next ten years he and his successor Allectus began the construction of forts on the southern and eastern coasts of Britain as a defence against the increasing raids of Saxon pirates. The stone fort at Cardiff resembles their work, and may be of this period, though it is equally likely to have been the work of Constantius Chlorus who in 296 re-united Britain with the Empire; it was presumably intended as a base for a detachment of the fleet. Subsequent repair of military communications is probably reflected in the later milestone inscriptions from near Port Talbot (753, iii–v).

Apart from coin finds, archaeological evidence sheds no light on the military history of the area after the first quarter of the 4th century. The coin series from Cardiff shows that occupation there continued up to the reign of Gratian (367–83). At Loughor, a coin of 260–8 (Gallienus) and one of 324–30 (Constantine II) were found in a layer of silt over the ruins of the recently discovered fort. The position would be well suited to a naval establishment subsidiary to that at Cardiff, but no structure of the appropriate date has been found.

For the greater part of the Roman period, Glamorgan was essentially part of the civil zone. The reduction in the intensity of military occupation a generation after the defeat of the Silures and the subsequent abandonment of all the forts seems to be accompanied by increasing Romanisation of existing farms and the establishment of new ones. The culmination of this process is reflected on the one hand by luxurious villas like that at Llantwit Major (758) and on the other by the stone fort at Cardiff, probably constructed for the protection rather than the domination of the surrounding countryside.

The evidence available from Llantwit Major is open to various interpretations; two have been published.[2] The villa seems to have been founded during the 2nd century with buildings of timber. These were replaced in stone, at some date not established with certainty.

The 4th century in Britain was marked by growing danger from pirates and raiders, culminating with a concerted attack by Picts, Scots and Saxons in 367. Of the 135 villas which have yielded relevant evidence almost half were abandoned at about that time, and many others show a reduction in prosperity. At Llantwit Major the coin sequence closes at about the middle of the century, but this need not preclude some later occupation. The oriented graves cut through the ruins of the main house could be those of people who lived in some unexplored part of the complex of buildings, but such conjecture lacks proof, as also does the suggestion that any part of the known group of buildings was the actual home of St. Illtud,[3] for nothing is recorded from the site which might represent the interval of several generations between the probable lifetime of the saint and the latest coins.

The structures in this section of the Inventory have been arranged under four main headings: Forts; Other Military Works; Roads; and Civil Sites.

FORTS

WITH the exception of *Bomium* (see p. 121), the positions are known of all eight of the forts built to consolidate the conquest. All seem to have been of typical standardised plan, rectangular with rounded corners and enclosing a regular arrangement of buildings. Some structural features have been discovered at all except Cardiff (735). Coelbren (731) and Gelli-gaer (737) are of particular importance, as both are unencumbered by later buildings, and should thus at some future time provide opportunities for complete excavation. At Gelli-gaer there is the further advantage that the earlier and later works are separated; during the first decade of the 2nd century a stone fort was built a short distance south of the earlier earth-and-timber structures. The Trajanic fort was excavated at the beginning of this century, and has long

[2] V. E. Nash-Williams, *Arch. Camb.*, CII (1953), pp. 89–163 (excavation report); G. Webster in *Roman Villa*, pp. 238–43; but see No. 761 below.
[3] J. Morris, 'The Dates of the Celtic Saints', *Journ. Theological Studies*, N.S. XVII, pt. 2 (1966), p. 379.

provided one of the best examples of the plan of a Roman *castellum*. The buildings have been reburied, and probably remain well-preserved.

The visible remains at Cardiff (735) are of the 3rd century, built in masonry in the style of the Saxon Shore defences. The reconstruction initiated by the 3rd Marquess of Bute gives a fine visual impression, unique in Britain, of such a fortress. The walls may now be considerably higher than in the original fort on this site, though they can be matched elsewhere, but all the Roman masonry has been carefully preserved and distinguished from the restorations, so that the archaeological interest is not affected.

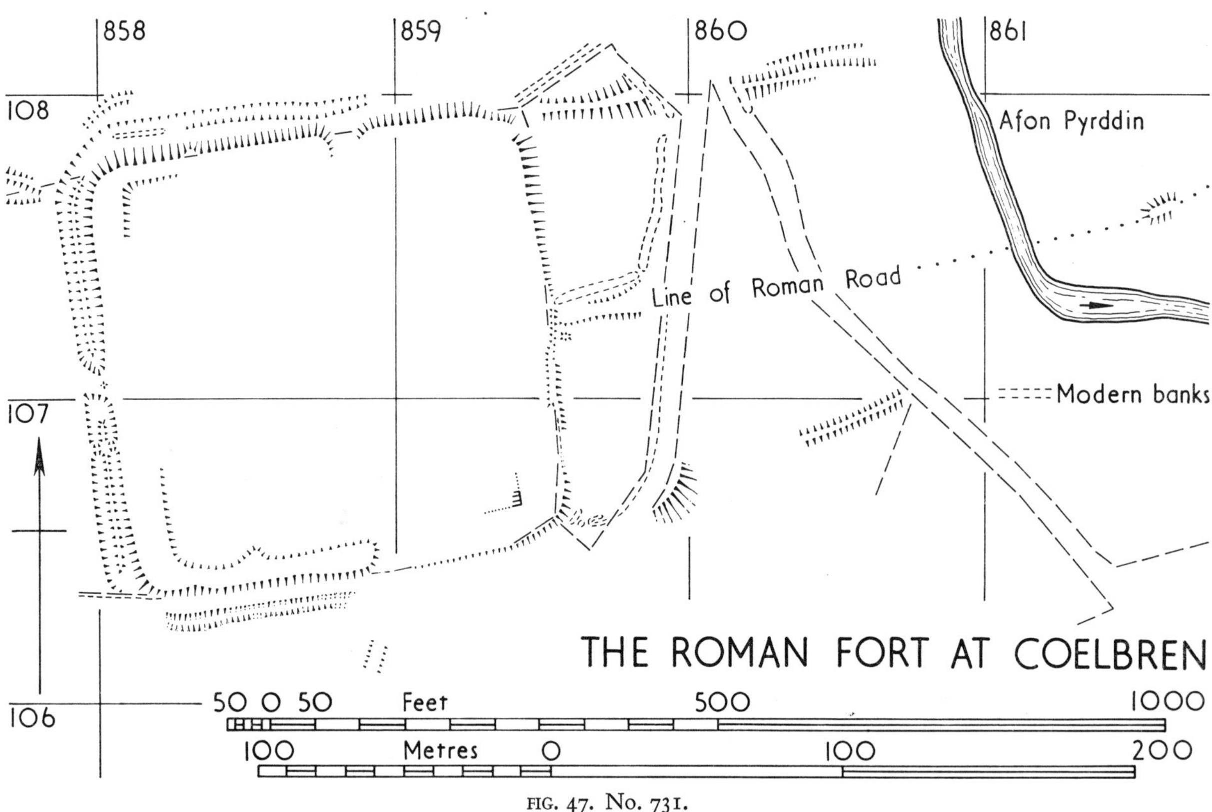

FIG. 47. No. 731.

(731) THE ROMAN FORT at COELBREN (Fig. 47 Plate 13) lies on the watershed between the Swansea and Neath Valleys, about halfway between Ystradgynlais and Glyn-neath. It is sited on a low ridge just to the W. of the junction of three streams, the Camnant, the Nant y Bryn and the Nant y Fedwen, which unite to form the Afon Pyrddin. The ground to the W. is occupied by a fairly extensive marsh, Gors Llwyn. The ridge, whose highest point is at 234 m above O.D., rises between 9 and 12 m above the adjacent marsh and stream beds. The long axis of the fort lies almost E.–W. and coincides with that of the ridge.

The main feature of the remains is an almost square earthwork with rounded corners, about 149 m long from E. to W. by 142 m wide (2·1 hectares), measured between the outer crests of the rampart. The interior is much ploughed down and the rampart survives only on the S. and W., in the form of a low bank from 9 to 15 m across, though its outer scarp, with a maximum height of 1·7 m, is visible also on the N. and E. Along the W. side, and the W. half of the S. side, are the remains of two external ditches with a combined width of about 10·5 m, and the outer ditch is also traceable along the W. half of the N. side. An entrance, with a causeway across the ditches, is visible at the middle of the W. rampart, and traces of entrances also remain on the N. and S. a little to the E. of the centre-line. The E. entrance is obscured by a modern bank.

Banks continue the lines of the N. and S. ramparts eastward for over 100 m. The area has been disturbed, so no E. boundary can be traced and the interpretation of these remains is uncertain. A section of the N. bank, E. of the modern road, showed that it was 6 m wide, of turf and upcast on a foundation of withies, and W. of the road the remains are almost as substantial as the fort ramparts.

There are three possible explanations of this feature. It can be regarded simply as an annexe to the main fort, but the rampart seems exceptionally massive for such a function. The marked drop in level at the modern road about 40 m E. of the existing rampart can be taken as evidence for an earlier fort of about 2·7 ha, with an annexe extending further E., but the same objection applies. Or the bank can be considered as the remains of a much larger early fort, about 250 by 150 m, and enclosing about 3·8 ha. This is exceptionally large and the proportions would be very unusual, but topography requires that the W. rampart of any hypothetical earlier fort should coincide with that now visible. This last explanation seems the most probable, for the large area is not unparalleled and the unusual proportions would be necessary owing to the shape of the ground; although the sections cut in 1904–7 give no support to the hypothesis of an earlier fort, they seem to be highly schematised.

The fort was excavated between 1904 and 1907 under the direction of Col. W. Ll. Morgan. The *Rampart* was sectioned at several places including all four angles. It was found to be a bank, preserved to a height of 0·9–1·2 m and spread to a width of about 10·7 m, though probably originally some 7·6–7·9 m wide, constructed of alternate layers of clay, turves and brushwood, mainly birch. Its outer portion was founded on a raft of oak logs, 5·2 m long and 20–30 cm in diameter, placed at right angles to the line of the rampart. In places the logs were in two lengths with a gap between, though the overall length was again about 5·2 m. The E. rampart, and part also of the N. half of the W. rampart, were founded on stones instead of logs. At the angles the foundation was more elaborate and consisted of two layers of logs, or of sawn boards up to 0·4 m wide, sometimes buttressed externally by oak piles 0·3 m square. These features may have been intended to support the weight of *ballistaria* (artillery platforms).

Outside the rampart was a berm 4·9 m wide. The *Ditches* were examined on the W. and N. sides of the fort, and along both sides were two in number, separated by a space varying in width from 2·1 to 4·6 m. They were V-shaped in section (possibly a truncated V, though this may only be due to insufficient clearance of the bottom of the ditch) and were both armed with a row of pointed oak stakes. The inner ditch was 2·8–3·4 m wide and at least 2·3 m deep; the outer was 2·1–2·5 m wide and at least 1·8 m deep.

The E. and W. *Entrances* were partially excavated though without much result. Traces of the road foundation were meagre and had probably been ploughed out. The causeway at the W. entrance was found to be an original feature; at either side of it the inner and outer ditches were connected by cross-ditches.

In the *Interior*, diagonal trenches yielded fragmentary remains of floors and buildings (apparently of wood) which were not recorded with sufficient accuracy to provide a coherent plan. Near the S.E. angle, layers of red ash and burnt material are probably to be connected with cooking operations in the lee of the rampart. A layer of gravel 0·5 m thick was doubtless the *intervallum* road, and traces of similar roads between the fort buildings were found elsewhere in the interior. Near the S.E. angle horizontal squared baulks of timber, 15 cm thick, represent sleeper beams at the end of a building, apparently a barrack block with its long axis parallel to that of the fort. At various places were found the rough cobbling of stone floors, and extensive layers of red ash or 'brick earth' which represent either floors or perhaps the collapsed remains of wattle-and-daub buildings destroyed by fire. These layers seem to have overlain a thin stratum of black earth which yielded most of the small finds, and it is possible that two periods of occupation are represented.

Small finds included Samian sherds of Drag. 29, 37, 15/17, 18 and 27, all of Flavian date; fragments of an *amphora*, a *mortarium*, *ollae*, a flagon, flanged bowls, a pot-lid, and a 'poppy-head' beaker (mostly late 1st to early 2nd century, though a few of the pieces are Hadrianic or Antonine); five melon beads; a *ballista* ball; pieces of window glass and of square bottles; iron nails; and a lump of fused lead. It is generally accepted that the fort was founded by Frontinus during his campaigns against the Silures in 74–78, but its occupation does not appear to have extended much beyond the middle of the 2nd century.

Outside the fort the causeways of the Roman roads leading to the S. and E. are visible. They are about 5·5 m wide and stand about 0·3 m high. That on the E. has a line of greener grass along its centre suggesting that a culvert may have existed here. Air photographs suggest the possibility of roads leading from the other two gates also. For 2 km to the S. the road is aligned on the existing fort. If the hypothesis of an earlier large fort is accepted, the gateways will almost certainly not have been in the same position, and it will follow that the system of engineered roads here was not laid out until the construction of the later fort, perhaps in the Antonine period.

The objects found are now at R.I.S.W., Swansea.

Arch. Camb., 1907, pp. 129–74; XCIV (1939), pp. 25–8; CXII (1963), pp. 43–5; *Roman Frontier*, pp. 81–3; *Journ. Rom. Stud.*, LI (1961), p. 126.

Cadoxton-juxta-Neath (E), Dulais Higher (C).
SN 81 S.E. (8590 1073) 23 ix 66 IV S.W.

(732) THE ROMAN FORT at PENYDARREN (Fig. 48) lay at about 215 m above O.D. on a spur overlooking the E. side of the Afon Taf valley above Merthyr Tudful. Nothing is now visible on the ground, which is partly built over and partly occupied by a sports stadium. The site of the fort was immediately to the S.W. of Penydarren House (now demolished). When this house was built in 1786, Roman bricks and a tessel-

lated pavement were found in digging the foundations. The bulk of the evidence relating to the fort was provided by excavations supervised by F. Treharne James prior to and during levelling operations for the construction of a football ground in the period 1902–05. This can now be supplemented by the results of selective excavations carried out by Dr. B. Swinbank (Mrs. Heywood) in 1957.

The 'paved causeway' discovered by James to the E. of the granary in 1905 (at SO 0510 0676) was clearly the stone foundation of the S.E. rampart; beyond it was the commencement of the fall into the fort ditch. Mrs. Heywood in 1957 located the E. angle and found the defences to be of a single structural period. The rampart, 8·2 m wide, rested on a stone foundation and was constructed of turves and clay over a core of stones.

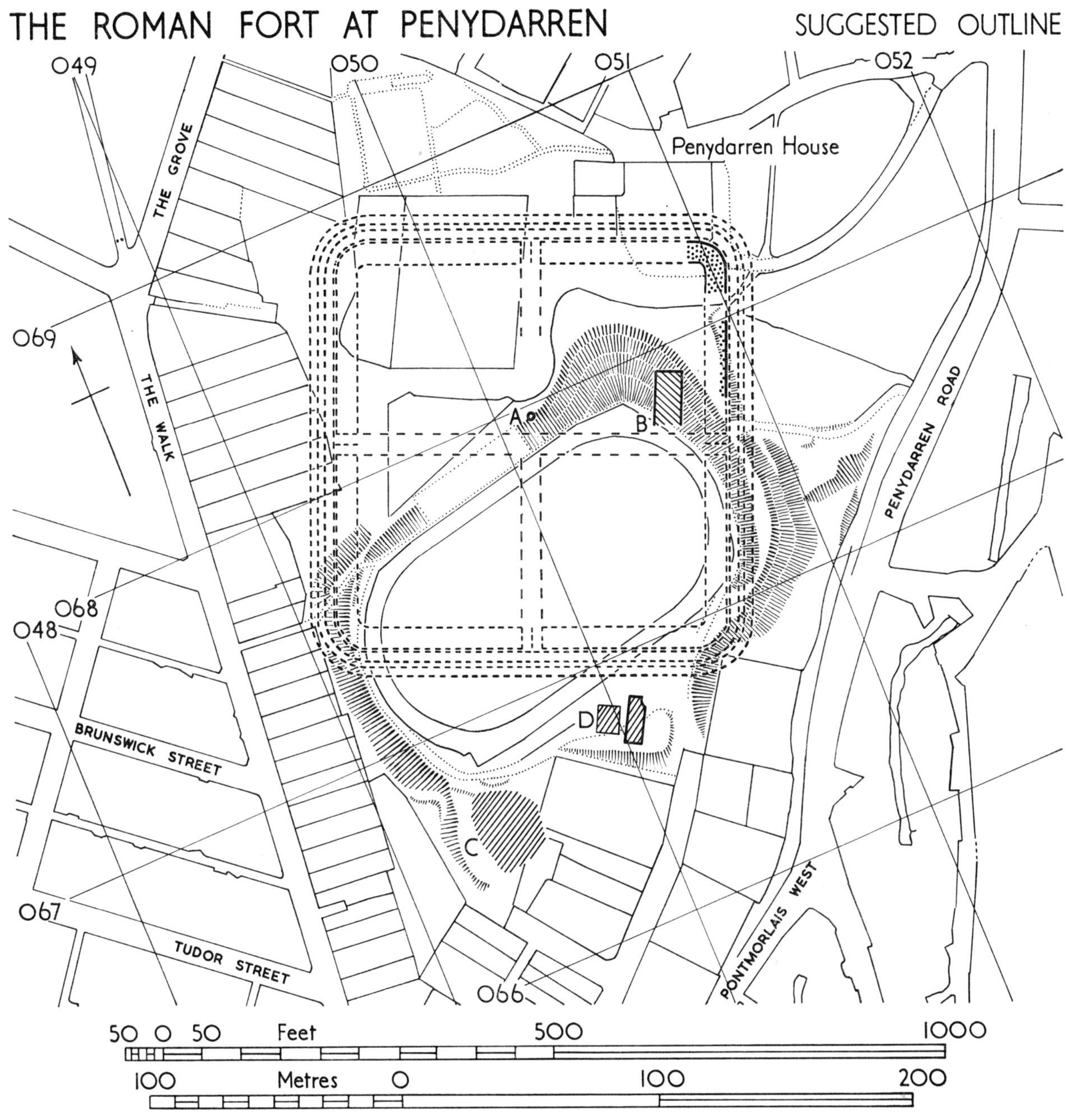

FIG. 48. No. 732.

Outside it lay a narrow berm (0·6 m wide) and two ditches, 4 m and 3 m wide respectively, separated by an interval of 2·5 m. At the angle a large post-hole for a timber tower was found in the stone core.

The size of the fort is unknown and the outline shown is conjectural. Haverfield assumed that the well discovered by James in 1905 lay at the centre of the fort, but this cannot be so since it is 76 m from (the outer face of) the S.E. rampart but only 67 m from the N.E. rampart. On the assumption that it is at least central in a N.W.–S.E. direction, and that the fort was square, the overall measurement between the outer faces of the rampart would be 152 m and the area of the fort would be 2·3 hectares. The *Via Principalis* would run from N.W. to S.E. just beyond the S.W. end of the granary, and the well would be in the courtyard of the *Principia*.

Internally, Mrs. Heywood found evidence of two periods of construction. Two sleeper trenches for timber buildings were sealed by the *intervallum* road and by the foundations of a stone building. James had found abundant remains of stone buildings though it is unlikely that they all lay within the defended area. The well (A on the plan) was at 0503 0678; it was stone-built, 4·6 m deep and 1·2 m in diameter. To the W. of it, at 0500 0680, the foundations of a wall running approximately E.–W. were found; this must have belonged to the *Principia* or possibly the *Praetorium*. Other walls, not planned by James, would seem to have been encountered by the levelling contractors. The most satisfactory discovery was of a stone granary 73 m S. of Penydarren House, at 0509 0676 (B on the plan). This was at least 18·3 m long N.–S. (its S. end was not found), and 9 m wide, with walls 0·8 m thick buttressed externally at intervals of 3 m. Transverse sleeper walls, each 0·5 m thick, spaced at intervals of from 0·9 to 1·8 m, had carried a floor which judging from the quantity of nails found had been of wood.

The remains of an extensive bath-building (C) lay to the S.W. of the fort. In 1902 a hypocaust was found 247 m S.W. of Penydarren House, at 0495 0666. Its concrete floor measured 9 m by 6·7 m and carried nine rows of brick pillars 0·2 m square, fourteen pillars to each row; broken tiles about 0·6 m square were also found, probably from the collapsed floor. At the N. end was a furnace with a narrow walled entrance. At 10 m to the E. was another hypocaust, 7 m by 6·4 m, apsidal to the N., and a paved and walled culvert. At 11 m S. of this was a small brick structure, 2·1 m by 1·2 m, and near it a wall running E. A little to the S.W., a third hypocaust was uncovered measuring 15·3 m by 5·5 m, with a pile of tufa voussoirs from a collapsed arch near its S. end. These discoveries do not allow the complete plan of the bath-building to be drawn, but at any rate indicate something of its extent; they cover an area of something like 40 m from N. to S., and 24·5 m wide.

North-east of the bath-building and closer to the fort, at 0501 0668, was a rectangular stone building (D) 15·3 m long from N. to S. and 5·2 m wide, divided into two rooms by a cross-wall 6·1 m from its S. end. On the W. it was separated by an alleyway from a rectangular pavement, 10·7 m by 8·5 m, with slots at regular intervals round its edge for wooden posts. The purpose of this building is obscure. Among the small finds was an interesting fragment of a Gaulish pipe-clay statuette of Venus.

Sporadic finds of pottery to the N. of the fort suggest (though rather uncertainly) that a Roman cemetery lay on the W. side of the road leading N. from the fort. In 1906 three vessels, including a Samian dish, were unearthed about 183 m N.W. of Penydarren House (this would be about 0497 0697), and later what appear to have been two cinerary urns described as of dark blue ware. In 1933 three complete vessels, one a Samian dish of form 18, were found a little further to the N., at 0502 0708; and in 1950 the foundations of a wall were revealed at about the same spot.

Small finds from the fort and its environs are fairly numerous and have been summarised by Nash-Williams. The datable material is almost all early and clearly indicates that the fort was founded by Frontinus in the period 74–78. It does not appear to have been held for very long. Recent re-examination of the pottery evidence indicates that occupation continued during the first third of the second century but no later.[1] Similar considerations at Gelli-gaer (737), together with the recognition of an earth-and-timber fort preceding the stone one there, now make it impossible to accept Haverfield's hypothesis that the latter structure was built *ca.* A.D. 100 to replace Penydarren.

The objects found are now at Cyfarthfa Castle Museum, Merthyr Tudful.

Arch. Camb., 1906, pp. 193–208. Haverfield, 'Military Aspects', pp. 142–9; *B.B.C.S.*, VII, i (Nov. 1933), p. 80; *Roman Frontier*, pp. 106–8; *Journ. Rom. Stud.*, XLVIII (1958), p. 131.

[1] Dr. G. Simpson, *Arch. Camb.*, CXII (1963), pp. 45–9.

Merthyr Tudful.
SO 00 N.E. (0503 0678) 7 ix 64 XII N.W.

(733) THE ROMAN FORT OF LEUCARUM, at Loughor,[1] (Fig. 49) stood on a ridge of rock on the E. bank of the Afon Llwchwr, where its marshy valley narrows before opening to the wide stretches of Burry Inlet. The Ordnance map records the former existence of a ford[2] about 60 m above the present bridge. A bath-house was discovered in 1851, and this, with various other discoveries (see below), confirmed the occupation of the area during the Roman period, but the position of the fort itself was not established until 1969. In that year, during excavations in the medieval castle, J. M. Lewis located the S.E. angle of the Roman defences[3]. Subsequently the investigation has been continued by R. J. Ling. Thanks are due to these excavators for the information on which the following summary is based; but the work is not yet complete and the conclusions are provisional.

The excavations have determined the positions of the ramparts on the N., E. and S., fixing the orientation of the enclosure, and its width of about 125 m. It is uncertain how far the fort extended to the W., and the intersecting railway lines may well have swept away the rampart in this direction. In 1971 traces of Roman buildings were discovered in the garden of Station House. The alignment of these buildings and their similarity to timber structures located in the N.E. area of the fort suggested that they were built within the

THE ROMAN FORT AT LOUGHOR
63
64
65
old ford
LOUGHOR
RIVER
KILN
81
CASTLE STREET
980
ROMAN
BUILDINGS
SITE-OF-
BATH HOUSE
79
78
POSSIBLE LINE OF
DEFENCE
CREMATION
BURIALS
50 0 50 Feet 500 1000
100 Metres 0 100 200

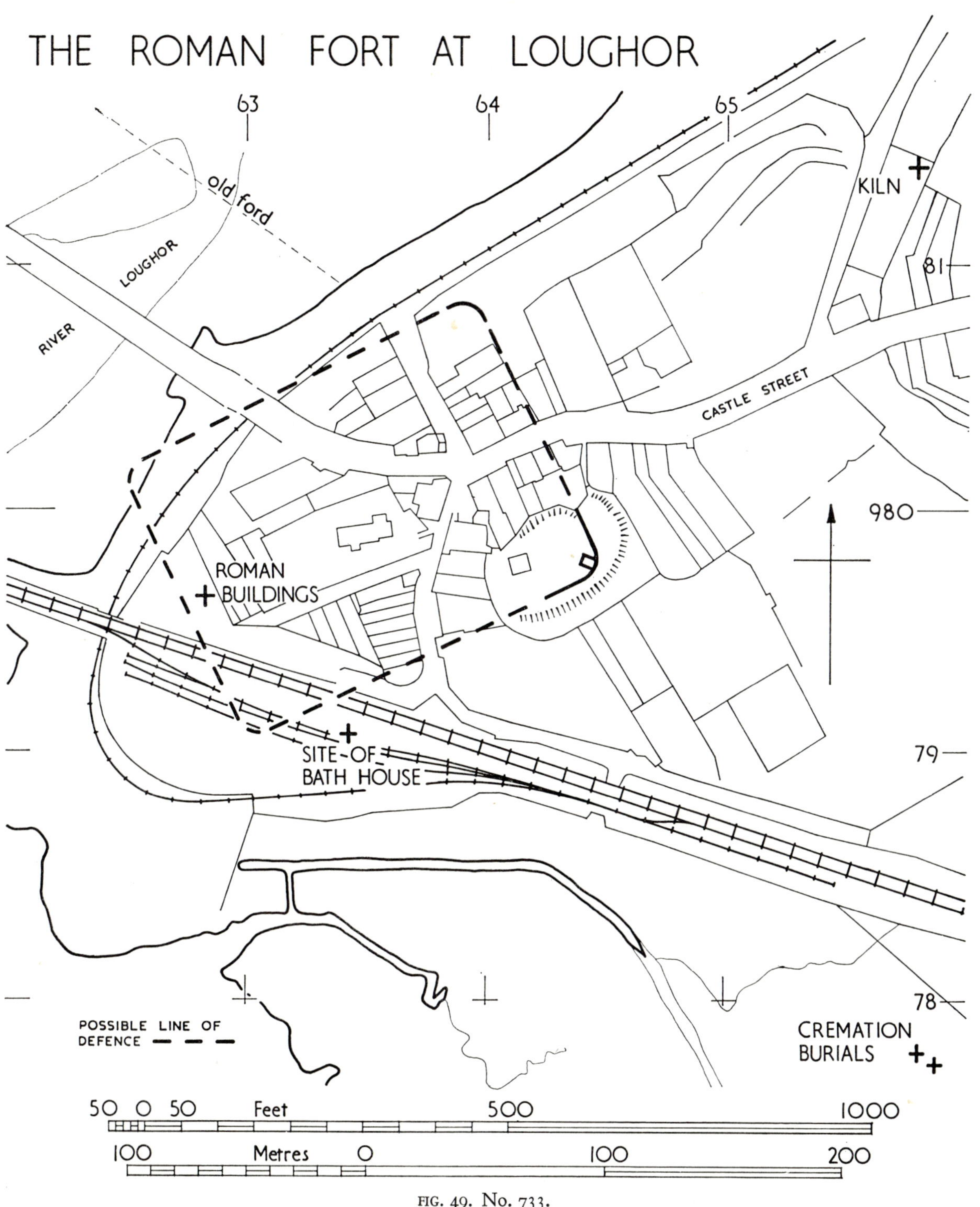

FIG. 49. No. 733.

defences. The possible line for the W. rampart shown on the plan gives a minimum westward extent in relation to these buildings, and follows a scarp across the angle of the two railway lines. This line would give a length of about 163 m and an area of just over 2 ha.

At the E. end, two periods of construction have been demonstrated. The earlier rampart was at least 6 m wide, of clay and turf on a raft of river cobbles, probably separated by a narrow berm from a ditch. Later, the ditch was packed solidly with clay and a masonry wall built against the cut-back face of the bank. In the S.E. angle, the only one examined, an internal turret was built against the wall, about 3 m square internally with a wall just over 1 m thick. The chronology and arrangement of the ditch-system are not yet certain, but two ditches seem to be associated with this phase.

The most important of the earlier discoveries was the bath-house. This was located in 1851, beneath the line of the track during the construction of the railway station, and thus just outside the S.W. corner of the fort, at about 5634 9791. It was 'arched over and left intact', but no mention is made of any provision for access.[4]

The only other structure was a roughly built ring of stonework, 2·5 m in diameter and up to 0·3 m high, about 200 m N.E. of the fort (5658 9814),[5] cleared by local residents some time before 1955. Pottery found on the same site in 1934 comprised bowls, jars and *mortaria* consistent with use from the late first to mid second century.

Former editions of the O.S. maps indicate the site of Leucarum at 5671 9777, about 200 m S.E. of the fort, with 'Church, site of' near by, at 5655 9779. There is no historical evidence for a church here. Close to this last point, at 5658 9777, on a low platform above the marsh, the Commission's investigators found two cremation burials exposed by drainage works. One burial was in an urn of grey ware, much damaged and lacking its rim but probably of the late first or early second century. It seems likely that a cemetery occupied this area, and that finds from it may have given rise both to the 'church' tradition and to the identification of the site as that of the fort.

In addition to various minor casual finds,[6] the town (or district near) has yielded a Roman altar re-used for an Ogam inscription (I iii 845) and a hoard of 60 coins covering the period 250 to 263,[7] now lost.

The recent excavations have produced pottery of Flavian date, so the foundation of the fort should probably be attributed to *ca.* A.D. 80, as part of the network set up after Frontinus' campaigns (p. 81). Its later history remains uncertain, but one coin of 260–8 (Gallienus) and one of 324–30 (Constantine II) occurred in a layer of silt above the ruins of the S.E. corner-turret. These, taken in conjunction with the hoard mentioned above, suggest that the position may have retained its importance in the third and fourth centuries as part of the coastal defence system based on Cardiff; but no structure of the appropriate period has yet been identified.

The *medieval castle* was built on a natural knoll within the S.E. angle of the Roman fort and began as an oval ring-work about 24 m from N.E. to S.W. by 18 m. The ruined Roman structures were cleared and levelled and a new ditch was cut around the fort angle and beyond the line of the Roman ditch, the vestiges of both being buried in the scarp on the N.E. and S.E. fronts. The destruction recorded at Loughor Castle in 1151 and its capture in 1215 probably relate to this phase.[8]

Later in the 13th century an almost square tower, with walls 1·83 m thick and measuring 7·3 m by 7·9 m externally, was built out over the S.W. scarp of the motte, and a curtain wall enclosed the summit. The curtain linked with the tower near the top of the scarp, leaving the bulk of the tower projecting down and over the scarp. A ground-level door in the tower communicated with the walled area of the summit. The excavations to date have not located the site of the main gate but this was probably placed in the curtain immediately N. of the tower. The capture of the castle is recorded in 1391.[9]

The site is much robbed and mutilated by recent tipping, and the ruined tower, which stands to a height of about 7·0 m, is the only masonry remaining above ground.

The objects found are now at R.I.S.W., Swansea.

[1] For an alternative identification see A. L. F. Rivet, *Britannia*, I (1970), p. 56.

[2] This could be crossed for four hours at each tide. Lewis, *Top. Dict.*, under Loughor.

[3] Thus confirming the observation by G. T. Clark that the castle mound is 'mixed up with the bank of a Roman Camp'. G. T. Clark, *Mediaeval Military Architecture* (2 vols., London, 1884), I, p. 122.

[4] Davies, *W. Gower*, I, p. 117; Morgan, *E. Gower*, p. 19.

[5] Information from O.S. records. The structure was left exposed and the pottery is unpublished. It was taken to the Secondary Modern School.

[6] A coin each of Domitian and Antoninus Pius, two of Trajan, querns and potsherds, Morgan, *E. Gower*, pp. 20–1; *Journ. Rom. Stud.*, XVII (1927), p. 186; *Arch. Camb.*, XCIV (1939), p. 29.

[7] *Journ. Brit. Arch. Ass.*, XII (1856), pp. 157, 239.

[8] *Brut.*, *s.a.* 1150 (for 1151), 1215; *Ann. Camb.*, *s.a.* 1154 (for 1151).

[9] Clark, *Cartae*, IV, p. 139.

Loughor (E), L. Borough (C).
SS 59 N.E. (5635 9800) 18 ix 69 XIV S.W.

(734) THE ROMAN FORT OF NIDUM at Neath (Fig. 50). The evidence of the name and the mileages given in the *Antonine Itinerary* have long suggested the site of this fort, but although scattered finds of Roman coins occurred in the Neath area, it was not until 1949 that its precise location was determined, during the opening of trenches for a new housing estate. The fort was low-lying, situated to the W. of the modern town at 11 m above O.D. on the W. bank of the Afon Nedd, about 110 m from the water's edge.

In 1949 excavations by V. E. Nash-Williams at SS 7470 9767, just S. of the present main road, revealed the south-eastern side of the S.W. gateway. The rampart facing was of stone, 2·1 m thick at foundation level. Attached to the back of it was a stone guard-chamber, 3·4 by 2·5 m internally, with walls 1·1 m thick and the remains of a doorway in the N.W. wall. A slab-covered drain followed the edge of the roadway, and the N. quoin of the tower suggested the abutment of an arch over the passage. Traces of an occupation layer under both rampart facing and guard-chamber indicated an earlier period, presumably associated with defences of earth and timber. Test cuttings also revealed traces of the rampart on the S.E. and S.W. sides of the fort, and located a latrine in the S. angle, with a stone-built culvert piercing the rampart.

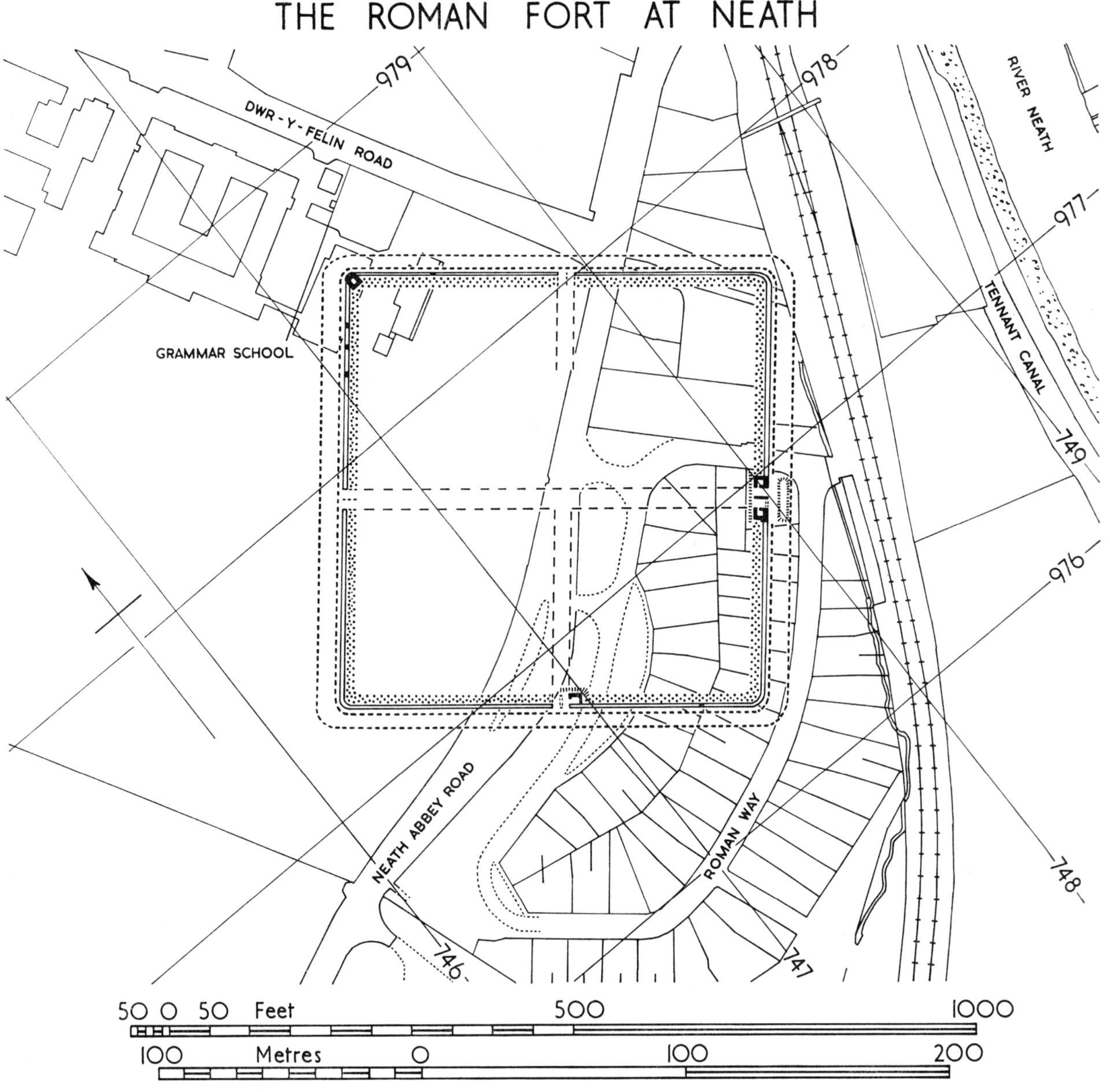

FIG. 50. No. 734.

In 1950 a section was cut through the S.W. defences at 7474 9764. The original rampart was a clay bank about 4·6 m wide and (as preserved) 0·6 m high, probably revetted with timber on both faces. Outside it lay a berm 1·5 m wide and a shallow V-shaped ditch 4·6 m wide and 0·9 m deep. The front of the rampart was subsequently revetted with a stone wall 1·7 m thick. Internally the rampart was separated by a space of 4·3 m from the *intervallum* road, 7 m wide, of pebbles edged on the outside by a slab-covered stone culvert. At the same time, the S.E. gateway was located and excavated, at 7479 9768. This location suggests that it was the *Porta Principalis Sinistra*, and that the S.W. gateway was the *Porta Praetoria*. The gateway was of characteristic plan and consisted of a roadway 7 m wide, probably with a central *spina*, between flanking guard-towers attached to the inside of the rampart-ends. Both towers measured about 3 m by 2·5 m internally. The footings of both the rampart and the rear walls of the guard-chambers continued unbroken beneath the roadway, possibly to serve as sills for the double doors of the passage. A substantial box-culvert emptied through the N.E. half of the passage, and a smaller weeping drain lay in the other half. The fort ditch (here 4·3 m wide and 1.2 m deep) continued uninterrupted across the front of the gateway and must have been spanned by a wooden bridge; the greater width of the berm at this point (3·7 m) was presumably to provide a firm base for the abutment of the bridge. The interior of the fort was also tested by cross-trenches at one or two points, but the remains encountered were slight; the general impression gained was that this part of the fort, probably the *Praetentura*, had been occupied by timber structures.

Both gateways are now preserved within iron railings, but otherwise the only visible evidence of the fort is the N.W. rampart, which can just be distinguished as a faint swelling of the ground in the school playing field to the N.W. of the main road. In 1958 this rampart was sectioned by Dr. Swinbank (Mrs. Heywood) and a tower in the N. angle was excavated. Three periods of occupation were distinguished, of which the third, representing rebuilding after abandonment, included the stone defences found elsewhere by Nash-Williams.

The N.E. rampart is less satisfactorily fixed than the N.W., but was encountered in 1954 during digging for gas mains, and again in 1958 and 1962. Sufficient is therefore known of the plan of the fort to indicate that it was almost square, measuring 160 m each way and covering 2·5 hectares. Small finds include roofing-, floor- and box-tiles; Samian ware ranging from Flavian to Hadrianic in date; fragments of *amphorae* (including an early carrot-shaped example, mid-1st century); *mortaria, ollae*, beakers, flanged bowls, pie-dishes, ring-necked flagons—mostly late 1st–early 2nd century but including one or two Antonine pieces; six coins from Augustus to Trajan (23 B.C.–A.D. 111); and miscellaneous objects including an inscribed slate gaming counter. The fort was evidently founded by Frontinus in the period 74–78, with defences of earth and timber, and wooden buildings. The rebuilding of the rampart and gateways in stone was tentatively dated by Nash-Williams *ca.* 100, but Mrs. Heywood and Dr. Simpson regard both the abandonment and subsequent rebuilding as occurring during the 2nd century. There seems little evidence of occupation after the Antonine period, though the mention of the fort in the *Antonine Itinerary* suggests that the place survived at least into the early 3rd century, even if only as a civil settlement.

The objects found are now at N.M.W.

B.B.C.S., XIII, iv (May 1950), pp. 239–43; XIV, i (Nov. 1950), pp. 76–9; *Journ. Rom. Stud.*, XLV (1955), pp. 121–2; XLIX (1959), p. 102; *Roman Frontier*, pp. 98–101; *Arch. Camb.*, CXII (1963), pp. 41–3.

Cadoxton-juxta-Neath (E), Neath (C).
SS 79 N.W. (7474 9773). 22 vi 64 XVI S.W.

(735) THE ROMAN FORT at CARDIFF (Fig. 51). The fort stands on almost level ground at about 12 m above O.D., on the E. bank of the Afon Taf. Its Roman name is unknown.[1] Soon after 1080 the site was selected for a Norman castle. This, and the medieval and modern buildings which succeeded it, will be described in detail in later volumes of the Inventory, but a summary account of their main features is given at the end of this entry.

The enclosure formed by the Roman walls is irregular, but approximates to a rectangle 185 m by 200 m to the outer wall-faces excluding towers, the long axis being about 15 deg. W. of N. The area enclosed, again excluding towers, is 3·7 hectares. If, as seems likely, the original design was symmetrical, the walls were reinforced by eighteen five-sided towers, two pairs forming N. and S. gateways, the remainder fairly evenly spaced round the perimeter with one at each corner; but for eight of these, on the W. side of the fort from the N.W. angle-tower to the S. gateway inclusive, no visible trace of Roman construction survives. The foundations and some of the superstructure of the remaining ten have been excavated. It is likely that the wall was accompanied by a ditch, but all evidence for it has been destroyed by later works.

To the E. of the line joining the N.W. corner to the S. gate, the ruins of the Roman wall were buried by a large earthen bank probably thrown up as part of the Norman defences. In 1889 part of the bank was removed, exposing the wall, which was subsequently cleared and rebuilt by the then Lord Bute, all the Roman masonry being preserved. Later work showed that the existing medieval walls on the S. and W. were built on Roman foundations, so the present enclosure follows the original outline almost exactly. In the rebuilt sections, the limit of the surviving Roman work is indicated by a course of coloured stone, and a covered tunnel provides access to the inner face of the S. wall and of the N.E. corner.[2] The reconstruction, although open to criticism in detail,[3] provides a good general impression of the appearance of a late Roman fortress.

The wall was founded on a filling of rounded river-boulders rammed in a trench 4·6 m wide by 0·6 m deep. Over this, on a layer of mortar, was a plinth-course, 3·4 m wide by 0·6 m high, still partly visible in places. The wall, approximately 3 m thick, was then built up with vertical faces to a height of 2·3 m, where it was reduced at the back by stepped courses, generally four, to a thickness of 2·4 m. Behind the wall was an earthen bank, still standing in places to a height of 3·7 m, but of uncertain width. There was a clear line of demarcation between this and the medieval bank which had covered and preserved it. The wall where best preserved stood 5·2 m high. If, as seems likely, one function of the bank was to provide access to the wall-walk, the original height of the masonry cannot have been much greater. The facing was composed of coursed blocks of limestone, and the core of river boulders set in mortar. The back, where protected by the Roman bank, was not weathered and had not been robbed of stone.

The wall-towers are of similar construction and are bonded into the main wall, except at the very bottom in some cases. Throughout the N. wall including the N.E. angle, they are founded on a rounded plinth as though their fronts were intended to be curved, not polygonal; and part of a similar plinth is incorporated in the first tower N. of the S.E. corner.

The towers as built are all five-sided and are very nearly symmetrical, but no two are identical in plan or dimensions. They decrease fairly steadily in size proceeding clockwise from the N.W. angle.[4] Their widths at the junctions with the

Surviving Roman walls shown in black
Moat
Medieval bank
Roman wall
Roman bank
10 0 10 Feet 30
5 0 Metres 5
SECTION THROUGH DEFENCES AT A-B
Well
A
B
100 0 Feet 100 200
10 0 10 Metres 80
THE ROMAN FORT AT CARDIFF CASTLE

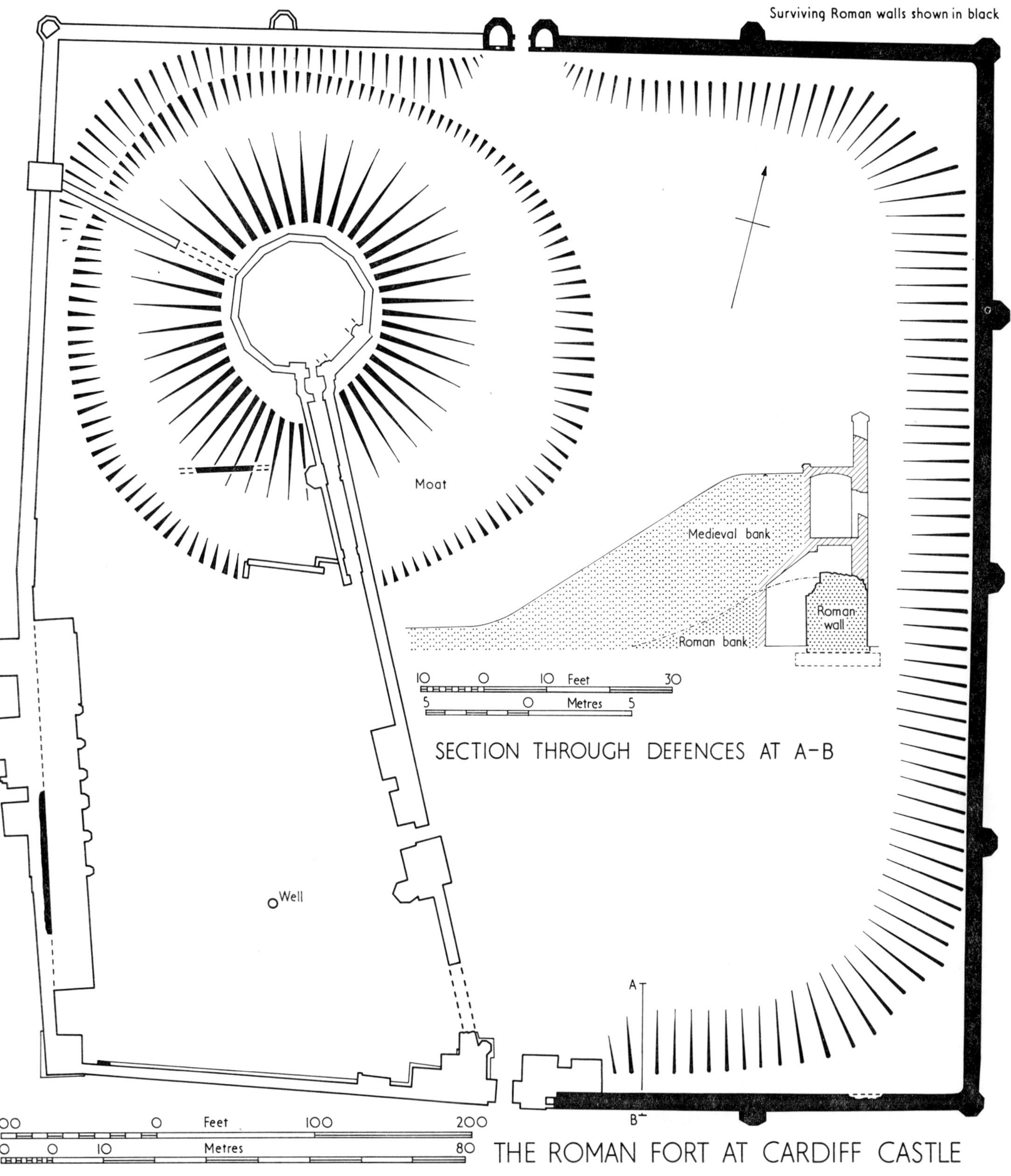

FIG. 51. No. 735.

curtain-wall range from 5·3 m to 4·7 m and their total projections from 3·4 m to 2·8 m. The facets range from 2 m to 1·7 m in length. In the surviving S. wall tower and at the S.E. and N.E. corners, the facets adjacent to the curtain are almost parallel; in the other towers they converge at angles of between 10 and 20°.

All the towers were solid except those at the N. gateway and at the middle of the E. wall; this last was solid for the lowest 2 m, but the upper part was hollow with outer walls 1 m thick. Ward regarded this as the remains of a postern-gate with access by a ladder from the rampart walk, but the N. side, where the doorway may have been, was destroyed.[5]

The N. gateway was protected by a pair of towers; it measured nearly 14·3 m wide overall and 6·1 m from back to front, and projected 3 m from the wall-face. Doorways in the S. walls led to the tower interiors, which were hollow and D-shaped, placed asymmetrically relative to the outside. The gate-passage was 3 m long with pairs of pilasters at both ends, projecting 0·3 m from the adjacent wall and leaving a clear passage of almost 3 m between them. Although by analogy with similar forts it seems likely that the gateway was arched, no voussoirs were in fact found. Pivot-stones remained, for a gate of two leaves between the outer pilasters.

These pivot-stones were embedded in the metalling of the uppermost of three road-surfaces, each formed of iron-clinker on a base of broken stone; the total thickness reached about 0·5 m. The pivot-stones associated with the earlier layers had apparently been hacked away. Beneath the lowest road-surface, and continuing right across the opening, the fort wall stood to a height of one course above the plinth, showing that the gateway was not part of the original design. Five courses remained beneath the E. guard-chamber.

Within the enclosure no systematic excavations have been recorded. Road-surfaces of iron-clinker have been found at a depth of about 1·5 m, indicating two streets crossing at right angles near the middle of the fort. Buildings are also said to have been uncovered, but the only wall now visible which is likely to be of Roman date runs roughly E.–W. for about 11·5 m from beneath the motte into the moat. Only one face is clear, but its thickness seems to be about 1 m.[6]

Evidence for a 1st-century fort

Finds of coins and pottery indicate that the site was occupied, almost certainly by a fort, before the end of the 1st century, but no structural remains of this period have been observed,[7] and occupation seems to have ceased before the middle of the 2nd century. The existing wall was built after 175, for a coin of about that date was found beneath the Roman bank near the S.E. corner; analogy with similar forts elsewhere suggests a date of *ca.* 300.[8]

The presence of early pottery, together with the evidence for changes in detailed design, especially at the corners and at the north gateway, raise the question whether the present walls may follow the outline of an earlier fort. This hypothesis cannot be conclusively proved or disproved without further excavation, but all the changes in design can be accounted for at least equally well as belonging to revision during construction of the later fort.

The setting out and construction of the surviving fort

The table below gives the distances between mid-points of towers or gateways and the directions of the outer wall faces measured for convenience clockwise relative to the axis joining the two gateways; no particular direction can be considered 'correct'. The distances and angles are believed to be within 0·1 m and 05 minutes of arc, except perhaps in the two stretches adjacent to the S.W. angle, where there has been much rebuilding and the exterior of the Roman work is not accessible.

North Wall		
N.W. Angle to W. Tower	46·7 m	
W. Tower–Gateway	46·6 m	90° 15′ (N.W. Angle to E. Tower)
Gateway–E. Tower	45·0 m	
E. Tower–N.E. Angle	46·9 m	90° 00′
East Wall		
N.E. Angle–N. Tower	51·1 m	179° 20′ (N.E. Angle to Mid Tower)
N. Tower–Mid Tower	50·0 m	
Mid Tower–S. Tower	50·0 m	180° 15′ (Mid Tower to S.E. Angle)
S. Tower–S.E. Angle	50·7 m	
South Wall		
S.E. Angle–E. Tower	40·1 m	268° 45′
E. Tower–Gateway	48·6 m	269° 55′
Gateway–S.W. Angle	89·2 m	273° 10′
West Wall		
S.W. Angle–bend in wall	94·1 m	355° 30′
Bend–N.W. Angle	104·9 m	1° 50′

The enclosure is thus an asymmetrical nine-sided polygon; the only two sections of wall either parallel or perpendicular to each other are the W. part of the N. wall and the S. half of the E. wall, and this could well be merely accidental. Bearing in mind the accuracy of which Roman military engineers were capable, the failure to give such a monumental structure any sort of true symmetry is surprising, and suggests that the setting-out was done in haste.

The view that two distinct structural periods are incorporated in the Roman work is supported by the facts that the tower foundations in places are of broken stone, unlike the boulders used for the main wall; that the lower courses are not always bonded to the wall; and that the lower courses of the wall were continuous across the north gateway. Against this, it may be noted that all changes in alignment occur at towers or gateways (except on the W. wall where no towers survive), implying that such features were envisaged at those points in the original design. An analogy to the use of separate foundations for the towers, and absence of bonding in the lower courses, is found at Verulamium, where the provision of brick quoins in appropriate positions shows that both wall and tower were contemporary.[9]

Taken as a whole, the evidence is in favour of the view that the work is all of one period.[10] In particular, the indications of the plan, that towers formed part of the original design although no work was done on them for a considerable time, gives strong support to the impression that all the features which suggest a long period of development can be better accounted for by the hypothesis that the whole work was pushed forward in great haste on account of some sudden emergency. This would not necessarily have been military. Indeed, the monumental character of the structure, together with the indications that insufficient time was allowed for preliminary work and that there were functionally unnecessary changes in design after building had started, combine to suggest most strongly that the apparent emergency was a result of some high-level administrative decision.

The sequence of events in the construction of the 3rd-century fort would seem, therefore, to have been as follows:

(i) The fort was set out, in haste, with markers at the four corners, the approximate mid-points of the E., S. and W. sides, and the two E. quarter-points in the N. and S. sides; this would seem to imply that towers were envisaged at these points, and hence, by symmetry, at the other quarter-points.

(ii) The footing-trench was dug, and the plinth laid. At this stage the corners were envisaged as quadrants of about 6 m external radius, and the plinth was laid to conform to this.

(iii) This design seems to have been given up before any part of the superstructure was built, for although there is a slight curvature in the wall where it approaches the angles, it is much less sharp than that of the plinth.

(iv) After work had started on the main wall and a few of the lowest courses had been laid, foundations were placed for the towers and their plinths formed, at least throughout the N. wall including the gateway and N.E. angle, and for the S. tower on the E. wall. These were designed for towers with rounded fronts. At this stage, also, the N. gateway was introduced into the design. Ward noted that the mortar in the section of wall across the entrance had set so hard that the stones had to be broken in order to level the space for the roadway. He records no evidence for any tower, other than those of the gateway, near the middle of the N. wall.

(v) Finally, apart from some evidence for repairs, the plan of the towers was changed from rounded to polygonal, and the whole defensive perimeter was carried up to its full height.

Post-Roman Structures

These will be described in detail in subsequent volumes. One incident in the history of the remains, however, must have preceded the erection of the Norman castle, for the Roman wall buried under the earthen bank had been extensively robbed of its squared facing-stones. These do not seem to have been used in the early castle, so it may reasonably be inferred that some considerable masonry buildings existed nearby before the Norman invasion. Had the stone been required merely for a causeway across marshy ground, it may be assumed that the rubble would also have been taken.

The fort, however, seems to have remained unoccupied until about 1080, when it was adopted by the Norman invaders as the site of one of their major castles. The earliest Norman castle is now represented by the earthworks of the motte and the substantial banks which covered the Roman wall on the N., E. and S. Nothing is known of how the defensive circuit was completed at this period. Masonry construction started late in the 12th century with the shell keep on the motte and perhaps some rebuilding on the line of the Roman walls, the fortifications being effectively finished during the 13th by the south gate, the adjacent Black Tower, and the link wall between it and the keep. Later defensive structures were the octagonal tower on the outer face of the W. curtain and the gateway and barbican a little S. of it. The tower is known to have been built by Richard, Earl of Warwick, early in the 15th century, and the barbican is probably of the same date. Finally, in the 16th century a rectangular bastion, the Herbert Tower, was added. During these centuries buildings were also erected against the inner face of the curtain, but such parts as survive have been obscured by later work. The link wall was removed during the 18th century when the enclosure was landscaped, and at the same time a large house was built against the W. curtain.

In 1865, Lord Bute (the 3rd Marquess, 1848–1900) set in hand an extensive programme of restoration and reconstruction, including the clearance and preservation of the Roman walls, already mentioned. The most remarkable work was the result of the free interpretation of the medieval spirit by the architect William Burges, exemplified particularly by the immense clock-tower at the S.W. corner of the Roman fort, by the spire added to the Earl of Warwick's Octagon Tower, and by the mass of elaborate interior decoration.

The objects found are now at N.M.W.

Information as to features not now visible is taken from papers by J. Ward in *Archaeologia*, LVII (1901), pp. 335–52; *Arch. Camb.*, 1908, pp. 29–64; 1913, pp. 159–64; and by R. E. M. Wheeler in *Antiq. Journ.*, II (1922), pp. 361–70. These describe successive stages in the investigation of the Roman walls. Their discovery in 1889, and the history of the medieval work, were described by G. T. Clark in *Arch. Camb.*, 1890, pp. 283–92, and 1862, pp. 249–71 respectively.

In addition to the sources cited in footnotes, see Haverfield, 'Military Aspects', pp. 154–8; *Roman Frontier*, pp. 70–3; *Arch. Camb.*, CXII (1963), pp. 69–72.

[1] The modern name means 'the fort on the Taf', early forms being *Kairdif, Cayrdif*; the Welsh form Caerdydd is not known before the 16th century (G. O. Pierce in *The Cardiff Region* (Cardiff, 1960), p. 175). The suggestion that the latter is derived from the name of Aulus Didius Gallus (as e.g. Lewis, *Top. Dict.*) can be dismissed as an antiquarian fantasy.

[2] In 1966 the features at this latter point were concealed by rubbish.

[3] In particular the original wall would not have incorporated a mural passage or the associated windows; and it is unlikely to have been more than 5·5 or 6 m high, as against the 11 m of the reconstruction.

[4] The N.W. angle-tower is entirely modern; even its foundations had been destroyed.

[5] The interior would accommodate a ladder 2·7 m long, hinged at the top. If such an arrangement existed, it would imply a total height of about 4·6 m to wall-walk level.

[6] G. T. Clark's plan (*Arch. Camb.*, 1890, opp. p. 288) suggests that it formed part of the keep defences, but it seems to lie at a much lower level.

[7] It is possible that the early fort may have been sited a little to the S. of the existing remains. One of Ward's informants reported that he had 'seen exposed during street alterations the remains of a thick wall, which appeared to run parallel with the south side of the castle area, at a distance of 450 feet (137 m), the south-east corner being immediately west of St. John's Church' (*Archaeologia*, LVII (1901), p. 349 n.). From the same area comes the earliest pottery recorded from Cardiff: Samian and coarse-ware sherds of the period 50–80, found during the building of Lloyd's Bank in High Street in 1892 (*Arch. Camb.*, 1893, p. 279).

[8] Cf. *B.B.C.S.*, XX, ii (May 1963), p. 217. Of the eleven coins after 175, ten are later than 265, the eleventh being dated 253. Five coins

found in the Roman level at the N. gateway cover the period from Victorinus to Julian (268–363) and prove that the gateway was in use till at least the middle of the 4th century; and coins of Valentinian I (364–375) and Gratian (367–383) found elsewhere indicate occupation into the late 4th century.

[9] R. E. M. and T. V. Wheeler, *Verulamium. A Belgic and two Roman Cities* (Soc. Ant. Research Rep., XI, Oxford, 1936), pp. 59–61.

[10] As argued by Wheeler, *Antiq. Journ.*, II (1922), p. 368.

Cardiff St. John (E), Cardiff (C).
ST 17 N.E. (1808 7659) 28 xii 66 XLIII S.E.

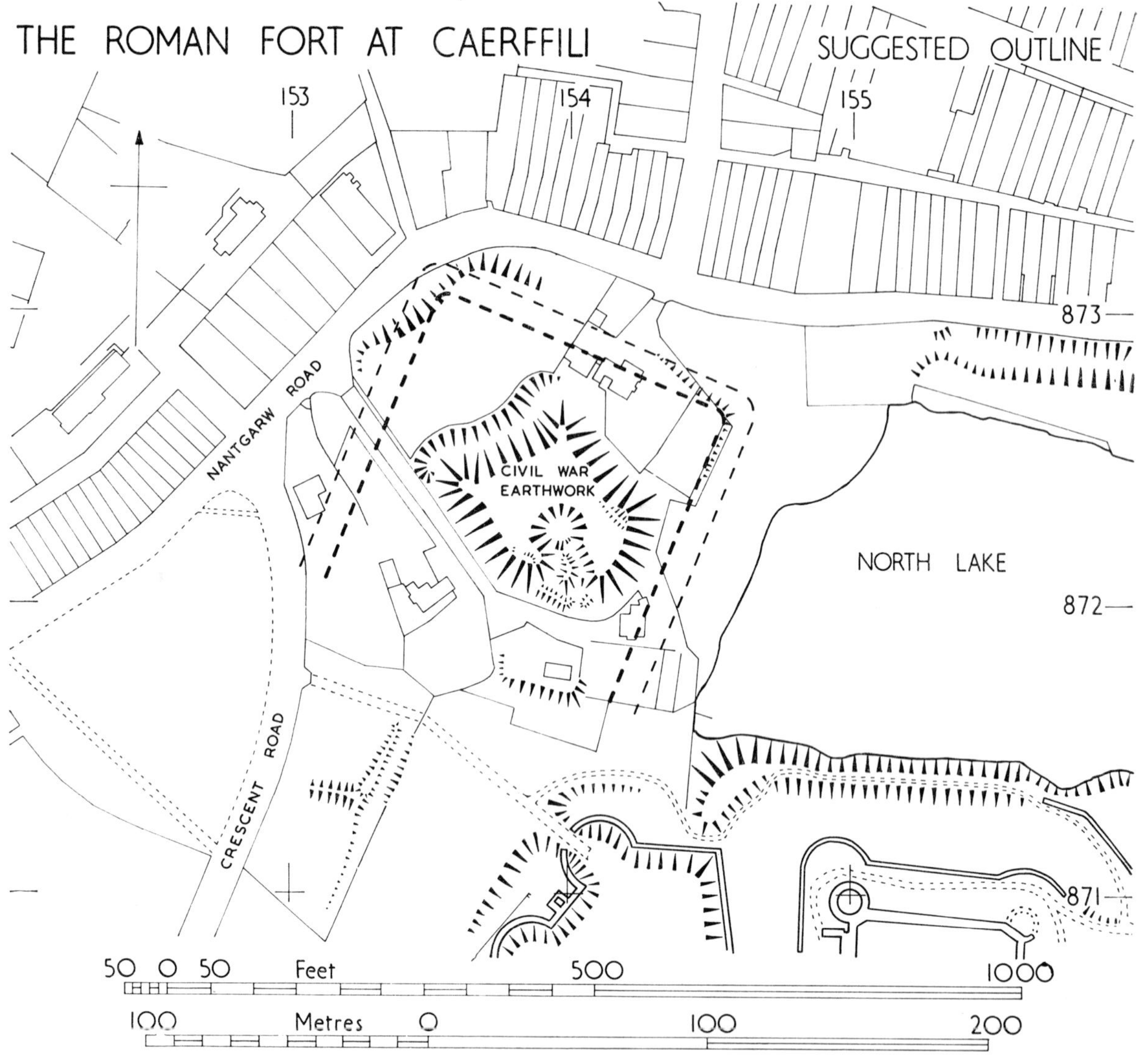

FIG. 52. No. 736.

(736) THE ROMAN FORT at CAERFFILI (Fig. 52) lay 180 m N.W. of the site of Caerffili Castle, at 90 m above O.D. Its existence was unknown until 1963, when its remains were brought to light in the course of excavations by Mr. J. M. Lewis, undertaken to examine the outer defences of the Castle. He located the N.W. angle and parts of the N.W. and N.E. defences, as well as some internal walls. Since only very short lengths of these latter were exposed, they have not been included on the plan. The extent and precise orientation of the fort are not known. In order to take account of what may be traces of the E. angle, the outline suggested here differs from that proposed by the excavator; but these traces are very slight and have been disturbed by the construction of a garden.

The defences comprised a rampart fronted by two ditches,

and had an overall width of 14·6 m. The rampart, of clay and turf on a cobbled base, was 7·3 m wide and preserved to a maximum height of 0·6 m. A post-hole suggested it had been fronted by a timber palisade. The ditches were about 1·5 m apart. Each was V-shaped, about 2·8 m wide at the top and excavated some 0·9 m into the subsoil. The spine between the ditches may have supported a bank of stones and clay.

Behind the rampart was an *intervallum* road about 2·8 m wide, with a drain along its outer edge. Beyond this, a trench through the N.W. defences near the N. angle revealed as many as four periods of construction; the presence of walls was indicated only by robber trenches. (i) A hearth against the inner edge of the road, and beyond it the N.W. wall of a building (Wall I). (ii) A paved floor overlying the hearth and terminated at the road edge by Wall II, 2·8 m from Wall I. (iii) The replacement of Wall II by another and narrower wall. (iv) A stone-lined post-hole dug through the road metalling.

Some 10 m behind the rampart a large ditch of Civil War date had destroyed the Roman levels for a distance of 11 m. At 2·8 m beyond this, the trench encountered Wall III, and 4·6 m further on, Wall IV. The excavator considered Walls I and III to define a building 10·1 m wide, separated by a stony path from Wall IV which was the N.W. end of a second building. The layout suggested that the trench had cut across the N.E. end of two barrack blocks; Wall II would seem to indicate that the outer of these was at some time widened by about 2·8 m.

Small finds included Samian ware of the last quarter of the 1st century; coarse pottery extending from the early Flavian period up to *ca.* 160; a lead weight and other lead fragments; and pieces of glass bottles of 1st–early 2nd century date. The excavator considered the fort to have been established *ca.* 75 and occupied at least till the middle of the 2nd century.

The objects found are now at N.M.W.

Arch. Camb., CXV (1966), pp. 67–87; *Roman Frontier*, pp. 64–5.

Eglwysilan
ST 18 N.E. (1538 8729) 3 i 67 XXXVII N.W.

(737) THE ROMAN FORT at GELLI-GAER (Fig. 53) lies 11 km N. of Caerffili, towards the southern end of a long broad ridge between the Taf and Rhymni valleys, at a height of 238 m above O.D. The earthworks are relatively well preserved. The site was excavated in 1899–1913 by the Cardiff Naturalist's Society under the general direction of J. Ward, and the results still provide a textbook example of the layout of a Roman *castellum.*

(A) The *Fort* itself, centred at ST 1341 9707 to the S.W. of the Rectory, now appears as a large square earthwork defined by a broad bank, best preserved on the S.W. where it is about 15 m wide, 0·8 m high above the ground level within the fort and 1·2 m high on the outer side, where also the ditch is visible. The N.W. and S.E. sides are less well preserved and are 7 m wide and 0·6 m high; the outer slope of the bank on the N.W. is truncated by the lane leading to the Rectory. The N.E. rampart is 10 m wide, 0·6 m high on its inner and 1·2 m high on its outer side. Depressions in the banks, between 8 and 10·4 m wide, mark the sites of the four gateways; that on the N.E. is the most pronounced.

Excavation showed that the fort was almost square, measuring between the outer faces of the rampart 123 m from N.E. to S.W. by 117·3 m (1·4 hectares). The defences consisted of a rampart 6·1 m thick, faced externally with coursed masonry 0·9–1·2 m thick and internally with a somewhat slighter wall; a berm 1·5 m wide; and a V-shaped ditch 5·8 m wide and 2·1 m deep. There were four angle-towers and eight other turrets symmetrically placed between the angles and the gateways; all these towers were of stone and measured internally 4·6 m by 3·5 m, with a doorway in the rear wall; the front wall was formed by the rampart facing but the remaining walls were not bonded into it, so that the towers were, constructionally at any rate, an addition to the stone rampart. The four gateways were symmetrically disposed and were of conventional plan: a double roadway with central *spina*, flanked on either side by a guard-chamber 3·4 m by 2·9 m with narrow doorway in the rear wall. At the S.W. gateway (the *Porta Decumana*) the sides of the ditch for a length of 5·5 m immediately in front of the entrance were stepped to receive the timber supports of a bridge.

Internally the buildings were all of stone. The centrally placed *Principia* (Building 7) measured 24·4 m by 21 m and consisted of an outer colonnaded court, an inner court or 'cross-hall', and a row of five small rooms at the rear, of which the central one was the *sacellum*. The outer court contained a well, and with the exception of the *sacellum* the rear rooms contained hearths or traces of fires. To the N.W. of the *Principia* stood the *Praetorium* (6), 22·6 m by 19·5 m, with rooms grouped round a tiny central court; debris showed that the building had a tiled roof and glazed windows. To the S.E. lay a walled open space of uncertain purpose, perhaps a forecourt to the hospital on its S.W. side. The central range of buildings was completed at each end by a granary (*horreum*; 5 and 8), 18 m by 10·4 m, with external buttresses and transverse sleeper walls, and a loading platform at each end.

North-east of these buildings lay the *Praetentura*, containing two pairs of L-shaped barrack blocks (12–15) with wooden verandahs, each *hemistrigium* measuring 44·2 m in length by 9·1 m wide at the narrow end. Behind these, a long building divided down the centre (9), 44·2 m by 12·5 m, with a water tank at the end next to the *Via Praetoria*, may have been a stable. Opposite it two smaller buildings (10–11) were perhaps storehouses. The *Retentura* was occupied by two more *hemistrigia* (1–2), not paired but disposed on either side of the *Via Decumana*; a building 45·1 m by 10·1 m with lateral wings (4), perhaps the fort hospital (*valetudinarium*); and another smaller rectangular building (3), possibly a magazine. The accommodation is consistent with a garrison in the form of a *cohors quingenaria* of 480 men, and the possible existence of a large stable suggests it may have been a *cohors quingenaria equitata* in which 120 of the men were mounted.

Trans. Cardiff Nat. Soc., XXXV (1903).

(B) Adjoining the fort on the S.E. was an *Annexe* (centred at 1349 9701), of which nothing remains except an inward-facing scarp, 3 m wide and 0·3 m high, along the N.E. side.

THE ROMAN FORT AT GELLI-GAER
SITE PLAN
D
RECTORY
C
A
B
E
E
SCHOOL
MOTTE
CHURCH
100 0 100 FEET 1000
100 0 METRES 200
PORTA DECUMANA
VIA DECUMANA
PRINCIPIA
VIA PRINCIPALIS
PORTA PRINCIPALIS DEXTRA
PORTA PRINCIPALIS SINISTRA
VIA PRAETORIA
PORTA PRAETORIA
1
2
3
4
5
6
7
8
9
10
11
12
13
14
15
AFTER J.W. RODGER 1902
100 50 0 50 100 FEET 250
10 0 50 METRES 100

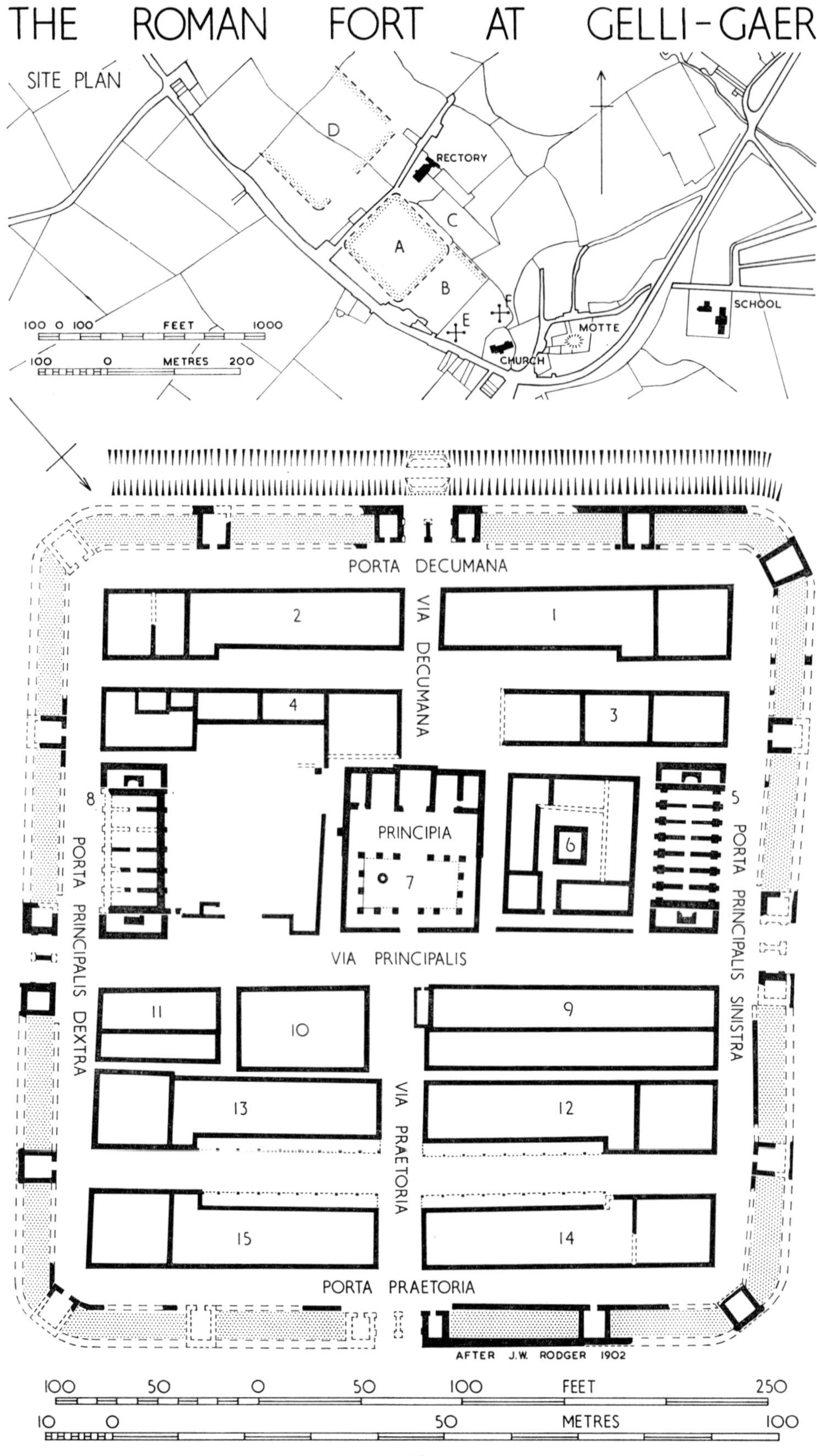

FIG. 53. No. 737.

This was approximately 119 m long from N.E. to S.W. by 65 m wide (0·75 hectare), and was bisected by a roadway leading direct from the *Porta Principalis Dextra* to a simple gateway in the S.E. wall of the annexe. The defences consisted of a stone wall 0·9 m thick, backed with earth; a berm 1·8–3·1 m wide; and a shallow V-shaped ditch 4·6 m wide. A small building 3·7 m by 2·8 m just within the N.E. angle of the gateway may have been a guard-chamber. The N.E. half of the annexe was occupied by the fort bath-house, 33·5 m long N.–S. by 19·8 m wide, comprising the usual suite of hot and cold rooms and including a circular *laconicum* or sweating chamber. Some of the rooms were decorated with painted wall-plaster. To the W. of the bath-house projected a courtyard, 19 m by 13 m, containing cooking ovens. The excavator considered the bath-house to be of more than one structural period, part of the remodelling being due to the fact that the builders misjudged the water-level and had to rebuild at a higher level.

The S.W. half of the annexe contained a rectangular yard, 27·5 m by 13·4 m, with a building 13·4 m by 5·8 m projecting from its S.E. wall. There was also an isolated rectangular structure, 11 m by 3·7 m. The purpose of these buildings is obscure.

Trans. Cardiff Nat. Soc., XLII (1909), pp. 25–69; XLIV (1911), pp. 65–91.

(C) Adjoining the N.E. side of the fort is a level area (centred at 1347 9713) some 116 m long from N.W. to S.E. by 49 m wide between the fort ditch and the crest of falling ground to the N.E. (0·5 hectare). Excavation disclosed this to be uniformly gravelled, and delimited on the S.E. by a V-shaped ditch 3·7 m wide and 1·5 m deep. In the excavator's opinion it was a *Parade Ground*.

Trans. Cardiff Nat. Soc., XLVI (1913), pp. 4–7.

(D) North-west of the fort, and centred at 1331 9723, is a large rectangular *Earthwork*, 174 m long from N.E. to S.W. by 128 m wide (2·2 hectares). It is still outlined by a faint bank about 12 m wide and 0·3 m high. The fact that its longer sides are parallel with the fort rampart and that its S.W. side is practically in line with the S.W. side of the fort proves a close connection between the two. Trenching by Ward disclosed it to be defended by a much ploughed-down earthen bank at least 6·1 m wide, fronted by two V-shaped ditches, each 3·4 m wide, separated by an interval of 2·3 m. There are traces of entrances about the middle of the N.E. side and about a third of the way along the N.W. side from the W. angle.

The purpose of the earthwork is uncertain. Ward suggested it was a temporary camp occupied during the construction of the stone fort, but recent opinion regards it as a pre-Trajanic earth-and-timber fort which was abandoned when the garrison moved into a brand-new stone *castellum*. Excavations in 1963 by M. G. Jarrett, in the S. angle, strengthened this supposition and revealed two periods of timber building, one of which (probably the later) ended in destruction by fire.

Trans. Cardiff Nat. Soc., XLVI (1913), pp. 13–19; *Journ. Rom. Stud.*, LI (1961), p. 126; LIV (1964), p. 152.

(E) South-east of the fort and just outside the annexe, at 1349 9696, a Roman tile- and pottery-kiln was discovered in 1913 during the digging of a grave in the churchyard. It was 2·5 m square internally, with walls 0·5 m thick; under the brick floor was a central vaulted main flue and six transverse flues on either side. Fragments of roofing tiles and *mortaria* were found in and around the kiln.

Trans. Cardiff Nat. Soc., XLVI (1913), pp. 7–13.

(F) A 'rough paving and Roman potsherds' are recorded as having been found during the digging of graves in the churchyard at 1356 9698.

Trans. Cardiff Nat. Soc., XLVI (1913), p. 20.

(G) To the S. of the fort and near the Harp Inn, at 1352 9683; Roman cinerary urns containing burnt bones were found in 1910. This would seem to indicate the presence of a Roman cemetery on the S.W. side of the road leading S.E. from the fort.

Among the numerous finds from the site the most important are probably the fragments of Trajanic building inscriptions.[1] Two were found in 1909 in the ditch filling near the S.E. gateway, and a further portion of the larger stone was found about the same place in 1957. A fourth stone was found in 1913 at the N.W. gateway. All three inscriptions appear to be similar and the largest surviving example has been restored as *[Imp(eratori) Ca]es(ari) divi | [Ner(vae) f(ilio) N]er(vae) Traiano | [Aug(usto) Ge]rm(anico) Dac(ico) pont(ifici) | [max(imo) t]rib(unicia) p(otestate) p(atri) p(atriae) co(n)s(uli) V | [imp(eratori) III]I | [leg(io) II Aug(usta)]*

The reference is to the fifth consulship of the Emperor Trajan (103–111), and it is generally accepted that these inscriptions date the building of the stone fort at Gelli-gaer to the first decade of the 2nd century. One of the fragments bears a line of letters which have been read . . . PAN . . . and interpreted as part of the name of the garrison, a *cohors Hispanorum* or *Pannoniorum*, but *Roman Inscriptions* questions this.

The chronology of the fort's history has been a matter of some debate. In 1903, after the main work on the site, Ward believed the fort to have been founded in, or soon after, the time of Frontinus (74–78), and abandoned by 100. This belief was based on the recovery of a quantity of Flavian pottery—mainly late Flavian—and seven coins of which five fall in the period 69–98, and on the apparent absence of rebuilding which seemed to favour a short occupation. The subsequent discovery of the building inscriptions and of further coins of which the latest was one of Hadrian dated between 119 and 138, led Haverfield to argue that the fort was founded *ca.* 105–110 and abandoned during the reign of Hadrian. This view was endorsed by most later authorities including Nash-Williams. But a recent important re-examination of the evidence by Dr. G. Simpson[2] has led her to suggest considerable modifications to the traditional chronology. While accepting the construction of the stone fort in the time of Trajan, she points out that the Flavian pottery must imply an earlier earth-and-timber fort which is probably to be equated with the large earthwork (D); that the datable evidence implies occupation throughout the 2nd century; that there is evidence of a withdrawal of the garrison, possibly in 196 when Clodius Albinus drained Britain of troops to dispute the Imperial throne with Septimius Severus; that after a period of devastation the garrison returned and was forced to carry out repairs including the rebuilding of the S.E. granary; and that late 3rd to mid-4th century pottery implies an even later occupation which may have included the reconstruction of the bath-house.

The objects found are now at N.M.W.

In addition to the sources cited above, see Haverfield, 'Military Aspects', pp. 130–42; *Roman Frontier*, pp. 88–91.

[1] *Roman Inscriptions*, Nos. 397–9; *Journ. Rom. Stud.*, XLVIII (1958), p. 151, No. 6; LII (1962), p. 193, No. 10; Simpson, *Britons*, pp. 22–3.

[2] *Arch. Camb.*, CXII (1963), pp. 49–66.

Gelli-gaer.

ST 19 N.W. (1341 9707) 22 xii 66 XX S.W.

OTHER MILITARY WORKS

In addition to the permanent forts, three other types of structure can be assigned to the Roman army. These are Marching Camps (738–41), Practice Camps (742–50), and Signal Stations (751–2).

Marching camps are large but lightly embanked enclosures, thrown up to protect the encampments of an army during campaigns or field exercises. The accepted view is that one legion required about 8 ha, so Blaen-cwm Bach (739) could have held the equivalent of three legions, Coelbren and Penycoedcae (738, 740) two each, and Twyn y Briddallt (741) perhaps one. Theoretically, a camp was constructed at every night's halt, but it seems impossible to reconcile this with the evidence from Glamorgan.[1] The camps there seem far too few and too widely spaced to provide even for a single campaign, yet the Silures were under attack during the periods 48–60 and 74–8. The known camps lie on the mountain ridges, which would seem to offer natural routes for the passage of armies. These uplands have suffered little disturbance, and are well covered by aerial photography, which led to the discovery of all four camps; it is unlikely, though not impossible, that any have been overlooked in this region.

Whether structural differences imply that camps belong to different campaigns is open to question, but it may be noted that the surviving gateway at Blaen-cwm Bach is protected by a short detached length of bank and ditch.[2] At Twyn y Briddallt a *clavicula* was used, a quadrantal length of bank curving inwards from one side of the gateway.[3] Traces at Penycoedcae suggest that the gates there were similarly protected, and Coelbren, where the gates are destroyed, seems likely from its position to belong to the same campaign as Ystradfellte, which also had a *clavicula*. Considered from another point of view, Twyn y Briddallt stands out in isolation, on account of the way in which its plan is adapted to the terrain. The other three show a rigid geometrical disdain for any surface irregularities.

Practice camps are small square earthworks thrown up by soldiers as part of their training.[4] They reproduce the essential features of the marching camps, having carefully rounded corners and protected gateways, but the area enclosed is far too small to be of any practical use. Nine have been identified in Glamorgan; they fall into three groups. Three (742–4) lie close to the fort at Loughor, and five (746–50) on the Common north of Gelli-gaer; this type of siting, well within a couple of hours' march of a known fort, is characteristic. The single example on Cefn Hirgoed north of Bridgend is similarly placed relative

[1] For general discussion of marching camps see *Arch. Roman Britain*, ch. II; G. Webster, *The Roman Imperial Army* (London, 1969), pp. 167–72. For those in Wales, *Roman Frontier*, pp. 123–6.

[2] This feature is generally referred to in recent literature as a *tutulus*, but in a recent discussion J. P. Wild suggests that the correct term should be *titulum*. The text quoted seems to imply that this word referred to the ditch, and the accompanying bank was called *sanctum*. *Arch. Camb.*, CXVIII (1969), pp. 133–4.

[3] The internal *clavicula* is not known to have been used in Britain after the Flavian period. *Journ. Rom. Stud.*, LIX (1969), p. 123.

[4] *Arch. Roman Britain*, pp. 12–13; R. W. Davies, *Arch. Camb.*, CXVII (1968), pp. 103–20.

to the suggested location of *Bomium*, but cannot safely be taken as supporting evidence for the position of that fort, for it is not itself a perfectly typical practice camp.

The two known *signal stations* (751–2) are also small square enclosures, each with a single entrance.[5] They lie on Hirfynydd, immediately adjacent to the Roman road connecting Neath and Coelbren. If they are regarded as part of a system for signalling between those places, at least two more await discovery, for they are not visible from either fort.

[5] *Arch. Roman Britain*, pp. 60–6; G. Webster, *The Roman Imperial Army* (London, 1969), pp. 247–8.

738–741. MARCHING CAMPS

(738) MARCHING CAMP near COELBREN (Fig. 54). The camp occupies part of a broad low ridge, rising to about 230 m above O.D. and bounded on all sides except the E. by the marshy valleys of the Camnant and Afon Pyrddin. The crest of the ridge runs almost due W. from the S.E. corner, so that most of the interior falls gently to the N., and overlooks the site of the fort (731) on the other side of the Camnant; the fort and camp are about 180 m apart. Most of the interior is peaty, and very wet in the N. half. The S.W. corner and about 60 m of the adjacent sides are lost in a marsh which drains into the Camnant.

The axis of the camp lies slightly W. of N. The N. and S. sides are almost parallel, true bearing 073°; the E. and W. sides run at 345° and 340° respectively. The camp is 438 m long, tapering from 332 to 305 m, the area being about 14 hectares. Where best preserved, in the S. half of the W. side, the defences consist of a bank and ditch about 4·6 m wide by 0·3 m high overall, but for most of the circuit except in the S.W. quarter they have been damaged by the construction of field banks on or very near their line. The rampart can be detected almost throughout the circuit, and the rounded corners (except the S.W.) remain recognisable; but all details of the entrances have been destroyed.

Cadoxton-juxta-Neath (E), Neath Higher (C).

SN 81 S.E. (8620 1025) 19 ii 68 IV S.W.

(739) MARCHING CAMP, BLAEN-CWM BACH (Fig. 55, Plate 13). The camp stands about 5 km E.N.E. of the Roman fort at Neath, at about 245 m above O.D., near the W. end of a ridge along which runs one of the ancient trackways called Cefn Ffordd. Its long axis lies 80° E. of N., corresponding roughly with that of the ridge. Compared with the other marching camps of the county, it is greatly elongated; it measures approximately 908 m by 295 m, and has an area of about 26·7 hectares, including a hectare of marshy ground. Its whole outline can be traced either on the ground or on air photographs, except at the S.E. corner which has been destroyed by the farm buildings of Blaen-cwm Bach, and for the W. half of the N. side which may never have been built, as the presence here of a steep natural scarp falling to marsh

made it unnecessary. The E. half of the N. side is overlooked by higher ground, but the position is otherwise good.

The enclosing bank and ditch are now about 4·6 m wide by 0·9 m high overall. The corners are boldly rounded, to a radius of about 21·5 m. Only one entrance survives, near the centre of the W. side. It is a simple gap about 7·6 m wide, protected by a *titulum* in the form of a rather slighter bank and ditch of similar length set parallel to the main rampart and 13·7 m from it.

The enclosure contains a small earthwork (627).

Llantwit-juxta-Neath (E), Tonna (C).

SS 79 N.E. (7960 9870). 8 x 58 XVI N.E.

(740) MARCHING CAMP, PENYCOEDCAE (Fig. 56), S. of Pontypridd on fairly level ground at about 230 m above O.D. The camp is nearly rectangular, with boldly rounded corners, and measures 478 m E.–W. by 320 m, enclosing 15·2 hectares, including about 3 hectares of marsh. It is overlooked by a large natural mound, Twyn Maes-y-grug, which stands about 137 m S. of the S.E. corner.

Where best preserved, the bank and ditch measure about 4·6 m wide and 0·9 m high overall, but only short lengths near and including the N.E. and S.E. corners remain undamaged, and the latter is much overgrown. The E. side can be traced on the ground, but most of the S. side has been destroyed though its line is still visible on aerial photographs. Much of the remaining circuit is followed more or less closely by modern field boundaries. No gates can be certainly identified, though there are gaps in the middle of the E. side (with a trace of a possible inturned *clavicula*) and in the apparently modern bank on the N. side, 274 m from the N.E. corner.

Llantwit Fardre (E), Pontypridd (C).

ST 08 N.E. (0670 8800) 7 x 58 XXXVI N.W.

(741) MARCHING CAMP, TWYN Y BRIDDALLT (Fig. 56), N. of Ferndale in the Rhondda-fach, at about 440 m above O.D., following the top of a ridge. The enclosing bank and ditch, where best preserved, measure about 5·5 m wide and 0·9 m high overall. The camp is set out to take advantage of the form of the ground instead of with geometrical regularity,

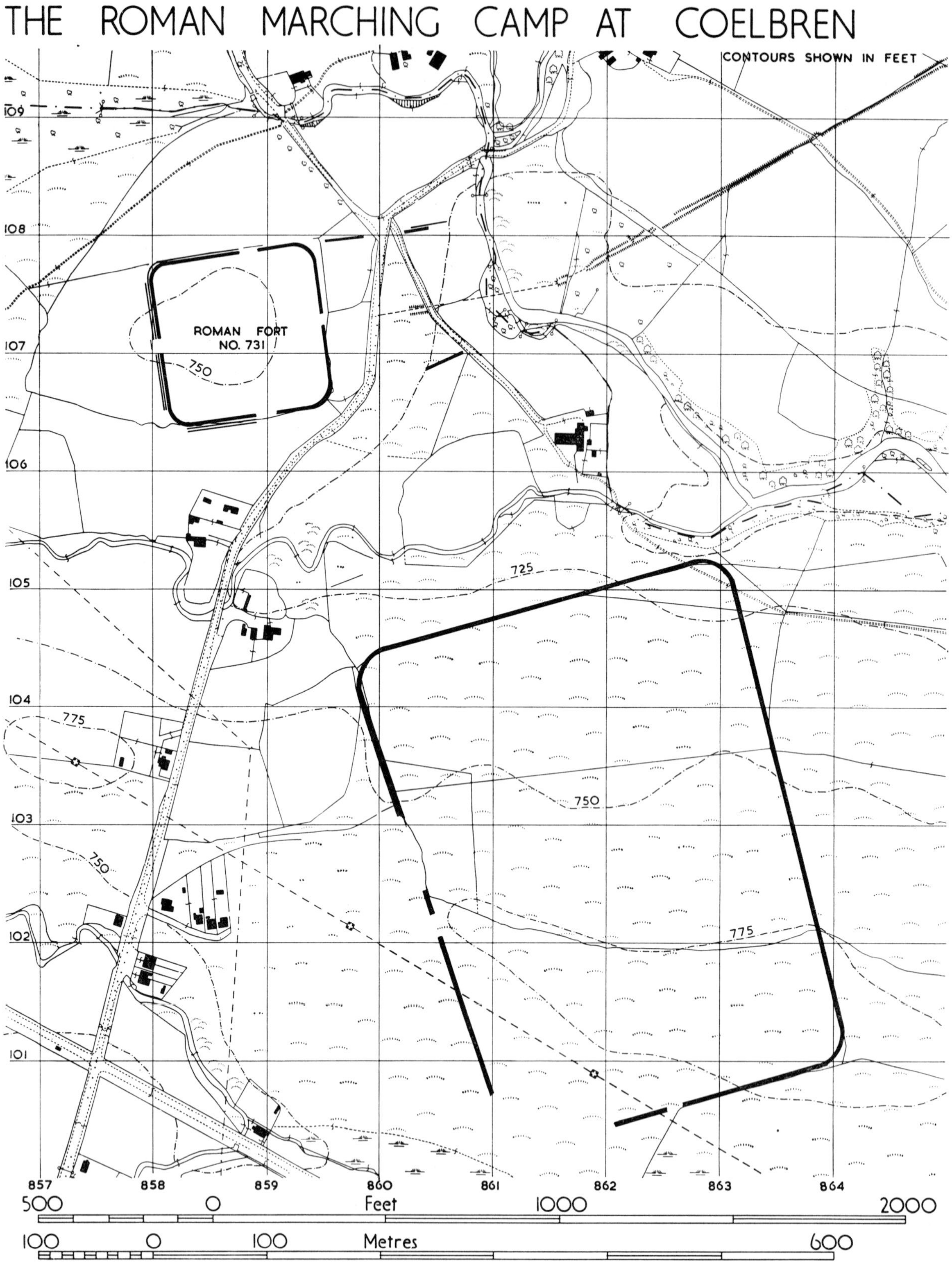

THE ROMAN MARCHING CAMP AT COELBREN

CONTOURS SHOWN IN FEET

ROMAN FORT
NO. 731

750
725
775
750
750
775

109
108
107
106
105
104
103
102
101

857 858 859 860 861 862 863 864

500 0 Feet 1000 2000

100 0 100 Metres 600

FIG. 54. No. 738.

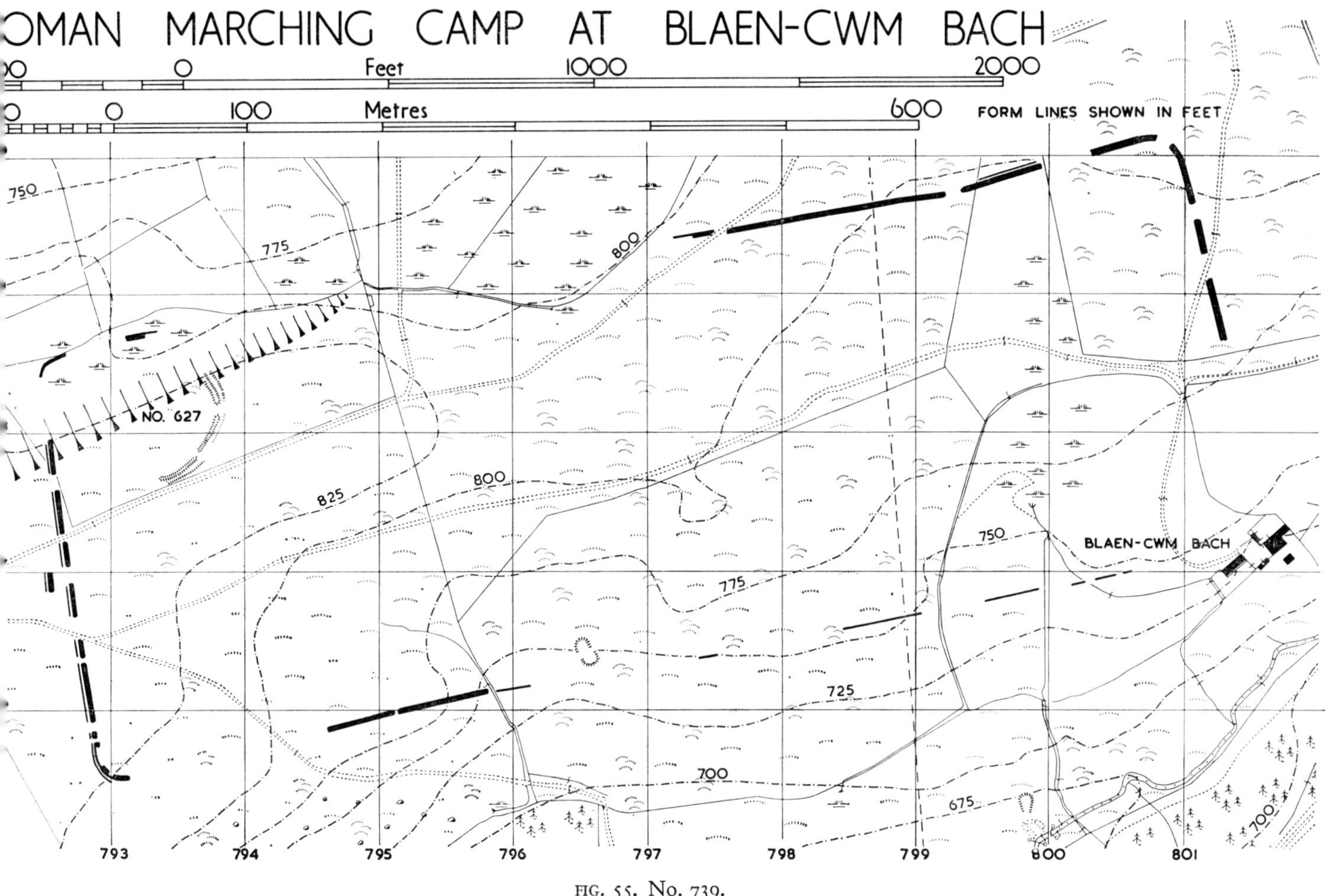

FIG. 55. No. 739.

and at the S.W. end the line of the rampart is interrupted by marshy hollows. Some at least of these breaks seem to be original, as the ends of the bank on each side of the N. marshy patch are neatly rounded. Overall, the enclosure measures about 402 m N.W.–S.E. and 183 m wide; the area is 7·3 hectares.

There are entrances on the N.W. and N.E. Each has an internal *clavicula* of about 7·6 m radius, formed by a bank about 3·6 m wide and 0·6 m high.

Aberdâr/Llanwynno (E), Aberdâr/Rhondda (C).

ST 09 N.W. (0015 9820) 10 x 58 XVIII N.E.–S.E.

742–750. PRACTICE CAMPS

(742) PRACTICE CAMP on STAFFORD COMMON S. of Gorseinon, in level marshy ground at 9 m above O.D. It consists of a rectangular enclosure with rounded corners, 53 m long from N.N.E. to S.S.W. by 46 m wide, defined by a slight bank 3 m wide and 0·2 m high. The bank is preserved only intermittently, mainly on the N. and E. sides and at the N.W. and S.W. angles. Along the E. side a modern field bank lies just within the rampart. The S. side is very indistinct and appears to have been dug away. In places an external ditch is visible, mainly at the N.W. angle where it is 2 m wide, and along the W. side and S.W. angle where it is traceable as a bank of reeds. There are no signs of entrances or internal structures.

Loughor (E), Gowerton (C).

SS 59 N.E. (5914 9731) 28 vi 61 XIV S.W.

(743–4) PRACTICE CAMPS on MYNYDD CARN-GOCH S.E. of Gorseinon. Two square earthworks with rounded corners are visible on level ground at 55 m above O.D. Both are greatly worn down, and the more easterly (744) has suffered from modern disturbance. Doubts might be entertained as to their character and antiquity, especially since they lie on an old golf course which has several rectangular earthworks that are nothing more than the old tees. But 743, in spite of its denuded

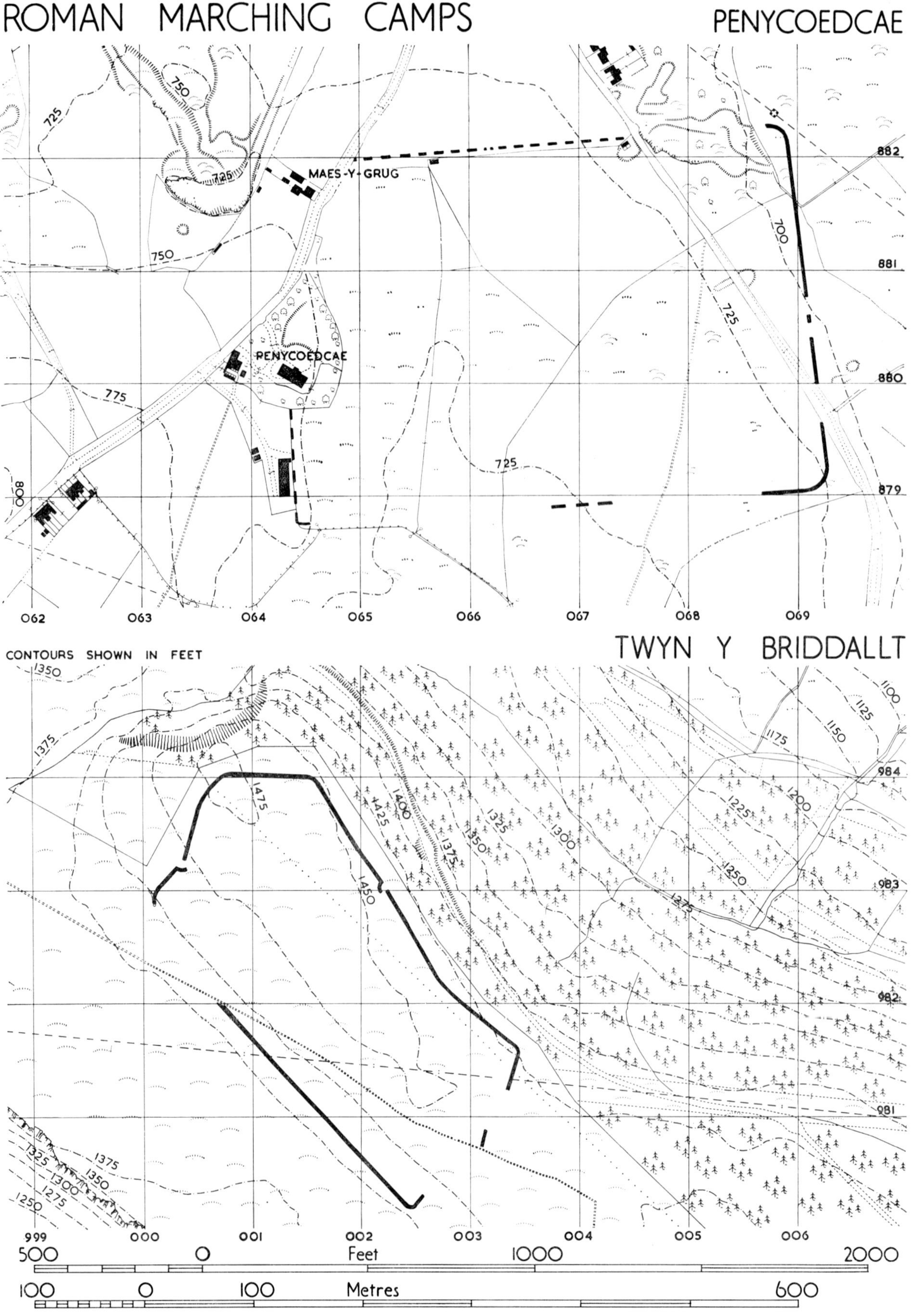

FIG. 56. Nos. 740, 741.

condition, is clearly recognisable as a practice camp; and both sites are mentioned as early as 1811.

Carlisle, *Top. Dict.*, s.v. 'Lloughor'; *Arch. Camb.*, 1886, p. 343; Morgan, *E. Gower*, p. 26.

(743) (Fig. 57.) The western camp is 23 m square, defined by a very slight bank about 2 m wide and 0·3 m high, outside which are traces of a ditch 1·5 m wide. In the middle of each side is an entrance, 1–2 m wide, with traces of a much worn-down *clavicula*.

Loughor (E), Gowerton (C).

SS 69 N.W. (6077 9718) 8 iv 69 XIV S.E.

(744) At 110 m E.N.E. of No. 743. 25 m square, defined by a bank 3 m wide and 0·4 m high, outside which a marshy area 1 m wide probably represents the ditch. There is a simple entrance 2 m wide in the middle of the S. side. There has been some dumping of earth on the W. side. Turf stripping in the interior a few years ago is said to have revealed a floor of slag and clinker; and at the time of examination slag, clinker and a concrete slab were found under the turf on top of the bank at the S.E. corner. The common was occupied by an army camp during the Second World War, and it is possible that this site was utilised as a hut base.

Loughor (E), Gowerton (C).

SS 69 N.W. (6086 9719) 8 iv 69 XIV S.E.

(745) PRACTICE CAMP (?) on CEFN HIRGOED N.E. of Bridgend, at 122 m above O.D. on ground with a slight fall to the S. A rectangular enclosure, measuring (between the crests of the bank) 43 m from E. to W. by about 34 m. It is defined by a bank 3–3·4 m wide and 0·3 m high, with an external ditch 0·3 m deep; the overall width of the defences is 5–5·5 m. An entrance 5·5 m wide is situated about the middle of the N. side. The defences are largely bracken-covered, and the S. end of the earthwork is mutilated by a footpath and quarry hollows.

Coety (E), C. Higher (C).

SS 98 S.W. (9228 8278) 25 vi 63 XXXIV S.E.

(746) PRACTICE CAMP W. of TY'R MYNYDD on Gelli-gaer Common, at about 277 m above O.D. on ground falling gently to the W. The only traces visible on the ground are low banks now much spread, but aerial photography and an earlier visit[1] showed it to have been a rectangular enclosure with rounded corners, 22 m long N.E.–S.W. by 20 m along the S.W. side. There is an entrance gap 10 m wide in the S.E. side, staggered so as to make the N.E. side of the earthwork only 16·5 m long. A drainage ditch has cut the enclosure into two unequal parts from N.E. to S.W.

[1] Dr. J. K. S. St. Joseph *in lit.*

Gelli-gaer.

ST 19 N.W. (1161 9862) 13 x 60 XIX N.E.

(747-50) PRACTICE CAMPS, FFOREST GWLADYS (on Gelli-gaer Common). Nos. 747 and 748 are E. of Capel Gwladys, 749 and 750 W. of Bargoed. 747 and 749 are closely similar both in size and plan, with gaps in the two longer sides, one simple and one with an internal *clavicula*. The ramparts of 747, 749 and 750 now appear as earthen banks accompanied by an external ditch, about 6 m wide and 0·9 m high overall where best preserved, though in places the height is only about 0·3 m and the ditch is often almost invisible. These three seem to be undisturbed.

(747) (Fig. 57, Plate 14). In moorland at 260 m above O.D., on a slightly raised promontory of dry ground between two marshy streamlets. 25 m by 20·7 m between the crests of the bank; entrances about 4·6 m wide.

Gelli-gaer.

ST 19 N.W. (1315 9908) 21 iv 64 XX N.W.

(748) At 347 m N. of No. 747, on fairly level ground at 275 m above O.D. It is almost square, measuring about 22 by 25 m along the centre-line of the banks; the longer axis is 18° E. of N. The banks are much spread by former cultivation, and now measure about 2 m by 0·2 m high. There is a trace of a gateway in the middle of the W. side, but no *clavicula* or *titulum* is visible. The E. side is almost obliterated, and there is no other original opening in the N. or S. side.

Gelli-gaer.

ST 19 N.W. (1315 9943) 7 vii 69 XX N.W.

(749) (Fig. 57, Plate 14). At 640 m E. of No. 747, in enclosed pasture on a fairly level summit at 290 m above O.D. 24·4 m by 20·7 m; E. entrance about 4·9 m wide, W. entrance 3·7 m.

Gelli-gaer.

ST 19 N.W. (1379 9917) 9 ix 69 XX N.W.

(750) At 73 m E. of 749 (Plate 14). About 39·5 m by 36·5 m overall, with its angles to the cardinal points. It has a plain gap in each of the longer (N.W. and S.E.) sides.

Gelli-gaer.

ST 19 N.W. (1386 9916) 21 iv 64 XX N.W.

Omitted and Doubtful Sites

(i) At the western edge of the summit plateau of Cefn Morfudd, E. of Neath, are thirteen small quadrangular earthworks. They are disposed in two groups. The first group of four extends in a line N.–S. between SS 7819 9750 and 7816 9735 (145 m), between 265 and 275 m above O.D. The second group of nine follows the 290 m contour from N.N.W. to S.S.E., from 7857 9720 to 7885 9664 (635 m). They are all approximately square in plan though the sides vary slightly in length and the corners are not always right-angles. The smallest is 10·7 m square, the largest 36·6 m, but the majority are about 23 m square. Each enclosure is bounded by a bank 3 m wide and 0·8 m high, with an external V-shaped ditch 2·8 m wide and a slight counterscarp bank. The angles are sharp, and there are no entrances. The purpose and date of these structures are obscure, and literature and local tradition are alike silent about them. They have none of the characteristics of genuine Roman practice camps, and the banks have a sharp and recent appearance. On the other hand the most southerly enclosure (7885 9664) is cut through by a boundary bank so that they must be earlier than the system of field-enclosures on the mountain. It is possible they may have been 'bee gardens', where the hives were kept during the summer months for the bees to gather honey from the heather. SS 79 N.E. (785 972) XVI S.W.

(ii) A short distance W. of 748, in the same field, a similar but slightly larger bank runs in three straight sections, 17 m at 100°, 17 m at 30° and 7 m at 300°. Its function is uncertain. It seems unlikely to be an unfinished practice camp, for the corners are sharp, and the first two sections are not at right-angles. ST 19 N.E. (1312 9944) XX N.W.

(iii) Golden Mile, near Cowbridge. Lewis (*Top Dict.*, s.v. Cowbridge) mentions two small camps about here. These cannot now be identified with certainty, and may have been practice camps; but it seems more likely that one was the enclosure on Mynydd Bychan (681). The other may have formed part of the early modern field system at Corrwg. SS 97 N.E. (96 76) XLI S.W.

751–752 SIGNAL STATIONS

(751) SIGNAL STATION on HIRFYNYDD (Fig. 57), at 451 m above O.D. on a broad mountain ridge with a superb outlook in all directions, extending as far as the Preseli Mountains in Pembrokeshire. The station stands on the line of the Roman road over Hirfynydd (see No. 755), and consists of an approximately square earthwork measuring (between the crests of the rampart) 19·5 m from N.W. to S.E. by 18·3 m. The defences comprise a low spread grassgrown bank, 1·8–3·7 m wide, with rounded corners and external ditch. Internally the bank is nowhere more than 0·3 m high; externally it is 0·3 m high along the S.E. and S.W. sides, 0·6 m along the other two sides, and 0·9 m at the W. angle. The single entrance lay at the middle of the S.E. side, facing the road. The ditch is 2·7–3·1 m wide and at the entrance is interrupted by a causeway about 3·7 m wide. There are no signs of internal structures. A deep trench N. of the site appears to be a recent quarry hollow.

Cadoxton-juxta-Neath (E), Dulais Higher (C).

SN 80 N.W. (8284 0663) 27 iv 64 IX N.E.

(752) SIGNAL STATION in RHEOLA FOREST, at 372 m above O.D. on the line of the Roman road over Hirfynydd (see No. 755). It consists of a portion of a small quadrangular earthwork, presumably square but the N.W. side has been destroyed during afforestation. It measures 9·1 m from N.E. to S.W. between the crests of the bank, which is 1·8–2·5 m wide and 0·3 m high, with rounded corners and an external ditch about 1·5 m wide. The height of the bank above the bottom of the ditch reaches 0·6 m at the E. and S. angles. There is a faint suggestion of an entrance and a causeway crossing a ditch about the middle of the S.E. side (probably the side adjoining the road, *cf.* No. 751).

Cadoxton-juxta-Neath (E), Dulais Lower (C).

SN 80 S.W. (8124 0401) 27 iv 64 IX S.E.

ROADS

So far as it affects Glamorgan, the general arrangement of the main road system is well established. It is essentially triangular, with the vertex at Brecon Gaer and the base running from Caerleon to Neath and produced westward to Carmarthen, but many details remain unknown. The only part of the system where substantial structural features are recorded is where the Neath to Coelbren 'Sarn Helen' follows the Hirfynydd ridge. This forms an interesting contrast to the meagre traces of the road running north from Cardiff, even where its line should appear on the undisturbed common land of Cefn Gelli-gaer. Much of the original Roman alignment of the east–west road has been preserved by the modern highway, but this seems to have destroyed every structural trace except about 200 m of *agger* on the ridge between the Ogmore and Ewenni rivers.

That other roads existed is certain, if only to serve the local needs of the small farms in the Vale; establishments such as that at Llantwit Major, in its prime, can hardly have been content to depend entirely on unmetalled trackways. Many of the existing roads in this region are quite well aligned and are followed for much of their lengths by parish boundaries. The possibility of a Roman origin for some of these cannot be completely dismissed, but proof is entirely lacking.

Ffordd y Gyfraith (I iii, p. 3) is the only trackway for which any positive case could be made out. The relevant part runs from just north of Laleston (SS 872 802) to Mynydd Baiden (SS 866 857), where it becomes a normal ridgeway. This length, of 5·5 km, is set out essentially in three straight sections, with angles on

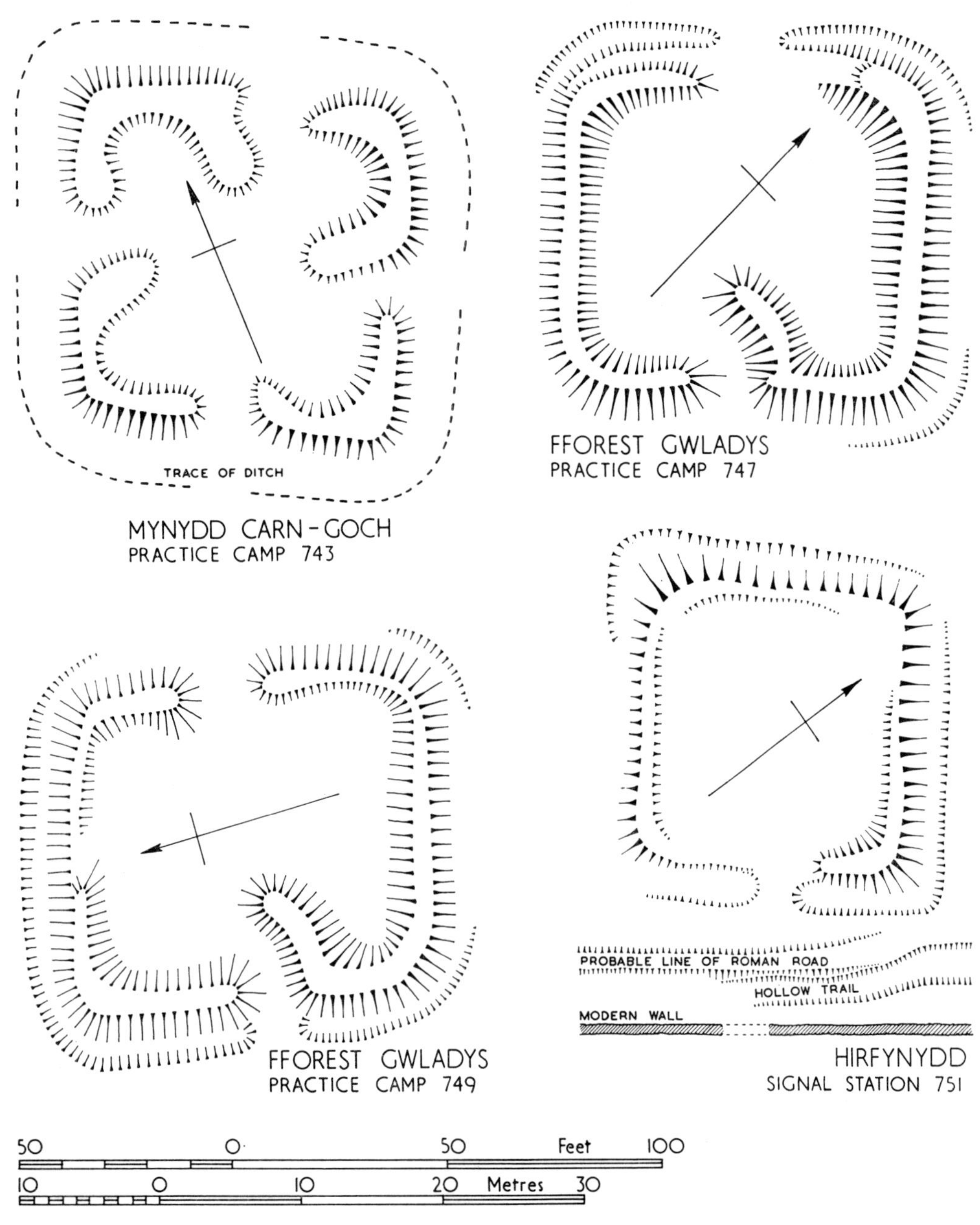

FIG. 57. Nos. 743, 747, 749, 751.

Cefn Cribwr (SS 865 822) and on a southern spur of Mynydd Baiden (SS 870 847); it also uses sharp zig-zags to descend steep slopes. These features are characteristic of known Roman roads, but it is difficult to see how this track could fit into the general network. In default of more positive proof, its Roman origin must remain doubtful.

Even for the three main roads, although their general routes are certain the exact details are not. The actual line of a length of Roman work can only be established either by the survival of structural features, such as an *agger* or paving, or by characteristically Roman setting-out. These are minimal requirements. The Cardiff–Neath road, for example, is set out characteristically, in an almost exact alignment from St. Hilary Down to Stormy Down; so although in the whole 17 km the only known structure to survive is the short length of *agger* near Bridgend, the greater part of this stretch can be accepted as following the Roman line. By contrast, although the section from Bonvilston to Cardiff includes some short straight lengths, the general route is quite un-Roman in planning. It is possible that some parts of the road may coincide with the Roman line, but no evidence to support this view has ever been published. Similarly, the traces visible on Cefn Gelli-gaer may represent the actual road leading north to Penydarren, but they are unconvincingly slight for Roman work. The nature of the evidence does not justify detailed mapping, and can be more satisfactorily and precisely defined by means of grid references. The entries dealing with the roads therefore fall into two parts: a general account of the route, which will be sufficient for most purposes; and a detailed description of the actual remains, based primarily on grid references, which will enable anyone who wishes to study the road in greater detail to locate its traces with precision on the ground or on a large-scale map.

The Roman milestones all occur in association with the Cardiff–Loughor Road (753) and are described in that entry. They have received definitive publication in the first volume of *Roman Inscriptions*.

(753) CAERLEON TO LOUGHOR. The existence of this road is attested by the Antonine Itinerary (Iter XII), which is discussed in relation to the position of *Bomium* (p. 121). In some earlier accounts the road is called *Via Julia Maritima*, but the name has no historical justification.[1] Except for a short length of *agger* S. of Bridgend no structural remains have ever been recorded, but for about 16 km the setting-out is typically Roman, in a long straight run between sighting-points. Elsewhere the exact line followed by the road is mostly uncertain, but its general direction is not in doubt. In the 20 km S.E. of Neath five milestones have been discovered; unfortunately none was certainly *in situ*.

Codrington,[2] followed by some later writers, suggests a line of road crossing the Taf near Llandaf, some 2 km above Cardiff Castle; but there is no evidence whatever to support this hypothesis.[3]

General description. Entering the county on the east, and passing close to the Roman fort at Cardiff (735), the modern A48 must follow the same general route as its precursor; but topography offers no reason why the road should not have been set out in the normal Roman way, so although some short lengths of the modern and ancient lines may coincide there is no convincing evidence for this until the approach to St. Hilary Down, some 20 km from the point at which it enters the county and 17 km W. of the fort at Cardiff. Here a short length of the modern main road, and a lane continuing the same line, run straight for a kilometre to the summit of the Down, followed by a parish boundary. From the summit the line of road points straight through Cowbridge for some 18 km towards Stormy Down, 6 km W. of Bridgend. Apart from a few small deviations, probably modern, existing roads follow the whole of this line except where it crosses the valleys of the Ogmore and Ewenni. Midway between these rivers, and close to the correct line of sight, a short length of *agger* survives; it is the only remaining fragment of the original road, and was discovered during search for the lost fort of *Bomium*, which probably stood near this point.

Westward from Stormy Down, the exact route again becomes uncertain. Existing roads continue the alignment fairly accurately to Mawdlam near Kenfig and then northwards along Water Street, which follows a generally fairly direct line. This route appears in Margam charters of the 13th century as *via regalis*,[4] and the 6th-century Pumpeius stone (I iii 849) stood close to it, but the milestones (i) and (ii) from the main street of Pyle and the Coal Brook, though not *in situ*, suggest that a more easterly route is likely. Sections of modern road for about 1·5 km N.W. of Stormy Down and N.W. and S.E. of Margam align fairly accurately, and may correspond to the Roman road, but in the absence of any structural evidence this cannot be accepted as certain. From Margam to Neath the milestones (iii) to (v) show that the Roman road must have followed much the same course as the modern one; but although the possible choice is restricted by the topography there is no evidence of any kind for the exact line, and no reason to assume that the two coincide.

West of Neath the road has been discussed by W. Ll. Morgan,[5] but although once again topography limits the choice of route there is no evidence of any kind until the Tawe is reached. In excavations for the canal, about 1·5 km above the bridge at Swansea, the old ford was discovered, constructed of beams of wood rebated together. This is very close to the line, produced, of a straight length of modern road which starts about 3 km from Swansea and continues in two straight sections to Loughor, passing near the practice camps on Mynydd Carn-goch (743–4). The modern road here probably corresponds to the Roman line, as suggested by Morgan.

The Milestones. This road is notable for having yielded five milestones, one with three inscriptions. All have been published with full discussion by R. P. Wright in *Roman Inscriptions* (*RIB*) and *Roman Frontier* (*RFW*),[6] from which the following extracts, with original entry numbers, are taken by permission.

(i) *RIB* 2251; *RFW* 10. Found shortly before 1845 in a wall opposite Pyle Cottage in the main street at Pyle (SS 8269 8222). Now in R.I.S.W. Museum, Swansea.

Imp(eratori) [C(aesari)] | M(arco) ⟨C⟩ Pia|uonio | Victor|ino Aug(usto)

'For the Emperor Caesar Marcus Piavonius Victorinus Augustus.'

A.D. 268–70.

(ii) *RIB* 2255; *RFW* 8. Found in 1926 in the bed of the Coal Brook, Margam, 290 m S.S.E. of Margam East Lodge (SS 8158 8486). Now in N.M.W.

Imp(eratori) C(aesari) | M(arco) C(assianio) L(atinio) | Pos|tum|o Au|g(usto) ⟨G⟩

'For the Emperor Caesar Marcus Cassianius Latinius Postumus Augustus.'

A.D. 258–68.

(iii) *RIB* 2254; *RFW* 18. Found in 1839 on the E. outskirts of Port Talbot near an old toll cottage beside the former main road (SS 7834 8734). Now in Margam Abbey Museum. Cast in N.M.W.

Im[p(eratori) C(aesari)] | Fla(uio) [Va]|l(erio) Maxi|mino | Inuic|to Au|gus(to)

'For the Emperor Caesar Flavius Valerius Maximinus Invictus Augustus.'

Maximinus Daia A.D. 309–13.

The stone was reused on the back for an early Christian inscription (I iii 846), *Hic iacit Cantusus pater Paulinus.*

(iv) *RIB* 2252–3, 2256; *RFW* 5, 13, 17. Found *ca.* 1847 on the W. side of the channel known as New Cut, Port Talbot, Aberavon (probably near SS 756 890). Now at Nottage Court, Porthcawl; cast in N.M.W. The stone has been used for three inscriptions:

Imp(erator) C(aesar) | M(arcus) A(ntonius) Gor|dianus | Aug(ustus)

'The Emperor Caesar Marcus Antonius Gordianus Augustus.'

Gordian III, A.D. 238–44.

Im[p(eratori)] | Caes(ari) | [Do(mino)] No(stro) V|[al(erio)] Lic|[in(io)] P(io) F(elici) A|[u]g(usto)

'For the Emperor Caesar, our Lord, Valerius Licinius Pius Felix Augustus.'

A.D. 308–24.

Imp(eratoribus) C|(aesaribus) Dio|cleti|ano | et MARI|[D]VRE | inu(ictis) A|ug(ustis)

'For the Emperor-Caesars Diocletian and [Maximian], Invicti Augusti.'

A.D. 286–305.

The original inscription to Maximian has been recut and partly obscured so as to read Maridure, perhaps referring to the Roman name of Carmarthen (Maridunum or Moridunum).

(v) *RIB* 2257; *RFW* 14. Found *ca.* 1892 beside the railway line at Melin Crythan (SS 7485 9682). Now in N.M.W.

Imp(eratori) | C(a)es(ari) | [D]io|[c]leti|[a]no | [A]ug(usto)

'For the Emperor Caesar Diocletianus Augustus.'

A.D. 284–305.

Since the stones had probably all been displaced before discovery, and the exact line of the road is unknown, it is impossible to determine whether they were part of an accurately spaced series. On the assumption that they were, the best estimates of their positions, measuring from stone (i), correspond to 2, 5, 7 and 13 'miles' of about 1420 m; but the agreement is not very satisfactory, for stone (iii) was found about 160 m E. of the theoretical position and stone (iv) nearly 200 m too far W.

The inscriptions seem to fall into two groups, three between A.D. 238 and 270 and four between 284 and 324. It has been suggested that the latter group is to be associated with development of the coastal defences implied by the construction of the stone fort at Cardiff[7] but the total number of inscriptions is far too small for the apparent grouping to have any statistical significance.

Details of route. In the first 20 km of the route, a possible fixed point is the bridge over the Ely river, at ST 1454 7683, which occupies the site of an ancient crossing, and is about 0·8 km N. of the villa (762). Even here, certainty is impossible, for the configuration of the valley below the bridge may well have changed since the Roman period. The section of road S.W. of the bridge may in part be on the Roman line, but older maps show it as rather more sinuous than it is now. The convincing section, E. of St. Hilary Down, starts at ST 0250 7390, and the summit of the Down, apparently a sighting point, is at 0143 1389. The corresponding sighting-point, Stormy Down, at the other end of this section, is at SS 8450 8045. Between these points a modern road follows the line with a few slight deviations, except from SS 9265 7735 to 8850 7888, where it is interrupted by the valleys of the Ewenni and the Ogmore. Between these two rivers the *agger* can be traced for about 200 m, from 9040 7827 to 9020 7834; it is now little more than 0·1 m high, and the edges cannot be precisely defined. In the whole section between St. Hilary Down and Stormy Down, although the trace of the road looks straight it in fact deviates slightly; the *agger* just mentioned lies about 100 m N. of the direct line.[8]

From Stormy Down to the Tawe above Swansea the exact

course is lost. The modern roads to Mawdlam (8065 8195) and thence along Water Street (to 8011 8558) follow fairly direct alignments but are far from truly straight. The short straight section which runs N.W. from Stormy Down (8450 8045 to 8356 8154) and those near Margam (8011 8558 to 7964 8620, 7917 8675 to 7900 8700, 7820 8790 to 7766 8855) coincide quite well with a straight alignment, but there is no structural evidence to confirm this route and the milestones (i) and (ii) were found some 300 and 500 m, respectively, from the direct line. They were not *in situ*, but seem unlikely to have been moved so far. The remaining milestones were also not *in situ*, and again merely confirm the general route.

West of Neath the line is lost for some 12 km, but Morgan records the discovery of a well-constructed ford when excavating for the 'Pottery lock' of the Swansea Canal. This name is now lost, but it seems to have been near 6611 9445; the line of the next straight section, produced, would cross the canal at about 6611 9468, 230 m further N. The straight line of modern road tentatively suggested as Roman by Morgan begins at 6320 6599 and continues to Loughor. Again structural evidence is lacking, but the setting-out seems characteristic and Morgan's identification is probably correct.

Margary, *Roman Roads*, p. 325 (Route 60c).

[1] The name *Via Julia* was first applied by Camden, misunderstanding a couplet by Alexander Neckham; *Maritima* was added by Colt Hoare. See J. E. Lloyd, 'Wales and the Past. Two Voices' (N.M.W. Inaugural Lecture, Cardiff, 1932), p. 14 and n. 2.

[2] T. Codrington, *Roman Roads in Britain* (3rd edn., London, 1918), p. 278.

[3] J. Ward, *Arch. Camb.*, 1903, p. 40.

[4] T. Gray, *The Buried City of Kenfig* (London, 1909), pp. 30–2. That the route was unlikely to be Roman was noted by Lady Fox, *Arch. Camb.*, XCIV (1939), p. 39.

[5] Morgan, *E. Gower*, pp. 15–19.

[6] *Roman Inscriptions*, pp. 704–5; *Roman Frontier*, pp. 182–8.

[7] R. E. M. Wheeler, *Trans. Cymmr.*, 1920–1, p. 92; R. P. Wright in *Roman Frontier*, p. 182; Simpson, *Britons*, pp. 168, 171.

[8] For simplicity, measurements have been taken, on the 6-in. O.S. map, from the straight line of the National Grid projection. At the point considered this lies 1·5 m S. of the Great Circle which would correspond to the true line of sight.

(754) CARDIFF TOWARDS BRECON via Gelli-gaer and Penydarren. The traces of this road are very slight indeed and would not be sufficient to establish that one existed were it not for the closely-set forts. These, however, imply some direct route from Cardiff to Brecon. There are two reasons for this lack of evidence: the line to be followed by the road is almost rigidly dictated by the topography, so that the characteristic Roman method of setting-out could seldom be used; and to judge from the fragments which seem to survive on Cefn Gelli-gaer, the road itself rarely consisted of more than a single thin layer of metalling.

General Description. For the first 11 km N. of Cardiff, as far as Caerffili (736), any attempt to define the exact line can only be guesswork. Various sections of modern road run fairly straight, and provide at least two possible alternative routes, but no part is sufficiently accurately aligned to demonstrate its Roman origin, and in this area the topography seems to offer no reason for any deviation from a straight run. Beyond Caerffili an old track still in use, Heol Lâs, follows a fairly direct route rather W. of N. along the E. spur of Mynydd Eglwysilan; this probably corresponds fairly closely to the Roman line, though it is not straight and no structural remains have been found. At the N. of the ridge, about 2 km S. of Nelson, a narrow lane runs E. of N. across a valley, leading fairly directly to the fort at Gelli-gaer (737); this probably succeeds the Roman road, and may follow its line in places. The track Heol Fawr, which leads direct to Nelson, has been claimed as Roman, but seems a less likely route to the fort. This line was favoured by Haverfield,[1] but at that time the existence at Gelli-gaer of an earlier fort, contemporary with Penydarren, had not been recognised.

From that fort the direction is again determined by a natural ridge, Cefn Gelli-gaer, and the modern road, known in part as Heol Adam or Adda, must be on or very near the Roman line. Further N., on the open common, are traces which in default of anything more convincing may be accepted as Roman.

The first trace occurs 4·5 km N. of the fort, as a slight bank about 100 m long, 80 m W. of the modern road. It is then lost for another 1·5 km, after which it reappears on about the same line, W. of the road. Hence it can be traced intermittently for nearly 3 km, first as a bank nearly 5 m wide with shallow side ditches about 3 m wide for 100 m, then for 140 m as a terrace widening from 4 to 6 m, then again after a break as a rather narrower bank not of uniform width for a further 590 m, passing about 70 m W. of the Early Christian stone (842) below Carn Bugail. It then becomes a terrace only about 2·5 m wide, which continues for another 200 m to end again a little N. of Pen-twyn. Near its N. end the terrace has been cut by a landslip crack, and no paving or metalling can be seen in the section. A kilometre further N., due W. of Fochriw, a group of hollow trails descends the steep hillside, and a further short length of terrace 82 m long continues to the modern road. From that point there is no trace in Glamorgan; the road must have curved westwards to reach Penydarren fort (732), and thence N. to reach Brecon. Haverfield states:[2] 'If its final goal was the Usk valley, it would naturally have run straight on, for no physical obstacle hindered it', but this is an astonishing simplification of the formidable task of getting a road across the Brecon Beacons.

This crossing lies in Brecknock, and thus outside the scope of the present volume, but it may be noted that the two possible alternatives[3] both display substantial engineering works, contrasting strongly with the character of the remains in Glamorgan.

Details of Route. Heol Lâs, the first section which can perhaps be regarded as of Roman origin, is first recognisable at ST 1475 8790, about 850 m from the N.W. gate of the recently discovered fort. The line of the existing track continues, as Heol Fawr, as far as Nelson (1137 9549), but the lane which seems more likely to be the successor of the Roman road branches off at 1256 9631, and runs fairly direct to the Gelli-gaer fort (737). Further N., the sections tentatively identified as parts of the original road are as follows:

A slight bank can be traced from 1126 0095 to 1120 0104; a rather clearer bank, nearly 5 m wide with shallow side ditches 3 m wide, standing about 0·5 m high above the ditch bottom, runs from 1069 0267 to 1063 0276; this is followed by a terrace, 4 m wide at its commencement and gradually widening to 6 m, from 1058 0285 to 1050 0296; after a gap, a bank 4 m wide with side ditches 2 m wide, and about 0·4 m high overall, extends from 1034 0323 to 1027 0340, where there is a break, beyond which the line of the *agger* seems to be displaced a short distance to the W.; it then continues as a bank 3 m wide with shallow side ditches 1 m wide and about 0·3 m high overall to 1023 0355, where it becomes a terrace 2·5 m wide which extends to 1018 0375; a section where a landslip crack crosses the terrace shows no trace of metalling. After another interval the line is picked up by a fine group of hollow trails, from 1012 0482 to 1002 0496. These are probably medieval or later, and have destroyed any Roman traces, but there is one more short length of terrace, 5·8 m wide, from 0996 0519 to 1993 0526.

Throughout the whole of the line along Cefn Gelli-gaer hollow trails follow the same general route as the supposed Roman road, and have crossed and obliterated it in some places, while in others the side-ditches seem to have been enlarged and deepened by use as trackways. This damage provides some evidence for the antiquity of the features recorded above, and may explain the apparent variations in width of the supposed *agger* and of the terraces.

Margary, *Roman Roads*, p. 337 (Route 621).
[1] Haverfield, 'Military Aspects', pp. 148–9.
[2] *Ibid.*, pp. 148–9.
[3] Either from SO 036 235 to SO 034 181 by the Taf Fechan valley, as indicated by the O.S. map and accepted by Margary; or the more probable route over Pen Milan to the Taf Fawr valley, from SO 001 238 via SN 992 220, recently identified by the staff of the Commission.

(755) NEATH TOWARDS BRECON via Coelbren (Sarn Helen).

General Description. This is the only Roman road in Glamorgan where good structural traces are recorded. The line must have been roughly that of the modern road running N.E. from Neath through Cadoxton, but the first visible remains appear after 5 km S. of Lletty'rafel-fawr where a short length of well engineered terraceway ascends a cliff. For the next kilometre the probable route is marked by a parish boundary and is followed by a lane, not Roman in its present form. Where this issues on to the open mountain the grass-grown *agger* becomes visible, 6 m wide and 0·5 m high, and Morgan, writing in 1907,[1] records that paving, with kerbs in places, could be traced with few interruptions from here as far as Coelbren. The *agger* can still be followed for about 1600 m, but it then enters the modern Rheola Forest, and has been replaced by a modern track for about 3 km. About half way along this afforested section it passes the remains of a signal station (752).

After emerging on to moorland the line follows the W. edge of the forest. At first it is marked by a hollow trackway across a marshy flat, but after about a kilometre the ground begins to rise and the road again becomes visible, the actual pavement being exposed where it tops the ascent. Just before reaching this point, a little W. of the road, is a small cairn (110a) which may have formed a base for an upright stone. The position would be consistent with the former presence of an Early Christian monument. From here the road can be followed to the second signal station (751). It may be noted that the two signal stations are two Roman miles apart, and that the more southerly (752) is very nearly equidistant from Neath and Coelbren, at 6 Roman miles from each, but this spacing is probably mere coincidence.

Over the stretch just mentioned, and N. of the signal station, the crest of the ridge is followed by a modern wall which indicates the line of the Roman road and of its medieval successor. The relationship of the three is shown in Fig. 57. The road survives as a low flat-topped ridge, from 3 to 4·5 m wide, W. of the wall, and the hollow trail usually runs between them, though it wanders somewhat and occasionally trespasses on to and obliterates the Roman road. There are old quarry scrapes along the W. side of the *agger* which may have served for its construction, but to judge from their condition are more likely to have provided material for the modern wall.

North-eastward from the signal station the *agger* can be traced for about 700 m, where it bends markedly more towards the E.; the bank is visible right round the angle, 3 m wide and 0·3 m high. Beyond this point the road is more broken, but it can be followed for another 850 m to its highest point, 477 m above O.D. There its trace is lost, but earlier accounts indicated that it followed the line of the wall along the ridge for nearly 2 km more, and then turned through a right-angle to run straight towards the S. gate of Coelbren. The Clwydi Banwen stone (841) stood near the angle. Where the line descended the hillside all trace has been destroyed by open-cast mining, but it is followed by the modern road through Banwen Pyrddin and a short length of *agger* survives just S. of the fort. Another short length leads from the E. gate towards the Afon Pyrddin, which here forms the county boundary.

Details of Route. The first appearance of the original road, near Lletty'rafel-fawr, is at SN 7891 0069, whence a track runs W. for 32 m and then turns sharply N. and ascends a cliff as a grassy terrace 3·5 to 5·5 m wide, issuing at the top (7891 0075) through a gap in the outcrop; the total rise is over 20 m. An old lane which has obliterated the Roman work is followed by the parish boundary for a kilometre, and where it issues on the open mountain, at SN 7940 0163, a grass-grown *agger* becomes visible, 6 m wide and 0·5 m high, which can be followed in two straight stretches joined by a curve for 1600 m. At 8023 0292 it enters Rheola Forest, and is replaced by a modern track for 3160 m, to 8222 0532, passing the signal station at 8124 0401. After leaving the forest a hollow trail across a marshy flat, from 8227 0554 to 8233 0565 and about 40 m W. of the existing track, may correspond to the original line. The small cairn (110a), is at 8229 0582. The road reappears at 8242 0606, and pavement is visible at 8248 0618. The *agger* continues in good condition for 700 m past the signal station (751) at 8284 0663 to a bend at 8326 0724, and can be traced, though less well preserved, to 8405 0768. The Clwydi Banwen stone stood at 8519 0855. The final straight section begins at 8558 0943, and continues to the S. gateway of the fort at Coelbren.

Margary, *Roman Roads*, p. 338 (Route 622).
[1] *Arch. Camb.*, 1907, pp. 130–3.

CIVIL SITES

THE extension of the Roman villa system of land-use from Somerset and the Cotswolds across the Severn and along the coast of South Wales has long been known. The Vale of Glamorgan has provided two good examples of villas whose details have been revealed by careful excavation: Ely near Cardiff (762) and Llantwit Major (758). In both cases the work was begun by John Storrie, to be continued at Ely by Wheeler and at Llantwit Major by Nash-Williams. Neither building was completely uncovered, and some problems remain unresolved at the latter site. A third establishment, at Whitton Lodge (761) south of St. Nicholas, has now been fully excavated by M. G. Jarrett. Its size justifies classing it as a villa, but it is not typical either in plan or position.

At present, only two Roman buildings are known in Glamorgan west of Llantwit Major, at Oystermouth (756) and near Porth-cawl (757). This apparent rarity is almost certainly misleading. In the neighbourhood of Barry,[1] fieldwork by Howard Thomas during 1956–7 identified twelve new Roman sites, including the villa at Whitton Lodge. Not all of these, as Thomas himself realised, were necessarily villas, but three have been accepted as such, at Moulton (759), Llanbethery (760) and Whitton Lodge. The nature of the other seven is not certain, but all have produced building debris, and actual walling has been found at three (765, 766, 768).[2]

Entries in this section of the Inventory are therefore restricted to sites where there is some evidence for masonry, implying Romanised civil occupation. Attention has been drawn above (p. 8) to the frequent occurrence of Roman pottery in hill-forts, to the settlement which remains visible in Caer Dynnaf (670), and to that which superseded the fortified enclosure on Mynydd Bychan (681). There seems to be no doubt that Whitton Lodge evolved from a pre-Roman establishment without any significant break in the occupation. At Moulton, too, the presence of iron-age material beneath the building suggests a similar development there.

In the context of fairly full Romanisation indicated by the villas and other buildings, the continued use of caves, apparently for dwelling-places, seems curious; material indicating some Roman activity has been found at Hound's Hole and Goat's Hole, Paviland (I i 4–5), Spritsail Tor (10), Culver Hole (9), Minchin Hole (12) and Lesser Garth near Radyr (19); the first five are in Gower. Culver Hole and Spritsail Tor were used for burials, and domestic occupation is not certain, but at Lesser Garth and Minchin Hole such use is indicated by domestic pottery, with hearths and evidence of metal-working at the latter. The last three remained in use into the Early Christian period, and Bacon Hole (14) seems also to have been inhabited then, though no Roman material was found there.

---

[1] *B.B.C.S.*, XVII, iv (May 1958), pp. 293–6.

[2] In the accounts of all these sites the Commission has been much assisted by unpublished information compiled by Miss V. G. Bishop (Mrs Swan) as an honours thesis for the University of Wales.

756–762 VILLAS

(756) ROMAN VILLA at OYSTERMOUTH CHURCH, at 9 m above O.D. near the shore of Swansea Bay. From the 17th century onwards, fragments of Roman mosaic pavement have been found during grave digging in the churchyard, especially on its N. side. Four pieces, found in 1860, are fixed to a mural tablet at the E. end of the N. aisle of the church; the tesserae are black, light cream, deep grey and red in colour, some forming a guilloche pattern. Sherds of black and red Roman pottery have also been found, and a small lead ingot (? Roman) with a stamped mark.

Two coins were found in 1822 'in digging foundations near Oystermouth'; one was of Caracalla, dated 213–17, the other of Severus Alexander (222–35). In 1837 a coin of Trajan dated 112–17 was found 'in digging a well at the Mumbles'.

Morgan, *E. Gower*, pp. 138, 140; *Arch. Camb.*, 1919, pp. 227–9; *Trans. Cymmr.*, 1965, p. 85.

Oystermouth.
SS 68 N.W. (6165 8802) 20 iii 67 XXXII N.E.

(757) ROMAN VILLA (?) at DAN-Y-GRAIG N.E. of Porthcawl, at 30 m above O.D. In 1850, during improvements to the grounds of the house, pieces of *opus signinum* flooring were found, together with fragments of painted wall-plaster, nails in a length of board, an iron key, and 'a coin of a Roman empress'.

Arch. Camb., 1853, pp. 96–7.

Newton Nottage.
SS 87 N.W. (8403 7803) 3 ii 67 XL S.W.

(758) ROMAN VILLA at CAE'R-MEAD near Llantwit Major (Fig. 58, Plate 15) on level ground at 76 m above O.D. The villa, the largest and best known in Glamorgan, was discovered and partly excavated in 1887–8 by J. Storrie,[1] and more fully examined by V. E. Nash-Williams in 1938–9 and 1948.[2] A small area was re-excavated in 1971[3] in order to resolve a discrepancy in the dating evidence.

The main outlines of the villa can still be traced; in places the tops of walls are visible, especially at the S.E. angle. The plan, as exposed by Nash-Williams, seems to be a fairly complete record of the stone buildings as they existed at the period of greatest prosperity, in the 4th century A.D. Traces of ruinous walls suggest a further courtyard to the N., and Storrie records a very large room here,[4] but the dimensions given by him do not agree with the indications now visible. No further discussion of this extension is possible without excavation.

Storrie cut an exploratory trench across the N. side of the villa through room 50, across the junction of rooms 7 and 8, and across the middle of room 14; rooms 7–9 and 14 were cleared. In rooms 8 and 9 he discovered the skeletons of three horses and thirty-seven humans, almost all male, scattered irregularly over a damaged mosaic floor; some of the skulls had been fractured by blows. He is explicit in distinguishing these remains from four formal interments found in the same rooms, and in one account the two groups are described as of different physique.[5] Two other formal burials were found near room 14.

In Nash-Williams's excavations rooms 8 and 9 were again cleared, together with the bath block (rooms 22–30) but most of his work was directed towards recovering the complete plan of the villa by following the lines of the walls. The adjacent earthworks were also partly investigated and the presence of ditches was demonstrated to N. and E. of the buildings; their full arrangement was not worked out.

The plan recovered was that of a villa of double courtyard type, with ranges of buildings round an inner courtyard on the W. and an outer yard on the E. The whole complex measured approximately 78 m from N. to S. by 73 m from E. to W. The main house comprised the N. and W. ranges round the inner courtyard. The S. end was linked by an enclosure wall to a single large rectangular building (Building B) facing the outer yard. The E. range comprised two long rectangular structures (Buildings A, C), while closing the outer courtyard on the N. and W. were two wings at right-angles to one another forming an appendage to the E. end of the N. range of the main house. The material used was local limestone and sandstone, supplemented with Bath stone for such features as columns, finials and ridge-pieces. The roofs were covered with slabs of Pennant sandstone, though the occurrence of tile-fragments suggested that part of the villa had at first been roofed with tiles. The profusion of nails indicated an extensive use of timber, probably for roof principals and rafters. Odd scraps of window-glass provided evidence for glazed windows. Interior walls were rendered in plain or tinted plaster, floors of living rooms were of *opus signinum*, and subsidiary buildings were paved with stone. Elaborate decoration of walls and floors was confined to the principal rooms.

The N. range, 36·6 m long and 10·5 m wide, comprised six rooms (8, 10–14) opening on the S. on to a portico or verandah with another room (9) at its E. end, connected to 8 by a wide opening to form in effect a single compartment. This seems to have been the principal apartment of the villa, having gaily coloured panelled or floriated patterns on the walls, and a patterned mosaic floor in four colours. It was the room in which the human skeletons had been found in 1888. Room 14, at the W. end of the range, was heated by a channelled hypocaust. Rooms 10–14 would seem to have been the main living apartments, including perhaps the dining room, a domestic shrine, and the kitchen.

The W. range measured 46·9 m long and 11·3 m wide, and opened on the E. on to a colonnaded verandah. There were seventeen rooms, of which rooms 22–30 comprised a complete suite of baths. This, though small, was remarkably complete and relatively well preserved, some of the walls still standing to a height of 1·8 m. A doorway at the N.E. corner gave access to a passage (room 22) and undressing room (*apodyterium*, room 23) occupying the N. end of the baths. The undressing room opened on the S. into a cold room (*frigidarium*, room 24) with an apse on the W. containing a *piscina* or cold plunge bath (room 27). On the E., the cold room opened into a warm room (*tepidarium*, room 25), and from this access was gained on the S. first to a hot room (*caldarium*, room 26) and then to a sweating chamber (*sudatorium*, room 29) with a hot bath (*alveus*, room 30) at its S. end. Another *sudatorium* (room 28) opened from the S. side of the cold room. Beyond the S. end of the baths lay a yard (rooms 32–33) with a furnace chamber (*praefurnium*, room 31) in its N.E. angle, from which a stoke-hole led to a suite of pillared hypocausts under rooms 30, 29, 26 and 25. Another stoke-hole in the N.W. angle of the yard led to a channelled hypocaust under room 28. The floors of the bath-house were of *opus signinum*, and the walls were rendered with painted plaster; the cold bath and perhaps also the adjoining *frigidarium* were ceiled with a stone vault.

The evidence showed that the baths and the adjacent rooms

THE ROMAN VILLA AT LLANTWIT MAJOR

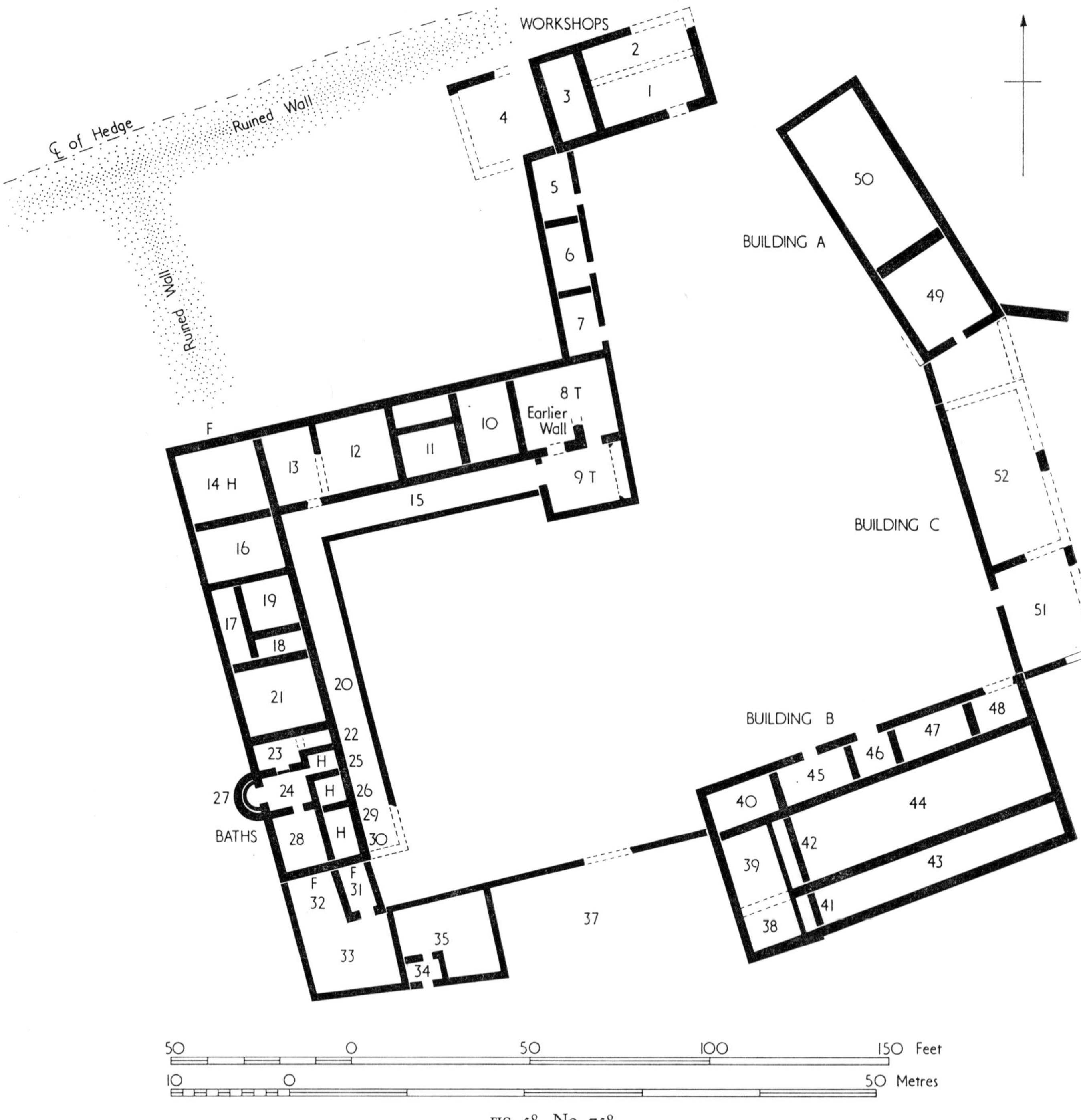

FIG. 58. No. 758.
H—Hypocaust, T—Tessellated pavement, F—Furnace chamber. After V. E. Nash-Williams and J. C. Storrie.

to the N. had been constructed together. After long use, the furnace chamber and the hot and cold plunge baths were remodelled and reduced in size. The date of this change was not determined but cannot have been earlier than the 3rd century. About the end of that century the baths were closed down and dismantled, except for the furnace chamber which was refloored and adapted for use as an iron foundry.

The S. range comprised two rooms (34–35) on the E. side of the yard attached to the bath-house; these were apparently of later date than the W. range. Building B, on the S. side of the outer yard of the villa, was a large basilican house, 29·6 m long by 14·6 m wide, probably the quarters of the servants and labourers working on the estate. The interior was divided into a central 'nave' (room 44) and flanking 'aisles' (rooms 43 and 45–48) except for a separate set of rooms (38–42) at the W. end.

The E. range consisted of two long buildings (C and A), each 23·4–23·8 m long and 7·9 m wide, set at a slight angle to one another. Each was divided into two rooms (Building C, rooms 51–52; Building A, rooms 49–50). Their purpose is uncertain but they were probably barns or stables.

The N. wing at the N.W. angle of the outer yard yielded evidence of industrial use and was probably a suite of workshops. It comprised a N. range (rooms 1–4) and a W. range (rooms 5–7) attached at its S. end to the N. range of the main house.

Small finds from the excavations were plentiful and included tiles and stonework (roof finials, portions of columns); painted wall-plaster and *opus signinum*; fragments of two sculptured figures; fragments of querns; window-glass; iron nails, knives, and horseshoes. Evidence for date was provided by plentiful pottery almost all dating between the mid-2nd and the 4th centuries, and by thirty-one coins ranging from Gallienus (253–68) to Constantius II (337–61). Out of five graves found in rooms 8 and 9 (including two of the four already noted by Storrie in those rooms) three proved to have been cut through walls, showing that this part of the buildings at least was completely ruined when the burials took place. Two more graves, not previously noted by Storrie, were found in rooms 10 and 15, bringing up to eleven the total number of formal interments recorded. All were oriented. The excavator considered that the thirty-seven other bodies noted by Storrie must also have been formal burials. The 1971 re-excavation located three other skeletons (see below).

Nash-Williams concluded that the stone buildings were essentially all of one build, *ca.* A.D. 150, and from the coin evidence deduced that the main (corridor) block was abandoned *ca.* 300, while Building B continued in use for at least another half-century. It thus became possible to regard the burials cut through the walls of the main block as having been deposited by the inhabitants of Building B. Recently, advances in the study of mosaic pavements[6] have shown that the corridor block must have been in use some half a century after the apparent date of desertion implied by the coins from it. Using this and other evidence, G. Webster[7] produced an alternative theory, suggesting that all the stone buildings date from *ca.* 300, replacing a timber villa; he accepted that the stone buildings were of one period, and that the human remains were probably burials by occupants of Building B.

The 1971 re-excavation was restricted to the opening between rooms 8–9 and to the adjacent end of the corridor; the primary objective was to resolve the discrepancy between the coin-evidence from the north wing and the new dating for the pavement. Several structural phases were identified, the earliest corresponding to a simple rectangular block with no (masonry) corridor; the wall of a room apparently identical in size to 10 and 11 was found beneath room 8 (Plate 15 bottom). This was subsequently extended to correspond to the present rooms 8–9, the corridor being added still later, probably (from the coin evidence) *ca.* 300. The mosaic thus falls into place as the latest structural alteration in a long history. The cross-wall which appears in Nash-Williams's photograph (Plate 15 top) seems to have been the work of Storrie; at each end it lies on top of the cement edging which he put in to protect the pavement.

The excavations also located two more formal burials in rooms 8–9, one cut through a wall, as well as a contorted skeleton about 0·2 m above the floor level in the corridor.

Certainty as to the history of the site must remain impossible without full excavation, but tentatively it appears likely[8] that the villa may have occupied the site of a pre-Roman enclosure, as at Whitton Lodge (761). The first Roman work included the simple rectangular block to the plan of which belong rooms 10, 11, and that newly identified under 8 (among others). After decline or abandonment in the early 3rd century a new burst of prosperity led to a sequence of building campaigns resulting in the extensive villa of which the plan is known. The mosaic represents the culmination of this development in the 4th century. The disuse of the baths and the use of parts of their outbuildings for metal-working seems to imply a further period of decline.

Storrie's careful distinction between the formal burials and the other human remains seems to justify his diagnosis of the latter as evidence for a massacre, and the contorted skeleton in the corridor may well belong to the same group. If so, it implies that the slaughter took place in a partly ruined building, the walls of which still stood to some height. In any case, the formal burials cannot have begun until the stumps of the walls were earth-covered. Since there is now no reason to suppose that any other room continued in use later than rooms 8–9, where the interments took place, there is nothing to support the suggestion that they were made by occupants of any portion of the villa. So far as present evidence goes, therefore, there is nothing to show that the inhabitants were Christians. The suggestion that the villa was eventually the home of St. Illtud[9] (*floruit ca.* 500) involves even greater difficulties, since it requires an occupation lasting several generations without leaving any trace.

The objects found are now at N.M.W.

[1] J. C. Storrie, *Trans. Cardiff Nat. Soc.*, XX (1888), pp. 49 ff.; see also n. 3.

[2] V. E. Nash-Williams, *Arch. Camb.*, CII (1953), pp. 89–169.

[3] On behalf of the Commission, under the direction of A. H. A. Hogg. Report forthcoming.

[4] *Arch. Camb.*, 1888, pp. 413–16, quoting an article in *The Athenaeum*, Oct. 20, 1888, No. 3182. The dimensions are given as 60 ft. by 51 ft. (19 by 15·5 m). In his MS. notes, it is described as 58 ft. 9 ins. E–W.

by 47 ft. 6 ins. (18 by 14·5 m), with the north wall 6 ft. 4 ins. thick (2 m).

[5] *Loc. cit.*, n. 4 above.

[6] The date of this mosaic probably falls well into the first half of the fourth century; D. J. Smith, *in lit.*, supplementing *Roman Villa*, p. 77, n. 4.

[7] G. Webster in *Roman Villa*, pp. 238–43.

[8] The arguments will be set out more fully in the report on the 1971 work.

[9] J. Morris, 'The Dates of the Celtic Saints', *Journal of Theological Studies*, N.S. XVII, pt. 2 (1966), p. 379.

Llantwit Major.
SS 96 N.E. (9588 6998) 20 vi 67 XLV S.W.

(759) ROMAN VILLA at MOULTON E. of Llancarfan, at 76 m above O.D. on the N. side of the valley of the R. Waycock. Evidence of Roman occupation was discovered by H. J. Thomas in 1956, and in 1958 a small amount of excavation was carried out. Four sites were explored on the edges of an area measuring some 165 m from N. to S. by 119 m wide. The occupied area must therefore have been of considerable extent.

(i) ST 0735 6955. A stone building associated with late 3rd–4th century pottery. Some of the rooms appear to have been faced with *opus signinum* and in at least one case with painted plaster. The building was roofed with sandstone slabs.

(ii) 0740 6970. Two periods of construction were identified. The first was represented by post-holes and by an E.–W. gully, probably the eaves-drip channel of a timber building at least 13 m long. This was associated with native iron-age-type pottery and with Samian ware implying an occupation that lasted into the early part of the 2nd century. The timber structure was succeeded *ca.* 125 by a rectangular stone building 14·9 m long from E. to W., and varying from 2·3 m to 3·4 m in width. This had a clay floor and was roofed with sandstone tiles, and was possibly a corridor-type villa of open E plan. The presence of large quantities of iron nails and cleats, and of *opus signinum* and coloured plaster, suggested that the building had an upper floor of timber with plastered walls. It remained in occupation till *ca.* 340, and in addition to pottery the small finds included two coins of Constantine I (307–37) and Constans (333–7), a 4th-century bronze spoon with decorated handle, an ornamental bronze boss, a whetstone, and iron slag.

(iii) 0745 6964. A paved area supporting a hearth and occupation soil containing coarse pottery of the late 3rd–4th centuries, a coin of Severina (wife of Aurelian, 270–75), iron nails and slag, etc.

(iv) 0747 6954. An occupation area which yielded 2nd–4th-century pottery and a 4th-century minim coin.

B.B.C.S., XVII, iv (May 1958), p. 294, no. 2.

Llancarfan.
ST 06 N.E. (0741 6963) 2 ii 67 XLVI S.W.

(760) ROMAN VILLA (?) at LLANBETHERY W. of Llancarfan, at 61 m above O.D. above the N.W. side of the deep valley of Pant y Coed. A stony ridge about 46 m long from N.W. to S.E., with a smaller mound at right-angles at its S.E. end, has yielded evidence of a Roman building, possibly a villa. Trenching at the S.E. end revealed a layer of rubble and occupation soil 0·6 m thick, with coarse pottery of the late 2nd–4th centuries, animal bones, iron nails and slag, roof- and box-tiles and three tesserae (?).

About 58 m to the S., at ST 0358 7019, was found in 1957 the lower part of a vessel of grey ware containing the remains of a hoard of Roman coins, the upper portion having been ploughed away. In all, 814 coins were recovered, which with the exception of six worn 3rd-century radiates were all Constantinian issues of the period 313–46, and mainly of the years 330–35.

B.B.C.S., XVII, iv (May 1958), p. 294, No. 3; cited in *Journ. Rom. Stud.*, XLVIII (1958), pp. 131–2; *Numismatic Chronicle*, 1960, pp. 253–66.

Llancarfan.
ST 07 S.W. (0355 7023) 5 iii 68 XLVI S.W.

(761) ROMAN VILLA near WHITTON LODGE S.S.E. of Bonvilston (Figs. 59, 60), on level ground at 88 m above O.D. The site was discovered by H. J. Thomas in 1956 and consists of a rectangular area about 65 m by 60 m, standing some 0·6 m above the general ground level. Excavations were initiated by Mr. Thomas in 1956–7 and revealed the existence of stone buildings grouped round a courtyard enclosed by a clay bank with external ditch. The site was subsequently damaged by ploughing, and rescue excavations were undertaken by M. G. Jarrett in 1965 on behalf of the Department of the Environment. The results were such as to justify total excavation, which was accomplished between 1966 and 1970, under the sponsorship of that Department and of the University College of South Wales, Cardiff. To date, only interim reports have been published,[1] with an incomplete plan.[2]

The most interesting and important discovery was that Roman buildings had been preceded by an early-iron-age farmstead (Fig. 59). This consisted of a number of circular wooden houses arranged round a yard, in the centre of which was a larger house. The whole was defined by a bank and ditch which were probably the earliest features of the site. The bank was 2–5 m wide, and the ditch 5–7 m wide and up to 2·6 m deep. The entrance to the farmstead was by a causeway over the ditch on the E. side; at least three successive timber towers preceded the (Roman) metalled road over this causeway. Although they were not precisely dated, it seems reasonable to suppose that one or more of these towers should be associated with the pre-Roman farm. The doors of the circular houses all faced directions between E. and S. The peripheral houses ranged between 9·5 m and 10·7 m in diameter, but the earlier and larger version of the central one was 14 m in diameter. The later version of this house appears to have had an inner ring of roof supports. It was clearly contemporary with the small round house to the north, to which it was joined by a timber fence. It is impossible to say how many of these circular structures were occupied at any one time. Near the S.E. corner of the yard was a rock-cut well 7·4 m deep; it was probably pre-Roman in origin, though it remained in use until the 4th century A.D. No other features are certainly pre-Roman, but between the entrance and the

S.E. angle were two grids of post-holes, 5·5 m and 6 m square respectively. These were interpreted as the remains of granaries with raised wooden floors; a similar structure may have underlain the W. building of the stone-built range. Any or all of them might be pre-Roman, as also some of the other timber features, which include partitions dividing the yard, and two or more rectilinear structures (one perhaps a granary) near the N.E. corner.

Dating evidence for the pre-Roman phase was imprecise. It included iron-age B pottery, with bead-rims and incised ornament which can be paralleled at Lydney and Glastonbury; brooches of Langton Down type; a coin of the Dobunni; and a number of characteristic glass beads. One of these was probably as early as the 4th century B.C., but the other material need not imply occupation before about 50 B.C.

Timber building continued into the Roman period. In the S.E. and S.W. angles of the yard were two houses, about 8 m square with rounded corners, that in the S.W. corner built over an earlier round house, and that in the S.E. probably over a granary. Neither was built before the last quarter of the 1st century A.D. From the early 2nd century the farmstead was transformed into ranges of rectangular stone buildings around a central courtyard. The ditch remained open until at least A.D. 200, and was eventually filled with limestone and tufa rubble from the demolition of one of the buildings of the villa. A metalled road led across the original causeway, and was associated with a walled entrance through the bank. The bank itself was levelled before the latest period of stone building in the E. range.

Though disposed around the central courtyard, the stone buildings (Fig. 60) form separate units and do not present a normal villa plan. Four, or possibly five, periods of construction were traced. The *W. range* consisted of a building 19·2 m long and 6·6 m wide, divided into four rooms, close to the S.W. angle. The *S. range* contained two buildings, each about 12 m by 5 m, separated by an interval of 14·5 m. The more westerly of these was fronted by a verandah 2 m wide; a room 7·2 m by 3·2 m was subsequently added to its E. end, and a small chamber 3 m square to its W. end. The latter may have been a cellar or unused hypocaust; early in the 3rd century it was used as a tip for domestic rubbish including painted plaster. The eastern building in the S. range had a long narrow chamber, 10·4 m by 2 m, added to its W. end; this was planned originally as a hypocaust but subsequently floored with wood, and finally (in the early 4th century) deliberately filled with rubble and plaster debris.

The only building in the *E. range* lay N. of the entrance. In the latest phase it was 18·9 m long by 7·5 m wide. In its S.E. angle was a slab-lined tank, ultimately filled with ash from an adjacent T-shaped corn-drying kiln; into this ash the body of a child had been inserted. Another T-shaped oven, rock-cut and lined with limestone slabs, was found outside the S.E. angle of the enclosure.

Three periods of stone building were detected in the *N. range*. The earliest was not earlier than *ca.* A.D. 200 but yielded no coherent plan; it appeared to run under the later E. range buildings. It was succeeded in the late 3rd century by a rectangular building of limestone blocks, 19 m by 11 m, running at a slight angle to the other buildings of the villa. The final period followed shortly afterwards, with little change of plan. The main entrance to the building lay on the N., away from the courtyard.

The finds from the excavation have not yet been published but include pottery and other objects of the 1st to 4th centuries, including a series of bronze brooches and a bronze steelyard with notches for positioning the weights. Two small moulded tablets of baked clay were found, both stamped from the same die with the letters BOV (see p. 121).

The excavator dates the Whitton farmstead to the period 50 B.C. to A.D. 330, and points out that although it is not a typical Roman villa, it throws interesting light on the romanisation of S. Wales. There were no indications of tessellated pavements, nor does there seem to have been a bath-suite. The only hypocausts were apparently never fired. But some of the walls were plastered and painted, and the stone buildings were substantial if not elaborate. Those in the N. and W. ranges might well have been two storeys high. If the later Roman levels were somewhat disappointing (due to destruction of floor levels by ploughing), the earlier phases were very rewarding. The site provides clear evidence of the transition from iron-age farm to Roman villa, with round houses giving place to sub-rectangular (probably soon after the Roman conquest), and with the gradual replacement of simple timber buildings by relatively complex and sophisticated stone structures in the 2nd and 3rd centuries.

[1] *B.B.C.S.*, XVII, iv (May 1958), pp. 293–4, No. 1; *Morgannwg*, IX (1965), pp. 91–5; X (1966), pp. 59–63; XI (1967), pp. 78–81; XII (1968), pp. 101–4; XIV (1970), pp. 84–8. Summaries are also given in *Journ. Rom. Stud.*, from 1958 onwards.

[2] *Journ. Rom. Stud.*, LIX (1969), p. 201, Fig. 26.

St. Lythans.
ST 07 S.E. (0811 7133) 7 v 62 XLVI S.E.

(762) ROMAN VILLA at ELY (W. Cardiff) (Fig. 61), at about 11 m above O.D. on the valley floor of the R. Ely, to the S.W. of the river. The ground is now a public park, in which a large oval area, overgrown with grass and weeds and standing some 0·6 m above the general field level, is all that remains to mark the site of the villa. Excavation has revealed the history of this building and has demonstrated that a major concern of its inhabitants at all times was the exclusion of unwelcome visitors, both human and animal. The site is low-lying and marshy and its choice must have resulted from the realisation that the discomforts and difficulties of the location were outweighed by the advantages of seclusion among the thickets of the swamp. Later the natural defences were augmented by artificial ones. The villa was partly excavated by J. Storrie in 1894; re-planned, and the evidence re-examined, by J. Ward in 1917; and thoroughly excavated by R. E. M. Wheeler in 1922.

The initial choice of site was dictated by the old course of the Caerau brook. The main stream flowed from W. to E. but at this point a branch diverged to the N. and then to the E. The villa was constructed in the angle; the branch channel was straightened and deepened to a depth of 1·5 m, the silt being

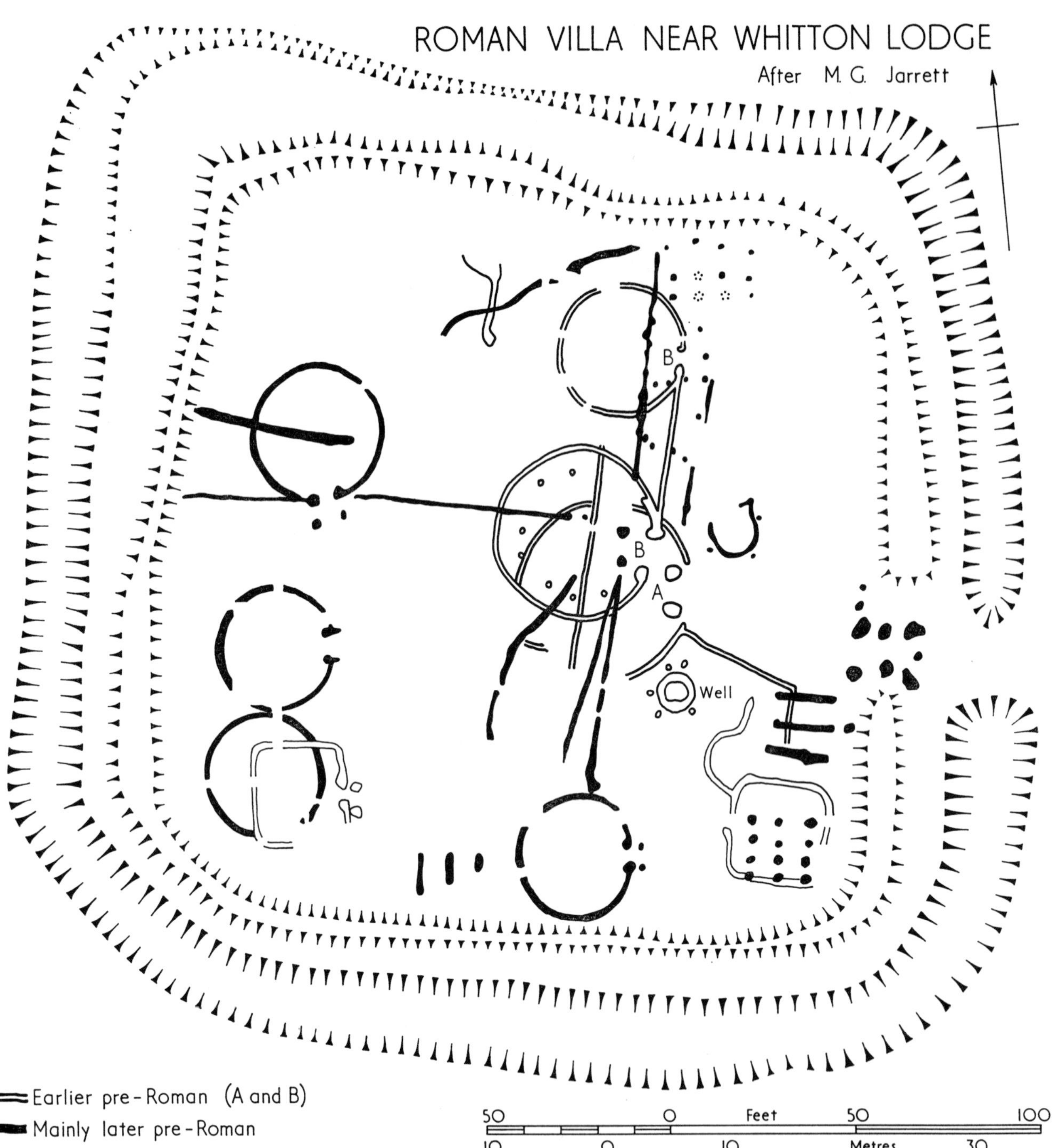

FIG. 59. No. 761, earlier phases.

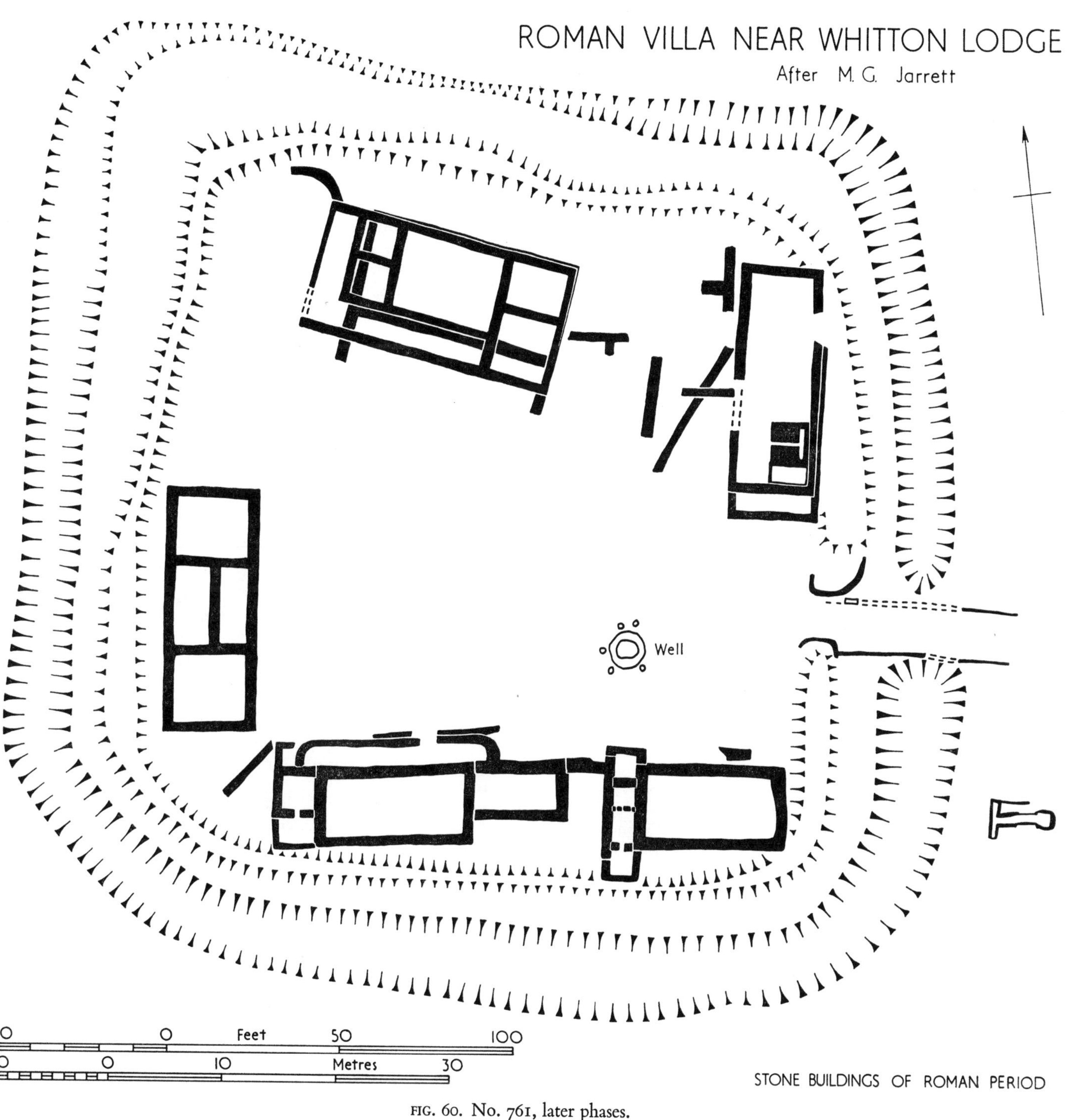

FIG. 60. No. 761, later phases.

thrown out on either side; this accounts for the vague banks originally visible on the W. of the site, and the inner cross-ditch in the N. part of the enclosure. The main block (Building I) was a rectangular house, with projecting wings on the S. enclosing a small paved and cobbled courtyard, approached by a road from the S. The house measured about 21·3 m by 18·3 m; its walls were of rubble with facings of limestone ashlar, and its roofs of tile. Along the S. front of the wings and enclosing the courtyard was a verandah (rooms 5–7) with a colonnade of Bath stone, and a mosaic floor to its central section; the edges of the courtyard had gutters to carry off rainwater from the roofs. The main part of the house consisted of four rooms: a central room (2); a single large room in the W. wing (1); and two rooms in the E. wing (3–4), the southern of which was heated by a channelled hypocaust. Along the back or N. side of the house were two long rooms (8–9). These and the verandah were doubtless of one storey while the central part of the house rose to two storeys.

The house had evidently undergone alterations during its lifetime, and indeed there was evidence that at one period it had been partly destroyed by fire. The walls may have been rebuilt in timber on stone foundations. The floors, originally of clay or slabs, were re-paved or relaid with *opus signinum*. The hypocaust in room 4 became disused and blocked. A circular oven was inserted in the verandah of the E. wing.

To the W. of the house was a large yard, 27·5 m by 15·2 m, and from its S.W. angle a rectangular block (Building II), 30·5 m by 9·1 m, projected to the S. This contained three rooms (12–14), paved with slabs and opening on the E. on to a corridor or verandah (15) with a tessellated pavement. A roadway approached the building from the E. Extending still further to the S. was a complete suite of baths, 27·5 m long by 6·1 m wide; these were an addition to the original plan though still of early date. They comprised a vestibule or undressing room at the S. end (16), followed by a cold room (17), a warm room (18), a hot room (19) with an apsidal plunge bath (20) on its W. side, another hot bath (21) and finally a furnace chamber (22) at the N. end. Rooms 18–21 were heated by pillared hypocausts.

At some stage of the occupation, the hypocaust flues became disused and choked with debris, and the whole bath-building was gutted and refloored. The decision to abandon the hypocausts here and in room 4 may have been forced on the owner of the villa by the difficulty of maintaining a hypocaust system on a site that was liable to floods. It was presumably at this time that a small rectangular chamber (11) was added to the S.W. angle of the main house, overlying the earlier verandah and an intervening layer of occupation soil and building stones. This new room had a floor of yellow cement and walls decorated with painted plaster; its E. half was raised in two steps, and the arrangement suggests a plunge-bath. From its N.W. angle a wall projected westwards.

Later still there were drastic changes in the layout of the site. The earlier ditch on the N. was filled in and a projecting room (10) built from the rear of the main block, partly across the ditch filling. The main house was surrounded with a rhomboidal enclosure measuring about 58 m long from E. to W. by 52 m wide, defended by a bank with external ditch. The defences were not of great strength; they survived at the time of excavation to a width of about 9 m, the bank being 0·3 m high internally and 0·6 m externally above the bottom of the ditch. On the W. they cut right across the earlier yard and over the N.E. angle of Building II, which must have been disused. At the same time an L-shaped outwork was built out from the N.W. angle of the new enclosure and southward along the W. side of Building II and the bath-house. Its purpose was less to protect these buildings (which indeed were no longer used) than to shelter cattle should the need arise; the absence of S. and E. sides to this larger enclosure can be explained by the marshy nature of the ground which probably constituted a sufficient obstacle in those directions. The stream was meanwhile diverted to flow along the new N. ditch.

Other discoveries throw light on the activities of the inhabitants. Immediately N. of Building II was a human skeleton in an E.–W. position, perhaps a Christian burial. Abundant traces of iron-working were found, and in the earlier excavations an actual foundry was discovered. This consisted of a small circular forge of masonry, with an adjacent casting floor of sand containing charcoal, though the main fuel seems to have been coal. Iron ore in the debris was of two different kinds, both involving transport from deposits several kilometres away, one at Rhiwbina and one at Wenvoe. Near the forge was also a pile of about 100 kg of manganese ore; its use in the casting process would be to produce a harder iron, virtually a steel; but not least in interest was the fact that it was not a Welsh ore and indeed resembles in composition certain Spanish ores.

Small finds from the excavations include eight coins of which the identifiable ones are Augustus (23 B.C.–A.D. 14), Nerva (96–98), Antoninus Pius (138–61), Claudius Gothicus (268–70), Carausius (287–93) and Constantine I dated 320–24; innumerable iron nails, staples, hooks and horseshoes; a lead strainer; bronze and bone pins; large quantities of iron slag; coal and charcoal; spindlewhorls; stone roofing slabs and roof tiles; window glass; bone counters; flints, including an arrowhead; a small quantity of Samian ware, and a greater amount of coarse pottery, some of it carefully repaired with rivets.

The history of the villa deduced by Wheeler is as follows:

(i) The initial construction of Buildings I and II took place in the first half of the 2nd century. The bath-house was added shortly afterwards.

(ii) Later, perhaps in the 3rd century, the main house was partly rebuilt, the bath-house was converted to other uses, and a new and smaller bath-building erected.

(iii) Building II was levelled and the banked and ditched enclosure was thrown up around the house about the beginning of the 4th century.

(iv) Occupation ceased *ca.* 325.

The objects found are at N.M.W.

Trans. Cardiff Nat. Soc., XXVI (1894), pp. 125–35; L (1917), pp. 24–44; LV (1922), pp. 19–45; *Journ. Rom. Stud.*, XI (1921), pp. 67–85; Wheeler, *P. & R. Wales*, pp. 257–8, Fig. 106.

Llandaf (E), Cardiff (C).
ST 17 N.W. (1472 7615) 8 vi 67 XLIII S.W.

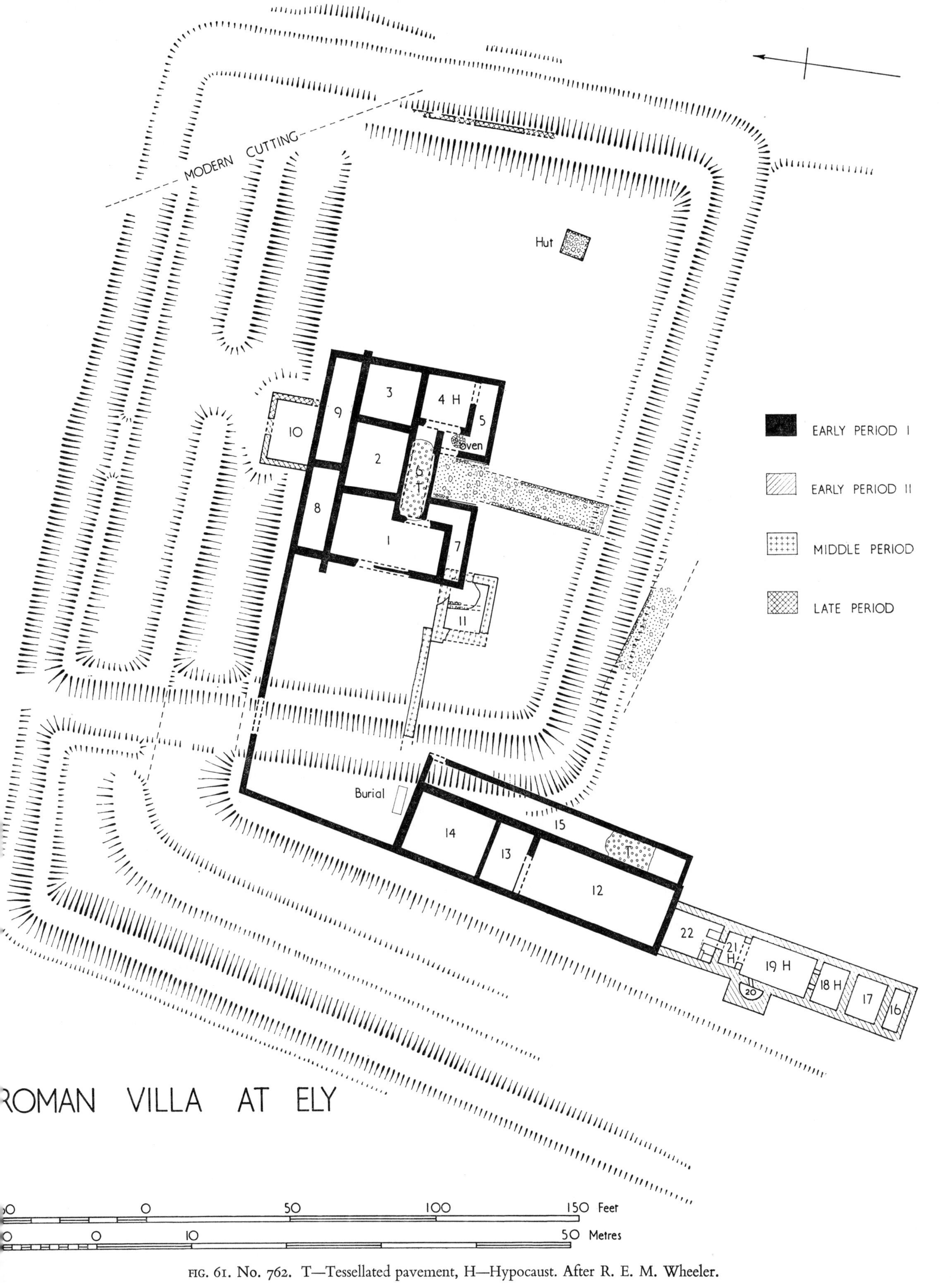

FIG. 61. No. 762. T—Tessellated pavement, H—Hypocaust. After R. E. M. Wheeler.

763–769. OTHER CIVIL SITES

The discoveries and trial excavations on sites 763–767 were by H. J. Thomas, those on 768–769 by G. Dowdell.

(763) ROMAN BUILDING (?) near LLANMIHANGEL (S. of Cowbridge), at 76 m above O.D. A slight mound is visible in the surface of a field N.W. of Pen-y-bryn farm. Ploughing has unearthed blocks of dressed limestone, presumably from walls, fragments of roofing slabs and tiles, lumps of ironstone and iron slag, and Samian and coarse pottery of the 2nd to 4th centuries.

Llanmihangel.
SS 97 S.E. (9840 7114) 18 iv 68 XLV S.E.

(764) ROMAN BUILDING at EAST ABERTHAW, at 24·5 m above O.D. In 1956, during the laying of a pipeline through the village, 2nd/3rd-century pottery was found in a layer of occupation soil 0·9 m thick, together with tiles, animal bones and shells. The site was in a garden on the N. side of Well Road. In 1959 a trench uncovered the remains of a stone building of two structural periods. The earlier structure had a narrow drystone wall and a clay floor which yielded 1st/2nd-century pottery, a *mortarium* stamp, and a late 1st-century bronze brooch. Subsequently the wall was widened, and other drystone walls were built which may have belonged to a T-shaped corn-drying oven. Abundant remains of shellfish were discovered, together with 3rd/4th-century pottery, a bronze bracelet, iron nails and slag, a strip of lead, and (surface find) a coin of Valentinian I (364–75).

B.B.C.S., XVII, iv (May 1958), p. 295, No. 7; *Journ. Rom. Stud.*, LI (1961), pp. 158–9.

Pen-marc.
ST 06 N.W. (0343 6670) 6 ii 67 L N.W.

(765) ROMAN BUILDING (?) near NURSTON (W. of Cardiff Airport), at 61 m above O.D. Ploughing in 1956–57 unearthed Romano-British pottery and iron clinker. Trial holes were subsequently dug at three sites:

(i) ST 0575 6775. Occupation soil and rubble containing 1st to 4th-century pottery and a glass bead.

(ii) 0570 6766. A rock-cut gully and a post-hole, which may have been associated with a timber building. The gully was filled with broken clay (? furnace lining), iron slag and coal, and also contained 2nd-century Samian pottery.

(iii) 0570 6780. A pit filled with burnt earth and roofing tiles.

The site has since been covered by an extension of the airport.

B.B.C.S., XVII, iv (May 1958), p. 295, No. 6.

Pen-marc.
ST 06 N.E. (0573 6773) 19 iv 68 L N.W.

(766) ROMAN BUILDING near COLD KNAP, Barry, on the shore of the Bristol Channel. In 1960 building operations revealed and later destroyed the walls of a sunken rectangular structure of dressed stone. It measured 6·4 m by 5·8 m; the walls were 0·6 m thick and survived to a height of 1·2 m. The interior had a cobbled floor on which was a thick layer of debris containing building stones and Roman tiles. Near the building were found a few fragments of Roman pottery including a sherd of 2nd-century Samian ware. 'Human remains' are recorded as having been found at this site in 1866 (O.S. maps of 1879).

Journ. Rom. Stud., LI (1961), p. 158.

Barry.
ST 06 N.E. (0993 6648) 6 ii 67 L N.E.

(767) ROMAN BUILDING (?) at BARRY CASTLE, at 52 m above O.D. Trenching during building operations in 1956 yielded evidence of Roman occupation beneath the castle and extending some 30 m to N. and E., the deposits being located as follows:

(i) ST 1012 6720. An occupation layer containing a fragment of late Antonine Samian ware, coarse ware of 3rd/4th-century date, and pieces of roofing tiles.

(ii) 1010 6722. A similar layer with minute fragments of 2nd-century Samian ware, coarse pottery, and tile.

(iii) 1008 6721. A similar layer containing tile fragments, and coarse ware of the 2nd to 4th centuries.

(iv) 1007 6719. A clay layer, perhaps the floor of a room, on top of a layer of stone rubble. Finds included a minute piece of 2nd-century Samian pottery, and coarse ware of the 3rd/4th centuries.

The evidence indicates Roman occupation extending over an area at least 30 m long from E. to W. by 25 m wide. Roman tiles and dressed tufa blocks were found in the E. range of the castle during its demolition in 1956.

B.B.C.S., XVII, iv (May 1958), p. 295, No. 8.

Barry.
ST 16 N.W. (1010 6721) 6 ii 67 L N.E.

(768) ROMAN BUILDING (?) near PALMERSTOWN (E. Barry), at 15 m above O.D. In 1953 a scatter of Romano-British pottery was revealed during ploughing. In 1956 a mound was noted at the site, and traces of two banks or walls at right-angles to one another. Trial holes dug in the field yielded limestone blocks, roofing slabs and tiles, a quantity of Samian and black burnished ware, a 3rd-century radiate coin, a flint barbed arrowhead and flint flakes.

St. Andrews (E), St. A. Major (C).
ST 16 N.W. (1420 6940) 18 iv 68 XLVII S.W.

(769) ROMAN BUILDING (?) on POP HILL S. of Dinas Powys, a little over 30 m above O.D. In 1957 ploughing brought up a scatter of Romano-British pottery. Trial holes revealed a paved floor and post-holes, together with rubble and roofing tiles; also a pit containing quantities of iron slag. Small finds included Roman pottery of 2nd to 4th-century date, a blue glass bead, and the upper stone of a rotary quern.

St. Andrews (E), St. A. Major (C).
ST 16 N.E. (1590 6998) 18 iv 68 XLVII S.W.

APPENDIX

The Glamorgan Section of Iter XII and the Site of Bomium

Bomium is recorded in Iter XII of the Antonine Itinerary[1] as being xv Roman miles (m p) from Nidum (Neath) and xxvii from Isca (Caerleon). There is no other evidence for its existence, but it fits so well into the pattern of Roman occupation in south Wales that it can almost certainly be accepted as a fort belonging to the same system as the others founded at the end of the 1st century. Unfortunately the text of the Iter contains copying errors and the exact routes followed between stations, and thus the true distances, are not always certain.

One error which can easily be eliminated is the intrusion of the greater part of another iter. When this has been done (see end) a list of nine stages remains, the separate distances of which add up to clxvi m p, while the total is stated to be clxxxvi; this strongly suggests that the errors are likely to be either straightforward omissions of x or v, or confusion of v with x.[2] In what follows, suggested amendments are restricted to those possibilities.

The overall distance along lines which are either certain or very probable[3] adds up to just over 162 English miles[4] via Loughor, which would give clxxxvi m p of 0·873 English miles; this gives better agreement than the customary value of 0·92 with all the distances in this iter. The alternative route through Hendy[5] amounts to just over 159 miles. To give satisfactory agreement with other distances this route requires the total to be corrected to clxxxi m p of 0·880 miles; but reasons are given below for rejecting it. The arguments for the position of Bomium are unaffected.

The overall distance from Neath to Caerleon is very near to 50 miles, depending on the exact route, and this corresponds to lvii m p of 0·873 miles. The distances in the text are xv and xxvii. There are several possible ways in which the necessary additional xv m p could be distributed, but the correction of xv and xxvii to xx and xxxvii is not only the simplest but places the lost fort in a very suitable position, just west of where the road crossed the Ewenni river.[6] This sort of location is typical of Roman forts in Wales, and none of the alternative emendations leads to a site with similar military advantages.[7] It has been suggested that two small bricks, stamped B O V and found at the Whitton Lodge villa,[8] justify regarding Bovium as the correct name, and indicate that the site should be nearby, but they are so small and easily portable that there seems to be no need to assume that they are of local origin. Even if the whole of the missing xv m p were added to the distance from Nidum, making it xxx (not xx as suggested), Bomium must still lie more than 4 km from the villa at which the bricks were found.

The most probable position for the lost fort is on a gently rounded hill about 2 km S. of Bridgend,

---

1 A. L. F. Rivet, 'The British Section of the Antonine Itinerary', *Britannia*, I (1970), pp. 34–82, espec. pp. 55–7.

2 *Ibid.*, pp. 39, 41, 50, 61.

3 Other assumptions as to routes, and more elaborate methods of calculation, give such closely similar results that discussion seems unnecessary.

4 For the purpose of this discussion, the English mile seems preferable to the kilometre as a unit.

5 Rivet, *op. cit.*, p. 56 suggests Hendy rather than Loughor as the site of Leucarum.

6 As indicated by Rivet, *op. cit.*, p. 57.

7 The spacing of the forts on this road seems unusually large, and the existence of two further posts between Neath and Cardiff might be expected. Roman pottery, probably from a settlement site, has been found at Cowbridge (*Western Mail*, May 16, 1962) and remains of masonry buildings associated with coins (Trajan to Constantine) are recorded from the site of the Town Hall. L. J. Hopkin-James, *Old Cowbridge* (1922).

8 *Journ. Rom. Stud.*, LVI (1966), p. 220 and n. 21. The dimensions of the unbroken specimen are given as 1 by $\frac{1}{2}$ by $\frac{9}{32}$ ins.

rising to 30 m above O.D. The grounds of the house Glanwenny (SS 9045 7815) are of about the right shape and area, but there is nothing visible at present which can be regarded as ancient.

As indicated above, a possible route from Moridunum to Nidum crosses the Afon Llwchwr near Hendy. This would make the overall total clxxxi but would require no emendation to the two stages of xv m p on either side of Leucarum. Indeed, the total distance Moridunum to Nidum by this line measures 26·6 miles, giving a total of 30·3 m p of 0·880 miles, in better agreement with the actual total Itinerary distances than the route via Loughor shown with the emended figures. On this route, though, the river crossing is 15·2 miles or 17·3 m p of 0·88 miles from Nidum, whereas the corresponding distance given for Leucarum in only xv m p. The site indicated for the fort would thus be more than 2 miles from the river from which it took its name. It seems preferable to accept the apparent error of a mile in the distance from Loughor to Neath, especially as the course of the road is uncertain. If the Tawe crossing were 1 km S. of the position assumed, the Loughor-Neath distance might easily be increased to 13·0 miles, or 14·9 m p of 0·873 miles, giving very close agreement with the xv of the Iter.

Iter XII (*Duplication of Iter XV omitted*)

Summary of *Iter* text	m p	Identification	English miles	m p of 0·873 miles	Suggested reading	Error to nearest m p
Muriduno	—	Carmarthen	—	—	—	—
Leucaro	xv	Loughor	17·6	20·2	xx	0
Nido	xv	Neath	12·0	13·7	xv	1
Bomio	xv	Glanwenny?	17·3	19·8	xx	0
Iscae	xxvii	Caerleon	32·6	37·2	xxxvii	0
Burrio	viiii	Usk	6·7	7·7	viiii	1
Gobannio	xii	Abergavenny	10·5	12·0	xii	0
Magnis	xxii	Kenchester	21·0	24·1	xxii	−2
Bravonio	xxiiii	Leintwardine	20·5	23·5	xxiiii	1
Viroconio	xxvii	Wroxeter	24·1	27·6	xxvii	−1
Totals	clxvi		162·3	185·8	clxxxvi	

Total according to text clxxxvi.

NAMES OF PLACES IN GLAMORGAN

THE written forms of place-names in Glamorgan may be grouped as follows:

(i) Welsh forms spelt according to established orthographical rules as recommended by the Board of Celtic Studies of the University of Wales.

(ii) Welsh forms commonly mis-spelt: e.g. Bettws *for* Betws, Coity *for* Coety, Merthyr Tydfil *for* Merthyr Tudful, Porthcawl *for* Porth-cawl, Rhossily *for* Rhosili.

(iii) Anglicised spellings of Welsh forms: e.g. Aberthaw *for* Aberddawan, Kilvey *for* Cilfái, Lisvane *for* Llys-faen, Llantwit *for* Llanilltud, Loughor *for* Llwchwr.

(iv) Non-Welsh forms, almost entirely of English origin: e.g. Cheriton, Oxwich, Reynoldston.

(v) Alternative Welsh and English forms for the same place: e.g. Abertawe/Swansea, Llandeilo Ferwallt/Bishopston, Llanilltud Gŵyr/Ilston, Tresimwn/Bonvilston.

In recent years, following the recommendations of the Board of Celtic Studies (see *Rhestr o Enwau Lleoedd: A Gazetteer of Welsh Place-names*, Cardiff, 1958), the Welsh spelling of forms in groups (ii), (iii) and (v) has become more generally adopted in official publications and notices. In this Inventory the correct Welsh forms of groups (ii) and (iii) are used where the differences are not likely to cause confusion in, for instance, the use of O.S. maps. The alternatives of group (v) are not normally used in the descriptive entries.

The two lists of place-names below are intended mainly to assist the reader, rather than to provide a comprehensive index. The first gives the English and anglicised forms alphabetically, with their correct Welsh equivalents, but only includes names which do not appear in the lists of Ecclesiastical and Civil Parishes (pp. xvii–xxiv), to which it is supplementary. The second list gives the correct spelling of Welsh names alphabetically, including the alternatives of group (v), and is more complete in order to serve as a cross-index both to the parish lists and to the Inventory text. No entries are included for the names of natural features which differ mainly in the choice between Welsh and English for a descriptive term, such as Mynydd or Mountain, Afon or River. The final column indicates that the form given in the second column is that used in the Ecclesiastical (E) or Civil (C) parish list, where the incidence of monuments in parishes is indexed.

English or anglicised form	*Correct Welsh form*
Aberthaw	Aberddawan
Bargoed	Bargod
Boverton	Trebefered
Candleston	Tregantllo
Crynant	Y Creunant
Cwmavon	Cwmafan
Dunraven	Dwnrhefn
Ely (place)	Trelái
Ely (river)	Elái
Glyn-neath	Glyn-nedd
Gower	Gŵyr
Kenfig Hill	Mynyddcynffig
Killay	Cilâ
Kilvey	Cilfái
Loughor (river)	Llwchwr
Miskin	Meisgyn
Mountain Ash	Aberpennar
Ogmore	Ogwr
Taff's Well	Ffynnon Taf
Van	Y Fan
Worm's Head	Pen Pyrod

Correct Welsh form	*English or anglicised form*			*Correct Welsh form*	*English or anglicised form*		
Aberafan	Aberavon	E		Llangynydd	Llangennith	E	C
Aberddawan	Aberthaw			Llanilltud Faerdref	Llantwit Fardre	E	C
Aberpennar	Mountain Ash			Llanilltud Fawr	Llantwit Major	E	C
Abertawe	Swansea	E	C	Llanilltud Gŵyr	Ilston	E	C
Yr As Fach	Nash		C	Llanilltud Nedd	Llantwit-juxta-Neath	E	
Yr As Fawr	Monknash	E	C	Llansanffraid-ar-Elái	St. Brides-super-Ely	E	C
Bargod	Bargoed			Llansanffraid-ar-Ogwr	St. Brides Minor	E	C
Y Barri	Barry	E	C	Llansawel	Briton Ferry	E	
Y Bont-faen	Cowbridge		C	Llantriddyd	Llantrithyd	E	C
Caerdydd	Cardiff	E	C	Llan-y-tair-mair	Knelston	E	C
Casllwchwr	Loughor (place)	E	C	Llwchwr	Loughor (river)		
Castell-nedd	Neath	E	C	Llwyneliddon	St. Lythans	E	C
Y Castellnewydd	Newcastle	E	C	Llys-faen	Lisvane	E	C
Cilâ	Killay			Meisgyn	Miskin		
Cilfái	Kilvey			Mynyddcynffig	Kenfig Hill		
Y Clun	Clyne		C	Ogwr	Ogmore		
Y Creunant	Crynant			Pen Pyrod	Worm's Head		
Cwmafan	Cwmavon			Pen-rhys	Penrice	E	C
Cynffig	Kenfig		C	Pen-y-bont ar Ogwr	Bridgend		C
Drenewydd yn Notais	Newton Nottage	E	C	Y Pîl	Pyle	E	C
Dwnrhefn	Dunraven			Porthceri	Porthkerry	E	C
Eglwys Fair y Mynydd	St. Mary Hill	E	C	Rugos	Rhigos		C
Yr Eglwys Newydd	Whitchurch	E		Y Rhath	Roath	E	
Elái	Ely (river)			Rhydri	Rudry	E	C
Y Fan	Van		C	Sain Dunwyd	St. Donats	E	C
Ffynnon Taf	Taff's Well			Sain Ffagan	St. Fagans	E	C
Glyn-nedd	Glyn-neath			Sain Nicolas	St. Nicholas	E	C
Gwenfô	Wenvoe	E	C	Sain Siorys	St. George	E	C
Gŵyr	Gower			Saint Andras	St. Andrews	E	C
Larnog	Lavernock	E	C	Sain Tathan	St. Athan	E	C
Lecwydd	Leckwith		C	Saint Hilari	St. Hilary	E	C
Llanbedr-ar-fynydd	Peterston-super-montem		C	Saint-y-brid	St. Brides Major	E	C
Llanbedr-y-fro	Peterston-super-Ely	E	C	Y Sgêr	Sker	E	
Llandeilo Ferwallt	Bishopston	E	C	Sili	Sully	E	C
Llandochau	Llandough	E		Silstwn	Gileston	E	C
Llandudwg	Tythegston	E	C	Trebefered	Boverton		
Llanddunwyd	Welsh St. Donats	E	C	Tredelerch	Rumney	E	
Llan-faes	Llanmaes	E	C	Trefflemin	Flemingston	E	C
Llan-fair	St. Mary Church	E		Tregantllo	Candleston		
Llanfeuthin	Llanvithyn		C	Tregatwg	Cadoxton-juxta-Barry	E	
Llanfihangel-ar-Elái	Michaelston-super-Ely	E		Tregolwyn	Colwinston	E	C
Llanfihangel y Bont-faen	Llanmihangel	E	C	Tre-gŵyr	Gowerton		C
Llanfihangel-y-fedw	Michaelston-y-Vedw	E		Trelái	Ely (place)		
Llanfihangel-ynys-Afan	Michaelston Higher		C	Trelales	Laleston	E	C
Llanfihangel-y-pwll	Michaelston-le-Pit	E	C	Tresimwn	Bonvilston	E	C
Llanfleiddan	Llanblethian	E	C	Uchelolau	Highlight	E	
Llangatwg Nedd	Cadoxton-juxta-Neath	E		Y Wig	Wick	E	C
Llan-giwg	Llanguicke	E	C	Ystumllwynarth	Oystermouth	E	C
Llangrallo	Coychurch	E	C				

GLOSSARY

WORDS adequately defined in the Shorter Oxford Dictionary are not included unless they have been used in a more specialised sense than is given there. The list is further limited by the exclusion of proper names and terms of cultural significance, as well as typological definitions of artifacts, which can be ascertained from standard works. Definitions are only given in the list when reference to an appropriate section of the Inventory will not suffice. Welsh words are indicated by (W). Terms special to Roman antiquities are indicated by (R): only the principal features of forts are included.

AGGER (R).—A continuous raised bank; the rampart of a fort, but also the visible mound of a road.
CLAVICULA (R).—See p. 98.
COUNTERSCARP BANK.—A subsidiary bank crowning the outer slope of the ditch of a hill-fort.
CWM (W).—A steep-sided valley interrupting a larger slope; *cf.* English 'coomb'.
HAFOD, HAFOTAI (W).—Dwelling(s) associated with summer pasturage.
HEMISTRIGIUM (R).—One of the pair of buildings which together form a *striga* (barrack block) in a fort.
LYNCHET.—A roughly levelled area formed by cultivation on sloping ground.
MARCHING CAMP (R).—See p. 98.
OPUS SIGNINUM (R).—A compound of lime and ceramic fragments used as foundation for pavements or wall-plaster, or as floor surfacing.
ORTHOSTAT.—An upright, earthfast stone.
PILLOW MOUND.—A ridged, artificial mound, thought to have served as a rabbit warren.
PLATFORM HOUSE.—A rectangular hut, usually of medieval date, with long axis roughly perpendicular to the contours, set on an artificially levelled platform.
PRACTICE CAMP (R).—See p. 98.
PRAETENTURA (R).—The area of a Roman fort in front of the headquarters buildings.
PRAETORIUM (R).—A building of domestic character, usually regarded as the commandant's house, placed at one side of the *principia* in a Roman auxiliary fort.
PRINCIPIA (R).—The headquarters building of a fort, centrally placed fronting the main cross-street.
RAMPART WALK.—The footway on top of a rampart, protected on the outer side by a parapet.
RETENTURA (R).—The area of a Roman fort behind the main cross-street.
RING-CAIRN.—A circular bank of stone surrounding a burial place.
SIGNAL STATION (R).—See p. 99.
TITULUM (TUTULUS) (R).—See p. 98.
-VALLATE (UNI-, BI-, TRI-, MULTI-).—Of hill-forts, indicates the number of main lines of defence, each consisting usually of bank and ditch.

INDEX OF NATIONAL GRID REFERENCES

THIS index gives the six-figure grid reference and corresponding monument number or page for every surviving structure mentioned in the Inventory, apart from roads and trackways for which the arrangement would be unsuitable. Its purpose is to simplify direct reference to the entry corresponding to a site located according to the National Grid, for which the proper name may be unknown or difficult to determine.

The references are classified according to the main categories of the Inventory, and lead not only to the descriptive entries of authentic sites, but to alternative categories where doubtful character has occasioned cross-reference in the text. Many rejected sites have been included under categories to which field archaeologists might be inclined to refer them on their own assessment.

The index for each of the three parts of Volume I contains no direct reference to the other two parts, which should be separately consulted when necessary.

HILL-FORTS AND RELATED STRUCTURES

G.R.	INV.
SN 618 068	616
SN 636 015	642
SN 670 063	p. 21b, after 616
SN 802 081	p. 72a, 'gaer' i
SN 838 000	618
SN 885 068	617
SN 944 064	p. 72b, 'gaer' ii
SO 027 040	619
SS 393 875	620
SS 398 925	612
SS 400 925	705
SS 407 928	706
SS 409 879	621
SS 414 873	697
SS 422 870	698
SS 422 898	707
SS 431 863	699
SS 434 860	622
SS 434 907	687
SS 436 908	646
SS 437 859	700
SS 437 906	688
SS 441 901	647
SS 443 927	689
SS 455 887	643
SS 461 935	622a
SS 469 913	674
SS 472 884	686
SS 483 899	644
SS 485 873	645
SS 505 924	665
SS 509 854	701
SS 518 879	675
SS 536 955	623
SS 546 938	649
SS 548 892	676
SS 550 947	624
SS 554 957	648
SS 567 866	702
SS 569 878	677
SS 588 875	703
SS 673 947	650
SS 675 943	651
SS 736 941	628
SS 748 954	626
SS 756 933	678
SS 765 936	629
SS 765 942	690
SS 768 981	p. 33a, after 651
SS 779 944	652 ii, iii
SS 781 944	652 i
SS 785 902	653
SS 788 917	679
SS 793 988	627
SS 799 867	625
SS 806 865	613
SS 812 885	654
SS 820 870	655
SS 820 940	658
SS 825 870	692
SS 831 861	656
SS 832 940	659
SS 833 880	657
SS 838 885	693
SS 840 807	632
SS 842 827	680
SS 863 779	691
SS 886 727	666
SS 888 780	630
SS 889 768	630a
SS 895 719	708
SS 897 717	631
SS 898 714	709
SS 914 684	667
SS 927 824	635
SS 939 813	636
SS 943 809	614
SS 948 852	634
SS 957 955	694
SS 958 795	633
SS 960 674	668
SS 963 756	681
SS 967 790	660
SS 971 796	p. 72b, 'gaer' iii
SS 973 849	637
SS 983 742	670
SS 994 665	669
ST 007 783	661
ST 021 744	695
ST 022 719	p. 72b, 'omit' i
ST 038 731	682
ST 039 790	p. 72b, 'omit' ii
ST 047 800	p. 72b, 'omit' iii
ST 050 870	639
ST 054 719	683
ST 054 734	638
ST 055 689	p. 72b, 'omit' iv
ST 059 700	615
ST 063 747	696
ST 064 832	672
ST 082 663	671
ST 085 791	662
ST 093 808	640
ST 100 901	p. 35b, after 663
ST 108 810	684
ST 121 702	p. 72b, 'omit' vi
ST 127 750	p. 72b, 'omit' v
ST 132 739	641
ST 133 750	673
ST 152 827	663
ST 168 669	704
ST 204 840	685

UNENCLOSED HUT SETTLEMENTS

G.R.	INV.
SN 922 018	711
SN 944 035	712
SN 951 035	713
SN 957 034	714
SO 012 053	715
SS 860 893	p. 78b, i (b)
SS 860 894	p. 78b, i (a)
SS 976 940	716
ST 006 836	p. 78b, ii
ST 074 975	p. 78b, iv
ST 088 839	p. 78b, iii

ROMAN FORTS

G.R.	INV.
SN 859 107	731
SO 050 067	732
SS 563 980	733
SS 747 977	734
SS 904 781	p. 122
ST 134 970	737
ST 153 872	736
ST 180 765	735

OTHER ROMAN MILITARY WORKS

G.R.	INV.	G.R.	INV.	G.R.	INV.
SN 812 040	752	SS 785 972 etc.	p. 103b, i	ST 116 986	746
SN 828 066	751	SS 796 987	739	ST 131 990	747
SN 862 102	738	SS 922 927	745	ST 131 994	748; p. 104a, ii
SS 591 973	742	SS 96 76	p. 104a, iii	ST 137 991	749
SS 607 971	743	ST 001 982	741	ST 138 991	750
SS 608 971	744	ST 067 880	740		

ROMAN CIVIL SITES

G.R.	INV.	G.R.	INV.	G.R.	INV.
SS 616 880	756	ST 035 702	760	ST 101 672	767
SS 840 780	757	ST 057 677	765	ST 142 694	768
SS 958 699	758	ST 074 696	759	ST 147 761	762
SS 984 711	763	ST 081 713	761	ST 159 699	769
ST 034 667	764	ST 099 664	766		

INDEX

Figures in brackets denote the serial numbers of monuments; the page number follows, with 'a' or 'b' indicating the left-hand or right-hand column respectively. References to the main site entries are printed in bold type.

Printed in England for Her Majesty's Stationery Office by
Ebenezer Baylis and Son Limited, Trinity Press, Worcester and London

Dd. 503868 K 12

(615, p. 20a) Castle Ditches, Llancarfan, from E.

(619, p. 22b) Gwersyll, from S.

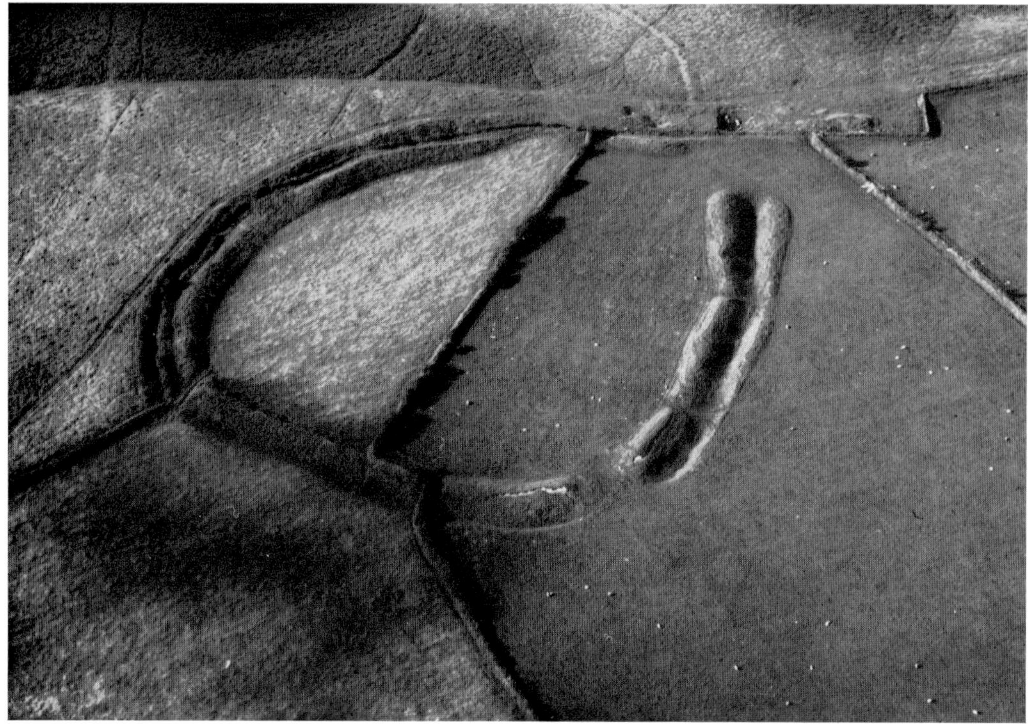

(637, p. 27b) Coedcae Gaer, from S.

(631, p. 26b) Cwm Bach, from S.E.

(657, p. 33b) Caer Blaen-y-cwm, from N.W.

(665, p. 36a) Cil Ifor Top, air view from S.E.

(665, p. 36a) Cil Ifor Top, ground view of S.E. end.

(666, p. 36b) Dunraven, from N.E.

(667, p. 38b) Nash Point, from S.E.

(668, p. 38b) Castle Ditches, Llantwit Major, from S.E.

(672, p. 43a) Caerau, Llantrisant, from N.E.

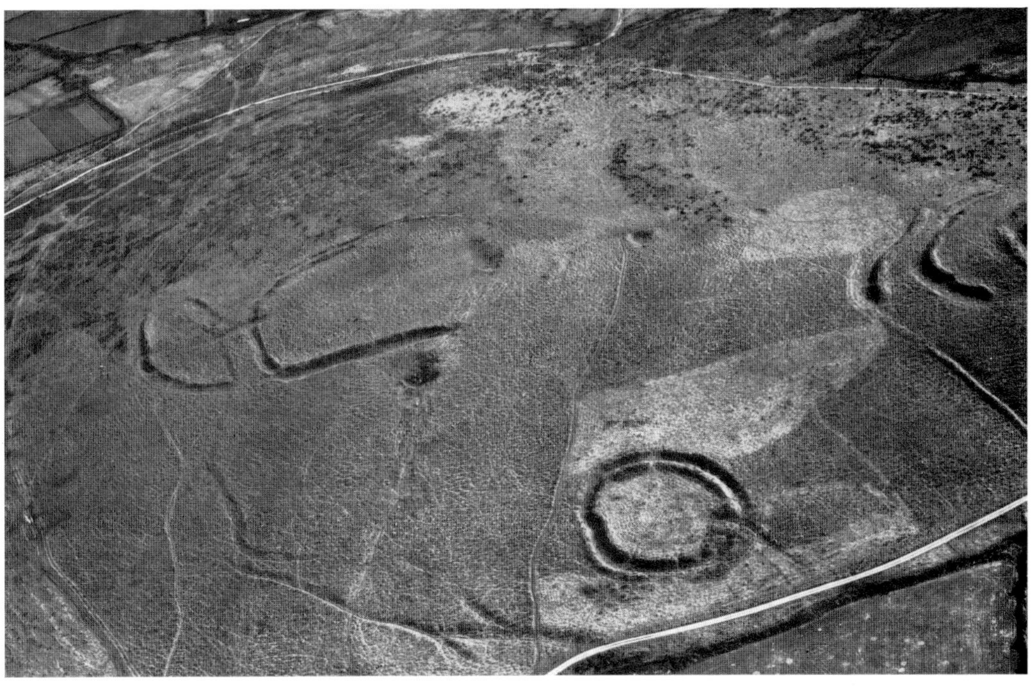

(688, p. 52b; 646, p. 31b; 687, p. 51b) Panoramic views of Down from N.E.

HILL-FORTS WITH WIDE-SPACED RAMPARTS

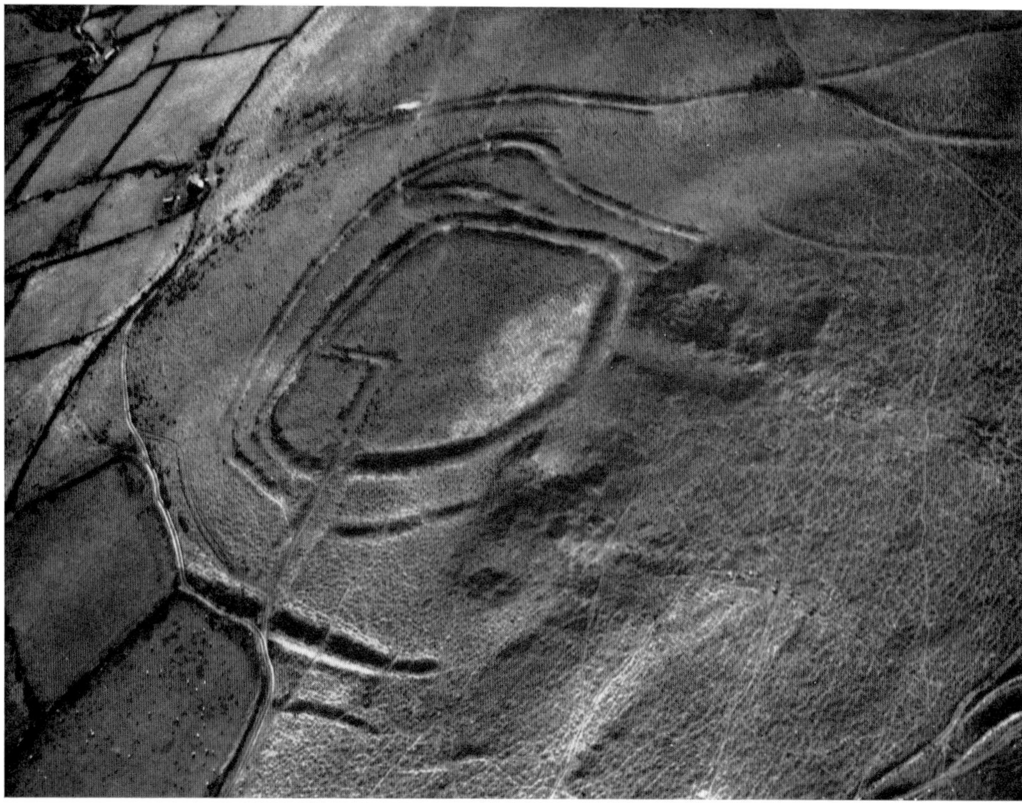

(689, p. 52b) The Bulwark, Llanmadog, from N.E.

(690, p. 55b) Gaer Fawr, from S.W.

(692, p. 57a) Moel Ton-mawr, from S.E.

(693, p. 57b) Y Bwlwarcau, from S.

HILL-FORT WITH WIDE-SPACED RAMPARTS and UNENCLOSED HUT SETTLEMENT

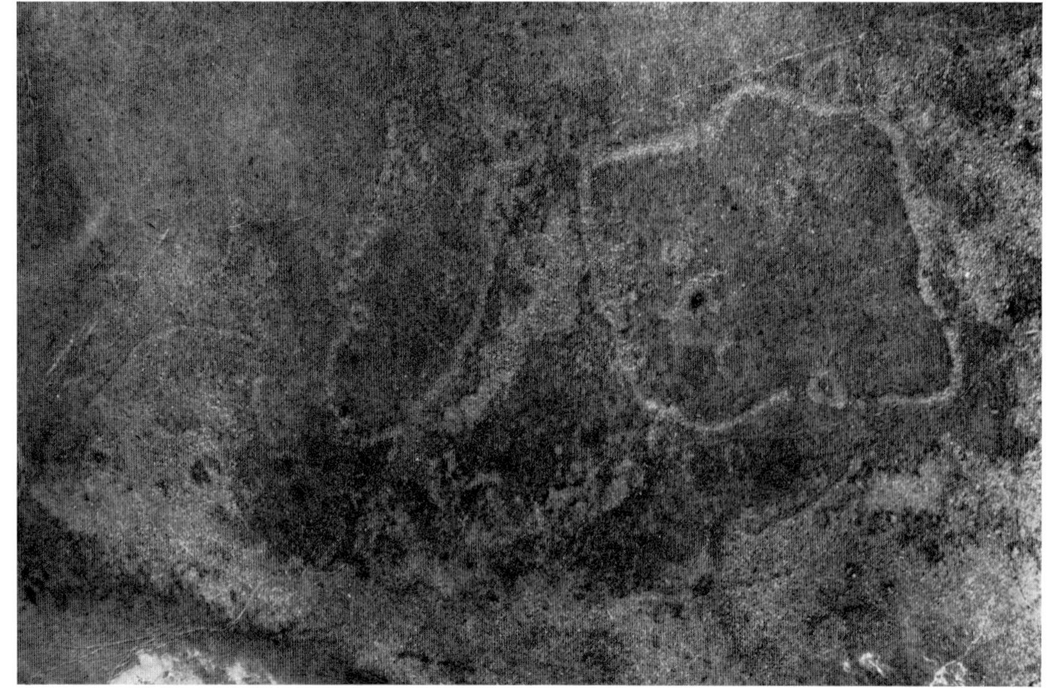

(715, p. 78a) Buarth Maen, from S.

(694, p. 61a) Maendy Camp, from S.E.

(699, p. 66a) The Knave, from S.E.

(711, p. 74a) above Garreg Lwyd, from E.

(714, p. 76a) Mynydd Cefnygyngon, main enclosure from N.E.

(731, p. 83a) Fort at Coelbren, from E.

(739, p. 99a) Marching camp, Blaen-cwm Bach, from S.W.

(747, p. 103b) Practice camp, Fforest Gwladys, from S.E.

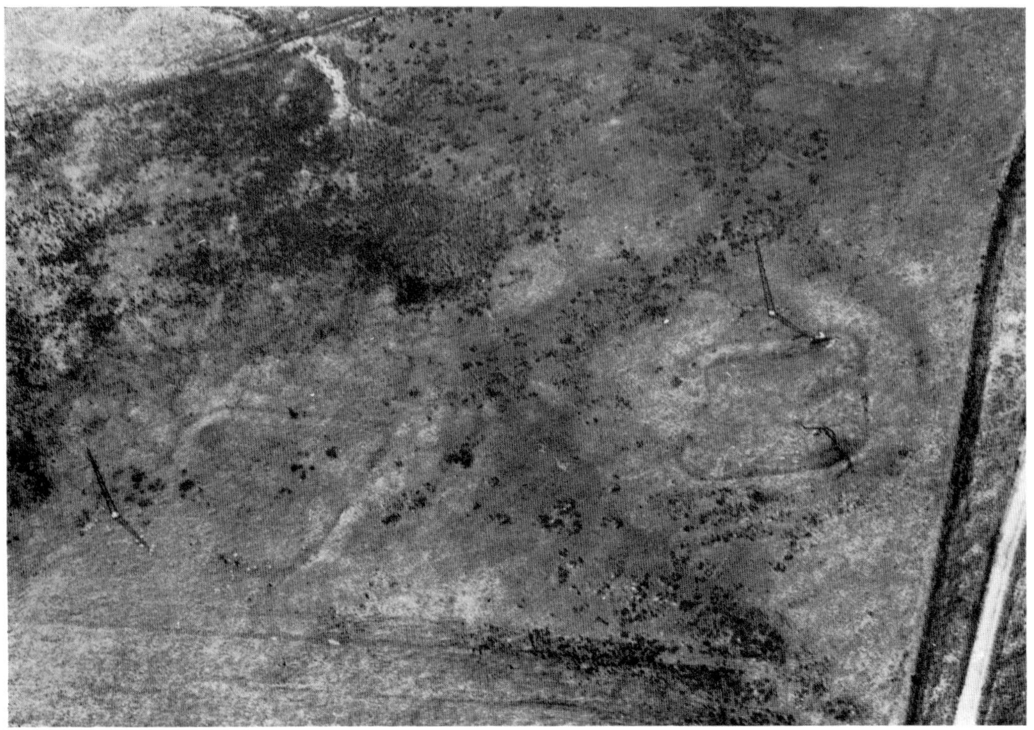

(749, 750, p. 103b) Practice camps, Fforest Gwladys, from N.E.

(758, p. 111a) Llantwit Major, division between rooms 8 and 9, from N.
1948 excavation, Nat. Mus. Wales. Scale in feet.

(758, p. 111a) Llantwit Major, division between rooms 8 and 9, from above.
1971 excavation, R.C.A.M. Scale in 0·2 m.